NEW STATISTICAL PROCEDURES FOR THE SOCIAL SCIENCES
Modern Solutions to Basic Problems

Rand R. Wilcox
University of Southern California

LEA LAWRENCE ERLBAUM ASSOCIATES, PUBLISHERS
1987 Hillsdale, New Jersey Hove and London

Lawrence Erlbaum Associates, Inc., Publishers
365 Broadway
Hillsdale, New Jersey 07642

Library of Congress Cataloging-in-Publication Data

Wilcox, Rand R.
New statistical procedures for the social sciences.

Bibliography: p.
Includes index.
1. Social sciences – Statistical methods.
2. Statistics. I. Title.
HA29.W522 1987 300'.1'5195 87-9001
ISBN 0-89859-936-9

Printed in the United States of America
10 9 8 7 6 5 4 3 2

Contents

To my wife, Karen

LIST OF SYMBOLS

$\surd$	SQUARE ROOT
α	ALPHA
β	BETA
γ	GAMMA
ξ	XI
ρ	RHO
δ	DELTA
η	ETA
μ	MU
Σ	SIGMA (UPPER CASE)
σ	SIGMA (LOWER CASE)
Ψ	PSI
τ	TAU
χ	CHI
ζ	ZETA
ν	NU

Preface

The first time I taught a graduate level analysis of variance course, I based my lectures on four recent and popular textbooks. My impression from these books was that not much had changed since I took the course in graduate school. However, when I started reading the journal articles on this topic, it soon became clear that many of the best known procedures should never be used. In particular, many journal articles had demonstrated that if certain commonly made assumptions are violated, procedures that are typically used can give highly unsatisfactory results. Moreover, new procedures had been developed for dealing with these problems, but there was no convenient way for students and researchers to learn these new techniques. The primary goal in this book is to supplement existing texts by bringing together many of these new procedures. Some procedures were previously impractical because appropriate tables were not available. This is the first book to include many of these tables.

A particularly important problem with the most frequently used procedures is the assumption that treatment groups have equal variances. It is probably fair to say that most researchers in the social sciences are more than willing to assume equal variances, yet among statisticians doing research on the analysis of variance, it is agreed that equal variances should not be assumed. In fact it has been demonstrated, using real data, that newer procedures that allow unequal variances can lead to drastically different results than those obtained using more conventional techniques where equal variances are assumed. What led to the widespread belief that equal variances can always be assumed, and why did statisticians change their mind about this view? How should the problem of unequal variances be addressed? Most researchers control power in terms of standardized differences, yet others find this approach to be completely unsatisfactory. What are the alternatives and what are their relative merits. What are the best multiple comparison procedures currently available? How should regression lines be compared in the analysis of covariance? These issues, and others, are discussed.

A difficulty with writing this book is that many results cannot be included because of space limitations. There is no doubt that nearly every statistician has opinions about what should be covered and what should be omitted in a book like this, and any two statisticians are not going to agree exactly on how to resolve this problem. Nevertheless, it is hoped that the new results covered in this book will be useful in many practical situations. One thing that should be evident from this book is that statistics is an evolving science. The approach used to solve the most basic questions may not be appropriate tomorrow.

Although the motivation for this book was to cover recent developments and to supplement existing texts, there is the problem that the training of students and researchers in statistics varies greatly. Accordingly, the first six chapters cover basic concepts without assuming any prior knowledge of statistics. Subsequent chapters cover many well known procedures, but most of these procedures are shown to be unsatisfactory, and they are included primarily to demonstrate their inadequacies.

Chapter seven is concerned with comparing the means of two treatment groups. Included is Welch's V and Chapman's exact heteroscedastic procedure. New tables are provided that greatly facilitate the use of Chapman's technique.

Chapter eight covers the conventional F test and demonstrates that violating the usual equal variance assumption severely affects both Type I errors and power. Both approximate and exact procedures for dealing with these problems are described. Similar results for the two-way ANOVA are described in chapter ten. Included is a simple procedure for handling unequal sample sizes in the first stage of the Bishop-Dudewicz ANOVA.

Chapter nine describes many new results on performing multiple comparisons. Included are the Kaiser-Bowden modification of Scheffe's procedure, Dunnett's T3 and C, as well as procedures proposed by Hochberg and Tamhane. This chapter also includes a guideline on how to choose a procedure.

Chapter eleven discusses repeated measures designs, and chapter twelve introduces ranking and selection techniques.

Chapter thirteen covers basic regression procedures and it includes some recent developments. Regression is a vast and rapidly growing field, and most of the new results cannot be covered in a single chapter. The emphasis here is on new procedures for comparing conditional means without the usual assumption of equal variances and equal slopes.

Chapter fourteen covers a few procedures in the analysis of categorical data.

Chapter fifteen discusses nonparametric procedures. Some researchers have argued that in addition to means, medians should be compared as well. This chapter includes a new procedure for comparing medians. The chapter describes several other procedures that are new including the Iman, the Quade, the Sandvik-Olson, and the Agresti-Pendergast.

There are many people who helped make this book possible. Particularly important was Norm Cliff. Without his help this book would have never been completed. I am grateful to Jerry Davison who also played an important role. Finally, a special thanks goes to all of my students who found many errors and made many helpful comments.

Rand R. Wilcox
Los Angeles, CA
1986

CHAPTER ONE

INTRODUCTION TO STATISTICS

It is probably fair to say that most undergraduates and beginning graduate students in the social sciences would never take a statistics course unless they were told they had to study statistics in order to get their degree. However, as students become more advanced, they realize that statistics is an invaluable tool for understanding the world in which we live. What makes the importance of statistics particularly obvious to anyone involved in research and experimentation is that most journal articles rely on statistical techniques when trying to make inferences about the people they are studying. Often I hear researchers saying that they wish they had a better understanding of statistical techniques. Fortunately, the application and correct interpretation of statistics can be accomplished without having an unusually strong background in mathematics--all that is required is a good background in high school algebra. While it is true that the theory of statistics can be mathematically complex, the point is that much of this theory need not concern those who are primarily interested in applying the techniques.

On the other hand, some theory is extremely important if you hope to avoid silly errors and erroneous conclusions when applying statistical procedures. Theory tells you precisely what a statistical procedure does. Perhaps the single most common error, even among experienced researchers, is making inferences that are not justified based on the statistical procedure that was used. Examples of where this problem occurs are given throughout the book.

While the emphasis in this book is on applications and recent developments in basic techniques, the first six chapters emphasize the basic theory needed to understand the most commonly used procedures. There is considerably more statistical theory than is covered in these chapters, but if too much emphasis is put on theory, it is easy to lose sight of how statistical procedures can be used to solve practical problems.

1.1 THE PURPOSE OF STATISTICS

To begin to understand why statistics is important, consider the following situations. Suppose you run some tests on manic depressives and you find that they have an unusually low level of some hormone that is suspected of influencing behavior. You might be tempted to conclude, or at least speculate, that this hormone has a relationship with being manic depressive. That is, you might think that all manic depressives have a lower than normal level of this hormone.

Next suppose you want to know how people feel about a particular political issue. For example, you might be interested in whether adults believe in banning all nuclear power plants. If you ask a few people about their attitudes on this subject, and most say that they favor a ban, you might want to conclude that most people in the United States have a similar attitude.

As a final situation, suppose you compare the SAT scores of ten students from high school A to the SAT scores of ten students from high school B. If seven students from high school A have scores above 600, while from high school B only 3 have scores above 600, you might suspect that the first high school has more students with scores above 600.

What do these three situations have in common? The answer is that in each case the goal is to generalize from a sample of subjects to some larger population of subjects. In the first situation some manic depressives were examined, and it was desired to generalize the findings to all manic depressives. In the second example you want to generalize to all adults in the United States, and in the third situation the goal was to generalize to all students in both high schools A and B. An obvious problem is that not every subject of interest can be examined. In this case, under what circumstances is it reasonable to generalize from the observations to the population that is of interest? Were enough subjects sampled in order to be reasonably certain that the generalizations are true, and if not, how many more observations do you need? If p_1 is the proportion of students in high school A who have scores above 600, and p_2 is the corresponding proportion for high school B, is it reasonable to assume $p_1=p_2$, and that the observed differences are due to chance, or is it more reasonable to conclude that $p_1>p_2$? These are just a few of the problems that can be solved with statistical techniques.

As one more illustration of how statistical procedures can be used, suppose you want to compare three drugs on their ability to lower blood pressure. One issue to be resolved is whether all three drugs are equally effective. It might be, for example, that observed differences among patients taking the drugs are due to chance fluctuations, and that for the typical person with hypertension, it makes little difference which drug is used. If you conclude there is a difference among the drugs, how certain can you be that the most effective drug will be correctly identified?

1.2 SUMMATION NOTATION

The first step is making sure you understand the basic notation used in statistics. To this end, suppose you conduct some experiment that involves n subjects. For instance, you might be interested in whether a special training program can affect a subject's score on the SAT exam. Further suppose that after the experiment is completed, the observed test score for the first subject is X_1, the observed score for the second is X_2, etc. For example, the values corresponding to X_1 and X_2 might be $X_1=600$ and $X_2=690$. Statistical procedures are based on arithmetic operations performed on the values $X_1,...X_n$. In order to describe these operations, a special notation is needed; it's called summation notation. The notation is quite simple, but you must be certain that you understand it, otherwise applying and understanding statistical techniques will forever remain a mystery.

The most basic operation is simply adding up the numbers $X_1,...X_n$. This is written as

$$\sum_{i=1}^{n} X_i = X_1+X_2+...+X_n.$$

The "i=1" just under the Σ, the Greek letter sigma, indicates that you start with the first observation, and the "n" just above the Σ indicates that the last term in the summation is X_n. If you see

$$\sum_{i=2}^{5} X_i,$$

you start with X_2 and end with X_5. That is,

$$\sum_{i=2}^{5} X_i = X_2+X_3+X_4+X_5.$$

The most common situation is where the summation is over all n values in which case

$$\sum_{i=1}^{n} X_i$$

is usually written as $\Sigma_i X_i$ or simply as ΣX_i.

<u>Example 1.2.1</u>. Suppose you measure n=3 subjects and the observed values are 5, 2, and 8. Then

$$\Sigma X_i=5+2+8=15$$

while

$$\sum_{i=2}^{3} X_i=2+8=10.$$

Let c be any number. The notation Σc means to take the number c and add it up n times. That is,

$$\Sigma c=c+c\ldots+c=nc.$$

Example 1.2.2.

$$\sum_{i=1}^{5} 4=20$$

Note that the usual algebraic operations can be applied. For instance,

$$\Sigma cX_i=c\Sigma X_i.$$

For the special case where $c=1/n$, $\Sigma X_i/n=(X_1+\ldots+X_n)/n$ which is usually written more simply as $\bar{X}$. That is, $\bar{X}$ represents the average of the numbers $X_1,\ldots X_n$.

It is quite common to want to add up some function of the X_i values. For instance, the sum of the squares of the X_i values is often important, and this operation is written as

$$\Sigma X_i^2=X_1^2+X_2^2+\ldots+X_n^2.$$

Notice that this quantity is usually different from $(\Sigma X_i)^2$ since

$$(\Sigma X_i)^2=(X_1+X_2+\ldots+X_n)^2.$$

Example 1.2.3. For the three values in example 1.2.1

$$\Sigma X_i^2=5^2+2^2+8^2=93,$$

$$(\Sigma X_i)^2=15^2=225,$$

and

$$\bar{X}=\Sigma X_i/3=(5+2+8)/3=5.$$

More generally, for any function of X_i that is of interest, say $g(X_i)$,

$$\Sigma g(X_i)=g(X_1)+...+g(X_n).$$

If $g(X_i)=X_i$, $\Sigma g(X_i)=\Sigma X_i$. If $g(X_i)=\surd X_i$ (the square root of X_i),

$$\Sigma g(X_i)=\Sigma\surd X_i=\surd X_1+\surd X_2+...+\surd X_n.$$

Some other algebraic manipulations should be mentioned. For instance,

$$\Sigma(X_i+c)=\Sigma X_i+\Sigma c$$

$$=(\Sigma X_i)+nc.$$

Also notice that $\Sigma X_i=n\bar{X}$, and so $\Sigma(X_i+c)$ could be written as $n\bar{X}+nc$. In a similar manner,

$$\Sigma(X_i-\bar{X})=\Sigma X_i-\Sigma\bar{X}.$$

But $\bar{X}$ is just a constant that does not depend on i, and so $\Sigma\bar{X}=n\bar{X}$. As a result,

$$\Sigma(X_i-\bar{X})=n\bar{X}-n\bar{X}=0.$$

Example 1.2.4. For the three values in example 1.2.1,

$$\Sigma(X_i-\bar{X})^2=(5-5)^2+(2-5)^2+(7-5)^2$$
$$=13.$$

Eventually a double subscript notation will be required. For instance, when studying the effects of training methods on SAT scores, you might have J=3 groups: subjects who receive method A, subjects who receive method B, and subjects in a control group who receive no special training at all. The notation X_{ij} refers to the observed value of the ith subject in the jth group.

Example 1.2.5. Suppose the scores for the subjects in J=3 groups are as follows.

Method A	Method B	Control
4	7	1
3	2	9

For instance, X_{11} refers to the first subject in the first group, and the observed value is 4. Similarly, X_{23} is the second subject in the third group, and the observed value is 9.

By definition

$$\Sigma_i \Sigma_j X_{ij} = X_{11} + X_{12} + \ldots + X_{1n} + \ldots X_{Jn}.$$

In example 1.2.5, $\Sigma_i \Sigma_j X_{ij} = 26$. If you see $\Sigma_i X_{ij}$, this means you sum over all values of i with j fixed. In example 1.2.5, $\Sigma_i X_{i2} = 7+2=9$. Similarly, $\Sigma_j X_{2j} = 3+2+9=14$.

Another common situation is where you have two or more observations for each subject. For instance, when training subjects for the purpose of increasing their SAT scores, you might want to take into account their score on an I.Q. test. In this case X_i might be the subject's score on the SAT exam, and Y_i might be the same subject's score on an I.Q. test. In this case the summation notation is extended in an obvious way. For instance,

$$\Sigma(X_i + Y_i) = (X_1 + Y_1) + (X_2 + Y_2) + \ldots + (X_n + Y_n)$$

$$= \Sigma X_i + \Sigma Y_i.$$

Two more examples are

$$\Sigma X_i Y_i = X_1 Y_1 + \ldots + X_n Y_n, \text{ and}$$

$$(\Sigma X_i)(\Sigma Y_i) = (X_1 + \ldots + X_n)(Y_1 + \ldots + Y_n).$$

Occasionally it will be necessary to use the notation $\Sigma_{i \neq j}$.

This just means that you sum over all possible values of i and j where $i \neq j$. For example, if n=3,

$$\Sigma_{i \neq j} X_i Y_j = X_1 Y_2 + X_1 Y_3 + X_2 Y_1 + X_2 Y_3 + X_3 Y_1 + X_3 Y_2.$$

Notice that

$$(\Sigma X_i)^2 = \Sigma X_i^2 + \Sigma_{i \neq j} X_i X_j. \qquad (1.2.1)$$

<u>Example 1.2.6.</u> For the three values in example 1.2.1,

$$\Sigma_{i \neq j} X_i X_j = 5(2)+5(8)+2(5)+2(8)+8(5)+8(2)=132.$$

As previously indicated, $\Sigma X_i^2 = 93$ and $(\Sigma X_i)^2 = 225$ which

verifies (1.2.1) for this special case since 225=93+132.

When working with probabilities, a slightly different form of the summation notation will be needed. For these cases you will be given a function f(x) which will be defined only for a specific set of values. Then $\Sigma f(x)$ means that the values of f(x) are added up over all possible values of x.

Example 1.2.7. If $f(x)=x^2$, and the only possible values of x are 1, 4 and 6, then

$$\Sigma f(x)=f(1)+f(4)+f(6)$$
$$=1^2+4^2+6^2$$
$$=53.$$

Another important quantity is $\Sigma xf(x)$. For the values in example 1.2.7,

$$\Sigma xf(x)=1(1^2)+2(2^2)+6(6^2)$$
$$=225$$

Example 1.2.8. If you are told that the possible values of x are -1, 0, and 1, and that f(-1)=.3, f(0)=.5, and f(1)=.2, then

$$\Sigma xf(x)=-.1,$$

$$\Sigma x^2 f(x)=(-1)^2(.3)+0^2(.5)+1^2(.2)=.5$$

and

$$\Sigma(x-.1)^2 f(x)=(-1-.1)^2(.3)+(0-.1)^2(.5)+(1-.1)^2(.2)=.53.$$

EXERCISES

1.1 Given the observations -2, 1, -1, 3, compute

a) ΣX_i

b) $\sum_{i=2}^{3} X_i$

c) ΣX_i^2

d) $(\Sigma X_i)^2$

e) $\Sigma_{i\neq j} X_i X_j$

f) $\bar{X}$

g) $\Sigma(X_i-\bar{X})^2$

h) $\Sigma 3$

i) $\Sigma(X_i+2)$

1.2 Using the data in example 1.2.5, compute

a) $\Sigma_i \Sigma_j X_{ij}^2$

b) $\Sigma_i X_{i3}$

c) $\Sigma_{i \neq j} X_{ij}$

d) $\Sigma_i \Sigma_j 3$

e) $\Sigma_{i \neq j} 2$

1.3 Suppose the possible values of x are 1, 2, and 3, and that f(1)=.1, f(2)=.7, and f(3)=.2. Compute

a) $\Sigma f(x)$
b) $\Sigma x f(x)$
c) $\Sigma x^2 f(x)$
d) $\Sigma 3f(x)$
e) Let $\mu=\Sigma x f(x)$ and compute $\Sigma(x-\mu)^2 f(x)$

1.4 Let the function f(x,y) be defined by the following table.

		Y	
		1	2
	1	.1	.1
X	2	.3	.05
	3	.3	.15

That is, the value of f(x,y) is given by the corresponding value in the table. For example, when X=2 and Y=1, f(2,1)=.3. Compute

a) $\Sigma_x \Sigma_y f(x,y)$
b) $\Sigma_y f(1,y)$
c) $\Sigma_x f(x,2)$
d) $\Sigma_x x f(x,1)$
e) $\Sigma_{x \neq y} f(x,y)$

f) $\Sigma_x \Sigma_y xyf(x,y)$.

1.5 Verify algebraically that

$$\Sigma(X_i - \bar{X})^2 = (\Sigma X_i^2) - n\bar{X}^2.$$

CHAPTER TWO

PROBABILITY

As indicated in chapter one, all statistical procedures are based on probability models, and so it is important for the student to master the basic principles of probability theory. The reader undoubtedly has some notion of what is meant by "probability," but experience has shown that it is important that the term "probability" be defined in a formal way. This is accomplished using the basic properties of set theory, and so the first goal is to quickly review the terms and operations of set theory that are needed. It might be mentioned that many books define probability as a proportion or relative frequency, but this approach is unsatisfactory for reasons that are impossible to explain at this point.

2.1 BASIC SET THEORY

The concept of a set or collection of objects is usually left undefined. That is, it is taken for granted that you know what is meant by a collection of objects. The starting point when dealing with sets is an exact rule for determining whether a particular object belongs to a set. For example, the set A might consist of the integers 0, 1, 2, and 3. Thus, it is clear that the numbers 1/2 and 14 do not belong to the set A.

As another example, a set might consist of all persons whose cholesterol level is over 200. Thus, a blood test can be used to determine whether a particular individual belongs to this set.

When an object belongs to a set, it is said to be an element of the set. For example, if the set A consists of all real numbers between 0 and 1, 1/4 is an element of A. In statistics the elements of a set usually consist of numbers, but in this chapter the emphasis is on elements that are events. For example, if you flip a coin and observe which side is facing up, the possible outcomes are a head, which will be represented by an H, or a tail, which will be represented by a T. Thus, the elements of the set are the events H and T.

Often the elements of a set are described using a brace notation. In the coin example, the set A is defined by $A=\{H,T\}$. If you see $A=\{1,4,13\}$, the set A consists of the elements 1, 4, and 13, while the set $A=\{a,b,g\}$ means the set consists of the letters a, b, and g.

In some instances not all of the elements of a set can be written down, in which case a slightly different notation is used. For example, $A=\{x:0\le x\le 2\}$ means that the set A consists of all real numbers between 0 and 2.

Definition 2.1.1. The set A_1 is a subset of the set A_2 if every element of A_1 is an element of A_2. In symbols, $A_1 \subset A_2$, which is read as A_1 is a subset of A_2. If $A_1 \subset A_2$ and $A_2 \subset A_1$, then $A_1 = A_2$ which means that every element of A_1 is an element of A_2, and every element of A_2 is an element of A_1. Put more simply, the elements of A_1 and A_2 are exactly the same.

Example 2.1.1. Suppose you have a ten-point scale for rating a subject's anxiety level toward statistics. The possible scores on this scale are the elements of the set $A=\{1,2,3,4,5,6,7,8,9,10\}$. Then $A_1=\{8,9,10\}$ is a subset of A because every element of A_1 is also an element of A. Similarly, $A_2=\{7\}$ is a subset of A, but $A_3=\{0\}$ is not.

Definition 2.1.2. If the set A has no elements, A is called the null set, written as $A=0$. Notice that for any set B, if A is a null set, $A \subset B$ because it is true that every element of A is an element of B.

Definition 2.1.3. The set of all elements that belong to at least one of the sets A_1 and A_2 is called the union of A_1 and A_2. This is written as A_1+A_2 (rather than using the usual symbol for union) which is read as A_1 union A_2. The definition is readily extended to any k sets. In particular, the union of the sets A_1, $A_2,\ldots,A_k$ is written as $A_1+A_2+\ldots+A_k$, and this union is the set of all elements that belongs to at least one of the sets $A_1,\ldots,A_k$.

Example 2.1.2. Consider again the ten-point anxiety scale. If $A_1=\{1\}$ and $A_2=\{8,9\}$, then $A_1+A_2=\{1,8,9\}$. If $A_3=\{10\}$, $A_1+A_2+A_3=\{1,8,9,10\}$.

Example 2.1.3. If $A_1=\{$all persons over six feet tall$\}$ and $A_2=\{$all persons over 200 pounds$\}$, then $A_1+A_2=\{$all persons over six feet tall or over 200 pounds$\}$.

Example 2.1.4. Suppose $A_1=0$ and A_2 is any set. Then $A_1+A_2=A_2$.

Definition 2.1.4. The set of elements belonging to both of the sets A_1 and A_2 is called the intersection of A_1 and A_2. The intersection of A_1 and A_2 is written as $A_1 \cap A_2$. More generally, the intersection of the sets $A_1,\ldots,A_k$ is the set of elements that belong to all of the sets $A_1,\ldots A_k$, and this intersection is written as $A_1 \cap A_2 \cap \ldots \cap A_k$.

Example 2.1.5. Suppose A_1={all persons who have heart disease}, and A_2={all persons who smoke}. Then $A_1 \cap A_2$ is the set of all persons who smoke and have heart disease. Notice that a person must have both characteristics to be a member of the set $A_1 \cap A_2$. For this reason, the symbol $\cap$ is sometimes read as "and." In the example, $A_1 \cap A_2$ means that a person smokes and has heart disease. This in contrast to the notation A_1+A_2, which refers to all persons who have heart disease or smoke, or both.

Example 2.1.6. Let A_1={3,4,5} and A_2={8,9,10}. Then $A_1 \cap A_2$=0, the null set, since there is no element that belongs to both A_1 and A_2.

Example 2.1.7. Consider two circles, and let A_1 be the set of points in the first circle, and A_2 the set of points in the second. The Venn diagrams in Figure 2.1.1 show the union and intersection of A_1 and A_2.

In some instances it is necessary to indicate the order in which set operations are performed, and this is done by using parentheses in the same way parentheses are used in elementary algebra. For instance, $(A_1+A_2)\cap A_3$ means that you first form the union of A_1 and A_2, and then you take the intersection of the resulting set with A_3. A Venn diagram of this set is shown in Figure 2.1.2. In other words, $(A_1+A_2)\cap A_3$ is the set of all points that belong to either A_1 or A_2, and belong to A_3.

Definition 2.1.5. It is often convenient to have a word that represents all the elements that are of interest in a given situation. For instance, if every subject is given a score that measures a subject's level of anxiety, and the integers 0,1,...,10 are the only possible scores, then the set A={0,1,...,10} is the largest possible set of interest. This set of all possible elements is called a space.

Example 2.1.8. You ask three persons whether abortion is immoral. If you ask persons to choose an integer between 0 and 3, where 0 means that they believe abortion is immoral, while 3 corresponds to the opinion that abortion is extremely immoral, then the space is the set {0,1,2,3}.

Definition 2.1.6. A simple experiment is defined to be an act or process that leads to some unambiguous outcome. A random experiment is a simple experiment where the outcome cannot be

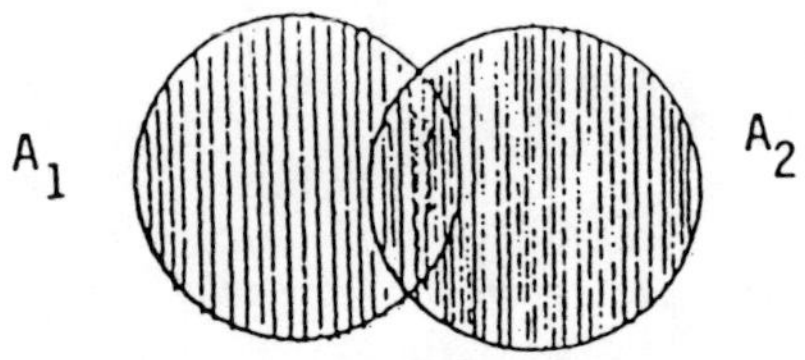

$A_1 + A_2$

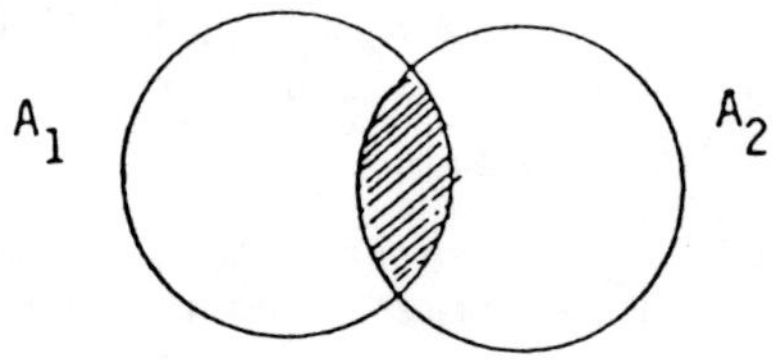

$A_1 \cap A_2$

Figure 2.1.1

The shaded area corresponds to the set indicated by the symbols

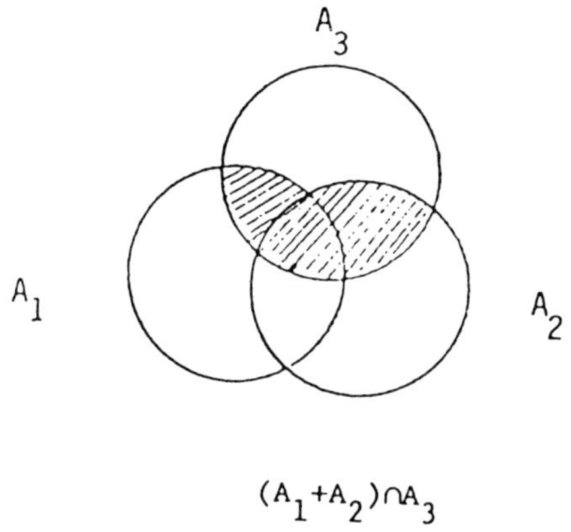

Figure 2.1.2

The shaded area corresponds to the set indicated by the symbols

predicted with certainty.

Example 2.1.9. A subject is given some aspirin, and an hour later it is determined whether there is any stomach damage. This simple experiment is also a random experiment because the outcome cannot be predicted--presumably this is why the experiment was conducted in the first place.

Example 2.1.10. Subjects take a twenty item vocabulary test and the outcome is the number of observed correct responses.

The important feature of simple experiments is that the outcome is unambiguous. In the vocabulary test, an item is scored either right or wrong, and this is the outcome that is of interest.

Definition 2.1.7. A *sample space*, which will be denoted by $\underset{\sim}{S}$, is the set of all distinct outcomes of some random experiment. Thus, a sample space is just the space associated with a particular simple experiment. The elements of a sample space are called *sample points* or *elementary events*. The space in example 2.1.7 is also a sample space, and the elements of the space are the integers 0, 1, 2, and 3. In example 2.1.9 the sample space is the number of correct responses, and the elementary events are the integers 0,1,...,20.

Definition 2.1.8. An event is any set consisting of elementary events. Alternatively, an event is any subset of $\underset{\sim}{S}$.

Example 2.1.11. In many instances it is events, rather than just elementary events, that are of interest. For instance, when using a ten-point scale to measure anxiety, you might be interested in the event of a score greater than or equal to 7. Thus, because you are using a ten-point scale, the event of interest is the set $A=\{7,8,9,10\}$.

Definition 2.1.9. The complement of a set A, written as $\bar{A}$, is the set of all elements in $\underset{\sim}{S}$ that are not in A.

Example 2.1.12. If $\underset{\sim}{S}=\{0,1,2,3,4,5,6,7,8,9,10\}$

and $A=\{7,8,9,10\}$, then $\bar{A}=\{0,1,2,3,4,5,6\}$. If $A=\{1\}$, then $\bar{A}=\{0,2,3,...,10\}$.

Example 2.1.13. If you flip a coin, in which case $\underset{\sim}{S}=\{H,T\}$, and if $A=\{H\}$, $\bar{A}=\{T\}$. If $A=0$, $\bar{A}=\underset{\sim}{S}$.

Definition 2.1.10. The sets A_1 and A_2 are mutually exclusive if $A_1 \cap A_2 = 0$. In terms of sample spaces, these events are mutually exclusive if they cannot occur simultaneously. More generally, if the k sets $A_1, \ldots, A_k$ are such that $A_i \cap A_j$, $i \neq j$, the k sets are said to be mutually exclusive. In other words, k sets are mutually exclusive if no two sets have any elements in common. That is, the k sets are mutually exclusive if any two of the k sets are mutually exclusive. If $A_1 + A_2 + \ldots + A_k = \underset{\sim}{S}$, the k sets are said to be exhaustive.

Example 2.1.14. For any set A, $\bar{A}$ and A are mutually exclusive and exhaustive.

2.2 PROBABILITY SET FUNCTIONS

Consider any sample space. It might help to keep in mind a specific case, and so in this section it is assumed that a random experiment is conducted where subjects are asked whether they agree that it is more difficult for women to succeed in business than it is for men. It is assumed that the subject either disagrees, has no opinion, or agrees, and so the sample space $\underset{\sim}{S}$ consists of these three simple events.

Definition 2.2.1. A probability set function is a rule, say Pr, that assigns a number to any subset A of $\underset{\sim}{S}$ with the property that

a) $Pr(A) \geq 0$

b) if $A_1, \ldots, A_k$ are mutually exclusive subsets of $\underset{\sim}{S}$,

$$Pr(A_1 + \ldots + A_k) = Pr(A_1) + \ldots + Pr(A_k)$$

and

c) $Pr(\underset{\sim}{S}) = 1$.

These properties stem from conventional notions of probabilities as proportions or relative frequencies. For example, if five of 30 subjects disagree with the statement described above, it is natural to suppose that if you arbitrarily choose one of the 30 subjects, the probability of a "disagree" response is 5/30. However, this probability is equal to 5/30 only if an additional condition is imposed (random sampling), which is formally described in the next chapter. The only point here is that if x of 30 subjects happen to disagree, of course $x/30 \geq 0$.

As for the second property of a probability set function, let A_1 be the event that a subject disagrees, and let A_2 be the event that a subject's response is "no opinion." The events A_1 and A_2

are mutually exclusive, and if x_1 of 30 subjects have a disagree opinion, and x_2 subjects have no opinion, the proportion of subjects who disagree or have no opinion is $x_1/30 + x_2/30$. In symbols we are supposing that $Pr(A_1)=x_1/30$, $Pr(A_2)=x_2/30$, and that $Pr(A_1+A_2)=x_1/30 + x_2/30$.

Several important properties of probability set functions can be derived using the basic principles of set theory. The first is that for any event A,

$$Pr(A)+Pr(\bar{A})=1 \tag{2.2.1}$$

which implies that

$$Pr(\bar{A})=1-Pr(A). \tag{2.2.2}$$

The reason is that A and $\bar{A}$ are mutually exclusive, and because

$$A+\bar{A}=\underset{\sim}{S},$$

it follows that

$$1=Pr(\underset{\sim}{S})=Pr(A+\bar{A})=Pr(A)+Pr(\bar{A}).$$

In particular, if A is the null set, $Pr(0)=0$. That is, the probability of the null set or empty set is zero because

$$Pr(0)=Pr(\bar{\underset{\sim}{S}})=1-Pr(\underset{\sim}{S})=1-1=0.$$

Another result is that for any event A,

$$0 \le Pr(A) \le 1. \tag{2.2.3}$$

This must be true because otherwise equation (2.2.1) would be violated. That is, if $Pr(A)>1$, and since $Pr(\bar{A}) \ge 0$, it would be true that $Pr(A)+Pr(\bar{A})>1$, which is impossible.

Let A_1 and A_2 be any two subsets of $\underset{\sim}{S}$. Then

$$Pr(A_1+A_2)=Pr(A_1)+Pr(A_2)-Pr(A_1 \cap A_2). \tag{2.2.4}$$

This last equation says that the probability of A_1 or A_2 is equal to the probability of A_1 plus the probability of A_2 minus the probability of A_1 and A_2.

Equation (2.2.4) can be established by first writing A_1+A_2 as the union of two mutually exclusive events. In particular,

$$A_1+A_2=A_1+(\bar{A}_1 \cap A_2). \tag{2.2.5}$$

But

$$A_2=(A_1\cap A_2)+(\bar{A}_1\cap A_2) \tag{2.2.6}$$

which is the union of two mutually exclusive events, and so

$$Pr(A_2)=Pr(A_1\cap A_2)+Pr(\bar{A}_1\cap A_2)$$

which means that

$$Pr(\bar{A}_1\cap A_2)=Pr(A_2)-Pr(A_1\cap A_2).$$

Substituting the right side of this last equation for $Pr(\bar{A}_1\cap A_2)$ in equation (2.2.5) establishes the desired result.

Example 2.2.1. Suppose you are interested in studying levels of income in relation to feelings of marital satisfaction. Further suppose subjects are classified into one of three income levels, say high, medium, and low, and these same subjects are also classified in terms of two categories of marital satisfaction, namely satisfied and not satisfied. Thus, any person in your study is assumed to belong to one of six mutually exclusive categories. For illustrative purposes it is assumed that the probabilities associated with the six categories are as follows:

Table 2.2.1

		INCOME LEVEL			
		High	medium	low	
Happily	Yes	.1	.2	.3	.6
Married	No	.05	.25	.1	.4
		.15	.45	.4	

For example, the probability that a subject is happily married and in a low income level is .3. The probability that a person is in a medium level income bracket and is unhappily married is .25. The event that a subject is happily married, regardless of income level, is the union of three mutually exclusive events, namely, (yes,low), (yes,medium) and (yes,high). Thus, the probability that a subject is happily married, which will be called event A, is .1+.2+.3=.6.

Now suppose you want to determine the probability of being happily married or having a high income. If B is the event that a person has a high income, then A+B is the union of four mutually exclusive events: (yes,low), (yes,medium), (yes,high) and (no,high). Thus,

$$Pr(A+B)=.1+.2+.3+.05=.65.$$

Instead of the above analysis, Pr(A+B) could also be determined using equation (2.2.4). In particular, Pr(A)=.6, Pr(B)=.15, and $Pr(A\cap B)=.1$. Thus,

$$Pr(A+B)=.60+.15-.1=.65$$

which agrees with the result given above.

In the illustration, determining Pr(A+B) was easily accomplished without resorting to equation (2.2.4). The primary purpose of the illustration was to put equation (2.2.4) on a more intuitive level. In many cases Pr(A+B) is not easily determined, in which case equation (2.2.4) can be useful.

2.3 CONDITIONAL PROBABILITIES

The notion of a conditional probability is one of the most important concepts in probability theory. In fact, it is common for persons to attempt to make inferences about conditional probabilities without fully realizing whether their conclusions are reasonable.

Suppose you observe an individual who can be classified as

A=wearing a black leather jacket, and

B=a person who engages in antisocial behavior.

Now suppose you observe another individual who belongs to category A. The temptation is to conclude that this person also belongs to category B, but to what extent is this conclusion reasonable?

Suppose you are told that within a particular neighborhood, $Pr(A\cap B)=.6$. If you go to this neighborhood and see someone wearing a black leather jacket, is there a high probability that the person also engages in antisocial behavior?

Conditional probabilities provide an answer to the problem just posed. Symbolically, conditional probabilities are written as

$$Pr(A|B)$$

which is read as the probability of event A given that event B has occurred. Similarly, Pr(B|A) is the probability of event B given that event A has occurred. In the illustration, the problem is determining Pr(B|A), which is the probability that a person engages in antisocial behavior given that the person wears a black leather jacket.

Definition 2.3.1. The conditional probability of event B, given that event A has occurred, is

$$\Pr(B|A)=\Pr(A\cap B)/\Pr(A) \qquad (2.3.1)$$

provided $\Pr(A)>0$.

A complete justification of (2.3.1) is not given here, but you can convince yourself that this is a reasonable definition of $\Pr(B|A)$ by examining Table 2.2.1. Suppose, for instance, you are interested in the probability of being happily married (event B, say) given that a person is in a low income bracket (event A). From Table 2.2.1, the event of being in a low income bracket is the union of two mutually exclusive events, namely, (yes,low) and (no.low). Thus,

$$\begin{aligned}\Pr(A)&=\Pr(\text{yes,low})+\Pr(\text{no,low})\\&=.3+.1\\&=.4\end{aligned}$$

Now think of the probabilities in Table 2.2.1 as relative frequencies. For convenience. assume the entries in the table are based on 100 subjects. Then 30/100 is the proportion who are in the (yes,low) category, while for the (no,low) category the proportion is 10/100. Suppose you are told that a person is in a low income bracket. Thus, this person is one of the 40 persons belonging to the last column of Table 2.2.1. Moreover, among these 40 persons, 30 of them are happily married. In other words, among the 40 persons having a low income, the proportion who are happily married is 30/40. Put another way,

$$\Pr(\text{happily married}|\text{low income})=30/40.$$

The essential feature of this argument is that the sample space has been changed from all married adults to all married adults who have a low income. If the definition of a conditional probability is applied instead, $\Pr(A\cap B)=.3$, $\Pr(A)=.4$, and so $\Pr(B|A)=.3/.4$, which agrees with the previous result.

Example 2.3.1. Consider again the illustration involving black leather jackets (event A) and antisocial behavior (event B). You are told that $\Pr(A\cap B)=.6$ so if $\Pr(A)=.9$, the probability of engaging in antisocial behavior, given that a person wears a black leather jacket, is

$\Pr(B|A)=.6/.9=2/3.$

From the definition of a conditional probability, it is seen that

$$\Pr(A\cap B)=\Pr(B|A)\Pr(A)$$

$$=\Pr(A|B)\Pr(B). \quad (2.3.2)$$

This result is called the multiplication rule.

Example 2.3.2. Suppose a jar contains 30 red marbles, 50 green marbles, and 20 blue marbles. Further suppose that the marbles are stirred and you draw two marbles without replacement. What is the probability of drawing a red marble on the first draw (event A), and a blue on the second (event B)? A reasonable approximation of Pr(A) is 30/100 since 30 of the 100 marbles are red. Given that a red marble is selected on the first draw, there are 99 marbles left, and so a reasonable approximation of $\Pr(B|A)$ is 20/99. Thus,

$$\Pr(A\cap B)=(30/100)(20/99)=.0606.$$

Example 2.3.3. In the previous example, suppose instead you want to know the probability of having a red and blue marble after two draws. This is different from the previous example because order does not matter here while before it did. That is, in the previous example you were interested in the event (R,B), i.e., a red on the first and a blue on the second. Now, however, the problem is to determine the probability of drawing a red marble on one of the two draws and a blue on the other. Of course there are only two ways this can happen. You either draw a red and then a blue, or a blue and then a red. Thus, you want to determine the probability of (R,B) or (B,R). These two event are mutually exclusive, and following the previous example, it is seen that Pr(R,B)=Pr(B,R)=.0606. Hence, the answer is .0606+.0606=.1212.

2.4 INDEPENDENT EVENTS

Another important concept, one that plays an integral role in statistical theory, is the notion of independent events. Basically the problem is finding a mathematical way of saying that two events are independent if the outcome of one does not affect the probability of the outcome of the other. Another way of saying this is that events A and B are independent if the occurrence or nonoccurrence of event B does not alter the likelihood of observing the event A. Writing this property in terms of conditional probabilities, events A and B are independent if

$$Pr(A|B)=Pr(A). \qquad (2.4.1)$$

But $Pr(A|B)=Pr(A \cap B)/Pr(B)$, and so (2.4.1) means that

$$Pr(A \cap B)=Pr(A)Pr(B). \qquad (2.4.2)$$

Thus, from equations (2.4.1) and (2.4.2), it seems reasonable to define independence as follows.

Definition 2.4.1. Events A and B are independent if and only if $Pr(A \cap B)=Pr(A)Pr(B)$. If $Pr(A \cap B) \neq Pr(A)Pr(B)$, the two events are said to be dependent.

Example 2.4.1. Consider again the probabilities in Table 2.2.1. Let A be the event a subject is happily married, and B be the event of having a low income. As previously explained, $Pr(A)=.6$. $Pr(B)=.4$, and $Pr(A \cap B)=.3$. But $.4(.6)=.24 \neq .3$, and so A and B are dependent.

Example 2.4.2. Suppose two patients have a particular psychological disorder, and each has a .3 probability of being cured without ever seeking professional help. If the probability of the first patient being cured is independent of the second patient being cured, then the probability that both patients are cured is $.3(.3)=.09$. From (2.2.1), the probability of no cure is $1-.3=.7$, and so the probability that neither patient is cured is $.7(.7)=.49$.

It should be mentioned that the property of independent events can be extended to any k events. In particular, if $A_1,\ldots A_k$ are independent events, then

$$Pr(A_1 \cap A_2 \cap \ldots \cap A_k)=Pr(A_1)Pr(A_2)\ldots Pr(A_k) \qquad (2.4.3)$$

2.5 THE BONFERRONI INEQUALITY

There are many instances where an investigator needs to know $Pr(A_1 \cap \ldots \cap A_k)$, but when the k events $A_1,\ldots,A_k$ are not independent, equation (2.4.3) cannot be applied. This problem occurs when applying multiple comparison procedures, which are described in chapter 9. Fortunately there is a simple approximation of $Pr(A_1 \cap \ldots \cap A_k)$ that is accurate in important situations. This is the Bonferroni inequality, which says that

$$\Pr(A_1\cap\ldots\cap A_k)\geq 1-\Sigma\Pr(\bar{A}_i)$$
$$=1-[\Pr(\bar{A}_1)+\ldots+\Pr(\bar{A}_k)] \qquad (2.5.1)$$

The inequality says that the probability that the events $A_1,\ldots,A_k$ occur simultaneously is at least as large as $1-\Sigma\Pr(\bar{A}_i)$. When $\Pr(A_1\cap\ldots\cap A_k)$ is close to one, the inequality in (2.5.1) is nearly an equality, and so for this particular case, $1-\Sigma\Pr(\bar{A}_i)$ provides a good approximation of the left side of (2.5.1). However, when $\Pr(A_1\cap\ldots\cap A_k)$ is not close to one, this approximation can be poor.

Example 2.5.1. Suppose you are studying three personality characteristics. Further suppose that previous studies show that the probabilites associated with these characteristics are $\Pr(A_1)=.9$, $\Pr(A_2)=.95$, and $\Pr(A_3)=.99$. If you want to know the probability that a person has all three characteristics simultaneously, you can approximate this probability using (2.5.1). In particular, $\Pr(\bar{A}_1)=.1$, $\Pr(\bar{A}_2)=.05$ and $\Pr(\bar{A}_3)=.01$. From (2.5.1),

$$\Pr(A_1\cap A_2\cap A_3)\geq 1-(.1+.05+.01)=.84.$$

That is, the probability of having all three characteristics is at least .84.

EXERCISES

2.1 Describe in words the set $A=\{x: x\geq 6\}$.

2.2 If $S=\{0,1,2,\ldots,12\}$, $A_1=\{2,4,6,8,10\}$, $A_2=\{1,3,5,7,8,9,10\}$, $A_3=\{3,5\}$ and $A_4=0$, determine

a) A_1+A_2
b) $A_1\cap A_2$
c) A_3+A_4
d) $A_1\cap A_4$
e) $A_1\cap A_2\cap A_3$
f) $\bar{A}_1$
g) $\bar{A}_1\cap\bar{A}_3$

2.3 If A_1=smokes marijuana, A_2=event a person has lung cancer, and A_3=event a person has emphysema, describe in words the event $A_1\cap A_2\cap A_3$.

2.4 Let S={all adult males}, and let A_1, A_2 and A_3 be defined as in 2.3 and let $\bar{A}_4=(A_1\cap A_2)$, $A_5=\bar{A}_1\cap(A_2+A_3)$ and $\bar{A}_6=(A_1\cap A_2\cap A_3)$. Describe in words $\bar{A}_1$, A_4 A_5 and $\bar{A}_6$.

2.5 Suppose A is a subset of B. If A+C=B and if A and C are mutually exclusive, what must C be equal to in terms of A and B?

2.6 Using the result of exercise 2.5, show that if A is a subset of B, then $Pr(A) \leq Pr(B)$.

2.7 Use Venn diagrams to verify equation 2.2.4

2.8 Referring to Table 2.2.1, determine

a) the probability of having a high income given that a person is happily married.

b) the probability of a high or medium income given that a person is happily married.

2.9 Assuming $Pr(B)>0$, verify that $Pr(A|B)$ is a probability set function.

2.10 Referring to example 2.3.2, what is the probability of a red marble on the first draw, or a blue marble on the second?

2.11 Again refer to example 2.3.2, but assume marbles are drawn with replacement, and that the outcomes of each draw are independent.

a) What is the probability of a red marble on the first draw, and a green on the second?

b) What is the probability of having one red and one green after two draws?

c) What is the probability of having two red marbles and one green after three draws?

2.12 Consider again example 2.3.2, and as in exercise 2.11, assume sampling is with replacement, but this time do not assume independence.

a) Using the Bonferroni inequality, what can be said about drawing a red marble on the first draw and a green marble on the second?

b) What is the minimum probability of drawing no blue marbles after two draws?

CHAPTER THREE

RANDOM VARIABLES, DISTRIBUTIONS AND ESTIMATION

3.1 RANDOM VARIABLES

In probability theory the sample space can consist of any collection of objects or events that are of interest. However, when trying to develop statistical techniques, it is convenient to restrict attention to sample spaces containing only numbers. Fortunately, for the problems considered in this book, assigning numbers to outcomes is a simple process. In many cases the numbers used to describe outcomes suggest themselves in an obvious way. For example, when measuring how much people weigh, a pointer on the scale might indicate the symbol "120," and so you would use 120 as the person's weight. In other cases numbers can be assigned in an arbitrary but convenient fashion that is appropriate for the problem at hand. For instance, if you want to conduct a study that deals with whether students pass (P) or fail (F) a statistics course, it turns out to be convenient to designate a "pass" with the number 1, and a "fail" with the number 0. The reader might not be completely convinced that assigning numbers to outcomes is always a simple matter, but eventually this will become clear.

Definition 3.1.1. A random variable, X, is a rule (or function) that assigns a unique number to any element of the sample space $\underset{\sim}{S}$. The set of possible values of the random variable X is called the space of X.

Example 3.1.1. Consider again the situation where students either pass or fail a course. Then the random variable X is defined by

$$X(P)=1$$

and

$$X(F)=0.$$

However, it is cumbersome to write X(P) and X(F), and so it is more common to simply say that X equals 1 or 0 according to whether a student passes or fails. The only reason for writing X(P)=1 was to emphasize that X is a function that assigns the number 1 to the event P.

From chapter two it is clear that when a sample space already consists of numbers, the probability of observing a particular number is already defined. In situations where numbers are assigned to events, such as in the example just given, again there is no problem in assigning probabilities to the values of a random variable. For instance, if the probability of a pass is Pr(P)=.7, then Pr(X=1)=.7. In general, if you have a probability set function for the sample space $\underset{\sim}{S}$, then you also have a probability set function for the corresponding random variable X. For random variables, however, it is more common to refer to a probability set function simply as a probability function, and this convention is followed henceforth.

Another common practice is to use lower case Roman letters to represent a particular value of a random variable, while upper case Roman letters denote a random variable. For instance, if you throw a die and count the number of spots facing up, the random variable X is a generic term for the number of spots, while the possible values of X are x=1,2,3,4,5, and 6. Many books never make a distinction between X and its values--usually the distinction is unimportant--but in this chapter there are a few instances where this distinction is useful. For discrete random variables it is also common to write Pr(X=x) simply as f(x), and this will be done here. However, for continuous random variables f(x) is <u>not</u> equal to Pr(X=x) although it is related to Pr(X≤x). This point is discussed in more detail in the next section.

<u>Example 3.1.2.</u> Suppose you develop a five-point rating scale for measuring the anxiety of students toward statistics. Then the random variable X would refer to the rating received by a particular subject, and the possible values of X are x=1,2,3,4, and 5, and f(x) represents Pr(X=x). More importantly, all of the results on probability set functions can be applied. For instance

$$\Pr(X\geq 3)=f(3)+f(4)+f(5)$$

because the event X≥3 consists of three mutually exclusive events, namely, X=3, X=4, and X=5. Once Pr(X≥3) has been determined, Pr(X<3) is easily found since Pr(X<3)=1-Pr(X≥3). The reason is that X≥3 is the complement of the event X<3.

It should be pointed out that the notion of a probability function of a single random variable is easily extended to two or more random variables. For instance, in chapter two an illustration was given involving two random variables: marital satisfaction and level of income. Let X be the random variable corresponding to marital satisfaction where X=1 indicates that a subject is happily married, while X=0 indicates that a subject is not. Next let Y be the random variable corresponding to the level of income. These levels will be denoted by 0,1, and 2 which indicate low, medium, and high income levels, respectively. Table 2.2.1 can now be written as shown in Table 3.3.1.

Table 3.1.1

		Level of Income			
		0	1	2	
Happily	1	.1	.2	.3	.6
Married	0	.05	.25	.1	.4
		.15	.45	.4	

In chapter two, the sample space was (yes,low), (yes,medium), etc., where a yes meant that a subject was happily married. Now the sample space consists of all pairs of numbers (x,y) where the possible values of x are x=0 and 1, and the possible values of y are y=0,1 and 2. The entries in Table 3.1.1 indicate the probability of observing (x,y). For instance, Pr(X=1,Y=1)=.2

The notation f(x) is also extended in an obvious way. In particular, f(x,y) refers to Pr(X=x,Y=y), and f(x,y) is called the joint probability function of X and Y. The term "joint" emphasizes that f(x,y) is the probability of having both X=x and Y=y. This is in contrast to the marginal probability function of X which refers to f(x). That is, the marginal probability function of X refers to Pr(X=x) regardless of what the value of Y might be. The term "marginal" is only used when you are working with the probability function of two or more random variables, and it indicates that one or more of the random variables is being ignored. For example, the joint probabilities of X and Y are contained in the six cells of Table 3.1.1, while the last column gives the marginal probability function of X, and the bottom row gives the marginal probability function of Y. As explained in chapter two, $Pr(X=1)=\Sigma_y f(1,y)=f(1,0)+f(1,1)+f(1,2)$ since (1,0), (1,1), and (1,2) are mutually exclusive events. Of course Pr(X=0) is determined in a similar manner. In fact it is generally true that

$$f(x)=\Sigma_y f(x,y)$$

where the summation is over all possible values of y, and

$$f(y)=\Sigma_x f(x,y)$$

where now the summation is over all possible values of x. It is noted that the term f(x,y) is easily extended to any n random variables, say X_1, $X_2,\ldots,X_n$. In this case

$$f(x_1,\ldots,x_n)=Pr(X_1=x_1,\ldots,X_n=x_n),$$

and $f(x_1,\ldots,x_n)$ is called the joint probability function of $X_1,\ldots,X_n$.

Finally, if $X_1,\ldots,X_n$ are independent random variables, then in terms of the notation just introduced,

$$f(x_1,\ldots,x_n)=f_1(x_1)f_2(x_2)\ldots f_n(x_n) \qquad (3.1.1)$$

where $f_1(x_1)$ is the marginal probability function of X_1, $f_2(X_2)$ is the marginal probability function of X_2, etc.

Definition 3.1.2. A random sample is a set of n independent observations, say $X_1,\ldots,X_n$ such that the probability function of X_1 is equal to the probability function of X_2, which is equal to the probability function of X_3, etc.

This definition says in effect that if $x_1,\ldots,x_n$ are values corresponding to $X_1,\ldots,X_n$, then $f_1(x_1)=f(x_1)$, $f_2(x_2)=f(x_2),\ldots,f_n(x_n)=f(x_n)$. That is, $X_1,\ldots,X_n$ have a common probability function which is called $f(x)$. Because $X_1,\ldots,X_n$ are independent,

$$Pr(X_1=x_1,\ldots,X_n=x_n)=f(x_1)f(x_2)\ldots f(x_n).$$

The concept of a random sample probably sounds much more complicated than it is actually is. Hopefully the following example will help clarify matters.

Example 3.1.3. Suppose for some population of subjects the possible values of X are 0,1,2, and 3, and that $f(0)=.2$, $f(1)=.1$, $f(2)=.4$, and $f(3)=.3$. Next suppose three subjects are selected and observed. Let X_1 be the observation corresponding to the first subject, X_2 the observation corresponding to the second subject, etc. For each X_i $(i=1,2,3)$ the possible values are, of course, 0,1,2, and 3. If the subjects are sampled in such a way that X_1, X_2, and X_3 are independent, and each has the probability function $f(x)$, then X_1, X_2, and X_3 constitute a random sample. For instance, the probability that the first subject has $X_1=1$, the second has $X_2=2$, and the third has $X_3=1$ is

$$f(1)f(2)f(1)=.1(.4)(.1)=.004.$$

Perhaps it should be noted that determining joint probabilities is important in some situations, but this is not the most important property of a random sample. The real importance of a random sample has to do with the estimation of population parameters which is discussed shortly.

A natural question to raise is how to ensure that a sample of subjects is indeed a random sample. One way to do this is to design your study so that every subject in the population has an equally likely chance of being selected and observed. This means, in particular, that all subjects have an equally likely chance of being the first subject sampled, all subjects have an equally likely chance of being the second subject sampled, etc. In this case, for any two subjects, say the ith and jth, $Pr(X_i=x)=Pr(X_j=x)$ for any x, and X_i and X_j are independent. In practice, though, this method is rarely used. One reason is that the population of subjects is often so large that it is difficult or even impossible to ensure that every potential subject has an equally likely chance of being included in the study. Another problem is that it is usually unclear just how large the population is, and in particular there is no list of the names of the persons in the population. Therefore, it is generally impossible to ensure that every potential subject has an equal chance of being included in your study. Also, even if the subjects could be randomly sampled, some might be unable or unwilling to participate in your study in which case the subjects you examine may not represent a random sample. About the only way around these problems is to assume your sample of subjects is "typical" of the population you are studying, and to temper your generalizations in light of the sampling problems you encounter. For example, if you take a telephone survey, your conclusions might only be valid for persons who were home the night you called and were willing to answer your questions.

It should be noted that the concept of a random sample can be extended to joint probability functions. Suppose for each subject in a study you observe two quantities, say X and Y. If for any two subjects, say the ith and jth, the joint events $(X_i=x_i, Y_i=y_i)$ are independent of the joint events $(X_j=x_j, Y_j=x_j)$, and if $f(x_i, y_i)$ is exactly the same for any subject, the pairs of observations $(X_1, Y_1), \ldots, (X_n, Y_n)$ is a random sample of size n.

3.2 CUMULATIVE DISTRIBUTIONS

Even more important than probability functions is the notion of a cumulative distribution, which is also known as a cumulative probability function, or simply as a distribution.

Definition 3.2.1. If f(x) is the probability function of the random variable X, the corresponding distribution is

$$F(x)=Pr(X\le x) \qquad (3.2.1)$$

The Discrete Case

While the notion of a distribution is simple, it is important to realize that the method of determining the distribution from the probability function of a discrete random variable is different from the situation where the random variable is continuous. In the discrete case you are always told what the possible values of the random variable X happen to be. In this case

$$\Pr(X \le x) = \Sigma_{y:y\le x} f(y)$$

where the summation is over all possible values of y that are less than or equal to x.

Example 3.2.1. Suppose the possible values of X are 0,1,2, and 3, and that f(0)=.05, f(1)=.2, f(2)=.3, and f(3)=.45. Thus, F(0)=.05, F(1)=.25, F(2)=.55 and F(3)=1.0.

Notice that if, for instance, you want to determine $\Pr(1 \le X \le 2)$, the answer is given by F(2)-F(0). In general, if the possible values of X, written in ascending order, are $x_1, \ldots, x_n$, $\Pr(x_i \le X \le x_j) = F(x_j) - F(x_{i-1})$.

Example 3.2.2. If the space of X is 1,2,3, and f(x)=x/6, then F(1)=1/6, F(2)=1/6+2/6=1/2, and F(3)=1.0.

The Continuous Case

So far the emphasis has been on discrete random variables. Such random variables are certainly important, but continuous random variables play an even more important role when applying statistical techniques. In contrast to the discrete case, the possible values of a continuous random variable (at least for all the cases considered in this book) are any real numbers in some interval [a,b]. That is, any real number satisfying $a \le x \le b$. In all cases that will be considered, you will be told what the values of a and b happen to be. The most important distribution is one where $a=-\infty$ and $b=\infty$, and this distribution is described in chapter five.

It should be mentioned that in the continuous case, f(x) is usually called a probability density function rather than just a probability function, as it was called in the discrete case. Also, any function such that $f(x) \ge 0$, and the area under the curve between a and b is equal to one, is called a probability density function.

In the discrete case, F(x) was determined by adding up all of the values of f(y) satisfying $y \le x$. For the continuous case, F(x) is the area under the probability density function and below the point x.

Example 3.2.2. A simple example will help clarify matters. Suppose the random variable X has the probability density function $f(x)=1$, $0 \le x \le 1$. This is known as the uniform probability density function. The area below $f(x)=1$ and between $x=0$ and $x=1$ is just the area of a square box having length one and height one. Thus, the area under the curve is one, and since $f(x) \ge 0$, $f(x)$ is a probability density function.

Suppose you want to determine $F(.7)$. This probability is the area of a rectangle having length .7 and height 1. Its area is $.7(1)=.7$, and so $F(.7)=.7$

Continuing the illustration, suppose you want to determine $\Pr(X \le .1 \text{ or } X \ge .8)$. The events $X \le .1$ and $X \ge .8$ are mutually exclusive, $\Pr(X \le .1)=.1$, $\Pr(X \ge .8)=.2$, and so $\Pr(X \le .1 \text{ or } X \ge .8)=.1+.2=.3$. Also notice that $\Pr(X \ge .8)=1-F(.8)$.

To further emphasize the difference between continuous and discrete distributions, by definition, in the continuous case, $\Pr(c \le X \le d)$, for any constants c and d, is the area under the curve $f(x)$ and between the points c and d. This is just a simple extension of how $F(x)$ was defined. In particular, $\Pr(c \le X \le d)$ is defined as $F(d)-F(c)$.

Now consider a specific point, say $x=.5$. Then $\Pr(X=.5)=F(.5)-F(.5)=0$. At first this result might seem strange because in general $f(x)>0$. For example, for the uniform distribution, $f(.5)=1$, but $\Pr(X=.5)=0$. The point is that in the continuous case, $f(x)$ does not tell you the probability of observing the value x--$f(x)$ is the probability of the event $X=x$ only in the discrete case.

Also note that for a continuous random variable, $\Pr(X<x)=\Pr(X \le x)$. The reason is that $\Pr(X \le x)$ is the union of two mutually exclusive events, namely, $X<x$ and $X=x$. But $\Pr(X=x)=0$, and so $\Pr(X<x)=\Pr(X \le x)$. Similarly, $\Pr(X>x)=\Pr(X \ge x)$.

Example 3.2.3. Suppose $f(x)=x$, $0 \le x \le \sqrt{2}$. The area under the line $f(x)=x$ and between 0 and $\sqrt{2}$ is $(1/2)(\sqrt{2})(\sqrt{2})=1$, and because $f(x) \ge 0$, $f(x)$ is a probability density function. Also, for any x between 0 and $\sqrt{2}$, $F(x)$ is the area of a triangle. For instance, $F(1)=(1/2)(1)(1)=1/2$. Similarly, $F(1.25)=(1/2)(1.25)^2=50/64$. Thus, $\Pr(1.0 \le X \le 1.25)=50/64 - 1/2=18/64$. To determine $\Pr(X \ge 1.0)$ simply note that it is equal to $1-\Pr(X<1.0)=1-1/2=1/2$.

Example 3.2.4. Suppose

$$f(x)=.1 \text{ for } 0 \le x \le 1$$

while

$$f(x)=.9 \text{ for } 1 \le X \le 2.$$

Then $F(.7)=(.1)(.7)=.07$, $F(1.3)=.1+.3(.9)=.37$,

$Pr(.7 \le X \le 1.3)=.03+.27=.3$, and $Pr(X \le 1.5)=.1+.5(.9)=.55$.

3.3 EXPECTATION

As previously indicated, the basic problem in statistics is using the observations from a random sample of subjects to make inferences about the events that are of interest in a particular situation. The purpose of this section is to describe the notion of expectation, which provides a link between the observations that are available from a specific study, and the probabilities that you are trying to determine. In addition, expectations provide a precise definition of the quantities that are of central interest in most studies. (These quantities are the population mean and population variance, which are defined below.) Again the problem is making inferences about these quantities based on the observations that result from some experiment, and the next chapter describes the most basic results on solving this problem. In every case the notion of expectation plays a central role.

The Discrete Case

Definition 3.3.1. Consider any discrete random variable X and let f(x) be the corresponding probability function. The expected value of X is defined to be

$$E(X)=\Sigma xf(x) \tag{3.3.1}$$

where the summation is over all possible values of X. In words, if every possible value of X is multiplied by the probability of observing this value, then the sum of these products is defined as the expected value of X. Frequently E(X) is written more simply as μ, which is called the population mean.

The quantity μ represents a "typical" or "central" value of the random variable X; it is the "average" of the these values. The more common notion of an average is the quantity $\bar{X}=(X_1+...+X_n)/n$ where $X_1,....,X_n$ are the observations resulting from some experiment. The quantity $\bar{X}$ is called a sample mean, and its connection with the population mean μ is discussed in the next chapter. The only goal here is to introduce the formal definition of μ.

Example 3.3.1. As a simple illustration, suppose subjects are asked to use a four-point scale to rate the importance of statistics in the social sciences. A rating of 1 indicates no importance while a rating of four indicates great importance. Thus, X would represent the ratings of subjects, and the possible values of X are x=1,2,3, and 4.

Now suppose that for the population of subjects you are studying, f(1)=.2, f(2)=.3, f(3)=.1, and f(4)=.4. (This probability function is used in the examples in the remainder of this chapter.) Then the mean or expected value of the rating for this population of subjects is

$$\begin{aligned}\mu&=E(X)\\&=1(.2)+2(.3)+3(.1)+4(.4)\\&=2.7.\end{aligned}$$

What will be needed are simple rules for determining expected values when a random variable is mathematically altered in some way. For example, it will be important to know how to determine the expected value of sample means and variances that are discussed in sections 3.7 and 3.8. Eventually these results will allow the reader to understand such notions as "degrees of freedom," and it will be a relatively simple matter to derive the expected value of the "sum of squares" terms in the analysis of variance models described in chapter eight.

<u>Expected Values of Functions of a Discrete Random Variable</u>

Let g(X) be any function of X. Then the expected value of g(X) is defined to be

$$E(g(X))=\Sigma_x g(x)f(x).$$

<u>Example 3.3.2.</u> Suppose $g(X)=X^2$. For the probability function used in example 3.3.1,

$$E(X^2)=\Sigma_x x^2 f(x)=1^2(.2)+2^2(.3)+3^2(.1)+4^2(.4)=8.7.$$

Certain functions are particularly important in statistics, and it is helpful to have rules of expectation for them. One of the simplest functions is g(X)=c where c is some constant. Then $E(g(X))=E(c)=\Sigma_x cf(x)$. But because f(x) is a probability function, $\Sigma_x f(x)=1$, so

$$E(c)=c \qquad (3.3.2)$$

That is, the expected value of a constant is equal to the constant.

<u>Example 3.3.3.</u> Next consider the function g(X)=X+c where again c is any real constant. Then

$$E(g(X))=E(X+c)$$
$$=\Sigma_x(x+c)f(x)$$
$$=\Sigma_x[xf(x)+cf(x)]$$
$$=E(X)+c$$

Thus,

$$E(X+c)=E(X)+c$$
$$=\mu+c \qquad (3.3.3)$$

In words, equation (3.3.3) says that if you add c to every value of X, then the average value of X, namely μ, is increased to $\mu+c$.

Example 3.3.4. If $\mu=10$ and $c=-3$, $E(X+c)=10-3=7$.

Example 3.3.5. It is important to realize that in practice, f(x) is usually not known, but nevertheless, μ is a constant. Thus,

$$E(X-\mu)=E(X)-E(\mu)=\mu-\mu=0.$$

Suppose instead the random variable X is multiplied by the constant c. That is, $g(X)=cX$. Then

$$E(cX)=\Sigma_x cxf(x)=c\Sigma_x f(x)=cE(X)$$
$$=c\mu \qquad (3.3.4)$$

This result is important when determining the expected value of the sample mean, as is demonstrated in chapter four.

Example 3.3.5. If $\mu=4$, $E(3X)=3\mu=12$.

Another important function is $g(X)=(X-\mu)^2$. By definition, the variance of X is

$$\sigma^2=E(X-\mu)^2.$$

The reason this quantity is important is discussed in the next chapter. For now the primary goal is to give the reader some idea of how expected values can be algebraically manipulated.

From the definition of the expected value of a function,

$$E(X-\mu)^2=\Sigma_x(x^2-2\mu x+\mu^2)f(x)$$

$$=E(X^2)-E(2\mu X)+\mu^2$$

$$=E(X^2)-2\mu^2+\mu^2$$

$$=E(X^2)-\mu^2. \qquad (3.3.5)$$

Thus, the variance can be written as

$$\sigma^2=E(X^2)-\mu^2 \qquad (3.3.6)$$

which is a useful result in some situations.

Example 3.3.6. For the probability function in example 3.3.1, it was found that μ=2.7. Thus, the variance is

$$\sigma^2=(1-2.7)^2(.2)+(2-2.7)^2(.3)+(3-2.7)^2(.1)+(4-2.7)^2(.4)$$

$$=.578+.147+.009+.676$$

$$=1.41.$$

In example 3.3.2 it was found that $E(X^2)=8.7$. Hence, the variance could have also been determined by computing $8.7-(2.7)^2=1.41$, which agrees with the computations given above.

3.4 EXPECTED VALUES INVOLVING TWO OR MORE RANDOM VARIABLES

In this section the notion of expected values is extended to two or more random variables. First consider two random variables, say X_1 and X_2. The most common way to think of these two measurements is that two subjects have been randomly sampled and that X_1 corresponds to the first subject while X_2 corresponds to the second. However, the results summarized here are quite general. For instance, X_1 and X_2 might represent two measurements taken on a single randomly sampled subject.

For notational convenience, let $X=X_1$, $Y=X_2$, and let f(x,y) be the joint probability function of X and Y. That is, f(x,y) is the probability that the values x and y both occur. Because f(x,y) is a probability function,

$$\Sigma_x\Sigma_y f(x,y)=1, \qquad (3.4.1)$$

$$\Sigma_y f(x,y)=f(x), \qquad (3.4.2)$$

and

$$\Sigma_x f(x,y)=f(y). \quad (3.4.3)$$

By definition, the expected value of any function of both X and Y, say g(X,Y), is defined by

$$E(g(X,Y))=\Sigma_x\Sigma_y g(x,y)f(x,y). \quad (3.4.4)$$

Example 3.4.1. Suppose g(X,Y)=X+Y. Then

$$E(X+Y)=\Sigma_x\Sigma_y(x+y)f(x,y)$$

$$=\Sigma_x x\Sigma_y f(x,y)+\Sigma_y yf(x,y).$$

From (3.4.2) and (3.4.3) this last expression is equal to

$$\Sigma_x xf(x)+\Sigma_y yf(y)=E(X)+E(Y).$$

In words, for any two random variables, the expected value of their sum is equal to the sum of the expected values. Notice that even though E(X+Y) is defined in terms of f(x,y), the joint probability function of X and Y, you do not need to know f(x,y) to determine E(X+Y)--if the marginal distributions of X and Y are known, E(X+Y) can be determined.

Proceeding as was done in the preceding section, it can also be shown that for any constant c, E[c(X+Y)]=cE(X)+cE(Y). For instance, if c=1/2,

$$E[(1/2)(X+Y)]=(1/2)E(X)+(1/2)E(Y).$$

Also, E(X-Y)=E(X)-E(Y).

Example 3.4.2. Suppose that for some population of subjects with hypertension, X_1 represents a subject's diastolic blood pressure, and X_2 is the same subject's diastolic blood pressure after some experimental treatment has been applied. Then X_1-X_2 represents the change in blood pressure and $E(X_1-X_2)$ is the expected or average change. If $E(X_1)=110$ and $E(X_2)=90$, then the average drop in blood pressure is $E(X_1-X_2)=110-90=20$.

Now consider any n random variables, say $X_1,\ldots,X_n$, having the joint probability function $f(x_1,\ldots,x_n)$. The expected value of $g(X_1,\ldots,X_n)$ is defined as

$$E(g(X_1,\ldots,X_n))=\Sigma\ldots\Sigma g(x_1,\ldots,x_n)f(x_1,\ldots,x_n),$$

where the summations are over all possible values of the x's.

Proceeding as was done for n=2, it can be seen that

$$E(\Sigma X_i)=\Sigma E(X_i). \quad (3.4.5)$$

That is, the expected value of the sum equals the sum of the expected values. More generally, for any constants $c_1, c_2, \ldots, c_n$

$$E(\Sigma c_i X_i)=\Sigma c_i E(X_i)$$

$$=\Sigma c_i \mu_i. \quad (3.4.6)$$

For instance, if $E(X_1)=3$, $E(X_2)=5$, $E(X_3)=6$, then $E(X_1+2X_2-4X_3)=3+2(5)-4(6)=-11$.

Another important function is $g(X_1, \ldots, X_n)=\Sigma X_i^2$. Proceeding as done for ΣX_i, it can be seen that

$$E(\Sigma X_i^2)=\Sigma E(X_i^2).$$

Consider any two random variables, say X and Y, and let g(X,Y)=XY. Then by definition,

$$E(XY)=\Sigma\Sigma xyf(x,y).$$

Now suppose X and Y are independent. That is, f(x,y)=f(x)f(y), in which case

$$E(XY)=\Sigma_x \Sigma_y xyf(x,y)$$

$$=(\Sigma xf(x))(\Sigma yf(y))$$

$$=E(X)E(Y). \quad (3.4.7)$$

Verbally, if two random variables are independent, the expected value of their product equals the product of their expected values. If, however, X and Y are dependent, E(XY) may or may not equal E(X)E(Y).

Some caution must be used when determining the expected value of the product of two random variables. A common mistake in connection with the F distribution (which is described in chapter six) is as follows. Suppose X and Y are independent, and that $E(X)=\mu_x$ and $E(Y)=\mu_y$. Further suppose you want to determine E(X/Y). It can be shown that the independence of X and Y implies that X and 1/Y are also independent, and so

$$E(X/Y)=E(X)E(1/Y).$$

But in general, $E(1/Y) \neq 1/\mu_y$, and so it would be incorrect to conclude that $E(X/Y)=\mu_x/\mu_y$.

3.5 EXPECTED VALUES OF CONTINUOUS RANDOM VARIABLES

All of the results concerning the expected value of discrete random variables also hold when the random variables are continuous. The only difference is that the summation terms used in the discrete case are replaced by an integral. There are no instances in this book where you are given the probability density function of a continuous random variable X and asked to determine E(g(X)) using integrals. However, it is important to realize that all of the rules of expectations that were derived above also apply when X is continuous.

As an illustration, suppose X is a continuous random variable having $E(X)=5$ and $\sigma^2=25$, and you are asked to determine $E(X^2)$. From (3.3.6), $E(X^2)=\sigma^2+\mu^2=25+5^2=50$.

3.6 OTHER CHARACTERISTICS OF PROBABILITY FUNCTIONS

A few other concepts related to probability functions need to be described.

Definition 3.6.1. A mode of a distribution is a value of X for which f(x) attains its maximum value. For a discrete random variable, a mode is a value of X for which no other value has a higher probability of occurring. An important point is that there can be more than one mode, and this is illustrated in the examples below.

Example 3.6.1. If the possible values of X are 0,1,2, and 3, f(0)=.25, f(1)=.3, f(2)=.05, and f(3)=.4, the mode is 3. If instead f(0)=f(1)=.1 and f(2)=f(3)=.4, there are two modes, namely, 2 and 3.

Example 3.6.2. If $f(x)=x$, $0 \le x \le \sqrt{2}$, the mode is $\sqrt{2}$.

Example 3.6.3. If $f(x)=x$ for $0 \le x \le 1$, and $f(x)=-x+2$, for $1<x\le 2$, the mode is x=1.

Definition 3.6.2. The median of a distribution is any point x such that $Pr(X<x) \le 1/2$ and $Pr(X \le x) \ge 1/2$.

Example 3.6.4. Suppose the cumulative distribution is given by F(0)=.2, F(1)=.5, F(2)=.6, and F(3)=1.0. (The only possible values of X are 0,1,2, and 3.) Then x=1 is a median because $Pr(X<1)=F(0)=.2\le 1/2$ and $Pr(X\le 1)=F(1)=.5$, which satisfies the definition of a median, since $.5\ge .5$. However, it is also true that $Pr(X<1.5)\le .5$ and $Pr(X\le 1.5)=.5$, and so 1.5 is also a median.

Example 3.6.5. If $F(x)=x^2/4$, $0\le x\le 2$, $x=\surd 2$ is a median because $Pr(X<\surd 2)=Pr(X\le \surd 2)=.5$.

As you have probably surmised by now, it is usually a simple matter to determine the median for a continuous random variable; the median is unique and it is just the point x such that $Pr(X\le x)=1/2$. However, if the median is defined to be the value x such that $Pr(X\le x)=1/2$, then for a discrete random variable, such as in example 3.6.1, there might be no median at all. From a practical point of view it turns out to be convenient to define the median in such a way that at least one median always exists, and this is why definition 3.6.2 is used.

Definition 3.6.3. Let p be any number such that $0<p<1$. A quantile of order p (or more simply, the pth quantile) of a distribution is a value of X, say x_p, such that $Pr(X<x_p)\le p$ and $Pr(X\le x_p)\ge p$. Another common term for x_p is (100p)th percentile. For the special case $p=1/2$, x_p is a median.

Example 3.6.6. In example 3.6.4, a 60th percentile, which is the same as a quantile of order .6, is 2. Similarly, 2.5 is a 60th percentile because $Pr(X<2.5)\le .6$, and $Pr(X\le 2.5)\ge .6$. In contrast, there is only one 95th percentile, namely 3. To verify that 3 is a 95th percentile, note that $Pr(X<3)=.6\le .95$, and $Pr(X\le 3)=1.0>.95$. To see that the 95th percentile is unique, suppose $x<3$. Then $F(x)\le .6$, and so x cannot be a .95 quantile. But if $x>3$, $Pr(X<x)=1.0$, and again x cannot be a .95 quantile. Thus, the only 95th percentile is 3.

In the continuous case the pth quantile is uniquely defined. It is the point x such that $F(x)=p$. In example 3.6.2, for instance, $F(x)=x^2/2$. Thus, the pth quantile is the point x such that $x^2/2=p$, and so the pth quantile is $x=\surd(2p)$.

3.7 ESTIMATION

The general goal of the remainder of this chapter is to begin to develop ways of making inferences about the quantities that characterize a population of subjects. Of particular importance are procedures that yield information about the value of μ, the population mean, and σ^2, the population variance. First, however, it may help to consider simple ways in which the population mean and sample mean are related. Once this is done, the importance of the population variance can be explained.

As already mentioned, the term "mean" or "average" usually brings to mind the sample mean $\bar{X}$. It turns out that $\bar{X}$ is related to μ in several ways, the most basic of which is through the sample probability function that is introduced next.

Definition 3.7.1. Let $X_1,\ldots,X_n$ be a random sample of size n from a discrete distribution, and let f_x be the number of times the value of x occurs among the values in the sample. Then the values f_x/n, for all possible values of X, are called a sample probability function.

Example 3.7.1. Suppose you randomly sample 65 subjects and give each a test to measure how open-minded they are. Suppose the frequencies of the scores are as follows:

x	f_x	f_x/n
1	5	5/65
2	10	10/65
3	20	20/65
4	17	17/65
5	13	13/65
	65	1.0

For example, among the 65 subjects, 20 got a score of 3. The relative frequency of the score is defined to be f_x/n, and the five values of f_x/n in the above table constitute a sample probability function.

As mentioned in chapter two, relative frequencies are related to probabilities in several ways and one of these ways is through the "law of large numbers." This law addresses the question of whether f_x/n is a reasonable approximation of $f(x)=\Pr(X=x)$. Basically this law says that as n, the sample size, gets large, you can be increasingly certain that the difference between f(x) and f_x/n is small. In fact, f_x/n converges to f(x). More precise descriptions of this law are covered in books on mathematical statistics--in fact several versions of this law exist--but these details are not important here. The only important point is that if you have a random sample of n subjects, f_x/n is a reasonable estimate of f(x).

Returning to the observed frequencies, suppose you want to use a single number to represent the "typical" score among the 65 subjects. One way to do this is to compute the sample mean $\bar{X}$. From the observed frequencies you know that five subjects got a score of 1, 10 got a score of 2, etc. Thus,

$$\Sigma X_i = 1+1+1+1+1+2+\ldots+5 = \Sigma_x x f_x.$$

Hence,

$$\Sigma X_i/n = \Sigma_x (x/n) f_x.$$

Consequently, another way of writing the sample mean is

$$\bar{X} = \Sigma x f_x/n.$$

By definition, the population mean is

$$\mu = \Sigma x f(x).$$

Because f_x/n is an estimate of $f(x)$, a reasonable approach to estimating μ would seem to be to replace $f(x)$, an unknown quantity, with f_x/n, a known quantity resulting from the sample of subjects. This is precisely what is done in practice, and so $\bar{X}$ provides an estimate of μ. In fact, the law of large numbers implies that as n gets large, $\bar{X}$ tends to be closer and closer to μ. That is, $\bar{X}$ converges to μ.

There are other ways of justifying $\bar{X}$ as an estimate of μ; one of these is considered below. The main goal here is to clarify the relationship between $\bar{X}$ and μ.

Example 3.7.2. You randomly sample five subjects and observe the values 10, 12, 18, 25, and 25. To determine an estimate of μ, compute $(10+12+18+25+25)/5=18$.

How else can $\bar{X}$ be justified as an estimate of μ? Put more generally, what criterion should be used when searching for an estimate of μ? One possibility is to search for a quantity that, on the average, is equal to μ. That is, if the experiment were repeated over and over again, and in every case n subjects are randomly sampled, it would be nice if the average of the estimates of μ were indeed equal to μ. Put in terms of the concepts developed so far, if the expected value of the estimate of μ is indeed equal to μ, it would seem to be a good estimate of μ.

Because it is assumed that $X_1,\ldots,X_n$ is a random sample, $E(X_1)=E(X_2)=\ldots=E(X_n)=\mu$. This is true because from the definition of a random sample, the X_i's have identical probability functions. Applying the rules of expectation,

$$E(\bar{X}) = E(\Sigma X_i/n) = \Sigma E(X_i/n) = \Sigma\mu/n = \mu.$$

In words, the expected value of $\bar{X}$ is μ, and this provides one more reason for estimating μ with $\bar{X}$.

3.8 THE POPULATION VARIANCE

Although $\bar{X}$ has been justified as an estimate of μ, it is far from clear whether this estimate gives you an accurate result. That is, is it reasonable to believe that $\bar{X}$ will be close to μ?

The first step in addressing this problem is finding a reasonable measure that indicates whether $\bar{X}$ can be expected to be close to μ. First consider the simplest case where you have a single observation X. Because $E(X)=\mu$, X is used as an estimate of μ. But is it reasonable to expect the observed value of X to be close to μ?

To help clarify matters, consider two probability functions:

x	$f_1(x)$	$f_2(x)$
-2	.05	.2
-1	.2	.2
0	.5	.2
1	.2	.2
2	.05	.2

The probability functions $f_1(x)$ and $f_2(x)$ both have means $\mu=0$. However, for the first probability function, $Pr(X=0)=.5$, while for the second $Pr(X=0)=.2$. Also, for the first probability function, $Pr(-1\le X\le 1)=.9$, while for the second, $Pr(-1\le X\le 1)=.6$. The point is that for $f_1(x)$, the value of X can be expected to be closer to μ than it is for $f_2(x)$.

To give a more concrete explanation, if you sample a subject and measure, say, this person's "level of ambition," and $f_1(x)$ is the probability function of the observed scores, chances are the subjects's observed response will be within one unit of the mean. If however $f_2(x)$ is the probability function, there is a good chance that the sampled subject will have a score of 2 or -2, which is as far away from the mean as is possible, and so the observed score has a good chance of yielding a much poorer indication of μ. Of course, the same is true if n subjects are randomly sampled. For $f_1(x)$, the observed scores will tend to be more tightly clustered around the population mean, μ, than they would if the underlying probability function were $f_2(x)$.

What will be needed is a single number that indicates the extent to which the value of X can be expected to be close to μ. It might seem that the average value of $X-\mu$ could be used, but this is unsatisfactory because it is always true that $E(X-\mu)=0$. Thus, this measure gives no indication of whether X can be expected to be close to μ. What turns out to be a very useful quantity for solving the problem at hand is $E(X-\mu)^2$. This quantity was mentioned in the section on expectation, and it is called the population variance, σ^2. Note that $(x-\mu)^2 \geq 0$ for any x, and so $\sigma^2 \geq 0$.

If you sample a single subject and if σ^2 is small, the observed value corresponding to this subject will tend to be close to μ. The extreme case is where $Pr(X=\mu)=1$, which implies that $\sigma^2=0$. If the values of X tend to be spread out, that is, they have a relatively high probability of not being close to μ, σ^2 will be large.

Example 3.8.1. Consider the two probability functions described above. For the first $\sigma^2=.8$, while for the second $\sigma^2=2.0$. Thus, if you were to sample from the first population, and then sample a subject from the second, you would expect the observation from the first population to be closer to its mean.

There are many ways in which the quantity σ^2 plays a role in determining whether you can expect an accurate estimate of μ, and they are described in subsequent chapters. For now, two problems need to be addressed. The first is measuring how well $\bar{X}$ estimates μ, and the second is that while σ^2 indicates how well X estimates μ, μ is not known, and so σ^2 is not known either.

First consider the problem of measuring whether $\bar{X}$ can be expected to be close to μ. As in the case n=1, it turns out to be convenient to use $E(\bar{X}-\mu)^2$. Note that $\bar{X}$ is a random variable, as is X, the mean of $\bar{X}$ is μ, and so $E(\bar{X}-\mu)^2$ is the variance of the random variable $\bar{X}$. As for the case n=1, this quantity measures the extent to which $\bar{X}$ can be expected to be close to μ.

It turns out that $E(\bar{X}-\mu)^2$ is related to σ^2. This can be established by applying the rules of expectation to the quantity $E(\bar{X}-\mu)^2$. In particular,

$$\begin{aligned} E(\bar{X}-\mu)^2 &= E(\bar{X}^2-2\mu\bar{X}+\mu^2) \\ &= E(\bar{X}^2)-2\mu E(\bar{X})+E(\mu^2) \\ &= E(\bar{X}^2)-\mu^2 \end{aligned} \qquad (3.8.1)$$

Next consider $E(\bar{X}^2)$. It is equal to

$$E(\Sigma X_i/n)^2=(1/n^2)E(\Sigma X_i^2+\Sigma_{i\neq j}X_iX_j).$$

Consider $\Sigma_{i\neq j}$. The number of terms in this summation is n(n-1). But this last equation is equal to

$$(1/n^2)[\Sigma E(X_i^2)+\Sigma_{i\neq j}E(X_iX_j)].$$

From equation (3.3.6), $E(X_i^2)=\sigma^2+\mu^2$, and because X_i and X_j are independent for $i\neq j$, $E(X_iX_j)=\mu^2$. Thus, the previous equation reduces to

$$(1/n^2)[\Sigma(\sigma^2+\mu^2)+\Sigma_{i\neq j}\mu^2]=(1/n^2)[n\sigma^2+n\mu^2+(n^2-n)\mu^2]$$

$$=\sigma^2/n+\mu^2.$$

Substituting this result for $E(\bar{X}^2)$ in equation (3.8.1) yields

$$E(\bar{X}-\mu)^2=\sigma^2/n. \qquad (3.8.2)$$

In words, if you randomly sample n observations from a distribution that has variance σ^2, the variance of $\bar{X}$ is σ^2/n.

Notice that as n gets large, σ^2/n approaches zero. That is, as the sample size increases, $\bar{X}$ becomes an increasingly more accurate estimate of μ because the variance of $\bar{X}$ is getting smaller. This result is consistent with the earlier observation that $\bar{X}$ approaches μ as n gets large.

3.9 THE DISTRIBUTION OF $\bar{X}$

It may help to emphasize that the sample mean $\bar{X}$ is a random variable that has a probability function. While there are no instances in this book where you will be required to derive the probability function of the sample mean, some results may be easier to understand if it is briefly indicated how the probability function of $\bar{X}$ could be determined for a discrete random variable.

Example 3.9.1 Suppose f(1)=.3, f(2)=.5, and f(3)=.2. If X_1 and X_2 are a random sample, X_1 and X_2 are independent, and each has the probability function just given. Thus, $f(x_1,x_2)$ is known and it is $f(1,1)=.3^2=.09$, f(1,2)=.15, f(1,3)=.06, f(2,1)=.15, f(2,2)=.25, f(2,3)=.1, f(3,1)=.06, f(3,2)=.1, and f(3,3)=.04.

Next note that the possible values of $\bar{X}$ are (1+1)/2=1.0, (1+2)/2=1.5, (1+3)/2=2, (2+1)/2=1.5, (2+2)/2=2, (2+3)/2=2.5, (3+1)/2=2, (3+2)/2=2.5, and (3+3)/2=3. The only way it is possible to have $\bar{X}=1$ is if $X_1=1$ and $X_2=1$. Thus, $Pr(\bar{X}=1)=f(1,1)=.09$. The event $\bar{X}=1.5$ consists of two mutually exclusive events, namely, $(X_1=1,X_2=2)$ and $(X_1=2,X_2=1)$. Thus, $Pr(\bar{X}=1.5)=f(1,2)+f(2,1)=.3$. The probability of observing the remaining values of $\bar{X}$ can be determined in a similar manner.

3.10 ESTIMATION OF THE VARIANCE

The previous section pointed out that the population variance is a useful quantity when measuring how well $\bar{X}$ estimates μ, but a practical problem is that f(x) is not known, and so σ^2 is unknown as well.

Because $\sigma^2=\Sigma_x(x-\mu)^2f(x)$, a reasonable estimate of σ^2 would seem to be $\Sigma(x-\mu)^2f_x/n$. However, this estimate of σ^2 is not very useful since it depends on the unknown quantity μ. But μ can be estimated with $\bar{X}$, which suggests that σ^2 be estimated with

$$\Sigma(X_i-\bar{X})^2/n \qquad (3.10.1)$$

While equation (3.10.1) is certainly a reasonable estimate of σ^2, will the average value of (3.10.1) equal σ^2? That is, is the expected value of (3.10.1) equal to σ^2?

To answer this question, first note that

$$\Sigma(X_i-\bar{X})^2=\Sigma(X_i^2-2\bar{X}(X_i)+\bar{X}^2)$$

$$=(\Sigma X_i^2)-2n\bar{X}^2+n\bar{X}^2 \quad \text{(because } \Sigma X_i=n\bar{X}\text{)}$$

$$=(\Sigma X_i^2)-n\bar{X}^2.$$

It was previously indicated that $E(\bar{X}^2)=\sigma^2/n+\mu^2$, which can be used to show that

$$E[\Sigma(X_i-\bar{X})^2/n]=(n-1)\sigma^2/n.$$

Thus, the expected value of equation (3.8.2) is <u>not</u> σ^2.

Next consider

$$s^2=\Sigma(X_i-\bar{X})^2/(n-1).$$

From the above results it can be seen that

$$E(s^2)=\sigma^2.$$

Hence, the expected value of s^2 is σ^2, and for this reason s^2 is used to estimate σ^2. The quantity s^2 is called the <u>sample variance.</u>

3.11 UNBIASED ESTIMATION, STATISTICS, AND PARAMETERS

In the preceding section, two parameters were identified (μ and σ^2), and a function of the observations was derived, say

$g(X_1,\ldots,X_n)$, with the property that $E(g(X_1,\ldots,X_n))$ equals the parameter being estimated. This approach to estimation is so common it has been given a special name. It is called unbiased estimation.

Definition 3.11.1 Let θ be any quantity that is defined in terms of some unknown probability function f(x). The quantity θ is called a population parameter.

The term "parameter" has been used in connection with μ and σ^2, but it is useful to have the formal definition just given.

Definition 3.11.2. Let $X_1,\ldots,X_n$ be a random sample of n subjects, and let $g(X_1,\ldots,X_n)$ be a function of $X_1,\ldots,X_n$ such that $E(g(X_1,\ldots,X_n))=\theta$. Then $g(X_1,\ldots,X_n)$ is called an unbiased estimate of θ.

Example 3.11.1. Suppose you want an unbiased estimate of the mean and variance of the triglyceride levels of psychology graduate students. If you randomly sample four students and observe the values 80, 90, 90, and 110, the unbiased estimate of μ is

$$\bar{X}=(80+90+90+110)/4=92.5.$$

The unbiased estimate of σ^2 is

$$s^2=[(80-92.5)^2+(90-92.5)^2+(90-92.5)^2+(110-92.5)^2]/3=158.3.$$

Definition 3.11.3. The quantity σ is called the population standard deviation. It is the square root of the variance.

Because s^2 estimates σ^2, a natural estimate of σ is s. However, s is a biased estimate of σ. An unbiased estimate is given by

$$\{1+1/[4(n-1)]\}s.$$

Definition 3.11.4. A statistic is any function of the random sample $X_1,\ldots,X_n$ that does not depend on any unknown population parameter.

Example 3.11.3. The quantities $\bar{X}$, s^2, and s are statistics, but the quantities μ, σ and $\bar{X}/\sigma$ are not.

Chapter one gave an informal description of the goals of statistics. Using the definitions just given, a more precise description of these goals can now be stated. Consider a population of subjects, and suppose you want to make inferences about certain parameters (e.g., μ and σ^2) associated with some random variable X. Inferences about these parameters are based on statistics, and the operation known as expectation is the link between the observations resulting from a particular experiment and the parameters being estimated.

EXERCISES

3.1 Suppose the possible values of the random variable X are -1, 0 and 1, and that f(-1)=.3, f(0)=.2 and f(1)=.5. Determine

a) $Pr(X \le 0)$
b) $Pr(X<0)$
c) $Pr(X \le .5)$
d) $Pr(X \le 2.0)$
e) $Pr(-.5 \le X \le .5)$

3.2 Suppose the random variables X and Y have a joint probability function as shown in the table.

		Y		
		1	2	3
	1	.05	.08	.02
X	2	.1	.1	.15
	3	.2	.3	0.0

Determine

a) $f(2,3)=Pr(X=2,Y=3)$
b) the marginal probability that Y=2
c) the marginal probability that X=3
d) $Pr(X \le 1 \text{ and } Y \le 2)$

3.3 You measure a single person's height (X) and weight (Y). Is it reasonable to believe that the two values (X,Y) constitute a random sample of size 2? Compare the answer to this problem to the answer to exercise 3.4.

3.4 As in exercise 3.3 you measure height and weight, but this time you have a population of 100 subjects and you sample 10 with replacement. If every time a subject is sampled, every subject has a .01 probability of being selected, and if the pairs of measures are (X_1,Y_1), (X_2,Y_2), ..., (X_{10},Y_{10}), is it reasonable to assume $X_1,\ldots,X_{10}$ is a random sample? What about $Y_1,\ldots Y_{10}$? What about the pairs of values $(X_1,Y_1),\ldots,(X_{10},Y_{10})$?

3.5 Suppose

$f(x)=.2$ for $0\le x\le 1$,
$f(x)=.3$ for $1<x\le 2$, and
$f(x)=.5$ for $2<x\le 3$.

Determine

a) $Pr(X\le .1)$
b) $Pr(X\le 1.3)$
c) $Pr(X<1.3)$
d) $Pr(X\ge 1.4)$
e) $Pr(.5\le X\le 2.5)$
f) $Pr(X\le .1$ or $X\ge 2.4)$
g) $Pr(X\le .4|X\le 2)$
h) $Pr(X=2.5)$

3.6 Suppose

$f(x)=x$ for $0\le x\le 1$ and
$f(x)=-x+2$ for $1<x<2$.

Verify that f(x) is a probability density function and devise an expression for F(x). Then determine

a) $Pr(X\le .5)$
b) $Pr(X\ge 1.5)$
c) $Pr(X\le .5$ or $X\ge 1.5)$
d) $Pr(.2\le X\le 1.8)$.

3.7 Determine the population mean μ and variance σ^2 for the probability function in exercise 3.1.

3.8 For the uniform distribution, $\mu=E(X)=1/2$ and $E(X^2)=1/3$. What is the variance? Also determine

a) $E(X+5)$
b) $E(6X)$

3.9 Suppose you have a random sample of 10 subjects, say $X_1,\ldots,X_{10}$, and that the corresponding probability function is that given in exercise 3.1. Determine

a) $E(\Sigma X_i)$
b) $E(\Sigma X_i/10)$
c) $E(\Sigma X_i^2)$

3.10 Repeat exercise 3.9, but this time assume the possible values of X are 1, 2 and 3 and that $f(1)=.5$, $f(2)=.4$, and $f(3)=.1$. Does $E(1/X)=1/\mu$?

3.11 Suppose you randomly sample five subjects and for each subject you measure blood pressure before receiving drug A, and 30 minutes after receiving drug A. For the i<u>th</u> subject, let X_i and Y_i represent blood pressure before and after, respectively. Thus,

$X_1,\ldots,X_5$ is a random sample, and so is $Y_1,\ldots,Y_5$.

a) Is it reasonable to assume X_i and Y_i are independent?

b) Is it reasonable to assume X_i is independent of X_j, $i \neq j$?

Suppose E(X)=120 and E(Y)=110 and determine

c) $E(\Sigma X_i - \Sigma Y_i)$

d) $E(\Sigma(X_i - Y_i)/5)$

e) Is X_1 independent of Y_2?

3.12 If X and Y are independent, E(X)=10, E(Y)=1, and $E(X-Y)^2=100$, what is the variance of X-Y? Hint: Let Z=X-Y, determine E(Z) and apply equation (3.3.6).

3.13 For the probability function in exercise 3.1, determine a mode, a median, and a 90th percentile.

3.14 Repeat exercise 3.13, but use the probability function in exercise 3.10.

3.15 You conduct an experiment and for a random sample of five subjects you observe the values 5, 8, 7, 9, and 11. What is the unbiased estimate of the mean, variance, and standard deviation?

3.16 Show that if c is a constant, and X has mean μ and variance σ^2, then the variance of X+c is also σ^2.

CHAPTER FOUR

BINOMIAL AND NORMAL DISTRIBUTIONS

Consider any random experiment where subjects are classified into one of two mutually exclusive categories. For example, subjects might either pass or fail a statistics course, survive or die after an operation, exhibit signs of schizophrenia or have no signs, etc. For these situations, a special probability function arises. Called the binomial probability function, it is one of the most important probability functions for discrete random variables. For a random sample of n subjects, it turns out that there is a simple expression for determining the probability that exactly x subjects will belong to the first category, and the remaining n-x belong to the second. Three goals in this chapter are to derive this expression, indicate some of the properties of the resulting probability function, and to briefly indicate how the probability function can be used. Additional applications are discussed in chapter five. Another goal is to introduce the normal distribution and to discuss some of its properties.

4.1 PERMUTATIONS AND COMBINATIONS

Permutations

The first step in deriving the binomial probability function is understanding the notion of a permutation. Starting with the simplest case, consider any two objects. For convenience, let these objects be the letters A and B. There are two possible sequences that can be formed from these two letters, namely, AB and BA. Notice that there are two ways of filling the first position in the sequence, and once this position is filled, there is only one letter left that can be used to fill the second position. Also, it is being assumed that order counts. That is, the sequence AB is different from the sequence BA. When order counts, a sequence of objects is called a permutation.

Now consider the letters A, B, and C. How many permutations are there? The answer can be derived by noting that there are three ways in which the sequence can start, namely with an A or a B or a C. Once one of these letters is put in the first position, there are two choices left for the second. For instance, if the first letter in the sequence is B, the second letter must be either an A or a C. Of course, once the first two positions have been determined, the third position is automatically determined as well.

More generally, suppose you have n objects. Then there are $n!=n(n-1)(n-2)\ldots(2)(1)$ permutations of these objects. (The term n! is read n factorial. For instance, 4!=4(3)(2)(1)=24.) To see this, note that there are n ways of filling the first position in the sequence. Once this position is filled, there are n-1 ways of filling the second, etc. This method of determining the number of sequences is an example of a "counting" rule.

Next suppose you have n objects and that x of these objects are selected. How many permutations of these x objects are there? Proceeding as in the previous paragraph, there are n ways of filling the first position, n-1 ways of filling the second, etc. The total number of positions being determined is x, and so the answer is

$$P(n,x)=n(n-1)\ldots(n-x+1)$$

$$n!/(n-x)! \tag{4.1.1}$$

<u>Example 4.1.1.</u> Suppose four horses compete in a race. Call them A, B, C, and D. You are allowed one guess as to which horse will finish first, and which will finish second. How many different guesses are possible? You could of course list all the guesses that are possible. The first is (A,B) meaning that horse A finishes first and B finishes second. The remaining possibilites are (B,A), (A,C), etc. However, a simpler method for determining the answer is to note you are interested in the number of permutations of x=2 objects selected from the n=4 horses. Thus, the answer is 4!/2!=12.

<u>Example 4.1.2.</u> A subject is told that three of nine chips are going to be selected from a container without replacement. If the chips are numbered one through nine, and if before each chip is selected the subject is asked to predict the number that will be chosen, what is the probability of a correct guess on all three draws if the subject guesses at random?

In this case order counts and there are x=3 chips drawn from a total of nine chips. Thus, there are 9!/6! possible outcomes, and only one of these outcomes correponds to a correct guess on all three draws. If the subject guesses at random, the probability of a correct prediction for all three draws is 1/(9!/6!)=6!/9!.

<u>Combinations</u>

In contrast to permutations are combinations where order does not count. For example, the combination of letters A, B, and C is just the set {A,B,C} which is the same as the set {A,C,B} which is equal to the set {B,C,A}, etc.

A fundamental result is that if x objects are selected from n objects, the number of possible combinations is

$$C(n,x)=n!/[x!(n-x)!]. \quad (4.1.2)$$

To verify this result, consider any combination of x objects. From (4.1.1) there are x! permutations of these x objects. But the total number of permutations is the total number of combinations multiplied by x!. In symbols,

$$P(n,x)=C(n,x)x!$$

Hence,

$$C(n,x)=P(n,x)/x!=n!/[x!(n-x)!].$$

Example 4.1.3. Consider example 4.1.1, but this time suppose you are asked to guess which two horses will be in first or second place. For instance, if you choose horses A and C, the events (A,C) and (C,A) are considered to be the same since the problem is not choosing which will be in first and which will be in second, but rather which two horses will occupy one of the first two positions. From (4.1.2) the total number of possible guesses is 4!/(2!2!)=6.

To illustrate the logic behind the derivation of (4.1.2), note that the results in example 4.1.3 could be obtained by first recalling that the total number of permutations is 4!/2! But for any two horses, there are 2 ways in which they can be arranged so that they occupy either first or second place. Thus, 2! permutations correspond to every combination, and so the number of combinations is (4!/2!)(1/2!) which agrees with the results given above.

4.2 DERIVATION OF THE BINOMIAL PROBABILITY FUNCTION

Consider a random sample of n subjects where each subject belongs to one of two categories. Traditionally these two categories are called "success" and "failure." If the ith subject is classified as being a success, set the random variable $X_i=1$; otherwise set $X_i=0$.

Let X be the total number of successes among the n subjects, and observe that because X_i equals one or zero, $X=\Sigma X_i$. The goal is to derive a simple expression for f(x), the probability of x successes among the n randomly sampled subjects.

Because $X_1,\ldots,X_n$ is a random sample,

$Pr(X_1=1)=Pr(X_2=1)=...=Pr(X_n=1)=p$, say. Set $q=1-p$ and consider any sequence of 1's and 0's. To take a specific case, suppose n=5 and consider the event (1,0,1,0,0). Thus, there are x=2 successes, and from the assumption of independence, the joint probability of these events is

$$Pr(1,0,1,0,0)=pqpqq=p^2q^3.$$

The important point is that for any sequence of 1's and 0's where there are exactly two successes in five trials, the probability of observing this sequence, assuming order counts, is p^2q^3. But these events are mutually exclusive. For instance, (1,0,1,0,0) is different from the event (0,0,0,1,1), and the probability of x=2 successes is the sum of the probabilities corresponding to all sequences having x=2 successes. If you list all sequences having two 1's and three 0's you will see that there are ten such sequences, and so the probability of x=2 successes is $10p^2q^3$.

In the general case where there are x successes among n subjects, each sequence having exactly x 1's and n-x 0's has probability

$$p^x q^{n-x}$$

of occurring. Thus, to determine the probability of exactly x successes, you need a simple expression that indicates how many sequences of 1's and 0's there are where there are exactly x 1's.

The answer is derived in basically the same manner as was the expression C(n,x). To illustrate the process, again consider the case x=2 and n=5. Every sequence consists of five objects, namely two 1's and three 0's. To emphasize that there are five distinct objects or subjects, a subscript will be added to each number. Thus, the five objects being considered are 1_1, 1_2, 0_1, 0_2, and 0_3. For the problem at hand, the sequence $(1_1,1_2,0_1,0_2,0_3)$ is the same as the event $(1_2,1_1,0_1,0_2,0_3)$. That is, the order of the objects 1_1 and 1_2 is being ignored. Consequently, when determining how many sequences of five objects there are where the order of the objects 1_1 and 1_2 is ignored, you must divide the number of permutations of these five objects by 2!. Similarly, you must also divide the number of permutations by 3! because the order of the objects 0_1, 0_2, and 0_3 is also being ignored. The result is that the number of sequences having exactly two 1's is 5!/[2!3!]=10

The same logic applies to the more general case where there are x successes in n trials. In particular, the number of sequences having exactly x 1's and n-x 0's is n!/[x!(n-x)!]. Moreover, the probability of exactly x successes in n trials is

$$f(x)=\binom{n}{x}p^x q^{n-x} \tag{4.2.1}$$

where $\binom{n}{x}=n!/[x!(n-x)!]$ is called the binomial coefficient.

<u>Example 4.2.1.</u> Six subjects are randomly sampled and given a new treatment for arthritis. If the probability of a cure is $p=1/2$, the probability of exactly $x=2$ cures among the $n=6$ subjects is

$$\binom{6}{2}(1/2)^2(1/2)^4=15/64.$$

<u>Example 4.2.2.</u> Consider the situation in example 4.2.1, but this time suppose you want to know the probability of obtaining at most 2 cures. This event is composed of three mutually exclusive events, namely, $x=0,1$, and 2 successes. Hence,

$$\Pr(X\le 2 \text{ successes})=1/64 + 6/64 + 15/64.$$

4.3 PROPERITES OF THE BINOMIAL DISTRIBUTION

Let $X_1,\ldots,X_n$ be a random sample where for any i, $1\le i\le n$, $\Pr(X_i=1)=p$, and let $X=\Sigma X_i$. That is, X is the number of successes. From the previous section the probability function of X is

$$f(x)=\binom{n}{x}p^x q^{n-x}$$

where $q=1-p$. Then

$$E(X)=E(\Sigma X_i)=\Sigma p=np.$$

In words, the population mean of a binomial probability function is

$$\mu=np. \tag{4.3.1}$$

Also,

$$E(X/n)=p. \tag{4.3.2}$$

In words, the number of observed successes divided by the number of observations is an unbiased estimate of p, the probability of a success.

To derive an expression for the variance, the following result will be used. Let $X_1,\ldots,X_n$ be n independent random variables having means $\mu_1,\ldots,\mu_n$ and variances $\sigma_1{}^2,\ldots,\sigma_n{}^2$, respectively. Then for any n constants, say $c_1,\ldots,c_n$, the variance of $Y=\Sigma c_i X_i$ is

$$\sigma_y^2=\Sigma c_i^2\sigma_i^2 \tag{4.3.2}$$

The proof of this result is not difficult but it is not given here.
Next consider the binomial probability function for the case n=1 where Pr(X=1)=p. Then

$$E(X^2)=0f(0)+1f(1)=p.$$

From equation (3.3.6), the variance of X is

$$\sigma^2=p-p^2=pq \tag{4.3.3}$$

Now consider the more general case where $X_1,\ldots,X_n$ is a random sample from a binomial probability function. From (4.3.2) and (4.3.3) the variance of ΣX_i, the probability of X successes, is

$$\sigma_x^2=\Sigma pq=npq. \tag{4.3.4}$$

(In this case $c_1=c_2=\ldots=c_n=1$.) Thus, the variance of the binomial probability function is npq, and the variance of X/n, the proportion of observed successes, is

$$(npq)/n^2=pq/n.$$

To facilitate the use of the binomial probability function, some values of $\binom{n}{x}p^xq^{n-x}$ are reported in Table A4. For instance, if you want to know the probability of exactly seven successes in 10 trials when p=.3, the answer is .009.

Notice that the largest value of p in Table A4 is .5. The reason in that for p>.5, the binomial probability function can be determined by setting p=q and looking up the entry corresponding to n-x successes. For example, to determine the probability of 7 successes when n=10 and p=.7, you simply refer to the entry in Table A4 corresponding to p=.3 and x=3, which is .2668.

Example 4.3.1. Suppose you are interested in determining whether height is related to the person who is elected President of the United States. If there is no relationship, and assuming there are only two candidates, you reason that among the n=10 previous elections, if the only thing you are told is which person is taller, then there should be a .5 probability of choosing the person who will win. For convenience, let p=Pr(taller candidate wins). If p=.5, then from Table A4, the most likely outcome is x=5 successes. That is, Pr(X=5)=.2461, and this is the largest probability when p=.5 and n=10. If you want to determine the two least likely outcomes, Table A4 indicates that these are the events X=0 and X=10 successes, each of which has a probability of .001. In fact, as the value of x moves away from x=5, the probabilities decrease. This property can be exploited to derive a method for deciding whether it is reasonable to assume p=.5 given that x successes are observed, but the details are postponed until the next chapter.

Example 4.3.2. Many students have trouble using Table A4 when p>.5. Accordingly, it may help to give a more detailed explanation of how it is used.

Suppose n=3 and p=.3. Table A4 gives you the values of f(x)=Pr(X=x). They are

X:	0	1	2	3
f(x):	.343	.441	.189	.027

Suppose you want the values of f(x) when p=.7. Because 1-.7=.3, you simply reverse the order in which the x values are written and leave the f(x) values where they are. This yields

X:	3	2	1	0
f(x):	.343	.441	.189	.027.

Thus, if p=.7, the probability of 2 successes is .441.

4.4 MAXIMUM LIKELIHOOD ESTIMATION

The binomial probability function provides a convenient way of illustrating yet another criterion that is often used when searching for an estimate of a parameter. The resulting estimate is called the maximum likelihood estimate and this approach to estimation can be traced to the German mathematician Karl Gauss. What is striking about this piece of history is that Gauss died many years before mathematical statistics, as we know it today, was ever invented!

Consider the case n=4 and suppose x=1 success is observed. From Table A4, the probability of a single success, when p=.5, is .4219 while if p=.05 the probability is .1715. Now suppose you are told that either p=.25 or p=.05. Which would you choose as your estimate of p given that x=1? Because x=1 is less likely to occur when p=.05, a more reasonable choice is p=.25. In fact, for n=4, it can be shown that for any value of p, $0 \le p \le 1$, the probability of observing the event X=1 attains its maximum possible value when p=.25.

More generally, the value of p that maximizes f(x), the likelihood of observing x successes, is x/n, and x/n is called the maximum likelihood estimate of p. This result can be established by viewing

$$\binom{n}{x} p^x q^{n-x}$$

as a function of p, with x fixed, and finding the value of p that maximizes this function. However, the details are not given.

Formal definitions of maximum likelihood estimates can be found in most books on mathematical statistics. In this book a simpler definition is used. Suppose X is a random variable and has a probability function f(x) which depends on some parameter θ. If X=x is observed, the value of θ, among all possible values of θ, that maximizes f(x) is the maximum likelihood estimate of θ.

One important feature of maximum likelihood estimates is that they are often easier to derive than are unbiased estimates. One way to derive a maximum likelihood estimate is through the following.

<u>Theorem 4.4.1</u>. Let $\hat{\theta}$ be the maximum likelihood estimate of the parameter θ. Then for any function $g(\theta)$,

$$g(\hat{\theta})$$

is a maximum likelihood estimate of $g(\theta)$. This theorem is a special case of a result derived by Zehna (1966).

<u>Example 4.4.1</u>. Let p be the probability of a success in a binomial probability function and suppose you want to estimate $\sqrt{p}$, the square root of p. Because x/n is a maximum likelihood estimate of p, $\sqrt{(x/n)}$ is a maximum likelihood estimate of $\sqrt{p}$.

4.5 THE NORMAL DISTRIBUTION

By far the most important distribution is the normal distribution that is described next. The distribution is sometimes called the Gaussian distribution in honor of Karl Gauss, who discovered it.

A continuous random variable is said to have a normal distribution if its probability density function has the form

$$f(x)=[1/\sigma\sqrt{(2\pi)}]e^{-(x-\mu)^2/2\sigma^2}, \quad -\infty\leq x\leq\infty, \tag{4.5.1}$$

where e, Euler's constant, is approximately equal to 2.71828. A graph of the normal distribution is given in Figure 8.2.1a in chapter eight. The mean and variance of this probability function are μ and σ^2, respectively. Equation (4.5.1) might seem rather formidable, but it is values of F(x) that are more important, and tables are available that give the value of F(x). Before describing how to use these tables, the following result is needed.

Theorem 4.5.1. If X has a normal distribution with mean μ and variance σ^2, then

$$Z=(X-\mu)/\sigma$$

has a normal distribution with mean 0 and variance 1. A normal distribution having mean zero and variance one is called a standard normal distribution.

The mean of Z is easily derived.

$$E(Z)=E[(X-\mu)/\sigma)]=\sigma^{-1}E(X-\mu)=\sigma^{-1}(\mu-\mu)=0.$$

Consequently, the variance of Z is

$$E[(X-\mu)/\sigma - 0]^2=\sigma^{-2}E(X-\mu)^2=\sigma^2/\sigma^2=1.$$

That Z has a normal distribution is not obvious, and a proof of this result goes beyond the scope of this book.

The practical importance of theorem 4.5.1 is that it provides a convenient way of evaluating F(x). In particular,

$$F(x)=Pr(X\le x)$$

$$=Pr(X-\mu\le x-\mu)$$

$$=Pr[(X-\mu)/\sigma\le(x-\mu)/\sigma]$$

$$=Pr(Z\le(x-\mu)/s)$$

where Z, as is assumed in the remainder of this chapter, has a standard normal distribution. Thus, to determine F(x), all that is required is a table of values for F(z), which is provided in Table A1.

Example 4.5.1. Suppose X has a normal distribution with $\mu=5$ and $\sigma^2=4$. Then

$$Pr(X\le10)=Pr[(X-5)/2\le(10-5)/2]$$

$$=Pr(Z\le2.5).$$

From Table A1 the answer is .994.

Example 4.5.2. The smallest value of z in Table A1 is zero, but F(z) can be evaluated for z<0 because f(z) is symmetric about the origin. Consequently, for z<0,

$$F(z)=1-F(-z).$$

For instance, for the normal distribution in example 4.5.1,

$$\begin{aligned}\Pr(X\le 2)&=\Pr(Z\le -1.5)\\&=1-F(1.5)\\&=1-.993\\&=.067.\end{aligned}$$

Example 4.5.3. Again consider the random variable in example 4.5.1 but this time suppose you want to compute $\Pr(1\le X\le 7)$. As before, the expression is transformed into an expression involving a standard normal random variable. In particular, the expression becomes

$$\Pr[(1-\mu)/\sigma\le (X-\mu)/\sigma\le (7-\mu)/\sigma]$$

$$=\Pr(-2\le Z\le 1)$$

$$=F(1)-F(-2).$$

Proceeding as in example 4.5.2, F(-2)=1-F(2)=1-.977=.023. F(1)=.841, and so the answer is .841-.023=.818.

Theorem 4.5.2. Let X_1, X_2,...,X_n be independent normal random variables having means μ_i and standard deviations σ_i respectively. Then for any set of constants c_1,...,c_n, not all zero,

$$Y=\Sigma c_i X_i$$

is normally distributed with mean $\Sigma c_i \mu_i$ and variance $\Sigma c_i^2 \sigma_i^2$.

The mean of Y follows from results on expectation, and the variance of Y follows from equation (4.3.2). The proof that Y is normally distributed is omitted.

An important special case of Theorem 4.5.2 is when X_1,...X_n is a random sample and c_1=,...=c_n=1/n. Then the theorem says that $\bar{X}$

is normally distributed with mean μ and variance σ^2/n.

Example 4.5.4. You have a random sample of 16 observations from a normal distribution with mean $\mu=26$ and standard deviation $\sigma=8$. Suppose you want to determine $Pr(\bar{X}\le 30)$. Because $\bar{X}$ is normally distributed with mean μ and variance σ^2/n, Theorem 4.5.2 says that $(\bar{X}-\mu)/(\sigma/\sqrt{n})=(\sqrt{n})(\bar{X}-\mu)/\sigma$ has a standard normal distribution. As a result,

$$Pr(\bar{X}\le 30)=Pr[(\sqrt{n})(\bar{X}-\mu)/\sigma\le(\sqrt{n})(30-\mu)/\sigma]$$

$$=Pr[Z\le(\sqrt{16})(30-26)/8]$$

$$=F(2)$$

$$=.977.$$

Using Table A1

Many students have difficulty getting used to Table A1. If this is the case for you, the following rules may help. There are four basic quantities that you need to be able to determine. The first two are $F(z)=Pr(Z\le z)$ when $z>0$ or when $z<0$ and the other two are $Pr(Z\ge z)$ when $z<0$ or when $z>0$. These quantities are determined as follows:

1. If $z>0$, $F(z)$ is determined simply by reading the value from Table A1. For example, if $z=.6$, $F(z)=.726$.

2. If $z<0$, look up $F(-z)$ and subtract it from 1. For example, if $z=-.6$, $F(z)=1-.726=.274$

3. If $z>0$ and you want to determine $Pr(Z\ge z)$, look up $F(z)$ and subtract it from 1. For example, $Pr(Z\ge .6)=1-.726=.274$.

4. To determine $Pr(Z\ge z)$ when $z<0$, look up $F(-z)$. Thus, $Pr(Z\ge -.6)=F(.6)=.726$.

4.6 THE CENTRAL LIMIT THEOREM

At first glance the normal distribution seems to have little practical value because it assumes the possible values of a random variable are any real number between $-\infty$ and ∞. Of course in practice, the values of a random variable are limited to some finite interval. The first step in realizing the practical importance of the normal distribution is provided through the central limit theorem. This theorem says that under very general conditions, if $X_1,...,X_n$ is a random sample from some probability density function, then as n gets large, $\bar{X}$ approaches a normal distribution with mean μ and variance σ^2/n, and so $(\sqrt{n})(\bar{X}-\mu)/\sigma$ approaches a standard normal distribution.

In an applied book it is impossible to give a complete description of the "general conditions" that ensure that the central limit theorem is true. Here it is merely stated that these conditions are indeed so general that for all practical purposes it can be assumed that $\bar{X}$ approaches a normal distribution.

Example 4.6.1. Suppose $X_1,...,X_{50}$ is a random sample from a binomial distribution, and suppose you want to know the probability that this sample will contain at most 30 successes when p=.5. Let $X=\Sigma X_i$. The central limit theorem says that $Z=(X/n - p)/\sqrt{(pq/n)}$ has, approximately, a standard normal distribution. Hence,

$$\Pr((X\le 30)=\Pr[(X/50 - .5)/\sqrt{\{(.5)(.5)/50\}} \le (30/50 - .5)/\sqrt{\{(.5)(.5)/50\}}$$

$$=\Pr(Z\le 1.41)$$

$$.92.$$

Example 4.6.2. Suppose $\bar{X}$ is based on a random sample of size 3 where $f(x)=1$, $0\le x\le 1$. This is the uniform distribution which has mean $\mu=1/2$ and variance $\sigma^2=1/12$. The distribution of $\bar{X}$ can be derived, but the resulting probability function is rather complicated. For practical purposes it is simpler to approximate the distribution of $\bar{X}$ with a normal distribution. For instance,

$$\Pr(.45\le\bar{X}\le.6)$$

$$=\Pr[(\sqrt{n})(.45-\mu)/\sigma \le (\sqrt{n})(X-\mu)/\sigma \le (\sqrt{n})(.6-\mu)/\sigma]$$

$$=\Pr[\sqrt{36}(.45-.5)\le Z\le\sqrt{36}(.6-.5)]$$

$$=F(.6)-F(-.3)$$

$$=.726-.382$$

$$=.344.$$

A natural issue to raise is how well a normal distribution approximates the distribution of $\bar{X}$. For most practical situations the approximation is quite good even when n is only moderately large. However, there are situations in which the approximation can be poor, even when n is large. For instance, for the binomial probability function, when p=1/2, the approximation works well, but as p gets close to zero or one the approximation becomes increasingly less accurate. In fact, it is quite poor for p close to 0 or 1. Additional comments about assuming $\bar{X}$ to be normally distributed are made throughout the book.

4.7 CONFIDENCE INTERVALS

Although σ^2 gives some indication of how well $\bar{X}$ estimates μ, there is an additional approach to describing the accuracy of $\bar{X}$ as an estimate of μ that will be seen to have considerable practical value. The idea is to find two numbers, say L and U, with the property that $\Pr(L \le \mu \le U)$ is reasonably close to one. That is, the goal is to find an interval that has a high probability of containing μ. Usually L and U are random variables, but as will be seen, there are a few important instances where L and U are constants. The interval(L,U) will be called a confidence interval for μ, and U-L is the length of the interval.

Suppose $\bar{X}$ is normally distributed with mean μ and variance σ^2/n. It is assumed μ is unknown, but that σ^2 is known. In practice σ^2 is usually unknown, and eventually the assumption that σ^2 is known will be dropped. The only goal here is to illustrate the notion of a confidence interval for the simplest case.

From the normality assumption, Table A1 tells us that

$$\Pr[-2 \le (\surd n)(\bar{X}-\mu)/\sigma \le 2\sigma) = .954.$$

Rearranging terms, the left side of this last expression becomes

$$\Pr(-2\sigma \le (\surd n)(\bar{X}-\mu) \le 2\sigma)$$

$$= \Pr(-2\sigma/\surd n - \bar{X} \le -\mu \le 2\sigma/\surd n - \bar{X})$$

$$= \Pr[\bar{X} - 2\sigma/\surd n \le \mu \le \bar{X} + 2\sigma/\surd n] \qquad (4.7.1)$$

Thus, with probability .954, the interval

$$(\bar{X} - 2\sigma/\surd n,\ \bar{X} + 2\sigma/\surd n) \qquad (4.7.2)$$

contains μ.

<u>Example 4.7.1</u> Suppose you are concerned about the levels of lead in persons living in Los Angeles. If $\bar{X}=84$, $\sigma=36$, and $n=16$, can you be reasonably certain that $\bar{X}$ provides an accurate estimate

of μ? To answer this question, assume normality and compute a .954 confidence interval. Using the results given above

$$\Pr[84-2(36)/\sqrt{(16)}\leq\mu\leq 84+2(36)/\sqrt{(16)}]$$

$$=\Pr(66\leq\mu\leq 102)=.954.$$

Thus, you can be reasonably certain that μ is in the interval (66,102). If in your judgment the length of the interval, namely 102-66=46, is reasonably small, $\bar{X}$ provides an accurate estimate of μ. From (4.7.2) it is seen that if you want a shorter confidence interval, use a larger value for n, i.e., a larger sample size. In fact, the length of the confidence interval is

$$(\bar{X}+2\sigma/\sqrt{n})-(\bar{X}-2\sigma/\sqrt{n})=4\sigma/\sqrt{n},$$

and so to obtain a confidence interval with length A, say, choose n such that $4\sigma/\sqrt{n}=A$. That is, randomly sample

$$n=16\sigma^2/A^2 \qquad (4.7.3)$$

subjects to obtain a .954 confidence interval.

More generally, suppose you want a $1-\alpha$ confidence interval. In other words, you want an interval such that with probability $1-\alpha$, the interval contains μ. (The reason for writing the probability requirement as $1-\alpha$ rather than just α is that this notation is consistent with certain conventions that are described in the next chapter.) Proceeding as was done above, determine the constant, say c, such that

$$\Pr(-c\leq Z\leq c)=1-\alpha \qquad (4.7.4)$$

This is accomplished by referring to Table A1 and determining c such that $\Pr(Z\leq c)=1-\alpha/2$. Then

$$\Pr(\bar{X}-c\sigma/\sqrt{n} \leq \mu \leq \bar{X}+c\sigma/\sqrt{n})=1-\alpha, \qquad (4.7.5)$$

and the length of the confidence interval is $2c\sigma/\sqrt{n}$.

Example 4.7.2. Consider again example 4.7.1, but this time suppose you want a .99 confidence interval for μ. Then $\alpha=.01$, $1-\alpha/2=.995$, and from Table A1, Pr $(Z\leq 2.57)=.995$, so c=2.57. Hence, according to (4.7.5),

$$(\bar{X}-2.57(36)(\sqrt{16}),\ \bar{X}+2.57(36)/(\sqrt{16}))=(60.87,107.13)$$

is a .99 confidence interval for μ. To get a confidence interval of length A, use

$$n=(2c\sigma/A)^2 \tag{4.7.6}$$

For instance, if in the illustration you want the length to be A=20, you need a sample of $n=[2(2.56)(36)/20]^2$ subjects.

As a final note, the central limit theorem can be used to derive a confidence interval for p, the probability of success in a binomial probability function. For a given value of α, determine the value of c satisfying (4.7.4). If x is the observed number of successes among n subjects, an approximate $1-\alpha$ confidence interval for p is

$$\{(x/n)-(c/\sqrt{n})\sqrt{[(x/n)(n-x)/n)]},$$
$$(x/n)+(c/\sqrt{n})\sqrt{[(x/n)(n-x)/n)]}\}.$$

However, several other confidence intervals have been proposed that give better results; the interested reader is referred to Blyth and Still (1983) and Blyth (1986).

EXERCISES

(The more difficult problems are marked with an asterisk.)

4.1 In a 26 letter alphabet, how many four letter sequences can be made where no letter is used more than once?

4.2 If a letter can appear as many times as you like, how many four letter sequences can be made? Hint: Use the "counting" rule that was used to derive equation (4.1.1). Again assume there are 26 letters.

4.3 A slot machine contains three wheels, each wheel has 12 symbols, and the same 12 symbols appear on each wheel.

a) How many outcomes are there where the symbols on all three wheels are all different? Assume order does not count. That is, you want the number of combinations.

b) How many outcomes are there where order counts. That is, determine the number of permutations.

c) How many outcomes are there where all three symbols are the same?

4.4 A committee of ten persons must select one member to be president, another to be vice president, and a third to be treasurer. How many different ways are there of filling these three positions from among the ten committee members?

*4.5 The Birthday Problem. Assume a person's birthday is equally likely to occur on any one of the 365 days in the year. What is the probability that among five persons, at least two persons have a birthday on the same day? Hint: First determine the number of possible outcomes in the sample space and then determine the probability that no two people have the same birthday.

4.6 Suppose the probability of eliminating a certain type of tumor with the usual method of treatment is $p=.5$. You have a new treatment, say method B. If method B has a probability of .7 of producing a cure, and you randomly sample 10 subjects, what is the probability that the number of cures under method B will be greater than or equal to the expected number of cures under the standard treatment?

*4.7 Refer to problem 4.6 and assume that the probability of a cure under method B is .55. Use the central limit theorem to determine how large a sample size, n, is needed so that if n observations are sampled from both the conventional method and method B, there will be a .99 probability that the number of cures under method B will be at least as large as the expected number of cures under the conventional method.

4.8 If $n=20$, what is $\Pr(2 \le X \le 18)$ where X is a binomial random variable with $p=.8$?

4.9 Twenty randomly sampled persons are asked to taste two drinks and to pick which they like best.

a) If 12 pick drink A, what is the maximum likelihood estimate of p, the probability of preferring drink A?

b) If $p=.5$, what is the probability that 12 or more of the twenty persons will pick drink A?

4.10 If $\Pr(Z \le z)=.4$, where Z is a standard normal random variable, what is the value of z?

4.11 If X is normally distributed with $\mu=30$ and $\sigma=4.5$, what is the value of $\Pr(X \le 35)$?

4.12 Suppose $n=25$ subjects are randomly sampled from a normal distribution with $\sigma=6$ and $\mu=80$. Determine

a) $\Pr(\bar{X} \le 82)$

b) $\Pr(79 \le \bar{X} \le 81)$

4.13 If $\bar{X}=80$, $\sigma=6$, and $n=25$, determine
a) a 95% confidence interval for μ
b) a 99% confidence interval for μ.

*4.14 Suppose X_1, X_2, and X_3 are three independent normal random variables having unknown means μ_1, μ_2, and μ_3, and variances 4, 9, and 16. If the observed values of these random variables are 200, 240, and 300, what is the 95% confidence interval for $\mu=\mu_1+2\mu_2-3\mu_3$?

References

Blyth, C. R. (1986) Approximate binomial confidence limits. Journal of the American Statistical Association, 81, 843-855.

Blyth, C. R. & Still H. (1983) Binomial confidence intervals. Journal of the American Statistical Association, 78, 108-116.

Zehna, P. W. (1966) Invariance of maximum likelihood estimation. Annals of Mathematical Statistics, 37, 744.

CHAPTER FIVE

HYPOTHESIS TESTING

So far the emphasis has been on basic theoretical results including the problem of how to estimate parameters associated with a particular population of subjects. This chapter introduces the basic results in an area of statistics that has played a central role in the social sciences. The general problem is making inferences about whether the parameters of a distribution satisfy certain properties that are of interest in a specific study. For example, in chapter four the issue was raised about whether there is any relationship between the height of the candidates who run for president of the United States and the person who wins the election. It was suggested that if there is no relationship, the probability of the taller person winning should be .5. Of course, even if $p=.5$, there is, for any x, $0 \le x \le n$, a positive probability of observing x successes in n trials, and so the issue is whether the observed number of successes is reasonably consistent with $p=.5$

As another example where hypothesis testing occurs, suppose two methods of dealing with a particular mental disorder are being studied. If n subjects receive the first method, and another n subjects receive the second, under what circumstances is it reasonable to conclude that there is no difference between the two methods. Alternatively, when should you conclude that one method is better than the other. For instance, if there are x_1 successes using method A and x_2 successes using method B, and if p_1 and p_2 are the corresponding probabilities of success, then $x_1 < x_2$ can occur even when $p_1 = p_2$, or even when $p_1 > p_2$. So how should you decide whether $p_1 = p_2$, and more generally, how can you design an experiment so that there will be a high probability of making a correct decision?

5.1 THE SIGN TEST

One of the simplest situations involving hypothesis testing is where the goal is to determine whether it is reasonable to believe that the probability of success for a binomial probability function is $p=.5$. In general, the hypothesis about a population parameter is called the <u>null hypothesis</u>, and it is indicated by the symbol H_0. A null hypothesis is called a simple hypothesis if it completely determines the distribution; otherwise it is called a composite hypothesis. For the problem at hand, the null hypothesis is

$$H_0: p=1/2, \tag{5.1.1}$$

and this is a simple hypothesis because it says that the distribution is a binomial distribution with p=1/2. That is, the null hypothesis tells you precisely what the values of f(x) are assumed to be. An example of a composite hypothesis is H_0:p≤1/2. Because p can be any value between 0 and 1/2, H_0 does not specify the values of f(x).

The alternative to the null hypothesis is indicated with the symbol H_1. For equation (5.1.1) the alternative hypothesis is

$$H_1: p \neq 1/2 \tag{5.1.2}$$

The goal is to devise a rule, called a test of a statistical hypothesis, for deciding which of these two hypotheses is to be accepted based on the outcome of an experiment. If, for example, x=2 successes are observed in a random sample of n=8 subjects, should H_0 be accepted, or should it be rejected in favor of H_1?

When answering this question, the convention is to first assume H_0 is true. For a simple hypothesis, this means that you have a specific probability model that tells you the likelihood of observing any possible outcome of the experiment. For instance, when p=1/2 and n=8, the possible outcomes and their probabilities are:

x:	0	1	2	3	4	5	6	7	8
f(x):	.004	.031	.109	.219	.273	.219	.109	.031	.004.

If your model is true, the most likely outcome is x=4. The three most likely outcomes are x=3,4, and 5. The five most likely outcomes are 2,3,4,5, and 6, etc. The point is that if H_0 is true, the observed number of successes should be close to x=4, and outcomes such as x=0 or 8 have a relatively low probability of occurring. This suggests that when testing the null hypothesis, when there are n=8 observations, H_0 should be rejected when X=0 or 8 because the probability of observing X=0 or 8 is only .008. If, for instance X=8, it is more reasonable to believe p is closer to 1 than it is to .5. For example, if p=.9, Pr(X=8)=.43.

Definition 5.1.1. Let H_0 be any null hypothesis about some parameter, and suppose it is decided H_0 is false if the observed value of some appropriate statistic is an element of some subset, C, of the sample space. The set C is called a critical region.

Example 5.1.1. Again consider the null hypothesis H_0:p=1/2. Suppose n=8 and for the reasons given above also suppose H_0 is rejected if X=0 or 8. Then the critical region is C={0,8}.

Testing H_0:p=1/2 in this way is called the sign test.

<u>Definition 5.1.2</u>. A Type I error is committed if H_0 is rejected when in fact H_0 is true. The probability of a Type I error will be denoted by α.

<u>Definition 5.1.3</u>. The significance level of a test of H_0 is the maximum probability of rejecting H_0 when H_0 is true. The reason for including the term "maximum" in this definition is explained shortly.

<u>Example 5.1.2</u>. In example 5.1.1 the significance level is f(0)+f(8)=.008. If instead the critical region is {0,1,7,8}, the probability of a Type I error is f(0)+f(1)+f(7)+f(8)=.07

<u>Example 5.1.3</u>. To illustrate the difference between a simple and composite hypothesis, suppose you have a new method, say method A, of treating anorexia nervosa. Also suppose method B is the standard method for treating this disorder and that after considerable experience it is known that under the standard method the probability of a cure is .6. You could test the hypothesis H_0:p=.6 where p is the probability of success under method A, but if you reject H_0 you would not necessarily want to use method A since it might be that p≤.6. One alternative approach is to assume p≤.6 and run an experiment to see whether p≤.6 is an unreasonable assumption in which case the new method should be used. Thus, the null hypothesis to be tested is H_0:p≤.6, and this is a composite hypothesis because it does not completely specify the values of f(x).

As before, the problem is arriving at a reasonable rejection region. When testing H_0:p=1/2, x=0 was part of the rejection region, but for H_0:p≤1/2 having x=0 in the rejection region makes little sense because if x=0, the estimate of p is zero, which is consistent with H_0. More generally, if p≤.6 is true, the estimate of p should have a value near or below .6.

It will help to consider a specific case, so suppose you have a random sample of n=12 subjects and consider the critical region x=12. The probability of observing X=12 depends, of course, on the actual value of p. For p≤.6 it can be shown that f(12) attains its maximum possible value when p=.6. Consequently, if H_0 is rejected when X=12, then from Table A4 the significance level is .002. If instead H_0 is rejected when X=11 or 12, the maximum probability of a Type I error is .02 where again it is assumed p=.6. In fact for any hypothesis of the form H_0:p≤p_0, where p_0 is a known constant, the significance level is determined by considering the case p=p_0. The same is true when testing H_0:p≥p_0.

Example 5.1.4. Suppose you want to test H_0:p≤.3. If you are asked to determine the largest possible critical region so that α≤.01 when n=11, the answer is C={8,9,10,11} in which case the significance level is .004. If instead C={7,8,9,10,11} is used, α=.021. These probabilities were determined by assuming p=.3 and referring to Table A4.

5.2 TYPE II ERRORS AND THE POWER OF THE SIGN TEST

Consider again the null hypothesis H_0:p=1/2 and suppose there are n=8 observations. As previously indicated, if H_0 is rejected whenever X=0 or 8 successes are observed, the probability of a Type I error is .008. It might seem, therefore, that this provides a satisfactory test of H_0 even though there were only 8 observations, but this is not necessarily the case.

Definition 5.2.1. A Type II error is committed if you fail to reject H_0 when H_0 is false.

For the sign test, suppose that unknown to you, p=.4. Then a correct decision is made if you reject H_0:p=1/2. If n=8 and the critical region is C={0,8}, a correct decision is made if the observed number of successes is 0 or 8, but an incorrect decision is made if X=1,2,3,4,5,6, or 7. Let β be the probability of a Type II error and note that β depends on the unknown value of p. To determine whether β is sufficiently small, it is customary to select some alternative value of p that is of interest (some value different from the hypothesized value), and calculate the corresponding value of β. If β is judged to be too large, some adjustment must be made so that β will have a more acceptable value. There are two ways in which β can be adjusted, and they are described momentarily. First, however, it is noted that when choosing a value for p at which β is to be evaluated, there are no rigid rules for determining which value you should pick, but for illustrative purposes the alternative value will be chosen so that the distance between H_0 and the alternative value is 10% of the range of possible p values. This arbitrary rule is used in later chapters.

Definition 5.2.2. The power of a statistical test is the probability of rejecting H_0. Thus, power is equal to 1-β.

Note that in the sign test, power is a function of p, and so it is more accurate to refer to power at a point or particular value of the parameter being tested. Occasionally the term power function is used, and this refers to $1-\beta(p)$ where $\beta(p)$ is the probability of a Type II error, and where β is written as $\beta(p)$ to emphasize that it is a function of p.

Returning to the illustration where n=8, C={0,8}, and the null hypothesis is H_0:p=1/2, let's compute the power of this statistical test when p=.4. Referring to Table A4 it is seen that when p=.4 the probability of 0 or 8 successes is .0175. In summary, when p=.4, you should reject H_0:p=1/2, but there is only a .0175 probability of doing so. Equivalently, there is a 1-.0175=.9825 probability of committing a Type II error.

One way to lower the probability of a Type II error is to increase the critical region. For instance, if you reject H_0 whenever the observed number of successes is 0,1,7 or 8, the power is increased to .115, and so the probability of a Type II error is .885. However, the probability of a Type I error has been increased to .0702. For the rejection region C={0,1,2,6,7,8} the power is now .3653, but the probability of a Type I error is .288.

An alternative way of adjusting the probability of a Type I and Type II error is to increase n. In general, if you want to ensure that both α and β do not exceed some predetermined value, you can accomplish this goal by choosing n sufficiently large. If, for instance, you want both α and β to be less than or equal to .1, you would choose an n and determine whether a critical region exists that satisfies this requirement. If not, you increase n and try again. Eventually n will be large enough. The value of n can also be determined through the central limit theorem, and this is illustrated in section 5.6.

Example 5.2.1. Suppose you want to test H_0:p=1/2 such that $\alpha \le .1$ and for p=.4, $\beta \le .2$. From the above discussion, satisfying this goal is impossible when n=8. Accordingly, consider n=9. To ensure that $\alpha \le .1$ it is seen from Table A4 that the largest possible critical region is C={0,1,8,9} in which case, for p=.4, the power is approximately .07, and so β still exceeds .2. Thus, n=9 still is not large enough. If instead n=15, the largest critical region satisfying $\alpha \le .1$ is C={0,1,2,3,4,5,10,11,12,13,14,15}, and when p=.4 the power is approximately .4 and so β is approximately .6. In this case β has a much more acceptable level, but an even larger sample size is needed to ensure that $\alpha \le .1$ and $\beta \le .2$. In fact the values in Table A4 are limited to $n \le 20$, and $n > 20$ is needed to solve this problem. An approximate solution is given in example 5.6.2.

5.3 COMPARING THE MEAN OF A NORMAL DISTRIBUTION TO A STANDARD

The previous section illustrated the basic approach and issues related to comparing a parameter to a known constant. A similar approach is used when comparing the mean of a normal distribution to a known constant, and the goal is this section is to illustrate how this is done.

Consider a normal distribution with mean μ and variance σ^2. In this chapter attention is restricted to the simplest case where σ is known. The goal is to test the simple hypothesis

$$H_0:\mu=\mu_0$$

where μ_0 is a known constant. For instance, it might be known that the average cholesterol level in adults is, say, 150, and you might want to know whether the average cholesterol level in Olympic athletes is also equal to 150.

As in the sign test, you can test the null hypothesis by assuming it is true and then determining whether the outcome of some experiment is reasonably consistent with this assumption. Thus, in the illustration, assume $\mu=150$ and suppose $\sigma=15$. Also suppose n=16 Olympic athletes have been randomly sampled and that their average cholesterol level is $\bar{X}=145$. Because normality is assumed, statements can be made about the likelihood of observing particular values of $\bar{X}$. For instance, the standard deviation of $\bar{X}$ is 15/4=3.75 and so from Table A1 it is known, for instance, that with probability .954, $\bar{X}$ will be within 2 standard deviations of μ. That is

$$\Pr\{\bar{X}-[2\sigma/\surd n] \leq \mu \leq \bar{X}+[2\sigma/\surd n]\}=.954.$$

The point is that you are assuming that $\mu=150$, which says that $\bar{X}$ will probably be within 2 standard deviations of 150, and so if $\bar{X}$ is more than 2 standard deviations away, this suggests that your model, and in particular your assumption that $\mu=150$, is unreasonable and should be rejected.

Summarizing and generalizing this argument, suppose you want the probability of a Type I error to be α when testing $H_0:\mu=\mu_0$. Let c be the constant such that

$$\Pr(-c\leq Z\leq c)=1-\alpha \qquad (5.3.1)$$

where Z is a standard normal random variable. Assuming H_0 is true,

$$\Pr[-c \leq (\surd n)(\bar{X}-\mu_0)/\sigma \leq c]=1-\alpha. \qquad (5.3.2)$$

Thus, if H_0 is rejected whenever

$$|(\surd n)(\bar{X}-\mu_0)/\sigma|>c, \qquad (5.3.3)$$

the probability of a Type I error is α. The quantity c is called the <u>critical value</u>. An alternative way of stating your decision rule is that you reject H_0 whenever μ_0 is not in the $100(1-\alpha)\%$ confidence interval for μ, the interval being

$$(\bar{X}-c\sigma/\sqrt{n},\ \bar{X}+c\sigma/\sqrt{n}).$$

<u>Example 5.3.1</u>. For the cholesterol illustration described above, $\mu_0=150$, $\bar{X}=145$, $\sigma=15$, and $n=16$. If you want to test $H_0:\mu=150$ in such a way that the probability of a Type I error is $\alpha=.01$, then from (5.3.1) and Table A1, the critical value is 2.58. Since

$$|(\sqrt{16})(145-150)/15|=1.33<2.58,$$

you do not reject H_0 because the value of $\bar{X}$ is within the range of values you would expect if H_0 were true. Moreover, the probability of a Type I error was .01.

<u>Example 5.3.2</u>. Consider the situation in example 5.3.1, but this time suppose $\bar{X}=140$ and $\alpha=.1$. Then the critical value is 1.645 and since

$$|(\sqrt{16})(140-150)/15|=2.67>1.645,$$

reject H_0. That is, you would conclude that the average cholesterol level in Olympic athletes is different from the average level in adults.

<u>Choosing α</u>

Of course the value of α actually used in a particular study is based on the judgment you make about the seriousness of a Type I error. The most common values are .01 and .05, although values as high as .25 have been used in published articles, while in other cases values smaller than .01 have also been used.

5.4 ONE-TAILED TESTS

When testing $H_0:\mu=\mu_0$, a so-called two-tailed test (also known as a two-sided test) was used. This just means that the rejection region consisted of both the upper and lower tails of the probability density function. In contrast is a one-tailed (or one-sided) test which occurs when testing $H_0:\mu\le\mu_0$ or $H_0:\mu\ge\mu_0$. A one-tailed version of the sign test was mentioned in section 5.1. The goal here is to consider a one-tailed test for the normal distribution.

To illustrate one type of situation where a one-tailed test might be used, suppose you believe that endurance-type exercises affect cholesterol levels. Continuing the illustration used above, this means that among Olympic athletes competing in events requiring endurance, you would expect to find $\mu<150$ where again μ is the expected cholesterol level of Olympic athletes and 150 is the expected level of adults. To test your suspicions about μ, you assume $\mu\geq150$, randomly sample n subjects and see whether $\bar{X}$ is sufficiently smaller than $\mu_0=150$ so as to suggest that $\mu\geq150$ is an unreasonable assumption. That is, you want to test

$$H_0: \mu\geq150.$$

Of course if $\bar{X}>150$ you would not reject H_0 because your estimate of μ is consistent with the hypothesis $\mu\geq150$. If, however, $\bar{X}$ is substantially smaller than 150, this suggests that H_0 should be rejected. For this reason, consider the rejection region

$$C=\{\bar{X}: \bar{X}\leq\mu_0-c\sigma/\surd n\}.$$

That is, reject H_0 if $(\surd n)(\bar{X}-\mu_0)/\sigma<-c$ where c is chosen so that $\Pr(Z\leq-c)=\alpha$. In this case the maximum probability of a Type I error can be shown to occur at $\mu=150$. As a result, the probability of a Type I error will be at most α.

Example 5.4.1. Consider again the situation where $\bar{X}=145$, $\mu_0=150$, $n=16$, and $\sigma=15$ and suppose you want to test $H_0:\mu\geq150$. If you want the probability of a Type I error to be .05, then from Table A1, $\Pr(Z\leq-1.645)=.05$, and so $c=-1.645$. Since $(\surd n)(\bar{X}-\mu_0)/\sigma=(\surd 16)(145-150)/15=-1.33>-1.645$, you do not reject H_0. If instead $\bar{X}=140$, $(\surd n)(\bar{X}-\mu_0)/\sigma=-2.67<-1.645$ and H_0 is rejected.

It should be remarked that $H_0:\mu\leq150$ can be tested in basically the same manner. The only difference is that this time c is chosen such that $\Pr(Z\leq z)=1-\alpha$ and you reject H_0 if $(\surd n)(\bar{X}-\mu_0)/\sigma>c$.

5.5 DETERMINING POWER WHEN COMPARING THE MEAN OF A NORMAL DISTRIBUTION TO A KNOWN CONSTANT

As was illustrated for the sign test, you cannot be sure that you have a reasonably accurate test of a null hypotheses unless you control the probability of both Type I and Type II errors. It is customary to first control α through the choice of the critical region and then determine whether the sample size is large enough so as to ensure that the power is reasonably close to one for some particular value of the parameter being tested.

The method for determining power, when testing hypotheses about normal distributions, is basically the same as it was for the sign test, and in some ways it is easier. To illustrate it, first consider the one-tailed test of $H_0:\mu\le\mu_0$. As previously explained, when testing this null hypothesis, the critical region is defined by the constant c where $Pr(Z\le c)=1-\alpha$,and where Z is a standard normal random variable.

Consider any number, say μ_1, where $\mu_1>\mu_0$, and suppose you want to determine how much power there is when $\mu=\mu_1$. By definition, power is just the probability of rejecting H_0 which is

$$Pr[(\sqrt{n})(\bar{X}-\mu_0)/\sigma>c] \tag{5.5.1}$$

when $\mu=\mu_1$. But when $\mu=\mu_1$, $(\sqrt{n})(\bar{X}-\mu_0)/\sigma$ is not a standard normal random variable. In order to evaluate (5.5.1), it must be converted into an expression involving a standard normal random variable. In particular, (5.5.1) is equal to

$$Pr[(\sqrt{n})(\bar{X}-\mu_1+\mu_1-\mu_0)/\sigma > c]$$

$$=Pr[(\sqrt{n})(\bar{X}-\mu_1)/\sigma > c-\{(\sqrt{n})(\mu_1-\mu_0)/\sigma\}]$$

$$=Pr[Z > c-\{(\sqrt{n})(\mu_1-\mu_0)/\sigma\}]. \tag{5.5.2a}$$

The quantities σ, n, μ_1, and μ_0 are known, and so (5.5.2a) can be evaluated. Of course, a similar expression can be derived when testing $H_0:\mu\ge\mu_0$. In this case power is equal to

$$Pr[Z<-c - (\sqrt{n})(\mu_1-\mu_0)/\sigma] \tag{5.5.2b}$$

Example 5.5.1. Suppose n=25, $\mu_0=150$, $\sigma=25$, $\alpha=.05$, and when testing $H_0:\mu\ge150$ you want to determine how much power there is when $\mu=145$. Because $\alpha=.05$, c=-1.645 and from equation (5.5.2b) the power is

$$Pr[Z < -1.645-\{(\sqrt{25})(145-150)/25\}]$$

$$=Pr[Z<-.645]$$

$$=.26.$$

If instead $\sigma=10$, the power is

$$Pr(Z<.855)=.80.$$

Example 5.5.2. Suppose it is known that the expected level of a particular neurotransmitter in adults is $\mu_0=12$ where the possible values are between 5 and 25. Also assume $\sigma=3.5$ and suppose that there is reason to believe that for individuals with a particular psychological disorder, μ, their expected level of this neurotransmitter, is larger than 12. Accordingly, you want to test $H_0:\mu\leq12$ to see whether your suspicion that $\mu>12$ can be verified. Suppose that because the range of possible values is 25-5=20, you decide to control power when $\mu-\mu_0=2$ where 2 was chosen because it is 10% of the range. Further suppose that when $\mu-\mu_0=2$ you want the power to be .8 when $\alpha=.05$. In the notation of equation (5.5.2) this means that $\mu_1=14$. How large of a sample do you need?

Because $\alpha=.05$, c=1.645, and so the power will be .8 when

$$\Pr[Z \geq 1.645-\{(\sqrt{n})(2)/3.5\}]=.8.$$

From Table A1, $\Pr(Z\geq-.84)=.8$. Thus, the power requirement will be satisfied if n is chosen such that

$$1.645 - (\sqrt{n})(2)/3.5=-.84.$$

which means that n=18.9, and so after rounding up, 19 subjects should be sample.

Determining the Sample Size

The results in example 5.5.2 can be generalized as follows. Let c be the critical value for testing $H_0:\mu\leq\mu_0$ for a given value μ_0, and suppose you want to determine the minimum value of n so that the power will be at least $1-\beta$ when $\mu-\mu_0=\delta$, say. That is, the difference between the actual value of μ and the hypothesized value μ_0 is δ. Then if b satisfies $\Pr(Z\geq b)=1-\beta$, the minimum value of n is

$$[(c-b)\sigma/\delta]^2 \tag{5.5.3}$$

This formula also holds when testing $H_0:\mu\geq\mu_0$ only c is chosen so that $\Pr(Z\leq c)=\alpha$, and b is chosen so that $\Pr(Z\leq b)=1-\beta$. If you are not able to specify a value for δ, you might plot the required sample size, n, for various δ values to at least gain some insight into how many observations are required for a specified value of β.

Example 5.5.3. Suppose the null hypothesis is $H_0:\mu\geq10$, and you want the power to be .9 when $\sigma=2$, $\alpha=.05$, and $\mu=9$. Then $\delta=9-10=-1$, c=-1.645, $\Pr(Z\leq b)=.9$, and so from Table A1, b=1.28. Substituting these results into equation (5.5.3), the required sample size is

$$[(-1.645-1.28)(2)/(-1)]^2=34.3$$

5.6 POWER OF A TWO-TAILED TEST

Not surprisingly, the power of a two-tailed test is determined in basically the same way as it was in section 5.5. Now the goal is to test $H_0:\mu=\mu_0$. Since H_0 is rejected whenever $|(\surd n)(\bar{X}-\mu_0)/\sigma|>c$, the power, when $\mu=\mu_1$, is

$$\Pr[(\surd n)(\bar{X}-\mu_0)/\sigma > c \text{ or } (\surd n)(\bar{X}-\mu_0)/\sigma < -c]$$

$$=\Pr[Z > c-\{(\surd n)(\mu_1-\mu_0)/\sigma\} \text{ or } Z < -c-\{(\surd n)(\mu_1-\mu_0)/\sigma\}]$$

$$=\Pr[Z > c-\{(\surd n)\delta/\sigma\}] + \Pr[Z < -c-\{(\surd n)\delta/\sigma\}] \qquad (5.6.1)$$

where $\delta=\mu_1-\mu_0$.

Example 5.6.1. Suppose you want to test $H_0:\mu=100$ with $\alpha=.05$. Then the critical value is $c=1.96$. If $n=36$ subjects are randomly sampled and $\sigma=20$, and if the actual value of μ is $\mu_1=105$, the power is

$$\Pr[Z > 1.96-(\surd 36)(5)/20] + \Pr[Z < -1.96-(\surd 36)(5)/20]$$

$$=\Pr(Z>.46)+\Pr(Z<-3.46)$$

$$=.32$$

If instead $\sigma=10$, the power is $\Pr[Z\geq-2.04]+\Pr[Z\leq-4.96]=.98$.

Example 5.6.2. In example 5.2.1 the problem was to test $H_0:p=1/2$ where p is the probability of success in a binomial probability function, and the goal was to determine a sample size and critical region such that $\alpha\leq.1$ and $\beta\leq.2$. As was indicated, the entries in Table A4 are not extensive enough to solve this problem, but an approximate solution can be had by applying the central limit theorem. When H_0 is true, $(\surd n)(x/n - 1/2)/\surd.25$ has, approximately, a standard normal distribution because the mean and variance of x/n, when p=1/2, are 1/2 and .25/n. Consequently, for $\alpha=.1$, reject H_0 whenever

$$|(\surd n)(x/n - 1/2)/\surd.25|>1.645. \qquad (5.6.2)$$

Now suppose that p=.4 in which case the left side of (5.6.2) is no longer a standard normal random variable. As a result, in order to determine the probability that equation (5.6.2) will be true, you must convert $\Pr[|(\sqrt{n})(x/n - 1/2)/\sqrt{.25}>1.645$ into an expression that involves a standard normal random variable. This can be accomplished by noting that when $p=.4$, the mean and variance of x/n is .4 and $.4(.6)/n=.24/n$, and so the probability of rejecting H_0 is equal to

$$\Pr[|(\sqrt{n})(x/n - 1/2)/\sqrt{.24}| > 1.645\sqrt{.25/.24}]$$

$$=\Pr[|(\sqrt{n})(x/n-.4+.4-.5)/\sqrt{.24}| > 1.645\sqrt{.25/.24}]$$

$$=\Pr(Z>.1(\sqrt{n})/(\sqrt{.24}) + 1.679) + \Pr(Z<.1(\sqrt{n})/(\sqrt{.24}) - 1.679) \qquad (5.6.3)$$

Because $1-\beta$ is close to one, the first term in (5.6.3) is nearly equal to zero, and so it can be ignored. Since $\Pr(Z<.84)=.8$, this means that n should be chosen so that

$$\{.1(\sqrt{n})/\sqrt{.24}\} - 1.679 = .84. \qquad (5.6.4)$$

Thus, about 152 observations are required.

5.7 SOME CONCLUDING REMARKS

One goal in this chapter was to provide some indication of how to determine critical regions when performing one-tailed and two-tailed tests. Although the techniques used in this chapter are indeed the ones used in practice, the reader may have some lingering doubts about whether alternative critical regions would be better in some sense. It turns out that a more formal criterion has been proposed for determining whether a particular critical region is optimal. This criterion ultimately leads to the Neyman-Pearson theorem, which describes how to obtain critical regions that have this optimal property. Here it is merely stated that when this theorem is applied to the problems considered in this chapter, it yields the critical regions described in previous sections.

Finally, when applying statistical techniques, it has been a common practice to set α equal to .05 or .01, but to simply ignore the problem of a Type II error. The examples in this chapter, particularly example 5.2.1, demonstrated that this practice can yield highly unsatisfactory results. Perhaps one reason power has frequently been ignored is that in most situations, σ^2 is unknown, in which case, from a theoretical point of view, power is more difficult to control. However, there are now simple methods for controlling power even when σ^2 is unknown and they are described in subsequent chapters.

EXERCISES

5.1 Nine subjects are asked whether they prefer drink A to drink B. If the observed choices are A,A,A,B,A,B,A,A, if p is the probability of choosing A, and if you want the probability of a Type I error to be $\alpha \le .1$, is it reasonable to believe that $p \le .5$?

5.2 In 5.1, what is the significance level and how much power was there when $p=.7$?

5.3 Repeat exercise 5.1, but this time test $H_0: p=1/2$.

5.4 If $n=14$ and $x=12$ successes are observed, would you reject $H_0: p=.5$ when $\alpha=.05$?

5.5 In exercise 5.4, determine α if the critical region is $C=\{0,1,2,12,13,14\}$, and then determine how much power there is when $p=.6$

5.6 In exercise 5.4, what must be done to lower β?

5.7 It is known that diabetes can affect eye sight. To learn more about this phenomenon, suppose you conduct a study designed to compare some characteristics of the eyes of diabetics to individuals who do not have the disease. If for non-diabetics the average value of this characteristic is known to be 18, and if for five randomly sampled subjects you observe the values 9, 10, 9, 14 and 7, is it reasonable to believe that diabetics have a mean at least as large as 18? Assume normality, $\sigma=5.8$, and $\alpha=.05$.

5.8 In exercise 5.7, test $H_0: \mu=18$

5.9 In exercise 5.7, how much power was there for $\mu=16$?

5.10 Test $H_0: \mu=25$ assuming $\bar{X}=30$, $\sigma=10$, $n=16$ and $\alpha=.01$.

5.11 Determine how much power there was in exercise 5.10 for $\mu=20$.

5.12 In exercise 5.7, how large a sample would you need so that when $\mu=16$, the power will be .9?

5.13 Repeat exercise 5.12 with $\beta=.2$.

5.14 To test $H_0: p \ge .7$ with $\alpha=.05$, how large of a sample should you use so that $\beta \leq .2$ when p=.5?

5.15 Solve problem 5.14, but this time $\alpha=.1$, and you want $\beta \leq .2$ when p=.6.

5.16 In example 5.6.2, if you want the power to be .8 when p=.3, what is the required sample size?

5.17 You conduct 10 independent experiments and each time you test $H_0:\mu=5$ using $\alpha=.05$. What is the probability of at least one Type I error?

CHAPTER SIX

STUDENT'S T, CHI-SQUARE AND F DISTRIBUTIONS

The general goal in most of the remaining chapters is to extend and generalize hypothesis testing techniques for normal distributions where the variances are unknown. First, however, a few more theoretical results are needed. Readers not interested in theory may skip this chapter.

6.1 THE CHI-SQUARE DISTRIBUTION

It has already been demonstrated that the transformation $Z=(X-\mu)/\sigma$ is important where X is a normal random variable having mean μ and variance σ^2. In particular, Z has a standard normal distribution. That is, Z has a normal distribution with mean zero and variance one. In this section the transformation $Y=Z^2$ is considered. The distribution of Y is so important it has been given a special name; it is called a chi-square distribution with one degree of freedom. A random variable having a chi-square distribution with one degree of freedom is usually written with the symbol

$$\chi_1^2.$$

The reason for the expression "one degree of freedom" is explained shortly. First, however, consider the properties of Y. Because Z has values between $-\infty$ and ∞, Y has values between 0 and ∞. Let E(Y) be the expected value of Y. Then

$$E(Y)=E(Z^2)=1,$$

since Z has mean zero and variance one, and because $E(Z^2)=\mu^2+\sigma^2$.

Next consider two independent standard normal random variables, say Z_1 and Z_2, and let

$$Y=Z_1^2+Z_2^2.$$

The distribution of Y is called a chi-square distribution with 2 degrees of freedom, and its mean is

$$E(Z_1^2+Z_2^2)=2.$$

More generally, let $Z_1,\ldots,Z_n$ be n independent standard normal random variables, and let

$$Y=\Sigma Z_i^2. \tag{6.1.1}$$

The distribution of Y is called a chi-square distribution with n degrees of freedom, and the usual symbol for representing such a distribution is

$$\chi_n^2.$$

For n<3, the shape of the probability function is as shown in Figure 6.1.1. For n=8 and n=11, the shape is as shown in Figure 6.1.2.The mean of Y is

$$\mu_y=n \tag{6.1.2}$$

and its variance can be shown to be

$$\sigma_y^2=2n. \tag{6.1.3}$$

In words, the mean of a chi-square distribution is its degrees of freedom, and its variance is two times its degrees of freedom. Moreover, as n gets large, Y approaches a normal distribution with mean n and variance 2n. Also note that if $X_1,\ldots,X_n$ is a random sample from a normal distribution,

$$\Sigma(X_i-\mu)^2/\sigma^2 \tag{6.1.4}$$

has a chi-square distribution with n degrees of freedom since $(X_i-\mu)/\sigma$ $(i=1,\ldots,n)$ are independent standard normal random variables.

Remember that the goal is to develop statistical procedures where σ^2 is not known. The strategy in solving this problem is to estimate σ^2 with s^2, the sample variance, and then take the distribution of s^2 into account when testing hypotheses about μ. Now $s^2=\Sigma(X_i-\bar{X})^2/(n-1)$ which is similar to $\Sigma(X_i-\mu)^2/\sigma^2$. The immediate goal is to exploit this similarity so that the distribution of s^2 can be determined.

Note that

$$\begin{aligned}\Sigma(X_i-\mu)^2&=\Sigma(X_i-\bar{X}+\bar{X}-\mu)^2\\&=\Sigma(X_i-\bar{X})^2+2(\bar{X}-\mu)\Sigma(X_i-\bar{X})+\Sigma(\bar{X}-\mu)^2\\&=\Sigma(X_i-\bar{X})^2+\Sigma(\bar{X}-\mu)^2\\&=\Sigma(X_i-\bar{X})^2+n(\bar{X}-\mu)^2\end{aligned} \tag{6.1.5}$$

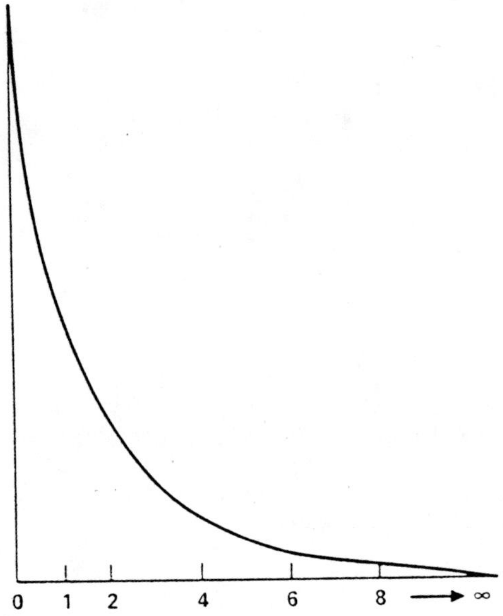

Figure 6.1.1
A Chi-Square Probability Density Function
With n Degrees Of Freedom, $n \leqslant 2$

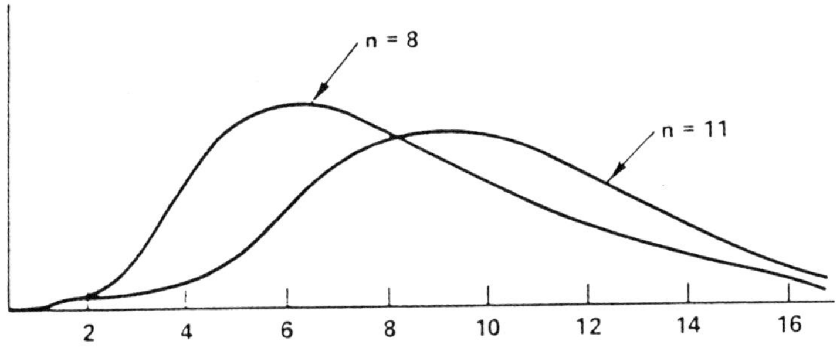

Figure 6.1.2
Two Chi-Square Probability Density Functions

since $\Sigma(X_i-\bar{X})=0$. But $n(\bar{X}-\mu)^2/\sigma^2$ has a chi-square distribution with one degree of freedom. The reason is that $\bar{X}$ is normally distributed with mean μ and variance σ^2/n, and so $(\sqrt{n})(\bar{X}-\mu)/\sigma$ has a standard normal distribution. But by definition, if you square a standard normal random variable, its distribution is a chi-square distribution with one degree of freedom.

It can be shown that if U and V are two independent chi-square random variables with n and m degrees of freedom respectively, then U+V has a chi-square distribution with n+m degrees of freedom. This result is not too surprising since if

$$U=\sum_{i=1}^{n} Z_i^2 \text{ and } V=\sum_{i=n+1}^{n+m} Z_i^2,\ U+V=\sum_{i=1}^{n+m} Z_i^2.$$

This suggests that $\Sigma(X_i-\bar{X})^2/\sigma^2$ has a chi-square distribution with n-1 degrees of freedom because from equation (6.1.5),

$$\Sigma(X-\mu)^2/\sigma^2=\{\Sigma(X_i-\bar{X})^2/\sigma^2\} + n(\bar{X}-\mu)^2/\sigma^2,$$

and because the other terms in this expression have chi-square distributions with n and 1 degrees of freedom, respectively. It turns out that this speculation is correct, but a proof requires techniques that go beyond the scope of this book. In summary,

$$(n-1)s^2/\sigma^2=\Sigma(X_i-\bar{X})^2/\sigma^2 \qquad (6.1.6)$$

has a chi-square distribution with n-1 degrees of freedom.

As was the case for the normal distribution, the percentage points of a chi-square distribution have been calculated for many important situations, and some of these percentage points are reported in Table A2. It should be noted that Table A2 follows the usual convention of letting χ_ν^2 represent a chi-square random variable with ν degrees of freedom. This convention is followed henceforth.

<u>Example 6.1.1</u>. Suppose you have a random sample of 10 observations from a normal distribution having variance $\sigma^2=8$. To determine the probability that s^2 will have a value less than or equal to 10, note that

$$\Pr(s^2\le 10)=\Pr\{(n-1)s^2/\sigma^2\le 9(10)/8\}$$

$$=\Pr(\chi_9^2 \le 11.25)$$

where χ_9^2 is a chi-square random variable with ν=n-1=9 degrees of freedom. From Table A2, $\Pr[\chi_9^2 \le 11.3887]=.75$, so $\Pr(s^2 \le 10)$ is approximately .75.

Because the percentage points of a chi-square distribution depend on the degrees of freedom, extensive tables cannot be included in a book, yet there are important situations where extensive tables are needed. From Hoaglin (1977), if you want to determine the value of y such that

$$\Pr(\chi_\nu^2 \le y)=1-\alpha \tag{6.1.7}$$

the answer is approximately

$$y=\{(\surd\nu)+2[-\log_{10}(\alpha)]^{1/2} - 7/6\}^2. \tag{6.1.8}$$

This approximation works well for $.005 \le \alpha \le .1$, but for $\alpha > .3$ it may be unsatisfactory. If you want to determine the value of q such that $q=\Pr(\chi_\nu{}^2 \ge y)$, for a given value of y, the answer is approximately

$$q=1-10^{-c} \tag{6.1.9}$$

where

$$c=[(\surd y) + 7/6 - (\surd\nu)]^2/4.$$

If you want to determine the value of y satisfying (6.1.7) when $\alpha \ge .9$, use

$$\{.9765(\surd\nu) - 1.4609(-\log_{10}[1-\alpha])^{1/2} + .59025\}^2 \tag{6.1.10}$$

Example 6.1.2. If $\sigma^2=8$ and n=10, in which case there are ν=n-1=9 degrees of freedom, and if you want to determine the value of y such that $\Pr\{(n-1)s^2/\sigma^2 \le y\}=.9$, equation (6.1.8) says that

$$y=[(\surd 9)+2\{-\log_{10}(.1)\}^{1/2} - 7/6]^2$$

$$=14.76. \tag{6.1.11}$$

From Table A2 the exact value of y is 14.69.

While equations (6.1.8) and (6.1.9) work well when $\alpha \le .1$ and $\alpha \ge .9$, their accuracy diminishes considerably for values outside this range. In this case the Wilson-Hilferty approximation can be used, which says that if z is the 100(1-α) percentile of a standard normal distribution, i.e.,

$$\Pr(Z \le z) = 1-\alpha,$$

the value of y satisfying (6.1.7) is

$$\nu[z(2/(9\nu))^{1/2} + 1 - (2/(9\nu))]^3. \qquad (6.1.12)$$

Hoaglin (1977) reports that this approximation works well for $\nu \ge 5$.

Confidence Intervals for σ^2

To obtain a 100(1-α)% confidence interval for σ^2, assuming normality, determine the constants y′ and y′′ such that

$$\Pr[\chi_\nu^2 \le y'] = \alpha/2 \text{ and } \Pr[\chi_\nu^2 \ge y''] = \alpha/2$$

in which case

$$\Pr[y' \le \chi_\nu^2 \le y''] = 1-\alpha.$$

Because $(n-1)s^2/\sigma^2$ has a chi-square distribution with ν=n-1 degrees of freedom, this last equation is equal to

$$\Pr[y' \le (n-1)s^2/\sigma^2 \le y'']$$

$$= \Pr[(n-1)s^2/y'' \le \sigma^2 \le (n-1)s^2/y']. \qquad (6.1.13)$$

Consequently, a 100(1-α)% confidence interval for σ^2 is

$$((n-1)s^2/y'', \ (n-1)s^2/y') \qquad (6.1.14)$$

Example 6.1.3. If you have 25 observations randomly sampled from a normal distribution, if s^2=20, and if you want a 90% confidence interval for σ^2, then $\alpha/2$=.05, and from Table A2, y′=13.85 and y′′=36.41. Hence, a 90% confidence interval for σ^2 is

$$(24(20)/36.41, \ 24(20)/13.85) = (13.2, \ 34.66).$$

Comparing σ^2 to a Known Constant

Suppose you want to test

$$H_0: \sigma^2 = \sigma_0^2 \qquad (6.1.15)$$

where σ_0^2 is a known constant and σ^2 is the variance of a normal distribution. A test of this hypothesis can be derived in much the same way as was the test of $H_0:\mu=\mu_0$. In particular, first assume H_0 is true. Then $(n-1)s^2/\sigma^2$ has a chi-square distribution with $\nu=n-1$ degrees of freedom. Consequently, for any α, if y′ and y′′ are chosen so that

$$\Pr[\chi_\nu^2 \le y'] = \alpha/2 \text{ and } \Pr[\chi_\nu^2 \ge y''] = \alpha/2,$$

then

$$\Pr[y' \le (n-1)s^2/\sigma^2 \le y''] = 1-\alpha \qquad (6.1.16)$$

When H_0 is true, $\sigma=\sigma_0$ and so if $(n-1)s^2/\sigma_0{}^2<y'$ or if $(n-1)s^2/\sigma_0{}^2>y''$, reject H_0, in which case the probability of a Type I error is α. This is the same as rejecting H_0 if $\sigma_0{}^2>(n-1)s^2/y'$ or if $\sigma_0{}^2<(n-1)s^2y''$ which in turn means that H_0 is rejected if $\sigma_0{}^2$ is not in the $100(1-\alpha)$% confidence interval for σ^2.

<u>Example 6.1.4</u>. Consider the situation in example 6.1.3, and suppose you want to test $H_0:\sigma^2=25$ with $\alpha=.1$. Because $y'=13.85$ and $y''=36.41$, and since $13.85\le 24(20)/25\le 36.41$, you fail to reject H_0. Alternatively, the 90% confidence interval is (13.2,34.66), this interval contains 25, so you would fail to reject H_0. If you wanted to test $H_0:\sigma^2=37$ with $\alpha=.1$, you would reject H_0 because 37 falls outside the 90% confidence interval.

It should be mentioned that there are many hypothesis testing procedures that are insensitive to typical departures from normality. This means that when observations are sampled from non-normal distributions, the probability of Type I and Type II errors can be determined fairly accurately by assuming normality. However, when testing (6.1.15) with equation (6.1.16), this is not the case. There are procedures for making inferences about variances that can be used when distributions are non-normal, and they are described in chapter eight.

6.2 STUDENT'S T DISTRIBUTION

The simplest situation where Student's t distribution arises is testing $H_0:\mu=\mu_0$ where μ_0 is a known constant, and μ is the mean of a normal distribution. Chapter five showed how to test H_0 when σ^2 is known. You simply reject H_0 if

$$|(\sqrt{n})(\bar{X}-\mu_0)/\sigma|>c \qquad (6.2.1)$$

where the critical value c is chosen so that $\Pr(-c\le Z\le c)=1-\alpha$, and as usual α is the Type I error probability. Equation (6.2.1) suggests that when σ^2 is unknown, you simply estimate σ^2 with s^2 and reject H_0 if $|(\surd n)(\bar{X}-\mu_0)/s|>c$. However, equation (6.2.1) is based on the assumption that $(\surd n)(\bar{X}-\mu_0)/\sigma$ is a standard normal random variable--the problem is that $(\surd n)(\bar{X}-\mu_0)/s$ does not have a normal distribution. It turns out that the shape of the distribution of $(\surd n)(\bar{X}-\mu_0)/s$ is similar to a normal distribution, in fact as n gets large its distribution approaches a normal distribution. However, for n small or even moderately large, approximating the distribution of $(\surd n)(\bar{X}-\mu_0)/s$ with a normal distribution can be unsatisfactory. What is needed is a way of evaluating the distribution of $(\surd n)(\bar{X}-\mu_0)/s$. About 100 years after Gauss derived the normal distribution, W. Gossett derived the distribution of $(\surd n)(\bar{X}-\mu_0)/s$, and it is called Student's t distribution. (Gossett published his results under the name "Student.") As will be seen, Student's t distribution plays an important role in many statistical procedures.

Theorem 6.2.1. If $X_1,\ldots,X_n$ is a random sample from a normal distribution, and if $\bar{X}$ and s^2 are the resulting sample mean and sample variance, then $\bar{X}$ and s^2 are independent random variables.

The validity of Theorem 6.2.1 is far from obvious. Indeed you would expect it to be false since $s^2=\Sigma(X_i-\bar{X})^2/(n-1)$ which is an expression involving $\bar{X}$. In fact, in general, s^2 and $\bar{X}$ are dependent, but when normality is assumed they are independent.

Definition 6.2.1. Let Z be a standard normal random variable, and let Y be a chi-square random variable with ν degrees of freedom where Z and Y are independent of one another. The distribution of

$$T_\nu=Z/[Y/\nu]^{1/2}$$

is called a Student's t distribution with ν degrees of freedom. (For convenience the subscript ν will usually not be written.) The range of possible values of T is from $-\infty$ to ∞. In addition, the distribution is symmetric about the origin, and its shape is very similar to the standard normal distribution. Percentage points of this distribution are given in Table A14. For instance, if $\nu=10$, $\Pr(T_{10}\le 1.812)=.95$. Because the distribution is symmetric about the origin, $\Pr(T\le -t)=\Pr(T\ge t)$.

If $X_1,\ldots,X_n$ is a random sample from a normal distribution, it has already been explained that $(\surd n)(\bar{X}-\mu)/\sigma$ has a standard normal distribution, and $(n-1)s^2/\sigma^2$ has a chi-square distribution with $\nu=n-1$ degrees of freedom. Also, these two quantities are independent of one another, and so

$$\{\surd n(\bar{X}-\mu)/\sigma\}/\{[(n-1)s^2/\sigma^2]/(n-1)\}^{1/2} =$$

$$(\surd n)(\bar{X}-\mu)/s \qquad (6.2.1a)$$

has a Student's t distribution with ν degrees of freedom. Note that the right side of (6.2.1a) is just $\surd n(\bar{X}-\mu)/\sigma$ with σ replaced by s.

Testing $H_0:\mu=\mu_0$ When σ^2 is Unknown

To illustrate how equation (6.2.1) is used, suppose you have a random sample of n=25 observations from a normal distribution,

$$\bar{X}=50,\ s^2=8,$$

and you want to test $H_0:\mu=48$ with $\alpha=.05$. When σ^2 is unknown, you cannot use $\surd n(\bar{X}-\mu)/\sigma$, but you can use $\surd n(\bar{X}-\mu)/s$. From Table A14, with $\nu=25-1=24$, $Pr(T_{24}\le 2.064)=.975$ which means that $Pr(T_{24}\le -2.064)=.025$, and $Pr(-2.064\le T_{24}\le 2.064)=.95$. This implies that when H_0 is true,

$$Pr(-2.064 \le (\surd n)(\bar{X}-\mu_0)/s \le 2.064)=.95,$$

and so if $|(\surd n)(\bar{X}-\mu_0)/s|>2.064$, reject H_0.

More generally, if you want the probability of a Type I error to be α, determine the value t such that

$$Pr(-t\le T_\nu \le t)=1-\alpha, \qquad (6.2.2)$$

and reject if

$$|(\surd n)(\bar{X}-\mu_0)/s)|>t. \qquad (6.2.3)$$

Confidence Interval for μ When σ^2 is Unknown

When σ^2 is unknown, the t distribution can also be used to derive a confidence interval for μ. The derivation is similar to the derivation for the case σ known; the result is that if

$$Pr(-t\le T_\nu \le t)=1-\alpha,$$

$$(\bar{X}-\{ts/\surd n\},\ \bar{X}+\{ts/\surd n\}) \qquad (6.2.4)$$

is a 100(1-α)% confidence interval for μ. Moreover, if μ_0 is contained in this interval, you would fail to reject $H_0:\mu=\mu_0$, and if μ_0 is not in this interval, you would reject. Verification of this statement is left as an exercise.

Example 6.2.1. Suppose the average diastolic blood pressure of adults is 80, and you want to know whether persons on a low sodium diet have a different average blood pressure. To find out, you randomly sample five subjects on low sodium diets and find that their blood pressures are 73, 95, 70, 80, and 72. The goal is to test $H_0:\mu=80$, and because σ^2 is unknown, the t distribution must be used. From the observations it is found that $\bar{X}=79$, and $s^2=105.75$. If the probability of a Type I error is to be $\alpha=.1$, then with $\nu=5-1=4$ degrees of freedom, the critical value is, from Table A14, $t=2.132$. The 90% confidence interval for μ is

$$79 \pm (2.132)(\sqrt{105.75})/(\sqrt{5}) = (69.2, 88.8)$$

Because $\mu_0=80$ is in this interval, H_0 is not rejected.

One-Tailed Tests When σ^2 is Unknown

For σ^2 unknown, a test of $H_0:\mu\le\mu_0$ or $\mu\ge\mu_0$ can be derived in the same manner as it was for the case σ known, the only difference being that the derivation is done in terms of the t distribution rather than the normal. The result is that if the probability of a Type I error is to be α, reject $H_0:\mu\le\mu_0$ if

$$(\sqrt{n})(\bar{X}-\mu_0)/s>t$$

where t is chosen so that $Pr(T\le t)=1-\alpha$, and T is a Student's t distribution with $\nu=n-1$ degrees of freedom. For $H_0:\mu\ge\mu_0$, reject if

$$(\sqrt{n})(\bar{X}-\mu_0)/s<-t.$$

6.3 DETERMINING THE SAMPLE SIZE AND CONTROLLING THE LENGTH OF THE CONFIDENCE INTERVAL FOR μ

In chapter four it was pointed out that for a normal distribution with known variance, you can determine the sample size n so that the length of the confidence interval for μ will be 2A, where A is some positive number you have chosen based on how accurate an estimate of μ you desire. A convenient feature of the solution (see equation 4.7.6) was that n can be determined prior to collecting your data. When σ is unknown, however, it can be shown (Dantzig, 1940) that if you want the length of the confidence interval to be 2A, there is no way for you to determine n prior to collecting your data. Instead a two-stage procedure must be used.

This just means that you must first collect a random sample of subjects, and then perform some calculations that tell you whether your sample size is large enough. If more observations are required, these calculations also tell you how many more observations are needed so that the length of the confidence interval will be at most 2A.

The procedure is as follows. Suppose you have a sample of n_0 subjects, s^2 is the usual unbiased estimate of σ^2, and let t be chosen so that

$$\Pr(-t \le T \le t) = 1 - \alpha \qquad (6.3.1)$$

where T is a Student's t random variable with $\nu = n_0 - 1$ degrees of freedom. Next compute

$$d = (A/t)^2 \qquad (6.3.2a)$$

and

$$n = \max\{n_0,\ [s^2/d]^\dagger + 1\} \qquad (6.3.2b)$$

where $[s^2/d]^\dagger$ is the integer portion of s^2/d. For example, if $s^2/d = 9.9$, $[s^2/d]^\dagger = 9$. The term "max" in equation (6.3.2b) just means that n equals the larger of the two values inside the braces. Stein (1945) showed that if $n = n_0$, no additional observations are needed, and

$$\Pr(\bar{X} - A \le \mu \le \bar{X} + A) \ge 1 - \alpha. \qquad (6.3.3)$$

That is, $(\bar{X}-A, \bar{X}+A)$ is at least a $100(1-\alpha)\%$ confidence interval for μ, and the length of this interval is 2A as was desired. If instead $n = [s^2/d]^\dagger + 1$, you must randomly sample an additional $n - n_0$ observations, compute $\bar{X}$ using all n observations, in which case

$$(\bar{X} - A,\ \bar{X} + A) \qquad (6.3.4)$$

is at least a $100(1-\alpha)\%$ confidence interval for μ. That is, (6.3.3) will be true. Although Stein's procedure is easy to use, the justification of his procedure is too involved to be given here.

Example 6.3.1. Suppose you are investigating a new method of teaching reading, and you want to estimate the average reading scores of subjects who have taken the course. Further suppose reading ability is measured with a 60-point test, and that you want a confidence interval for μ that has length 6, and you want the probability that μ will be in this interval to be at least .9. Thus, 2A=6, and so A=3. Finally, suppose $n_0=5$ subjects have been sampled and that their reading scores are 20, 27, 18, 12, and 23. Then s^2=31.5. From Table A14, with $\nu=n_0-1=4$ and $\alpha=.1$, the value of t satisfying (6.3.1) is t=2.132, and so

$$d=(3/2.132)^2=1.98$$

and

$$[s^2/d]^{\dagger}+1=15+1=16.$$

This means you need a total of n=max{5,16}=16 observations. You already have 5, so $n-n_0=11$ additional observations are required. Suppose you randomly sample 11 additional subjects and the scores are 26,26,28,29,30,31,31,35,15,18, and 18. The sample mean of all 16 observations is 24.2, and so with probability at least .9, the interval

$$(24.2 \pm 3)=(21.2,27.2)$$

contains μ.

<u>Controlling Power</u>

Stein's procedure for controlling the length of the confidence interval can also be used to control power when testing $H_0:\mu=\mu_0$. As before, you first randomly sample n_0 subjects and compute s^2. Next compute n using equation (6.3.2b), sample an additional $n-n_0$ observations, and compute $\bar{X}$ using all n observations. If H_0 is rejected whenever

$$|(\surd n)(\bar{X}-\mu_0)/s|>t \qquad (6.3.6)$$

where t satisfies

$$\Pr(-t\le T\le t)=1-\alpha, \qquad (6.3.7)$$

and T is a Student's t random variable with $\nu=n_0-1$ degrees of freedom, the probability of a Type I error is α, and the power when $\mu=\mu_1$ is at least

$$1-\Pr[-t+(\mu_0-\mu_1)/\surd d \le T \le t+(\mu_0-\mu_1)/\surd d] \qquad (6.3.8)$$

It is important to notice that in equations (6.3.7) and (6.3.8), the degrees of freedom are n_0-1, not n-1. Also, in equation (6.3.8), s is based on only the first n_0 observations. It is tempting to reestimate s^2 using all n observations, and then reject H_0 according to whether (6.3.6) is true. However, there are no theoretical findings on what the resulting probability of a Type I and Type II error might be. On the other hand, there are two-stage procedures where the sample variance is reestimated (Hewett & Spurrier, 1983), but these procedures do not control power.

Example 6.3.2. Consider again example 6.3.1. Suppose you want to test $H_0{:}\mu=26$, and suppose you want to determine how much power there was when $\mu=20$. From the original sample of n_0 subjects, $s^2=31.5$, and so

$$n^{1/2}(\bar{X}-\mu_0)/s=(16)^{1/2}(24.2-26)/(31.5)^{1/2}$$

$$=-1.283.$$

If $\alpha=.1$, then with 4 degrees of freedom, $t=2.132$, and since $|-1.283|<2.132$, you fail to reject H_0.

Also suppose you want the length of the confidence interval to be $2A=6$. From example 6.3.1 $d=1.98$, and so to determine how much power there was for $\mu=20$, you must evaluate

$$\Pr[-2.132+(26-20)/(1.98)^{1/2} \le T \le 2.132+(26-20)/(1.98)^{1/2}]$$

$$=\Pr(2.12\le T\le 6.4).$$

From Table A14, $\Pr(T\ge 2.12)$ is approximately .05, and $\Pr(T\le 6.4)$ exceeds .995. Hence, $\Pr(2.12\le T\le 6.4)$ is approximately .05, and so power is $1-.05=.95$.

When applying Stein's procedure, rather than choosing d to control the length of the confidence interval, you can choose d in terms of how much power you want. If you want the power to be at least $1-\beta$ for a given value of β, simply choose d so that equation (6.3.8) equals $1-\beta$. Equivalently, choose d so that

$$\Pr(-t+(\mu_0-\mu_1)/\surd d \le T \le t+(\mu_0-\mu_1)/\surd d)=\beta,$$

where again the degrees of freedom are $\nu=n_0-1$. The important point is that you choose d prior to collecting your data, and the value of d guarantees that the power will be at least $1-\beta$.

Example 6.3.3. You have a random sample of $n_0=25$ subjects, and you find that $s^2=4$. If you want to test $H_0{:}\mu=50$ with $\alpha=.05$, and if you want the power to be at least .9 when $\mu=45$, do you have enough observations? To find out, first note that the critical value, with $\nu=24$ degrees of freedom, is $t=2.064$. Thus, you must choose d so that

$$.1=\Pr(-2.064+\{(50-45)/\sqrt{d}\} \le T \le 2.064+\{(50-45)/\sqrt{d}\}). \quad (6.3.9)$$

From Table A14, $\Pr(T\le 1.318)=.9$, and so consider choosing d such that

$$-2.064+\{(50-45)/\sqrt{d}\}=1.318.$$

(Simplified rules for determining d are given in equations 6.3.10 and 6.3.11.) Then d=2.186, and since $\Pr(T\le 2.064+\{5/\sqrt{2.186}\})$ is approximately equal to one, equation (6.3.9) is approximately true. That is, d=2.186 will satisfy the power requirements you have specified.

Next compute

$$n=\max\{25,[4/2.186]^{\dagger}+1]\}=25.$$

This means that no additional observations are needed.

It might help to note that when determining d, when $\mu_0-\mu_1>0$, you can, for all practical purposes, choose d such that

$$\Pr(-t+(\mu_0-\mu_1)/\sqrt{d} \le T)=\beta \quad (6.3.10)$$

and when $\mu_0-\mu_1<0$, you choose d such that

$$\Pr(T \le t+(\mu_0-\mu_1)/\sqrt{d})=\beta. \quad (6.3.11)$$

If, for example, $\mu_0-\mu_1>0$, $\Pr(T\le t+(\mu_0-\mu_1)/\sqrt{d})$ will be close to 1 in which case β, the probability of a Type II error, is nearly equal to the left side of equation (6.3.10).

One-Tailed Tests

Stein's procedure can also be used to test $H_0:\mu>\mu_0$. The only difference from the two-tailed test is that you reject H_0 if

$$(\sqrt{n})(\bar{X}-\mu_0)/s < -t.$$

Again you first sample n_0 observations, compute s, and then compute n with equation (6.3.2). Next, sample an additional $n-n_0$ observations and compute $\bar{X}$ using all n observations. The power of the test is at least

$$\Pr(T \le -t+(\mu_0-\mu_1)/\sqrt{d}),$$

and so again d can be chosen to control power. For H_0: $\mu<\mu_0$ the power is at least

$$Pr(T \geq t+(\mu_0-\mu_1)/\surd d).$$

6.4 APPROXIMATING THE PERCENTAGE POINTS OF STUDENT'S T DISTRIBUTION

While the percentage points of the t distribution reported in Table A14 are the ones most frequently needed, there may be situations where other percentage points are required. Extensive tables are impractical in textbooks, and so an approximation is given instead. Let t be the $100(1-\alpha)$ percentage point of a t distribution with ν degrees of freedom. That is,

$$Pr[T_\nu \leq t]=1-\alpha.$$

From Koehler (1983),

$$t^{-1} \doteq -.0953-\{.631/(\nu+1)\} + \{.81/[-\underline{\ln}(2\alpha(2-2\alpha))]^{1/2}\}$$
$$+.076\{[(2\pi)^{1/2}-.5]2\alpha\nu^{1/2}\}^{1/\nu}. \quad (6.4.1)$$

where $\underline{\ln}$ is the natural logarithm. This approximation is very accurate for $.001 \leq \alpha \leq .2$ and $\nu \geq 8$, and it gives good results for ν as small as 3. For a table of t values that is more extensive than Table A14, see Federighi (1959).

Example 6.4.1. Suppose you want to determine t for $\nu=16$ and $\alpha=.05$. From equation (6.4.1), 1/t is approximately

$$.0953 - \{.631/17\} + .81/[-\ln(.1(2-.1))]^{1/2} +$$
$$.076\{[(2\pi)^{1/2}-.5](.1)(4)\}^{1/16}.$$

$$=.5711,$$

and so

$$t=1/.5711=1.75.$$

The exact value is 1.76.

6.5 THE F DISTRIBUTION

As will be seen in chapter eight, another important distribution is the F distribution which arises as follows. Let U and V be two independent random variables where U has a chi-square distribution with ν_1 degrees of freedom, and V has a chi-square distribution with ν_2 degrees of freedom. Then the distribution of the random variable

$$F=[U/\nu_1]/[V/\nu_2]$$

is called an F distribution with ν_1 and ν_2 degrees of freedom. Some percentage points are given in Table A3. Notice that a chi-square distribution assumes you are sampling from a normal distribution, and so the F distribution assumes normality as well. The mean of an F distribution is

$$\mu=\nu_2/(\nu_2-2).$$

This is an unexpected result since the mean depends on ν_2 but not ν_1. The variance is

$$\sigma^2=\{2\nu_2^2(\nu_1+\nu_2-2)\}/\{\nu_1(\nu_2-2)^2(\nu_2-4)\}$$

and the possible values of F range from zero to ∞.
Table A3 gives the value of F, say f, such that

$$\Pr(F\le f)=1-\alpha$$

for $\alpha=.05$ and .01. If you want to determine f where $\Pr(F\le f)=\alpha$, this can be accomplished from the relationship

$$\Pr(F_{\nu_1,\nu_2}\le f)=\Pr(F_{\nu_2,\nu_1}\le 1/f).$$

In words, to determine f, you reverse the degrees of freedom, look up the $1-\alpha$ quantile $f_{1-\alpha}$, and compute $1/f_{1-\alpha}$.

Example 6.5.1. Consider an F distribution with $\nu_1=8$ and $\nu_2=9$ degrees of freedom, and suppose you want to determine the value f such that $\Pr(F\le f)=.05$. To do this, reverse the degrees of freedom so that $\nu_1=9$ and $\nu_2=8$, refer to Table A3 and determine the $1-\alpha$ quantile. The answer is 3.39. Then $f=1/3.39=.295$. That is, $\Pr(F\le .295)=.05$.

To illustrate how the F distribution is used, suppose you have two independent groups with means μ_1 and μ_2, and standard deviations σ_1 and σ_2, respectively. The most common goal is to test $H_0:\mu_1=\mu_2$, but suppose you want to test $H_0:\sigma_1=\sigma_2$. This hypothesis can be tested with the procedure described in the next paragraph, but it should be emphasized that in practice you will rarely if ever want to use this procedure for comparing variances. The reason is that if you randomly sample observations from a non-normal distribution, the procedure described here can give you a poor indication of the probability of a Type I error. Instead you should test for equal variances using the Brown-Forsythe procedure which is described in chapter eight--their procedure works well even when the normality assumption is violated. The goal in this section is merely to give you some experience with how the F distribution is used.

Suppose n_j subjects are sampled for the j<u>th</u> group (j=1,2), and let $s_1{}^2$ and $s_2{}^2$ be the corresponding sample variances. Thus, $s_j{}^2$ is an unbiased estimate of $\sigma_j{}^2$. It is assumed that the subjects under treatment A are different from the subjects under treatment B, and so $s_1{}^2$ and $s_2{}^2$ are independent. Then $(n_1-1)(s_1/\sigma_1)^2$ and $(n_2-1)(s_2/\sigma_2)^2$ are independent chi-square random variables having $\nu_1=n_1-1$ and $\nu_2=n_2-1$ degrees of freedom. If $H_0:\sigma_1=\sigma_2$ is true,

$$F=\{(n_1-1)s_1^2/[\sigma_1^2(n_1-1)]\}/$$

$$\{(n_2-1)s_2^2/[\sigma_2^2(n_2-1)]\}$$

$$=s_1^2/s_2^2$$

has an F distribution with $\nu_1=n_1-1$ and $\nu_2=n_2-1$ degrees of freedom. When H_0 is true you would expect $(s_1/s_2)^2$ to have a value close to $\nu_2/(\nu_2-2)$, the mean of F, and so if this ratio is unusually small or large, reject H_0. More specifically, if you want the probability of a Type I error to be α, reject H_0 if

$$s_1^2/s_2^2<f_{\alpha/2}, \text{ or if } s_1^2/s_2^2>f_{1-\alpha/2},$$

where f_α is the 100α percentile of an F distribution with ν_1 and ν_2 degrees of freedom.

<u>Example 6.5.2</u>. Suppose 31 subjects are taught reading under method A, and another 25 subjects receive method B. After the instruction is complete, suppose each subject takes a reading ability test, and that the sample variances of the test scores for the two groups are $s_1{}^2=50$ and $s_2{}^2=60$. To test $H_0:\sigma_1=\sigma_2$ with $\alpha=.05$, compute $F=s_1{}^2/s_2{}^2=.883$. From Table A3,

$$f_{.025}=.467 \text{ and } f_{.975}=2.14.$$

Because .467≤.883≤2.21, fail to reject H_0.

6.6 THE NON-CENTRAL CHI-SQUARE DISTRIBUTION

A generalization of the chi-square distribution is the non-central chi-square distribution which plays an important role in chapter ten, and so a few of its properties are briefly mentioned.

Let $U_1,\ldots,U_m$ be independent normal random variables with means $\mu_1,\ldots,\mu_m$ and variances all equal to one. Then the distribution of

$$\chi_m^2(\delta)=\Sigma U_i^2 \tag{6.6.1}$$

is called a non-central chi-square distribution with non-centrality parameter $\delta=\Sigma\mu_i{}^2$ and degrees of freedom m. When $\delta=0$, (6.6.1) reduces to the (central) chi-square random variable which was discussed in section 6.1. The mean and variance of $\chi_\nu{}^2(\delta)$ are $\nu+\delta$ and $2(\nu+2\delta)$, respectively.

Some percentage points of the non-central chi-square distribution are reported by Johnson and Pearson (1969). If their table is unsatisfactory in a given situation, the following approximation, due to Pearson (1959), can be used.

Let

$$b=-\delta^2/(\nu+3\delta)$$

$$c=(\nu+3\delta)/(\nu+2\delta)$$

$$f=(\nu+2\delta)^3/(\nu+3\delta)^2.$$

Then

$$\Pr\{\chi_\nu{}^2(\delta)\le x\} \doteq \Pr\{\chi_\nu{}^2\le(x-b)/c\} \tag{6.6.2}$$

where $\chi_\nu{}^2$ is a central chi-square random variable with f degrees of freedom. The right side of (6.6.2) can be evaluated with equation (6.1.9) or with Table A2. Also, from equation (6.1.8), you can determine the value of x such that

$$\Pr\{\chi_\nu^2(\delta)\le x\}=1-\alpha.$$

Example 6.6.1. Suppose $\nu=7$, $\delta=4$, and you want to determine the value x such that

$$\Pr\{\chi_\nu^2(\delta)\le x\}=.95.$$

Then b=-.842, c=1.2667, and f=9.349. The value of y such that $\Pr\{\chi_f^2 \le y\}=.95$ is, from equation (6.1.8),

$$y=[(9.349)^{1/2}+2(-\log_{10}(.05))^{1/2}-(7/6)]^2=17.41$$

Thus, (x-b)/c=(x+.842)/1.2667=17.41, and so x=21.2. The exact value is 21.228.

6.7 THE NON-CENTRAL F DISTRIBUTION

Another important distribution is the non-central F distribution. The only goal here is to indicate, for future reference, how this distribution is defined.

Let U and V be two independent random variables where U has a non-central chi-square distribution with non-centrality parameter δ and ν_1 degrees of freedom, and V has a central chi-square distribution with ν_2 degrees of freedom. The distribution of

$$F=[U/\nu_1]/[V/\nu_2]$$

is called a non-central F distribution with ν_1 and ν_2 degrees of freedom and non-centrality parameter δ. For a summary of the properties of this distribution, see Johnson and Kotz (1970).

6.8 THE NON-CENTRAL T DISTRIBUTION

If U is a normal random variable with mean δ and variance one,

$$T=U/[\chi_\nu^2/\nu]^{1/2} \tag{6.8.1}$$

has a non-central t distribution with non-centrality parameter δ and ν degrees of freedom. In (6.8.1), χ_ν^2 is a chi-sqaure random variable that is independent of U. An approximation of $\Pr(T\le t)$, proposed by Johnson and Welch (1940), is

$$\Pr\{T\le t\} \doteq \Pr\{Z\le(t-\delta)/[1+(t^2/(2\nu))]^{1/2}\} \tag{6.8.2}$$

where Z is a standard normal random variable. For additional approximations, see Johnson and Kotz (1970), and Kraemer and Paik (1979).

6.9 THE BETA DISTRIBUTION

Another important distribution is the beta distribution. Unlike all of the other distributions in this chapter, the beta distribution is defined on the interval [0,1]. The distribution depends on two parameters r and s where $r>0$ and $s>0$. If Y has a beta distribution with parameters r and s, $Pr(Y \le y)$ can be determined from the extensive tables compiled by Pearson and Johnson (1968). When r and s are integers, the probability density function reduces to

$$f(y)=\{(r+s-1)!/[(r-1)!(s-1)!]\}y^{r-1}(1-y)^{s-1}.$$

One important feature of the beta distribution is that it usually provides an excellent approximation of a unimodal distribution defined on a finite interval. The beta distribution is seen to be important in chapters 14 and 15.

EXERCISES

All of the exercises in this chapter assume sampling is from a normal distribution.

6.1 If Y_1 has a chi-square distribution with 5 degrees of freedom, and Y_2 has a chi-square distribution with 7 degrees of freedom, and if Y_1 and Y_2 are independent, what is $Pr\{Y_1+Y_2 \le 14.85\}$?

6.2 If $s_1{}^2$ and $s_2{}^2$ are independent sample variances from a normal distribution with $\sigma^2=8$, and if $s_1{}^2$ is based on 5 observations, and $s_2{}^2$ is based on 10 observations, determine

$$Pr\{4s_1^2+9s_2^2 \le 221.52\}.$$

6.3 In problem 6.2, determine the value of y such that

$$Pr\{s_1^2 \le y\}=.9$$

6.4 Solve problem 6.3 using equation (6.1.8).

6.5 Suppose for a random sample of $n=14$, $s^2=10$. Determine a .99 confidence interval for σ^2.

6.6 Referring to exercise 6.5, test $H_0:\sigma^2=12$. Use $\alpha=.05$

6.7 Suppose $s^2=30$ with $n=15$. Test $H_0:\sigma^2<12$. Use $\alpha=.01$

6.8 Referring to definition 6.2.1, what is the distribution of T^2 if T is a Student's t random variable with ν degrees of freedom?

6.9 Suppose $\bar{X}=30$, $s^2=4$, and $n=25$. Test $H_0:\mu=34$ with $\alpha=.01$.

6.10 Suppose a scale for measuring maturity has been developed and that after extensive testing, the average score on this scale for children in grade 3 is found to be $\mu_0=36$. Further suppose 24 grade 3 children with I.Q.'s above 120 are given the same measure and, their average score on the maturity scale is 42. If $s^2=9$, is there reason to believe that the average score of children with I.Q.'s above 120 is different from 36? Use $\alpha=.01$.

6.11 In problem 6.10, obtain a 90% confidence interval for μ, the average maturity scores for grade 3 children having I.Q.'s above 120.

6.12 Referring to problem 6.10, suppose you want the probablity to be at least .95 that a confidence interval with length 2 will contain μ. Did you sample enough observations? If not, how many more observations are required?

6.13 Referring to problem 6.10, how many observations do you need so that power will be at least .9 when $\mu=38$, $\mu_0=36$ and $\alpha=.05$?

6.14 Use equation (6.4.1) to determine t so that $\Pr(T\le t)=.99$ when $\nu=20$. Compare your answer to the value of t in Table A14.

6.15 You have two independent groups with $n_1=9$, $n_2=11$, $s_1^2=1.8$, $s_2^2=2.3$. Test $H_0:\sigma_1^2=\sigma_2^2$ with $\alpha=.05$.

6.16 Use (6.6.2) to determine y such that $\Pr(\chi_4^2(16)\le y)=.95$.

References

Dantzig, G. (1940) On the non-existance of tests of "Student's" hypothesis having power functions independent of σ Annals of Mathematical Statistics, 11, 186.
Federighi, E. T. (1959) Extended tables of the percentage points of Student's t-distribution. Journal of the American Statistical Association, 68, 683-691.
Hewett, J. & Spurrier, J. (1983) A survey of two-stage tests of hypotheses: Theory and application. Communications in Statistics--Theory and Methods, 12, 2307-2425.
Hoaglin, D. (1977) Direct approximations for chi-squared

percentage points. Journal of the American Statistical Association, 72, 508-515.
Johnson, N. & Kotz, S. (1970) Continuous univariate distributions-2 New York: Wiley.
Johnson, N. & Pearson, E. (1969) Tables of percentage points of non-central χ. Biometrika, 56, 255-272.
Johnson, N. & Welch, B. (1940) Applications of the noncentral t distribution. Biometrika, 31, 362-389.
Koehler, K. (1983) A simple approximation for the percentiles of the t distribution. Technometrics, 25, 103-105.
Kraemer, H & Paik, M. (1979) A central t approximation to the non-central t distribution. Technometrics, 31, 357-360.
Pearson, E. (1959) Note on an approximation to the distribution of non-central χ^2. Biometrika, 46, 364.
Pearson, E. & Johnson, N. (1968) Tables of the incomplete beta function. Cambridge: University Press.
Stein, C. (1945) A two-sample test for a linear hypothesis whose power is independent of the variance. Annals of Mathematical Statistics, 16, 243-258.

CHAPTER 7

COMPARING TWO MEANS

So far, hypothesis testing procedures have been limited to situations where a parameter is compared to a known constant. This problem occurs in practice, but a more common problem is comparing two or more unknown parameters to one another. This chapter considers the simplest of these problems, namely comparing the means of two normal distributions.

7.1 COMPARING THE MEANS OF TWO INDEPENDENT NORMAL DISTRIBUTIONS

It will help to keep a specific problem in mind, so suppose you want to compare two methods of teaching reading. A basic issue is whether it makes any difference, on the average, which teaching method is used. To find out, suppose you randomly assign n_1 subjects to method 1 and n_2 subjects to methods 2. After the course is completed, the subjects take a test that measures their reading ability. Let X_{ij} be the observed score of the i<u>th</u> subject in the j<u>th</u> group, $i=1,\ldots,n_j$; $j=1,2$.

It is assumed that:

1) $X_{11}, X_{21},\ldots,X_{n_1,1}$

   is a random sample from a normal distribution with mean μ_1 and variance σ_1^2. These are the observations from group 1.

2) $X_{12}, X_{22},\ldots,X_{n_2,2}$

   is a random sample from a normal distribution with mean μ_2 and variance σ_2^2. These are the observations from group 2.

3) The observations $X_{11},\ldots,X_{n_1,1}$

   are independent of $X_{12},\ldots,X_{n_2,2}$.

4) $\sigma_1^2=\sigma_2^2$.

Comments about these assumptions are made at the end of this section.

In the illustration, the goal is to determine whether there is any difference between the average reading scores for the subjects who receive teaching method 1 as opposed to method 2. Thus, the goal is to test

$$H_0:\mu_1=\mu_2. \tag{7.1.1}$$

Let $\bar{X}_1=\Sigma X_{i1}/n_1$ and $\bar{X}_2=\Sigma X_{i2}/n_2$ be the sample means corresponding to the two groups. By assumption, $\bar{X}_1$ and $\bar{X}_2$ are independent normal random variables, and so from Theorem 4.5.2,

$$Y=\bar{X}_1-\bar{X}_2$$

is normally distributed with mean

$$\mu_y=\mu_1-\mu_2$$

and variance

$$\sigma_y^2=(\sigma_1^2/n_1)+(\sigma_2^2/n_2).$$

Let

$$s_y^2=\{\Sigma(X_{i1}-\bar{X}_1)^2+\Sigma(X_{i2}-\bar{X}_2)^2\}/[n_1+n_2-2], \tag{7.1.2}$$

$$s_1^2=\Sigma(X_{i1}-\bar{X}_1)^2/(n_1-1),$$

$$s_2^2=\Sigma(X_{i2}-\bar{X}_2)^2/(n_2-1),$$

and let σ^2 be the common value of $\sigma_1{}^2$ and $\sigma_2{}^2$. That is, for notational convenience, let $\sigma_1=\sigma_2=\sigma$. Then

$$s_y^2=[(n_1-1)s_1^2+(n_2-1)s_2^2]/(n_1+n_2-2),$$

and since $E(s_1{}^2)=\sigma_1{}^2$ and $E(s_2{}^2)=\sigma_2{}^2$,

$$E(s_y^2)=\sigma^2.$$

Thus, $s_y{}^2$ is an unbiased estimate of σ^2. Also, $(n_1-1)s_1{}^2/\sigma^2$ and $(n_2-1)s_2{}^2/\sigma^2$ are independent chi-square random variables with n_1-1 and n_2-1 degrees of freedom. From section 6.1, the sum of two independent chi-square random variables with ν_1 and ν_2 degrees of freedom is again a chi-square random variable, but with $\nu_1+\nu_2$ degrees of freedom. Thus,

$$\{(n_1-1)s_1^2+(n_2-1)s_2^2\}/\sigma^2 \tag{7.1.3}$$

has a chi-square distribution with $(n_1-1)+(n_2-1)=n_1+n_2-2$ degrees of freedom.

When $H_0:\mu_1=\mu_2$ is true,

$$(n_1 n_2)^{1/2}(\bar{X}_1-\bar{X}_2)/[(n_1+n_2)\sigma^2]^{1/2} \quad (7.1.4)$$

has a standard normal distribution. This result can be used to show that

$$T=[n_1 n_2/(n_1+n_2)]^{1/2}(\bar{X}_1-\bar{X}_2)/s_y \quad (7.1.5)$$

has a Student's t distribution with $\nu=n_1+n_2-2$ degrees of freedom. Note that because $\sigma_1=\sigma_2$ is assumed, $\sigma_1{}^2/\sigma_2{}^2=1$, and so equation (7.1.5) does not depend on any unknown parameters--its value depends only on quantities that are known as a result of your experiment. If, however, $\sigma_1\neq\sigma_2$, the unknown values σ_1 and σ_2 do not cancel, and so equation (7.1.5) cannot be evaluated.

Because $\mu_y=\mu_1-\mu_2$, $H_0:\mu_1=\mu_2$ is the same as $H_0:\mu_y=0$, and so testing $H_0:\mu_1=\mu_2$ is the same as comparing a parameter to a known constant, which was covered in chapter five. Thus, you reject H_0 if

$$|T|>t$$

where now T is given by equation (7.1.5), and t is chosen so that

$$\Pr(-t\leq T_\nu\leq t)=1-\alpha$$

where T_ν is a Student's t random variable with $\nu=n_1+n_2-2$ degrees of freedom. As will be shown in section 7.3 (see equation 7.3.10), the smaller the variance of $\bar{X}_1-\bar{X}_2$ happens to be, the more power you will have when testing H_0.

Example 7.1.1. Continuing the illustration where two methods of teaching reading are being investigated, suppose $n_1=15$ subjects receive the first method, and $n_2=12$ subjects receive method 2. Further suppose that for the first group, the scores on the reading test yield $\bar{X}_1=50$ and $s_1{}^2=10$, and for the second group, $\bar{X}_2=60$ and $s_2{}^2=12$. The degrees of freedom are $\nu=15+12-2=25$. If the probability of a Type I error is to be $\alpha=.05$, then from Table A14, t=2.060. The value of equation (7.1.5) is

$$T=\{[15(12)/(15+12)]^{1/2}(50-60)\}/\{[14(10)+11(12)]/25\}^{1/2}$$

$$=-7.82.$$

Because $|T|>2.060$, you reject H_0 and conclude there is a difference between the two methods.

One-Tailed Tests

The hypothesis $H_0:\mu_1<\mu_2$ can also be tested. You simply reject H_0 if T>t where t is the 1-α quantile of a Student's t distribution with $\nu=n_1+n_2-2$ degrees of freedom. To test $H_0:\mu_1>\mu_2$, reject if T<t, where now t is the α quantile of Student's t distribution.

Effect of Unequal Variances

Many books still claim that violating the equal variance assumption has little effect on the t-test. Assuming normality, Ramsey (1980) has shown that this is indeed the case provided the sample sizes are equal. For instance, if $n_1=n_2=15$ and $\alpha=.05$, the actual Type I error probability will not exceed .06. However, when the sample sizes are unequal, the t-test given above may not provide adequate control over both Type I error and power. For instance, if $n_1=21$, $n_2=41$, $\sigma_1=4,\sigma_2=1$, and you test at the $\alpha=.05$ level, the actual probability of a Type I error is approximately .15. It might seem that $\sigma_1/\sigma_2=4$ is unrealistically large, but Fenstad (1983) argues that this is not the case, and a survey of educational studies by Wilcox (1987) supports Fenstad's view. You might be tempted to use the t-test anyway if the sample variances are nearly equal (or if you test $H_0:\sigma_1=\sigma_2$ and fail to reject), but for reasons outlined in chapter eight, it is better simply to abandon the t-test and use Welch's V which is described below. Another reason for abandoning the t-test is that if the variances are nearly equal, Welch's V performs about as well as the t-test. If the variances are fairly unequal, Welch's V still performs well in situations where the t-test gives poor results.

7.2 APPROXIMATE SOLUTION WHEN $\sigma_1\neq\sigma_2$ (WELCH'S V)

When $\sigma_1\neq\sigma_2$, Welch (1937) suggested testing $H_0:\mu_1=\mu_2$ by computing an appoximate 100(1-α)% confidence interval for $\mu_1-\mu_2$, and rejecting H_0 if this interval does not contain zero. (Following Fenstad, 1983, this procedure will be called Welch's V.) Welch's confidence interval is given by

$$(\bar{X}_1-\bar{X}_2)\pm AB$$

where

$$A=\max\{(\sqrt{m_1})t_1,\ (\sqrt{m_2})t_2\},$$

$$m_i=[(n_i-3)/(n_i-1)],\ i=1,2$$

t_i (i=1,2) is the $1-\alpha/2$ quantile of a Student's t distribution with n_i-1 degrees of freedom, and

$$B=\{[s_1^2/(n_1m_1)] + [s_2^2/(n_2m_2)]\}^{1/2}.$$

Welch's U statistic (not given in this chapter) is also a well known procedure for comparing pairs of means, but Fenstad (1983) found that Welch's V statistic gives better results. The probability of a Type I error is not exactly α when using Welch's V, but it is fairly close.

Example 7.2.1. Suppose you want to test $H_0:\mu_1=\mu_2$, and you observe the following data.

Group 1	Group 2
1	2
2	3
3	2
2	4
2	2
	4
	4

The sample means are $\bar{X}_1=2$ and $\bar{X}_2=3$, and the sample variances are $s_1{}^2=.5$ and $s_2{}^2=1.0$. Further suppose you do not want to assume $\sigma_1=\sigma_2$. Then Welch's V can be used, in which case, when $\alpha=.05$, $t_1=2.776$ (with $\nu=n_1-1=4$), $t_2=2.447$ (with $\nu=7-1=6$), $m_1=2/4$, $m_2=4/6$

$$B=\{[4(.5)/5(2)] + [6(1.0)/7(4)]\}^{1/2}=.645$$

$$A=\max\{(2/4)^{1/2}2.776,\ (4/6)^{1/2}2.44\}=1.998,$$

and so an approximate $100(1-\alpha)$% confidence interval for $\mu_1-\mu_2$ is

$$-1\pm.645(1.998)=(-2.289,\ .289).$$

This interval contains zero, and so you do not reject H_0.

Effect of nonnormality

If n_1 or n_2 is less than or equal to 10, both the t-test and Welch's V may be affected by nonnormality (Tiku and Singh, 1981; Yuen, 1974). Usually this means that the actual probability of a Type I error will be less than the nominal α level. For example, with $\alpha=.05$, the actual probability of a Type I error can be as low as .02. As the sample sizes increase from 10 to 20, all indications are that the effects of nonnormality disappear rapidly. For a procedure that is robust to both nonnormality and unequal variances, see Tiku and Singh (1981).

7.3 EXACT PROCEDURE FOR CONTROLLING POWER AND HANDLING UNEQUAL VARIANCES

Both Chapman (1950) and Ghosh (1975b) have proposed exact two-stage procedures for controlling power and handling unequal variances. The first stage consists of sampling some observations, and performing some calculations that tell how many more observations, if any, are required. The second stage consists of sampling any additional observations that are needed and completing the analysis. When testing $H_0:\mu_1=\mu_2$, Chapman's procedure guarantees that the power will be exactly $1-\beta$ for a given value of $\mu_1-\mu_2$, and that the probability of a Type I error will be exactly α regardless of what the variances might be. Controlling power in this manner is impossible when using a single-stage procedure such as Welch's V or the t-test. Ghosh's procedure also guarantees that the Type I error probability will be exactly α, but in contrast to Chapman's procedure, the power will be at least $1-\beta$. Thus, in this sense, Ghosh's procedure has an advantage over Chapman's since it has more power.

An important feature of both Chapman's and Ghosh's procedures is that they control power and determine sample sizes in terms of some value for $\delta=\mu_1-\mu_2$ that is judged to be important in a given situation. Some readers might be familiar with methods that control power in terms of $\Delta=(\mu_1-\mu_2)/\sigma$ where by assumption $\sigma_1=\sigma_2=\sigma$. It has been argued that if $\mu_1\neq\mu_2$, chances are $\sigma_1\neq\sigma_2$. As illustrated in chapter eight, having $\sigma_1\neq\sigma_2$ can affect power when the difference between two treatment groups is measured in terms of δ rather than Δ. Some authorities prefer to measure differences with Δ, but this practice has met with several criticisms which are described in section 7.4. A method for controlling power in terms of Δ is described at the end of this section.

Ghosh's Procedure

First Stage

Suppose n_0 observations have been randomly sampled from each treatment group. Let $Y_i=X_{i1}-X_{i2}$ be the difference between the ith subject in the first group and the ith subject in the second, $i=1,\ldots,n_0$; and let $s_y{}^2$ be the usual sample variance of the Y_i's. That is,

$$s_y^2=\Sigma(Y_i-\hat{\mu}_y)^2/(n_0-1)$$

where

$$\hat{\mu}=\Sigma Y_i/n_0.$$

Let t be the $1-\alpha/2$ quantile of a Student' t distribution with $\nu=n_0-1$ degrees of freedom. Since $H_0:\mu_1=\mu_2$ is the same as testing $H_0:\mu_y=0$, Stein's procedure can be applied to the Y_i's. If you want the power to be at least $1-\beta$ when $\mu_1-\mu_2=\delta_0$, say, let

$$a=t-(\delta_0/\surd d),\ b=-t-(\delta_0/\surd d),$$

and choose d so that

$$\Pr(T\le b)+\Pr(T\ge a)=1-\beta \qquad (7.3.1)$$

where T is a Student's t distribution with $\nu=n_0-1$ degrees of freedom. When $\delta_0\ge 0$, (7.3.1) is nearly equal to $\Pr(T\ge a)$, and when $\delta_0<0$ it is nearly equal to $\Pr(T\le b)$. If for instance $\delta_0\ge 0$, d can be determined fairly accurately by choosing a so that $\Pr(T\ge a)=1-\beta$ and solving for d.

Second Stage

Compute

$$n=\max\{n_0,\ [s_y^2/d]^\dagger+1\} \qquad (7.3.2)$$

where $[s_y^2/d]^\dagger$ is the integer portion of s^2/d. The second stage of Ghosh's procedure consists of sampling $n-n_0$ additionalobservations from each treatment group, say X_{ij} $(i=n_0+1,\ldots,n;\ j=1,2)$, and computing

$$\bar{Y}=\Sigma_{i=1}^{n}(X_{i1}-X_{i2})/n \qquad (7.3.3)$$

where the summation is over all n observations. You reject H_0 if the confidence interval

$$\bar{Y}\pm(s_y/\surd n)t$$

does not contain zero where t is chosen so that $\Pr(T\le t)=1-\alpha/2$, and where T is a Student's t random variable with $\nu=n_0-1$ degrees of freedom. Note that the degrees of freedom are n_0-1, not $n-1$. Also note that Ghosh's procedure assumes that initially you have n_0 observations sampled from each treatment group. If instead you initially sample n_1 observations from the first group and n_2 from the second, and if $n_1 \neq n_2$, you can use Chapman's procedure, which is described below.

Example 7.3.1. Suppose you have two groups each containing five randomly sampled subjects. The first group consists of psychology majors and the second consists of English majors. Each subject is asked to use a ten-point scale to rate how much they like a particular movie. Suppose you want to know whether the average rating of the two groups is different, you want $\alpha=.05$, and you want the power to be at least .9 when $\mu_1-\mu_2=1.0$. Thus, $\delta_0=1$ and $1-\beta=.9$. If the ratings and the corresponding differences are

Group 1	Group 2	$Y_i=X_{i1}-X_{j1}$
1	8	-7
5	2	3
6	5	1
7	7	0
9	3	6

then $s_y^2=23.3$ is the sample variance of the Y_i's. From Table A14, with $\nu=4$ degrees of freedom, $Pr(T\geq-1.533)=.9$, and $t=2.776$. Thus, $a=-1.533$, and because $\delta_0>0$, choose d so that

$$2.776-(1/\surd d)=-1.533.$$

Solving for d yields $d=.054$, and so $b=-2.776-1/\surd .054=-7.08$. Since $Pr(T\leq-7.08)\doteq.001$, the power will be at least $Pr(T\geq a)+Pr(T\leq b)\doteq.901$. (The notation $\doteq$ means "approximately equal to.")

Continuing the calculations,

$$n=\max\{5,\ [23.3/.054]^{\dagger}+1\}=432.$$

Thus, you need an additional 432-5=427 observations randomly sampled from each group. If the sample means of these 432 observations are $\bar{X}_1=6.5$ for the first group, and $\bar{X}_2=5.5$ for the second, then $\bar{Y}=6.5-5.5=1.0$, and the confidence interval for $\mu_1-\mu_2$ is

$$1.0\pm2.776(23.3/432)^{1/2}=(.36,\ 1.64).$$

This interval does not contain zero, and so you reject H_0.

As in Stein's procedure, it should be emphasized that s_y^2 is based on the initial sample of n_0 observations. Once the additional $n-n_0$ observations are available, you do not recalculate

s_y^2. In contrast, $\bar{X}_1$ and $\bar{X}_2$ are based on all n observations when computing the confidence interval.

Chapman's Procedure

First Stage

Suppose you have n_1 observations randomly sampled from the first treatment group, and n_2 observations randomly sampled from the second. Let

$$V_j=\Sigma_i X_{ij}$$

be the sum of the observations for the jth group, j=1,2, where the summation is over i=1 to n_j, and let s_j^2 be the corresponding sample variances. Next compute

$$N_j=\{n_j+1,\ (s_j^2/d)|+1\},\ j-1,2$$

which is the total number of observations required from the jth group. Note that under Chapman's procedure, at least one additional observation must be sampled. If you want the length of the $100(1-\alpha)\%$ confidence interval for $\mu_1-\mu_2$ to be 2A, set $d=(A/c)^2$, where c is the $1-\alpha/2$ percentage point of the difference of two independent Student t random variables, which is read from Table A12. For example, if $\nu_1=5$, $\nu_2=6$ and $\alpha=.05$, then $\alpha/2=.025$ and c=3.536. Be sure to notice that when you refer to Table A12, you look up the entry corresponding to $\alpha/2$, not α, because you are testing a two-sided hypothesis. If the value of c you need is not in Table A12, an accurate approximation of c when both ν_1 and ν_2 are reasonably large, say greater than 10, is

$$c=z(2)^{1/2}\{1+16^{-1}[(n_1-1)^{-1}+(n_2-1)^{-1}](z^2+5)\} \qquad (7.3.4)$$

where z is chosen so that $Pr(Z\leq z)=1-\alpha/2$, and where Z is a standard normal random variable. (Equation 7.3.4 is based on an approximation proposed by Ghosh, 1975a.) That is, z is read from Table A1. This completes the first stage of your experiment.

Second Stage

In the second stage you randomly sample an additional N_j-n_j observations from the jth group, and compute

$$U_j = \sum_{i=n_j+1}^{N_j} X_{ij}.$$

In words, U_j is the sum of the observations in the j<u>th</u> group observed in the second stage.

To illustrate the computations, suppose the observed data is as shown in Table 7.3.1.

Table 7.3.1

First Stage Data				
Group 1			Group 2	
9	1	15	7	15
10	10	15	8	20
15	20	25	2	24
20	30	30	16	3
15	10	5	10	5
Second Stage				
16			15	
18			20	
14			13	
12			17	

Then $n_1=15$, $n_2=10$, $N_1-n_1=4$, $N_2-n_2=4$,

$$V_1=9+10+...+5=230$$

$$V_2=7+8+...+5=110$$

$$U_1=16+18+14+12=60$$

and $$U_2=15+20+13+17=65.$$

For technical reasons the confidence interval for $\mu_1-\mu_2$ is not based on the sample means. Instead you compute

$$b_j=(1/N_j)+ \{[n_j(N_jd-s_j^2)]^{1/2}/[(N_j-n_j)s_j^2]^{1/2}\}/N_j \quad (7.3.5)$$

and

$$\tilde{X}_j=\{[1-(N_j-n_j)b_j]/n_j\}V_j + b_jU_j \tag{7.3.6}$$

The 100(1-α)% confidence interval is

$$(\tilde{X}_1-\tilde{X}_2)\pm A.$$

Example 7.3.2. As a simple illustration, suppose you have already sampled n_1=10 and n_2=15 observations from the two treatment groups and you find that $s_1{}^2$=1.2 and $s_2{}^2$=0.8. Also suppose you want a 95% confidence interval with length 2A=4, and so A=2. From Table A1 with α=.05, z=1.96. From (7.3.4)

$$c=(\surd 2)(1.96)[1+.0114((1.96)^2+5)]=3.051$$

is the approximate value for c. If instead you use Table A12 to determine c, ν_1=9, ν_2=14, $\alpha/2$=.025, and for the entry in Table A12 corresponding to .025, you find that c=3.098. This value of c is more accurate and should be used.

Continuing the calculations with c=3.051,

$$d=(2/3.051)^2=.4297,$$

and so

$$N_1=\max\{11,3\}=11.$$

Similarly, N_2=16. Thus, one additional observation is sampled from both treatment groups.

Next you compute $\tilde{X}_1$ and $\tilde{X}_2$ using equation (7.3.6). In the illustration, N_1=11, and so

$$b_1=\{1+[10(11(.4297)-1.2)]^{1/2}[(11-10)1.2]^{-1/2}\}/11$$

$$=.584.$$

The quantity b_2 is determined in a similar manner. If, for example, $\tilde{X}_1$=12 and $\tilde{X}_2$=10.5, then a 95% confidence interval for $\mu_1-\mu_2$ is

$$(\tilde{X}_1-\tilde{X}_2-A,\ \tilde{X}_1-\tilde{X}_2+A)=(-.5,\ 3.5).$$

This interval contains zero, and so $H_0:\mu_1=\mu_2$ is not rejected.

Determining the Power of Chapman's Procedure: An Alternative Approach to Choosing d

Using Chapman's procedure, you reject $H_0:\mu_1=\mu_2$ if $|(\tilde{X}_1-\tilde{X}_2)/\surd d|>c$, where c is read from Table A12 (the entry corresponding to $\alpha/2$), or c is computed from equation (7.3.4). Let's suppose you have chosen a value for d and you want to determine how much power there will be when $\delta=\mu_1-\mu_2=\delta_0$, say, where δ_0 is some constant you have chosen that represents a difference between μ_1 and μ_2 that is of interest to you. As usual, let Z be a standard normal random variable, and define the function D(x) by

$$D(x)=Pr(Z\le x/\surd 2)-A(32\surd 2)^{-1}(\nu_1^{-1}+\nu_2^{-1})(x^2+10) \quad (7.3.7)$$

where $\nu_1=n_1-1$, $\nu_2=n_2-1$,

$$A=x\{1/\exp(x^2/4)\}/(2\pi)^{1/2}$$

and exp is the exponential function. That is, $\exp(x)=e^x$ where e is Euler's constant, which is approximately equal to 2.7182818. The power of Chapman's procedure is approximately

$$1+D[-c-(\delta/\surd d)]-D[c-(\delta/\surd d)]. \quad (7.3.8)$$

<u>Example 7.3.3</u>. Suppose d=.04, c=3.0, $n_1=11$, $n_2=16$, and you want to determine how much power there is for $\delta=\mu_1-\mu_2=1.0$. Then $\nu_1=10$, $\nu_2=15$, $-c-\delta/\surd d=-8$, $c-\delta\surd d=-2$,

$$(2\pi)^{-1/2}(1/\exp[x^2/4])=.1467,$$

and

$$D(-2)=.08-[(-2)(.1467)(32\surd 2)^{-1}(10^{-1}+15^{-1})(4+10)$$

$$=.0815.$$

D(-8) is nearly equal to zero, and so the power will be 1-.0816=.9175.

If instead you want to determine d so that the power will be $1-\beta$, you can use Table A5, which gives the value of $\delta/\surd d$ for $\alpha=.05$ and .01, and $1-\beta=.8$ and .9. The table assumes you have already specified the value of δ that is of interest to you. It should also be noted that for convenience the table assumes that $\nu_2\le\nu_1$. Since it is completely arbitrary which group is called group 1, it does not matter whether $n_1<n_2$ or $n_2<n_1$. For instance, if in example 7.3.3 you want power to be .9, you have $n_1=11$ and $n_2=16$.

To use Table A5 simply set $\nu_1=\max\{n_1-1,n_2-1\}$ and set $\nu_2=\min\{n_1-1,n_2-1\}$ in which case $\nu_1=15$ and $\nu_2=10$. With $\delta=1.0$, Table A5 says that the power will be .9 if $\delta/\surd d=5.0$. Since $\delta=1.0$, you can solve for d yielding d=.04.

To give you a slight hint about why Chapman's procedure is valid, Stein (1945) showed that $(\tilde{X}_j-\mu_j)/\surd d$ has a Student's t distribution with $\nu_j=n_j-1$ degrees of freedom, j=1,2. This result can be used to derive a confidence interval for $\mu_1-\mu_2$ in terms of the distribution of the difference of two independent Student t random variables. Equation (7.3.4), which gives the critical value c, is an approximation of the $1-\alpha/2$ quantile of this distribution. If $Y=T_1-T_2$, where the T_j's are independent Student's t random variables with ν_j degrees of freedom, Table A12 gives the value c such that $\Pr\{-c\le Y\le c\}=1-\alpha$.

Controlling Power and Determining Sample Sizes When $\sigma_1=\sigma_2$

In some cases, Stein-type procedures (two stage procedures that control power) will be impractical if additional observations are required. If it takes six months to get results on n_0 observations, and you find that an additional $n-n_0$ subjects are needed, it will be another six months before the experiment is complete. If $\sigma_1=\sigma_2=\sigma$, say, and if you are willing to specify how much power you want in terms of $(\mu_1-\mu_2)/\sigma$, rather than $\mu_1-\mu_2$, you can determine how large of a sample you need so that power will be reasonably large without first sampling any observations. When $\sigma_1=\sigma_2$, the random variable T, defined by equation (7.1.5), has a non-central t distribution with $\nu=n_1+n_2-2$ degrees of freedom and non-centrality parameter

$$\delta=(\mu_1-\mu_2)/\{\sigma^2[(1/n_1)+(1/n_2)]\}^{1/2}.$$

Thus, when the variances are equal, the power of the two group t-test is

$$\Pr\{T_\nu(\delta)<-t\}+\Pr\{T_\nu(\delta)>t\} \quad (7.3.9)$$

where $T_\nu(\delta)$ is a non-central t distribution with $\nu=n_1+n_2-2$

degrees of freedom, and non-centrality parameter δ, and t is the critical value. When in fact $\sigma_1\neq\sigma_2$, equation (7.3.9) may not give an accurate indication of power. (Further details are given in chapter eight.) For comments on the relative merits of measuring treatment effects in terms of $(\mu_1-\mu_2)/\sigma$, as opposed to using $\mu_1-\mu_2$, see section 7.5.

From section 6.8, (7.3.9) is approximately equal to

$$\Pr\{Z \le (-t-\delta)/[1+t^2/(2\nu)]^{1/2}\} + \Pr\{Z \ge (t-\delta)/[1+t^2/(2\nu)]^{1/2}\} \qquad (7.3.10)$$

Notice that as σ gets small, with μ_1 and μ_2 fixed, δ increases, and so from (7.3.10), the power increases as well. In general, the smaller the variances are, the more power there will be for a given value of $\mu_1-\mu_2$.

Example 7.3.5. Suppose that prior to conducting your experiment, you want to know how much power there will be when $(\mu_1-\mu_2)/\sigma=1.0$, $n_1=n_2=10$, and $\alpha=.1$. Then $\nu=18$, and for a two-tailed test $t=1.734$, and

$$\delta=1.0/[(1/10)+(1/10)]^{1/2}=2.236.$$

From (7.3.10), the power of the t-test is .68. If more power is required, larger sample sizes would be used.

7.4 MEASURING TREATMENT EFFECTS

Suppose you test and reject $H_0:\mu_1=\mu_2$ with $\alpha=.0001$. It is tempting to conclude that there is a large difference between μ_1 and μ_2, but this conclusion is not necessarily correct. The t-test merely tells you whether $\mu_1=\mu_2$ is a reasonable assumption. If $\mu_1-\mu_2=.000001$, H_0 should be rejected, since it is false, even though the difference between the means would seem to be trivial. The important point is that if n_1 and n_2 are large relative to σ_1 and σ_2, you will have a high probability of rejecting H_0 even when α and $\mu_1-\mu_2$ are small. Note that if n_1 and n_2 are large relative to $s_1{}^2$ and $s_2{}^2$, T can be large even when $\bar{X}_1-\bar{X}_2$ is small, and so you will reject H_0. In fact it often happens that H_0 is rejected even though the estimate of $\mu_1-\mu_2$, namely $\bar{X}_1-\bar{X}_2$, is small.

Let $\delta=\mu_1-\mu_2$. If you can specify how large a value is important to you, the two-group t-test, which was described in section 7.1, can be used to test whether δ is large. For instance, you might want to test

$$H_0:\delta=\delta_0$$

where δ_0 is the minimum value of δ that is considered a large difference. Choosing a value for δ_0 is not an easy task, but in many situations, with experience, researchers are able to determine a value for δ_0 that should be considered.

Let's suppose you have chosen a value for δ_0, you assume $\sigma_1=\sigma_2$, and you want to test

$$H_0:\delta=\delta_0.$$

You simply compute

$$A=[n_1n_2/(n_1+n_2)]^{1/2},$$

$$B=\{[(n_1-1)s_1^2+(n_2-1)s_2^2]/(n_1+n_2-2)\}^{1/2},$$

and $$T=A(\bar{X}_1-\bar{X}_2-\delta_0)/B.$$

If $|T|>t$, where t is the $1-\alpha/2$ quantile of a Student's t distribution with $\nu=n_1+n_2-2$ degrees of freedom, reject H_0.

An alternative and fairly simple method for indicating the magnitude of δ is to report a confidence interval for $\mu_1-\mu_2$. If the confidence interval is (1,11), it is reasonable to conclude that $\delta\geq1$ while if the confidence interval is (5,7), you would conclude that $\delta\geq5$. Note that in both cases the center of the confidence interval, which is $\bar{X}_1-\bar{X}_2$, is 6. It is quite common for researchers to simply report whether $H_0:\mu_1=\mu_2$ was significant at a specified α level. It is clear, though, that reporting confidence intervals provides a much better indication of how to interpret the results of an experiment. Not only does it tell you whether a significant result was obtained, it tells you something about the magnitude of δ. As a result, it is recommended that when comparing two means, YOU SHOULD ALWAYS REPORT THE CONFIDENCE INTERVAL FOR $\mu_1-\mu_2$.

It should be mentioned that when $\sigma_1=\sigma_2=\sigma$, some researchers prefer to measure treatment effects with

$$\Delta=(\mu_1-\mu_2)/\sigma,$$

rather than δ. It is noted, though, that Δ is only defined when $\sigma_1=\sigma_2$. You can test $H_0:\sigma_1=\sigma_2$ using the Brown-Forsythe procedure described in chapter eight, but keep in mind that it is the power of the Brown-Forsythe procedure that is important for the problem at hand. That is, if you fail to reject $H_0:\sigma_1=\sigma_2$, it is only reasonable to conclude $\sigma_1=\sigma_2$ if the power of the Brown-Forsythe procedure is reasonably large. A criticism of δ is that the units used in a particular study are often arbitrary, and since Δ is unitless, Δ should be preferred over δ. However, when making judgments about whether a treatment effect is large, Gibbons, Olkin, and Sobel (1977) argue that is is easier to make judgments in terms of δ rather than Δ. Finally Kraemer and Andrews (1982) argue that Δ implicitly assumes normality, an assumption that is rarely if ever met. Estimation of Δ is discussed in section 8.7. For a method of comparing Δ to a known constant, see Kraemer (1983). For a method of comparing δ to δ_0 when $\sigma_1 \neq \sigma_2$ and μ_1 is the mean of a control group, see Wilcox (1985).

7.5 COMPARING THE MEANS OF DEPENDENT GROUPS

The two group t-test described in section 7.1 assumes that $\bar{X}_1$ and $\bar{X}_2$ are independent random variables. In practice this independence is assured by randomly assigning subjects to the first treatment group, and a different random sample of subjects to the other. In many instances, though, it is convenient, even desirable, to have $\bar{X}_1$ and $\bar{X}_2$ be dependent random variables. To understand why requires some basic facts about a quantity called the correlation coefficient which is denoted by the Greek letter ρ. The properties of the correlation coefficient are described in chapter thirteen. For now it is merely pointed out that if X and Y are any two random variables, the correlation between them is defined to be

$$\rho = \mathrm{COV}(X,Y)/(\sigma_x \sigma_y), \tag{7.5.1}$$

where

$$\mathrm{COV}(X,Y) = E[(X-\mu_x)(Y-\mu_y)]$$

is called the covariance between X and Y. It can be shown that $-1 \le \rho \le 1$. From equation (3.4.7), if X and Y are independent, $\rho=0$. It can also be shown that the variance of X-Y is

$$\mathrm{VAR}(X-Y) = \sigma_x^2 + \sigma_y^2 - 2\rho\sigma_x\sigma_y. \tag{7.5.2}$$

The important point in this section is that as ρ increases from -1 to 1, VAR(X-Y) decreases. Thus, as ρ gets closer to one, X-Y becomes an increasingly more accurate estimate of $\mu_x - \mu_y$.

To illustrate why (7.5.2) is important in hypothesis testing, suppose you want to determine whether a particular training program affects a person's endurance. You could randomly assign n_1 subjects to the training program, and a different sample of n_2 subjects could be used as a control group. That is, the second group receives no special training at all. If the means of the two groups are μ_1 and μ_2, you could test $H_0: \mu_1 = \mu_2$ to determine whether the training has any effect. Because the variances of $\bar{X}_1$ and $\bar{X}_2$ are σ_1^2/n_1 and σ_2^2/n_2, from (7.5.2) the variance of $\bar{X}_1 - \bar{X}_2$ is

$$\sigma_1^2/n_1 + \sigma_2^2/n_2 - 2\rho\sigma_1\sigma_2/(n_1n_2)^{1/2}.$$

Thus, when $\rho>0$, the variance of $\bar{X}_1-\bar{X}_2$ will be smaller than when $\bar{X}_1$ and $\bar{X}_2$ are independent (i.e., when $\rho=0$). If, for instance $\sigma_1{}^2=5$, $\sigma_2{}^2=10$, $n_1=n_2=1,5$ and $\rho=0$, the variance of $\bar{X}_1-\bar{X}_2$ is 5/15 + 10/15=1.0. But if the correlation between $\bar{X}_1$ and $\bar{X}_2$ is $\rho=.5$, the variance of $\bar{X}_1-\bar{X}_2$ is only .53.

Returning to the illustration, suppose instead of assigning different subjects to the two treatment groups, you randomly sample n subjects, measure their endurance before training, and then measure their endurance after the training is complete. If μ_1 is the average endurance before training, and μ_2 is the average endurance after training, you can test $H_0:\mu_1-\mu_2=0$ as follows. Let X_{i1} be the observed endurance of the i<u>th</u> subject before training, and let X_{i2} be the observed endurance of the same subject after training is complete. Then $\bar{X}_1-\bar{X}_2$ is an unbiased estimate of $\mu_1-\mu_2$. This is true because even though $\bar{X}_1$ and $\bar{X}_2$ are dependent random variables, $E(\bar{X}_1-\bar{X}_2)=E(\bar{X}_1)-E(\bar{X}_2)=\mu_1-\mu_2$. Because X_{i1} and X_{i2} are observations from the same subject, you cannot assume X_{i1} and X_{i2} are independent. But when X_{i1} and X_{i2} are dependent normal random variables, it can be shown that $D_i=X_{i1}-X_{i2}$ is normal with mean $\mu_d=\mu_1-\mu_2$. Thus, $H_0:\mu_1=\mu_2$ is the same as $H_0:\mu_d=0$.

Let

$$s_d^2=\Sigma(D_i-\bar{D})^2/(n-1)$$

be the sample variance of the D_i's where $\bar{D}=\Sigma D_i/n$. Testing $H:\mu_d=0$ is the same problem covered in section 6.2. You simply compute

$$T=(\surd n)\bar{D}/s_d.$$

The degrees of freedom are $\nu=n-1$. If $|T|>t$, where t is the $1-\alpha/2$ quantile of a Student's t distribution with ν degrees of freedom, reject H_0.

Consider the illustration where endurance is measured before and after training, and suppose n randomly sampled subjects agree to take part in your experiment. If $\rho>0$, the variance of $\bar{X}_1-\bar{X}_2$ is smaller under the dependent group case, and so the power might be substantially larger. Chapter thirteen explains how to test $H_0:\rho<0$. However, if each subject receives the training, and you find that $\rho<0$, you still must use the dependent group t-test since $\bar{X}_1$ and $\bar{X}_2$ are dependent, and the power might be considerably less than what it would have been if independent groups were used. If for the i<u>th</u> and j<u>th</u> subjects in your study you suspect that $X_{i1}\leq X_{j1}$ implies that $X_{i2}\leq X_{j2}$, then you can expect to find $\rho>0$, in which case the dependent group t-test might be considered. Experience with a certain type of problem often gives you some indication about whether $\rho>0$ can be expected. However, even $\rho>0$ does not necessarily mean that the dependent t-test will have more power than the t-test for independent groups. For a guideline on when the dependent t-test is preferrable, see chapter eleven.

Summary of Assumptions

As in the t-test for independent groups, it is assumed that observations are randomly sampled from a normal distribution. However, it is not assumed that $\sigma_1=\sigma_2$. In addition, the observations from the two groups are not assumed to be independent.

Example 7.5.1. Continuing the illustration, suppose n=6 subjects are randomly sampled, and their endurance is measured before and after training. Let's assume the results are as follows:

Before Training	After Training	$D_i=X_{i2}-X_{i1}$
60	75	75-60=15
50	70	70-50=20
55	80	80-55=25
70	80	80-70=10
45	50	50-45=5
70	85	85-70=15
		$\Sigma D_i=90$

The sample mean and variance of the D_i's is $\bar{D}=90/6=15$

and $s_d^2=250/5=50$. To test $H_0:\mu_d=0$, compute

$$T=(\surd 6)(15)/(\surd 50) = 5.196.$$

If $\alpha=.01$, then with $\nu=6-1=5$ degrees of freedom, Table A14 says that the critical value is t=4.032. Since 5.196>4.032, reject H_0 and conclude that the average endurance is different after training.

Another common situation where dependent group t-tests are used is with paired observations. In example 7.5.1 you might randomly sample n identical twins, and the first twin might receive the training while the second receives no training at all. In this case X_{i1} and X_{i2} are the observations corresponding to the ith pair of twins, X_{i1} is the observation corresponding to the twin receiving training, and X_{i2} is the observation for the corresponding twin who received no training at all.

As final comment, the test $H_0:\mu_1=\mu_2$ described in this section does not assume $\sigma_1=\sigma_2$. Thus, if for two independent groups, $\sigma_1\neq\sigma_2$, but $n_1=n_2$, the Type I error probability will be exactly α if you use the solution described here, but the degrees of freedom will only be $\nu=n-1$, while in section 7.1, $\nu=2n-2$. This means that you may have substantially less power using the solution described in this section when in fact you have independent groups. For independent groups it is recommended that you use Welch's s V, or Welch's adjusted degrees of freedom procedure, which is described in chapter nine.

7.6 DEPENDENT GROUP T-TEST WHEN THERE ARE MISSING OBSERVATIONS

The dependent group t-test described in the previous section assumes you hou have n pairs of observations (X_{i1},X_{i2}), $i=1,\ldots,.n$. To test $H_0:\mu_1=\mu_2$ you form the random variable $D_i=X_{i1}-X_{i2}$, and then test $H_0:\mu_d=0$. A common problem is that one of the two values, X_{i1} or X_{i2}, may be missing. For instance, in example 7.5.1, you might observe the ith subject's endurance before training (the value of X_{i1}), but if this subject does not complete the training, X_{i2} is not known. An obvious solution is to just throw out the value of X_{i1} and assume you have only n-1 observations. It turns out, though, that if you know X_{i1}, but not X_{i2}, you can still use X_{i1} when testing $H_0:\mu_d=0$.

Bhoj's Procedure

Bhoj (1978) proposed a procedure for handling missing observations that assumes the observations are missing from both groups. Bhoj assumes that the pairs of values (X_{i1},X_{i2}) have been observed for $i=1,2,\ldots,n$. It also assumes that for n_1 subjects, X_{i1} is known, but X_{i2} is not known. Similarly, for n_2 subjects, X_{i2} is observed, but X_{i1} is missing. For situations where $n_1=0$ or $n_2=0$, the procedure proposed by Lin (1973) can be used, which is described below. (See equation 7.6.5.) For notational convenience the observations are assumed to be arranged as follows.

$$X_{11}, X_{21},\ldots,X_{n1} \quad X_{n+1,1},\ldots,X_{n+n_1,1}$$

$$X_{12}, X_{22},\ldots,X_{n2} \qquad\qquad X_{n+1,2},\ldots,X_{n+n_2,2}$$

It will help to explain Bhoj's procedure using some real data, so suppose you have the following observations.

Group 1: 4 2 3 5 1 7

Group 2: 3 2 4 1 6 9 8

Then for the first group, $X_{11}=4$, $X_{21}=2$, $X_{31}=3$, $X_{41}=5$, $X_{51}=1$ and $X_{61}=7$. The value of n is 4 since there are four pairs of observations for which there are no missing values. There are two observations in the first group for which the corresponding observations are missing in the second group, so $n_1=2$. Similarly, $n_2=3$.

Solution for Equal Variances ($\sigma_1=\sigma_2=\sigma$)

For convenience it is assumed that $n_1 \le n_2$. When the variances are equal, compute $\nu_1=n-1$, $\nu_2=n_1+n_2-2$, and

$$T=(\surd n)(\bar{X}_1-\bar{X}_2)/s + (\tilde{X}_1-\tilde{X}_2)/[s_1^2(1/n_1 + 1/n_2)]^{1/2} \qquad (7.6.1)$$

where

$$\bar{X}_1=\Sigma_{i=1}^{n} X_{i1}/n, \quad \bar{X}_2=\Sigma_{i=1}^{n} X_{i2}/n$$

$$\tilde{X}_j=\Sigma_{i=n+1}^{n+n_j} X_{ij}/n_j, \quad j=1,2$$

$$s^2=\Sigma_{i=1}^{n}(X_{i1}-X_{i2}-\bar{X}_1+\bar{X}_2)^2/(n-1), \text{ and}$$

$$s_1^2=\{\Sigma_{i=n+1}^{n+n_1}(X_{i1}-\tilde{X}_1)^2 + \Sigma_{i=n+1}^{n+n_2}(X_{i2}-\tilde{X}_2)^2\}/(n_1+n_2-2).$$

In words, $\bar{X}_1$ is the sample mean of the observations in the first group for which there are no missing observations. Thus, in the illustration,

$$\bar{X}_1=(4+2+3+5)/4=3.5.$$

Similarly,

$$\bar{X}_2=(3+2+4+1)/4=2.5.$$

The quantity $\tilde{X}_1$ is the sample mean of the observations in group 1 for which the corresponding observation in group 2 is missing. In the illustration,

$$\tilde{X}_1=(1+7)/2=4.0.$$

Similarly,

$$\tilde{X}_2=(6+9+8)/3=7.67.$$

The quantity s^2 is the sample variance of the difference scores where there are no missing observations. An equivalent way of computing s^2 is to compute $D_i=X_{i1}-X_{i2}$ $(i=1,\ldots,n)$, and then

$$s^2=\Sigma(D_i-\bar{D})^2/(n-1),$$

where $\bar{D}=\Sigma D_i/n$. In the illustration, $D_1=4-3=1$, $D_2=0$, $D_3=-1$, $D_4=4$, so $\bar{D}=1$, and

$$s^2=[(1-1)^2+(0-1)^2+(-1-1)^2+(4-1)^2]/3=4.67.$$

The quantity

$$s_1^2=[(1-4)^2+(7-4)^2+(6-7.67)^2+(9-7.67)^2+(8-7.67)^2]/3=7.56.$$

Thus,

$$T=(\surd 4)(3.5-2.5)/(\surd 4.67) + (4-7.67)/[7.56(.5 + .33)]^{1/2}$$

$$=.925-1.462$$

$$=-.537$$

Note that (7.6.1) is just the sum of two t-tests, one for dependent sample means, and one for independent sample means. The first t-test uses the pairs of observations, and the second uses the values where one value is missing. Thus, the distribution of T, when H_0 is true, is the distribution of the sum of two independent Student t random variables.

Critical values for Bhoj's procedure are in Table A12. Table A12 assumes $\nu_2\le\nu_1$, but if $\nu_1\le\nu_2$ you can determine the critical value simply by reversing the degrees of freedom. For example, if $\nu_1=3$ and $\nu_2=6$ with $\alpha/2=.025$, you refer to Table A12 and read the value corresponding to $\nu_1=6$ and $\nu_2=3$. The answer is 4.002.

If the critical value, t, is not in Table A12, t can be approximated with

$$t=z(\surd 2)[1+\{(1/\nu_1)+(1/\nu_2)\}(z^2+5)/16] \qquad (7.6.2)$$

where z is chosen so that $Pr(-z\le Z\le z)=1-\alpha$, where Z is a standard normal random variable, $\nu_1=n-1$, and $\nu_2=n_1+n_2-2$. As usual, if

$|T|>t$, reject H_0. In the illustration, if $\alpha=.05$, (7.6.2) gives 4.04. If $\nu_1\geq 10$ and $\nu_2\geq 10$, (7.6.2) gives an excellent approximation of t.

Solution for Unequal Variances ($\sigma_1\neq\sigma_2$)

When $\sigma_1\neq\sigma_2$, Bhoj (1978) recommends testing $H_0:\mu_1=\mu_2$ using

$$T=(\sqrt{n})(\bar{X}_1-\bar{X}_2)/s + (\sqrt{n_1})(\tilde{X}_1-\tilde{X}_2)/s_2 \qquad (7.6.3)$$

where again, for notational convenience, it is assumed that $n_1\leq n_2$. In equation (7.6.3),

$$s_2^2=\Sigma_{j=1}^{n_1}(w_j-\bar{w})^2/(n_1-1),$$

where

$$w_j=X_{n+j,1}-\{(n_1/n_2)^{1/2}\}X_{n+j,2} \quad (j=1,\ldots,n_1),$$

and

$$\bar{w}=\Sigma w_j/n_1.$$

For instance, for the sample data described above, because $n_1=2$, there are two w_j values, namely

$$w_1=1-(2/3)^{1/2}(6)=-3.899, \text{ and } w_2=7-(2/3)^{1/2}(9)=-0.348.$$

Thus, $\bar{w}=-2.12$, and $s_2{}^2=6.3$. The other quantities in equation (7.6.3) are the same as they were in equation (7.6.1). Again the critical value is read from Table A12, but now the degrees of freedom are

$$\nu_1=n-1 \text{ and } \nu_2=n_1-1.$$

If the critical value is not in Table A12, use equation (7.6.2) to determine t.

The assumption $\sigma_1=\sigma_2$ can be tested using results in chapter fifteen (the Sandvik Olson procedure) for dependent groups, chapter eight describes a test for independent groups, and both of these tests are robust to non-normality. That is, they control the Type I error probability when the normality assumption is violated. However, it is not recommended that you test for equal variances because for reasons given in chapter eight, the test for equal variances may not have enough power to detect unequal variances in situations where the assumption $\sigma_1=\sigma_2$ should be abandoned. Instead, simply use the procedure that allows $\sigma_1\neq\sigma_2$.

The procedures just described are special cases of a general technique that was studied by Bhoj. It is noted that Bhoj described an alternative but more complicated procedure that might give shorter confidence intervals. (Also see Tamhane, 1979.)

The Lin-Stivers Procedures for Missing Observations, $\sigma_1 \neq \sigma_2$

Lin and Stivers (1974) proposed testing $H_0: \mu_1 = \mu_2$ for dependent groups with

$$W = (\bar{Y}_1 - \bar{Y}_2)/(h_1 + h_2 + h_3)^{1/2} \tag{7.6.4}$$

where

$$\bar{Y}_1 = \Sigma_{i=1}^{n+n_1} X_{i1}/(n+n_1),$$

$$\bar{Y}_2 = \Sigma_{i=1}^{n+n_2} X_{i2}/(n+n_2),$$

$$h_1 = n(A - 2a_3)/B,$$

$$A = [(n+n_2)a_1/(n+n_1) + (n+n_1)a_2/(n+n_2)],$$

$$B = (n-1)(n+n_1)(n+n_2),$$

$$a_1 = \Sigma_{i=1}^{n} (X_{i1} - \bar{X}_1)^2,$$

$$a_2 = \Sigma_{i=1}^{n} (X_{i2} - \bar{X}_2)^2,$$

$$a_3 = \Sigma_{i=1}^{n} (X_{i1} - \bar{X}_1)(X_{i2} - \bar{X}_2),$$

$$h_2 = n_1 b_1/[(n_1 - 1)(n+n_1)^2]$$

$$b_1 = \Sigma_{i=n+1}^{n_1} (X_{i1} - \tilde{X}_1)^2,$$

$$h_3 = n_2 b_2/[(n_2 - 1)(n+n_2)^2]$$

and

$$b_2 = \Sigma_{i=n+1}^{n_2} (X_{i2} - \tilde{X}_2)^2.$$

The terms $\bar{X}_1$, $\bar{X}_2$, $\tilde{X}_1$, and $\tilde{X}_2$ are defined the same way they were in Bhoj's procedure. When H_0 is true, W in equation (7.6.4) has, approximately, a Student's t distribution with

$$\nu = (h_1 + h_2 + h_3)^2 / \{[h_1^2/(n-1)] + [h_2^2/(n_1 - 1)] + h_3^2/(n_2 - 1)]\}$$

degrees of freedom. If $|W| > t$, where t (read from Table A14) is the critical value corresponding to ν and some value of α that you have chosen, reject H_0.

Example 7.6.1. Consider again the situation where a subject's endurance is measured before and after training, and suppose the results are

Before: 5 4 3 4 2 7 - -

After: 6 6 5 7 4 - 6 8.

Thus, for the first n=5 subjects, measures are available for both testings. For the sixth subject, the first observation is known, but the subject's endurance after training was never obtained. Thus, $n_1=1$, Also, the last two subjects did not have their endurance measured before training, and so $n_2=2$. To evaluate equation (7.6.1), you compute

$$\bar{X}_1=(5+4+3+4+2)/5=3.6,$$

$$\bar{X}_2=5.6$$

$$s^2=[(-1+2)^2+...+(-2+2)^2]/4=.5$$

$$\tilde{X}_1=7/1=7,$$

$$s_1^2=[(7-7)^2+(6-7)^2+(8-7)^2]/1=2,$$

and

$$T=(\surd 5)(3.6-5.6)/(\surd .5)+(7-7)/[(\surd 2)(1/1+1/2)^{1/2}]$$

$$=6.32.$$

For $\alpha=.05$, Table A1 says that z=1.96 (remembering to divide α by 2 since a two-tailed tests is being used), and from equation (7.6.2), the critical value is approximately

$$t=1.96(\surd 2)[1+(1/16)(1/4+1/1)(1.96^2+5)]=4.687.$$

Because 6.32 >4.687, reject $H_0:\mu_1=\mu_2$.

For $\sigma_1\neq\sigma_2$, you compute $w_1=1$, $w=1$, and $s_2{}^2=0/0$. Thus, Bhoj's procedure cannot be used when $n_1=1$ because you are dividing by zero.

Suppose instead the observations are

Before: 5 4 3 4 2 7 4 - -

After: 6 6 5 7 4 - - 6 8.

Then $n_1=n_2=2$,

$$w_1=7-(2/2)^{1/2}(6)=1,$$

$w_2=4-(2/2)^{1/2}(8)=-4$,

so $\bar{w}=-1.5$, $s_2{}^2=(1+1.5)^2+(-4+1.5)^2=12.5$, $\tilde{X}_1=5.5$, $\tilde{X}_2=7$, so

$$T=[(\surd 5)(3.6-5.6)/\surd 5] + [(\surd 2)(5.5-7)/\surd 12.5]=-6.925.$$

Since $\nu_1=4$, and $\nu_2=n_1-1=1$, equation (7.6.2) yields t=4.687, and because 6.925>4.867, reject H_0.

As for the Lin-Stivers procedure, consider the second data set where $n_1=n_2=2$. Then

$$\bar{Y}_1=(5+4+3+4+2+7+4)/7=4.14.$$

$$\bar{Y}_2=42/7=6.0$$

$$a_1=(5-3.6)^2+...+(2-3.6)^2=5.2,$$

$$a_2=(6-5.6)^2+...+(4-5.6)^2=5.2$$

$$a_3=(5-3.6)(6-5.6)+...+(2-3.6)(4-5.6)=4.2$$

$$b_1=4.5,\ b_2=2,\ A=10.4,\ B=196,$$

$$h_1=5(10.4-2(4.2)0/196=.051,$$

$$h_2=2(4.5)/7^2=.184$$

$$h_3=2(2)/49=.082,$$

$$\nu=2.41$$

and

$$W=-1.86/\surd .317=-3.30.$$

From Table A14, with $\alpha=.10$, the critical value is between 2.92 and 2.35. Because $-3.3<-2.92$, reject H_0.

When both ν_1 and ν_2 are less than 5, and if $\nu_1\neq\nu_2$, critical values for Bhoj's procedure are not available from Table A12, and so the critical value must be determined from (7.6.2). The same is true when $\nu_2=1$. In this case the Lin-Stivers procedure may give better control over Type I error probabilities. It should be emphasized though that more research is needed to determine which procedure is best for these special cases. If the critical value can be determined from Table A12, or if both ν_1 and ν_2 are greater than or equal to five, Bhoj's procedure is recommended based on the information that is currently available.

Solution When There Are Missing Observations from One Group Only

Both of the procedures described above assume that n_1 and n_2 are both greater than or equal to two. That is, it is assumed that there are missing observations from both groups. For the case where there are missing observations from only one group, the procedure proposed by Lin (1973) can be applied.

The notation used to described Bhoj's procedure is adopted here, only it is assumed that $n_2=0$, and that $n_1>1$. Compute

$$N=n+n_1,$$

$$\lambda=n/N,$$

$$\bar{W}_1=\Sigma_{i=1}^{N}X_{i1}/N,$$

$$a_{jk}=\Sigma_{i=1}^{n}(X_{ij}-\bar{X}_j)(X_{ik}-\bar{X}_k) \quad j,k=1,2;$$

$$b=\Sigma_{i=n+1}^{n+n_1}(X_{i1}-\tilde{X}_1)^2,$$

$$\Delta_1^2=(\lambda^2 a_{11}-2\lambda a_{12}+a_{22})/(n-1),$$

and

$$\Delta_2^2=(1-\lambda)^2 b/(N-n-1).$$

When $\mu_1=\mu_2$,

$$T=(\bar{W}_1-\bar{X}_2)/[\Delta_1^2/n + \Delta_2^2/(N-n)]^{1/2} \qquad (7.6.5)$$

has, approximately, a Student's t distribution with degrees of freedom

$$\nu=[(\Sigma\Delta_i^2/m_i)^2]/[\Sigma\Delta_i^4/(m_i^2(m_i-1))]$$

where $m_1=n$ and $m_2=N-n=n_1$. As usual, you reject $H_0:\mu_1=\mu_2$ if $|T|$ exceeds the $1-\alpha/2$ quantile of a Student's t distribution with ν degrees of freedom.

For alternative procedures for handling missing observations, see Ekbohm (1976), Morrison (1973) as well as Mehta and Gurland (1973). Some readers might be familiar with the "EM" algorithm for handling missing observations, but it is not included here because of the difficulties summarized by Carter and Yang (1986, p. 2508).

Finally, it should be mentioned that there is an alternative procedure for testing hypotheses based on what is called Fisher's randomization test. Occasionally this method is recommended by some researchers, but the reader is advised to read Basu's (1980) criticisms of this technique before it is used.

EXERCISES

7.1 Suppose you want to determine whether bilingual students score higher on the verbal section of the SAT exam as compared to student's who speak only one language at home. To find out, you randomly sample 10 bilingual student's, and 10 students who are not bilingual. If the sample means and variances are $\bar{X}_1=580$, $\bar{X}_2=560$, $s_1^2=100$, $s_2^2=121$, is it reasonable to believe the means are equal? Use $\alpha=.05$, and assume $\sigma_1=\sigma_2$.

7.2 Test $H_0:\mu_1>\mu_2$ using $\bar{X}_1=5$, $\bar{X}_2=8$, $s_1^2=3$, $s_2^2=4.5$, $n_1=n_2=16$. Assume $\sigma_1=\sigma_2$ and use $\alpha=.01$.

7.3 Use Welch's V test to solve 7.1.

7.4 Referring to problem 7.1, use Ghosh's procedure to determine whether your sample size is large enough so that $1-\beta\geq.9$ when $\mu_1-\mu_2=40$. Assume $s_y^2=200$. If not, how many more observations are required?

7.5 Repeat 7.4, but use Chapman's procedure.

7.6 Suppose you want to test $H_0:\mu_1=\mu_2$ with $\alpha=.05$. If $\sigma_1=\sigma_2=\sigma$, and $n_1=n_2=15$, what is the power when $(\mu_1-\mu_2)/\sigma=1.5$?

7.7 In problem 7.6, suppose you want to determine power when $\mu_1-\mu_2=5$. What is your answer?

7.8 Suppose a ten-point scale is used to measure the level of schizophrenia in patients before and after a new treatment. Suppose the results are

Before:	4	5	4	8	7	7
After:	3	4	5	4	6	8

Is it reasonable to assume $\mu_1=\mu_2$? Use $\alpha=.01$

7.9 In exercise 7.8, suppose you have three additional subjects with "before" scores but no "after" scores, and that you also have four subjects with an "after" score, but no "before" score. If the value of equation (7.6.1) is T=2.2, would you reject $H_0:\mu_1=\mu_2$ with $\alpha=.05$? Assume $\sigma_1=\sigma_2$.

7.10 Consider exercise 7.9 but do not assume $\sigma_1=\sigma_2$. What is the critical value?

7.11 Suppose you conduct a study on identical twins and that one twin receives treatment A, and the other treatment B. Suppose the observations are:

A:	8	12	14	7	9	10	12	10	-	-
B:	12	11	13	8	5	-	-	-	10	14

When applying Bhoj's test for dependent groups, where $\sigma_1\neq\sigma_2$, what are the values of w_j, n_1, and $\bar{w}$? Test $H_0:\mu_1=\mu_2$ with $\alpha=.05$.

7.12 Using the data in 7.11, use the Lin-Stivers procedure to test $H_0:\mu_1=\mu_2$ with $\alpha=.01$.

7.13 In exercise 7.11, what is the unbiased estimate of $\mu_1-\mu_2$?

7.14 Describe in general terms how you would use Stein's procedure to test $H_0:\delta=\delta_0$ where $\delta=\mu_1-\mu_2$ and δ_0 is a known constant.

References

Basu, D. (1980) Randomization analysis of experimental data: The Fisher randomization test. Journal of the American Statistical Association, 75, 575-582.

Bhoj, D. S. (1978) Testing equality of means of correlated variates with missing observations on both responses. Biometrika, 65, 225-228.

Carter, R. L. & Yang, M. C. K. (1986) Large sample inference in random coefficient regression models. Communications in Statistics--Theory and Methods, 15, 2507-2525.

Chapman, D. G. (1950) Some two-sample tests. Annals of Mathematical Statistics, 21, 601-606.

Ekbohm, G. (1976) On comparing means in the paired case with incomplete data on both responses. Biometrika, 63, 299-304.

Fenstad, G. (1983) A comparison between U and V tests in the Behrens-Fisher problem. Biometrika, 70, 300-302.

Ghosh, B. K. (1975a) On the distribution of the difference of two t-variables. Journal of the American Statistical Association, 70, 463-467.

Ghosh, B. K. (1975b) A two-stage procedure for the Behrens-Fisher problem. Journal of the American Statistical Association,

70, 457-462.
Gibbons, J., Olkin, I. & Sobel, M. (1977) Selecting and ordering populations: A new statistical methodology. New York: Wiley.
Kraemer, H. (1983) Theory of estimation and testing effect sizes: Use in meta-analysis. Journal of Educational Statistics, 8, 93-101.
Kraemer, H. & Andrews, G. (1982) A non-parametric technique for meta-analysis effect size calculation. Psychological Bulletin, 91, 404-412.
Lin, P. (1973) Procedures for testing the difference of means with missing data. Journal of the American Statistical Association, 66, 634-636.
Lin, P. & Stivers, L. (1974) On the difference of means with incomplete data. Biometrika, 61, 325-334.
Mehta, J. & Gurland, J. (1973) A test for equality of means in the presence of correlation and missing values. Biometrika, 60, 211-212.
Morrison, D. (1973) A test for equality of means of correlated variates with missing data on one response. Biometrika, 60, 101-106.
Ramsey. P. (1980) Exact Type I error rates for robustness of Student's t test with unequal variances. Journal of Educational Statistics, 5, 337-349.
Stein, C. (1945) A two-sample test for a linear hypothesis whose power is independent of the variance. Annals of Mathematical Statistics, 16, 243-258.
Tamhane, A. (1979) A comparison of procedures for multiple comparisons of means with unequal variances. Journal of the American Statistical Association, 74, 471-480
Tiku, M. L. & Singh (1981) Robust test for means when population variances are unequal. Communications in Statistics--Theory and Methods, A10, 2057-2071.
Welch, B. (1937) The significance of the difference between two means when the population variances are unequal. Biometrika, 29, 350-362.
Wilcox, R. (1985) On comparing treatment effects to a standard when the variances are unknown and unequal. Journal of Educational Statistics, 10, 45-54.
Wilcox, R. (1987) New designs in analysis of variance. Annual Review of Psychology, 38, 29-60.
Yuen, K. K. (1974) The two-sample trimmed t for unequal population variances. Biometrika, 61, 165-170.

CHAPTER EIGHT

ONE-WAY ANOVA

8.1 INTRODUCTION

Perhaps the most common mistake when interpreting statistical results is making inferences that are not justified based on the procedure that is being used. This is certainly true for the F test discussed in this chapter, and so some nontechnical comments about this test may be helpful. To illustrate what the F test in the analysis of variance (ANOVA) model can and cannot do, suppose you want to conduct a study on how room characteristics affect the scores of examinees on aptitude tests. Further suppose three situations are of interest: normal rooms, rooms where there are disturbing noises outside, and sound proof rooms with "dead" walls. That is, the walls are constructed so that sound cannot reverberate off of them.

Among the population of subjects that might be tested, let μ_1, μ_2, and μ_3 be the average test scores under the conditions just described. You might want to know which of these means is largest, or whether any pair of means is substantially different from one another, but before addressing these questions a more fundamental goal is determining whether indeed there are any differences among the means. That is, the goal is to test

$$H_0: \mu_1 = \mu_2 = \mu_3,$$

and more generally where there are J treatment means the goal is to test

$$H_0: \mu_1 = \mu_2 = \ldots = \mu_J. \qquad (8.1.1)$$

The F test used to test (8.1.1) can also be used to measure the inequality among the means, but these measures can be unsatisfactory for reasons that are explained in section 8.3. Moreover, the F test that is developed in the next two sections does not provide a direct indication of how certain you can be that the treatment group with the largest mean will be correctly identified based on the subjects in your study. Of course in some situations knowing this probability can be crucial. For example, if several methods for treating dyslexia (a disorder affecting reading ability) are being investigated, once it is decided that there is a difference among the procedures, it is important to know how certain you can be that the best treatment is correctly selected. Methods for dealing with this problem are discussed in chapter twelve. There is also the problem of controlling the probability of correctly determining which means are substantially different rather than just statistically significant. Two means, say μ_1 and μ_2, are "significantly" different if $\mu_1 \neq \mu_2$. By substantially different is meant that the difference between the means is "reasonably large." The results in section 8.3 are used to test for significant differences, and in the past these results have been used by some to infer that the means are substantially different as well. This may be inappropriate, though, because means can be significantly different yet have nearly equal values.

As will be explained in section 8.8, the F test derived in section 8.3 actually tests much more than (8.1.1). In some cases this may be desirable, but in other situations interest may focus on making all pairwise comparisons of the means only. Depending on the Type I error probability that is desired, procedures other than the F test may be more appropriate. This issue is discussed in section 9.5.

Assumptions

Let X_{ij} be the outcome measure of the ith randomly sampled subject in the jth treatment group (i=1,...,n; j=1,...,J). For the moment, primarily for notational convenience, it is assumed that all treatment groups have exactly n subjects. Let σ_j be the standard deviation of the outcome measures for the jth group. It is assumed that

a) The X_{ij}'s are independent,

b) the observations within any treatment group are normally distributed, and

c) $\sigma_1 = \sigma_2 = \ldots = \sigma_J$. (8.1.2)

When (8.1.2) is true, it is said that the variances are homogeneous, or that the homogeneity of variance assumption is satisfied. Heteroscedastic variances just means that some of the variances are not equal. That is, (8.1.2) is violated. There are practical situations where violating (8.1.2) can seriously affect the Type I error probability and power of the F test (e.g., Brown and Forsythe, 1974a; Ramsey, 1980; Scheffe, 1959). It is sometimes argued that with equal sample sizes, the F test performs well when equation (8.1.2) is violated, but as illustrated in section 8.5, this is not always true when J>2 treatment groups are being compared. Approximate methods for handling unequal variances are described in section 8.6, and exact methods are described in section 8.12.

The normality assumption will rarely if ever be met exactly, but it appears that typical departures from normality have little effect on the F test (Tan, 1982). However, it should be emphasized that there are nonnormal distributions where an F test can have a Type I error probability that is substantially different from the nominal level. Unfortunately, there is no completely satisfactory method for determining when the departure normality is extreme enough so as to substantially affect the Type I error probability and power of the F test. Some progress has been made on obtaining an alternative to the F test that is robust to nonnormality (Schrader & Hettmansperger, 1980). For a discussion of a second alternative to the F test, see Still and White (1981).

8.2 AN INTUITIVE LOOK AT HOW TO PROCEED

To gain some insight into how the analysis of variance model works when testing (8.1.1), consider J=3 treatment groups and suppose H_0 is true. Because the variances are assumed to be equal, and because the distributions are assumed to be normal, the distributions are indistinguishable from one another as shown in Figure 8.2.1a. If n observations are randomly sampled from each treatment group and the sample mean is computed for each, the sample means will tend to be more spread out when H_0 is false than they are when H_0 is true. The problem is to determine how much variation among the sample means can be expected when H_0 is true, and if the variation is larger than what is expected by chance, this suggests that the null hypothesis is false.

To be a little more specific, again suppose n subjects are randomly sampled from each of the J treatment groups. These observations are shown in Table 8.2.1. The sample mean for the j<u>th</u> group is represented by

$$\bar{X}_j=\Sigma_i X_{ij}/n.$$

Also let

$$s_j^2=\Sigma_i (X_{ij}-\bar{X}_j)^2/(n-1)$$

be the unbiased estimate of $\sigma_j{}^2$, the variance of the j<u>th</u> treatment group. Because it is assumed that the $s_j{}^2$'s all estimate the same quantity, σ^2, an intuitive estimate of σ^2 is

$$\Sigma_j s_j^2/J.$$

This is in fact the estimate of σ^2 that is used, and it is called the <u>mean square within groups</u> (MSWG) which is discussed in more detail in the next section.

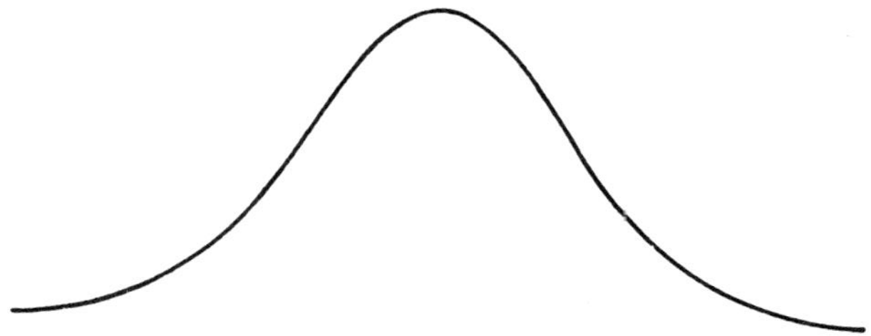

Figure 8.2.1a

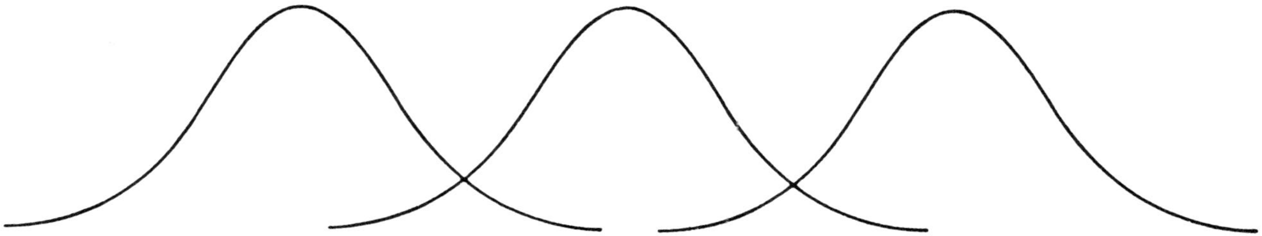

Figure 8.2.1b

Next suppose H_0 is true and consider

$$\Sigma_j(\bar{X}_j-\bar{X})^2/(J-1)$$

where

$$\bar{X}=\Sigma_j\bar{X}_j/J.$$

The quantity $\bar{X}$, which is also equal to $\Sigma_i\Sigma_jX_{ij}/(nJ)$, is called the grand sample mean. (It's the sample mean of all nJ observations.) The quantity $\Sigma_i(\bar{X}_j-\bar{X})^2/(J-1)$ is the sample variance of the sample means. The point is that when H_0 is true, the $\bar{X}_j$'s are independent random variables arising from the same distribution. But from equation (3.8.2) the variance of $\bar{X}_j$ is σ^2/n, and so

$$E\{\Sigma_j(\bar{X}_j-\bar{X})^2/(J-1)\}=\sigma^2/n.$$

Table 8.2.1

Randomly Sampled Observations for J Treatment Groups

Group 1	Group 2	...	Group J
X_{11}	X_{12}		X_{1J}
X_{21}	X_{22}	...	X_{2J}
		.	
		.	
		.	
X_{n1}	X_{n2}		X_{nJ}

It follows that

$$E\{n\Sigma_j(\bar{X}_j-\bar{X})^2/(J-1)\}=\sigma^2.$$

The quantity

$$n\Sigma_j(\bar{X}_j-\bar{X})^2/(J-1)$$

is called the <u>means square between groups</u> (MSBG). But the further apart the treatment group means, as in Figure 8.2.1b, the more variation we would expect among the sample means. In fact when the null hypothesis is false,

$$E(MSBG)=\sigma^2+n\Sigma_j(\mu_j-\mu)^2/(J-1) \quad (8.2.2)$$

where

$$\mu=\Sigma_j\mu_j/J$$

is the grand population mean. Thus, if MSBG is substantially larger than MSWG, this suggests that $n\Sigma_j(\mu_j-\mu)^2/(J-1)>0$, which can only happen when the μ_j values are not all equal.

To establish (8.2.2), let $\alpha_j=\mu_j-\mu$, and consider the random variable $\bar{X}_j-\alpha_j$. Because $\Sigma\alpha_j=0$, $\Sigma_j(\bar{X}_j-\alpha_j)/J=\Sigma\bar{X}_j/J=\bar{X}$. That is, $\bar{X}$ is the sample mean corresponding to the random variables $\bar{X}_j-\alpha_j$ $(j=1,\ldots,J)$. For any j, $E(\bar{X}_j-\alpha_j)=\mu$, and the variance of $\bar{X}_j$ is the same as the variance of $\bar{X}_j-\alpha_j$. Thus, $\Sigma(\bar{X}_j-\alpha_j-\bar{X})^2/(J-1)$ is just the usual sample variance for the random variable $\bar{X}_j-\alpha_j$, and $\bar{X}_j-\alpha_j$ has variance equal to σ^2/n. That is,

$$E\{(\bar{X}_j-\alpha_j-\bar{X})^2/(J-1)\}=\sigma^2/n.$$

Also note that $E(\bar{X})=\mu$. Hence,

$$\Sigma_j(\bar{X}_j-\bar{X})^2=\Sigma_j(\bar{X}_j-\alpha_j-\bar{X}+\alpha_j)^2$$

$$=\Sigma_j(\bar{X}_j-\alpha_j-\bar{X})^2+2\alpha_j(\bar{X}_j-\alpha_j-\bar{X})+\alpha_j^2.$$

This last equation can be used to show that

$$E\{\Sigma_j(\bar{X}_j-\bar{X})^2\}=(J-1)\sigma^2/n + \Sigma\alpha_j^2 \quad (8.2.2a)$$

Equation (8.2.2) follows.

To summarize the point of this section, if H_0 is true, both MSBG and MSWG estimate the same quantity, namely σ^2, but if H_0 is false, $E(MSWG)=\sigma^2$ still holds, but MSBG estimates $\sigma^2+\{n\Sigma\alpha_j^2/(J-1)\}$. If H_0 is true, $\Sigma\alpha_j^2=0$; otherwise $\Sigma\alpha_j^2>0$. What is needed is a method for determining whether the difference between MSBG and MSWG is due to chance, or because $\Sigma\alpha_j^2>0$. Such a method is derived in the next section.

8.3 FORMAL DESCRIPTION OF THE ONE-WAY FIXED EFFECT MODEL, AND THE DERIVATION OF THE F TEST

As in the previous section, X_{ij} represents the i<u>th</u> randomly sampled observation in the j<u>th</u> treatment group, and $\alpha_j=\mu_j-\mu$ where $\mu=\Sigma\mu_j/J$ is the grand mean. The treatment groups are assumed to have equal variances which can be written as $VAR(X_{ij})=\sigma^2$.

Let

$$\epsilon_{ij}=X_{ij}-\alpha_j-\mu.$$

Then

$$X_{ij}=\mu+\alpha_j+\epsilon_{ij} \tag{8.3.1}$$

This is called the one-way fixed effect model. It might appear to be an arbitrary and uninteresting way to proceed, but (8.3.1) turns out to be a convenient way of deriving various results. Note that from exercise 3.16,

$$VAR(X_{ij})=VAR(\epsilon_{ij})=\sigma^2.$$

Also observe that

$$\mu_j=E(X_{ij})$$
$$=E(\mu+\alpha_j+\epsilon_{ij})$$
$$=\mu+\alpha_j+E(\epsilon_{ij})$$
$$=\mu_j+E(\epsilon_{ij}).$$

Thus,

$$E(\epsilon_{ij})=0.$$

Another important result (but one that is far from obvious) is that if the X_{ij}'s are normally distributed, the ϵ_{ij}'s are normally distributed as well.

Some additional notation is needed, namely,

$$\bar{\epsilon}_j=\Sigma_i\,\epsilon_{ij}/n$$

and

$$\bar{\epsilon}=\Sigma_j\,\bar{\epsilon}_j/J.$$

With the results in the previous section in mind, consider the quantity

$$\Sigma_i \Sigma_j (X_{ij}-\bar{X})^2$$

$$=\Sigma_i \Sigma_j (X_{ij}-\bar{X}_j)^2+n\Sigma_j (\bar{X}_j-\bar{X})^2 \quad (8.3.2)$$

The quantity

$$SST=\Sigma_i \Sigma_j (X_{ij}-\bar{X})^2$$

is called the total sum of squares. The quantity

$$SSWG=\Sigma_i \Sigma_j (X_{ij}-\bar{X}_j)^2$$

is called the sum of squares within groups. Another common term for SSWG is "sum of squares error term." The quantity

$$SSBG=n\Sigma_j (\bar{X}_j-\bar{X})^2$$

is called the sum of squares between groups. Thus, (8.3.2) can be written as

$$SST=SSBG+SSWG.$$

Next the quantity SSWG is examined in terms of results in chapter 6. In particular it will be shown that $SSWG/\sigma^2$ has a chi-square distribution. To see this, first observe that for any value of j, it follows from section 6.1 that $\Sigma_i (X_{ij}-\bar{X}_j)^2/\sigma^2$ has a chi-square distribution with n-1 degrees of freedom. Thus, from section 6.1, $\Sigma_j \Sigma_i (X_{ij}-\bar{X}_j)^2/\sigma^2$ has a chi-square distribution with J(n-1) degrees of freedom. Moreover, this implies that

$$E(SSWG/\sigma^2)=J(n-1)$$

since the mean of a chi-square distribution is its degrees of freedom, and so

$$E(SSWG)=J(n-1)\sigma^2. \quad (8.3.3)$$

A similar result will be established for SSBG assuming that the treatment groups have equal means (i.e., that H_0 is true). Referring to (8.3.1),

$$\bar{X}_j=\Sigma_i X_{ij}/n$$

$$=\Sigma_i (\mu+\alpha_j+\epsilon_{ij})/n$$

$$=\mu+\alpha_j+\bar{\epsilon}_j$$

$$=\mu+\bar{\epsilon}_j$$

where the last equality follows from the fact that $\alpha_j=0$ under H_0. Also, $\bar{X}=\mu+\bar{\epsilon}$, so

$$n\Sigma(\bar{X}_j-\bar{X})=n\Sigma(\mu+\alpha_j+\bar{\epsilon}_j-\mu-\bar{\epsilon})^2$$

$$=n\Sigma(\bar{\epsilon}_j-\bar{\epsilon})^2.$$

But under the assumptions of the ANOVA model, $\bar{\epsilon}_j$ is normally distributed with mean zero and variance σ^2/n. Thus,

$$SSBG/\sigma^2=n\Sigma(\bar{\epsilon}_j-\bar{\epsilon})^2/\sigma^2$$

is distributed as a chi-square random variable with J-1 degrees of freedom. Moreover, this result establishes that

$$E(SSBG)=(J-1)\sigma^2. \tag{8.3.4}$$

If SSWG and SSBG are divided by their respective degrees of freedom, the results are called the mean square within groups (MSWG) and the mean square between groups (MSBG), which were introduced in the previous section. For the one-way fixed effect model being considered here,

$$MSBG=SSBG/(J-1)$$

and

$$MSWG=SSWG/[J(n-1)].$$

From (8.3.3) and (8.3.4),

$$E(MSWG)=\sigma^2, \tag{8.3.5}$$

and

$$E(MSBG)=\sigma^2, \tag{8.3.5a}$$

assuming H_0 is true, which agrees with the results in section 8.2. When H_0 is false, (8.3.5) still holds, but (8.3.5a) does not.

One final result, given without proof, is that SSWG and SSBG are independent. Thus, referring to the definition of an F distribution in chapter six,

$$F=\{(SSBG/\sigma^2)/(J-1)\}/\{(SSWG/\sigma^2)/(J(n-1))\}$$

$$=MSBG/MSWG \qquad (8.3.6)$$

has an F distribution with J-1 and J(n-1) degrees of freedom when H_0 is true. The point is that if F is large, (8.2.2) suggests that $n\Sigma\alpha_j^2/(J-1)>0$, i.e., H_0 is false. Accordingly, reject H_0 if

$$F > f$$

where f is the 1-α quantile of the F distribution with ν_1=J-1 and ν_2=J(n-1) degrees of freedom. As usual, α is the Type I error probability that the experimenter wants to allow.

There is one point that cannot be stressed too strongly--a large F value does not necessarily mean that there are any large differences among the means. The reason is that E(MSBG) is a function of σ^2, $\Sigma\alpha_j^2$ and n/(J-1), while E(MSWG)=σ^2 regardless of whether H_0 is true. Referring to (8.2.2), it is seen that when H_0 is false, E(MSBG) can be made as large as you want simply by choosing n large. Because E(MSWG) does not depend on n, it is always possible to choose n so that F will be large, when H_0 is false, no matter what the magnitude of $\Sigma\alpha_j^2/(J-1)$ happens to be, and so a large F does not necessarily mean that $\Sigma\alpha_j^2$ itself is large. Overall measures of the inequalities of the means are discussed in section 8.7.

8.4 SUMMARY OF CALCULATIONS, INCLUDING UNEQUAL n's

A summary of the calculations for performing an F test are shown in Table 8.4.1. Many computer programs are available for performing an ANOVA, but if these are not available, the formulae in Table 8.4.1 are easier to use when calculating the sum of squares terms than are the equations given previously.

TABLE 8.4.1

Summary of Calculations

$A=\Sigma_i \Sigma_j X_{ij}^2$

$B=\Sigma_i \Sigma_j X_{ij}$

$C=\Sigma_j \{\Sigma_i X_{ij}\}^2/n_j$

$N=\Sigma n_j$

$SST=A-\{B^2/N\}$

$SSBG=C-\{B^2/N\}$

$SSWG=SST-SSBG$

The degrees of freedom are $\nu_1=J-1$ and $\nu_2=N-J$

As an illustration, suppose the experiment for the effects of room characteristics has been carried out, and the observations are as shown in Table 8.4.2. Then the results of the ANOVA would be reported as

Source	Sum of Squares	DF	Mean Squares	F
BETWEEN GROUPS	28.8	2	14.4	1.14
WITHIN GROUPS	88.1	7	12.59	

For α=.05 the critical value is f=4.74, and so H_0 would not be rejected.

TABLE 8.4.2

Sample Observations for J=3 Groups

Group 1	Group 2	Group 3
9	16	7
10	8	6
15	13	9
	6	
$\Sigma X_{i\,1}=34$	$\Sigma X_{i\,2}=43$	$\Sigma X_{i\,3}=22$

$A=9^2+10^2+...+9^2=1097$, $B=9+10+...+9=99$,
$C=34^2/9 + 43^2/4 + 22^2/3=1008.9$
$N=3+4+3=10$
$SST=1097-99^2/10=116.9$
$SSBG=1008.9-99^2/10=28.8$
$SSWG=116.9-28.8=88.1$

8.5 TESTS FOR EQUAL VARIANCES AND THE EFFECTS OF UNEQUAL VARIANCES ON TYPE I ERROR PROBABILITIES AND POWER

At one time the assumption of equal variances used to be tested, but it was found that the test typically used was sensitive to departures from normality. It was also thought that having unequal variances had little impact on the actual Type I error probability, particularly when an equal number of observations is sampled from each treatment group. Now, however, it is realized that unequal variances can have a substantial effect on both Type I error probabilities and power (Brown & Forsythe, 1974a; Hsu, 1938; Scheffe, 1959; Rogan & Keselman, 1977; Tomarken and Serlin, 1986). More accurate and more extensive simulation studies (Bishop, 1976; Rogan & Keselman, 1977; Wilcox, Charlin & Thompson, 1986) show that even with equal sample sizes, unsatisfactory results can be obtained.

To give you some idea about the effects of having unequal variances, the actual probability of a Type I error (estimated via monte carlo techniques based on 10,000 iterations) are shown in Table 8.5.1a. The nominal level is $\alpha=.05$, and as is evident, the actual level can be quite different. For example, with $J=4$, $\sigma_1=\sigma_2=2$, $\sigma_3=\sigma_4=1$, $n_1=6$, $n_2=10$, $n_3=16$, and $n_4=20$, the actual probability of a Type I error is approximately .147. Bradley (1978, 1980) has argued that in order for a statistical procedure to be considered robust when $\alpha=.05$, the actual probability of a Type I error should be between .025 and .075. This is sometimes called Bradley's liberal criterion. His conservative criterion is that the actual α level should be between .045 and .055. Notice that even with equal sample sizes, and 50 observations per group, the F test is not robust according to Bradley's liberal criterion.

For J treatment groups, let θ be the ratio of the largest standard deviation to the smallest, and notice that in Table 8.5.1a, θ is as large as 4. Some readers might feel that this is unrealistically large, but Fenstad (1983) argues that having θ as large as 4 is not extreme, and a survey of educational studies (Wilcox, 1987a) supports Fenstad's view. Results in Box (1954) are often cited to support the view that the F test is robust to unequal variances, but Box's results were limited to $\theta\leq\surd 3$. Another important result is that it appears that as J gets large, the F test becomes increasingly more sensitive to unequal variances.

It is tempting to use the F test if the sample variances appear to be equal, or to test for equal variances using the Brown-Forsythe procedure that is described below and use the F test if the test for equal variances is not significant. However, this approach can be unsatisfactory for reasons that are explained below.

TABLE 8.5.1a

Actual Type I Error Probabilties When α=.05

Sample Sizes	σ_j's	Pr(Type I Error)
(4,8,10,12)	(2,2,1,1)	.125
	(1,2,3,4)	.028
	(4,3,2,1)	.173
	(1,1,1,4)	.041
	(4,1,1,1)	.279
(11,11,11,11)	(1,1,2,2)	.062
	(4,1,1,1)	.109
(6,10,16,20)	(2,2,1,1)	.147
	(4,3,2,1)	.194
	(4,1,1,1)	.275
(50,50,50,50)	(4,1,1,1)	.088
(6,10,15,18,21,25)	(2,2,2,1,1,1)	.150
	(4,1,1,1,1,1)	.309

Table 8.5.1b

Power of the F Test When $\Sigma\alpha_j{}^2$=1 and α=.05

Sample Sizes	Standard Deviations	Power
6,6,8,8	3,2,2,1	.195
	1,2,2,3	.083
6,10,16,20	3,1,1,1	.444
	1,1,1,3	.079

Suppose you want to control power in terms of $\Sigma\alpha_j{}^2$. A practical problem is knowing to what extent power is affected, for a given value of $\Sigma\alpha_j{}^2$, by the variances. Table 8.5.1b shows that the variances can have a pronounced effect. For example, for sample sizes 6, 10, 16, and 20, and standard deviations 3,1,1, and 1, the power is .444 while if the standard deviations are 1,1,1, and 3 the power is .079. Methods for controlling power in terms of $\Sigma\alpha_j{}^2$ are described in section 8.12.

The Brown-Forsythe Test for Equal Variances

Brown and Forsythe (1974b) proposed that

$$H_0:\sigma_1^2=\sigma_2^2=\ldots=\sigma_J^2 \tag{8.5.1}$$

be tested as follows. First compute the median for each treatment group, say M_j. A summary of how to compute the median is given in Table 8.5.2. Next, for each X_{ij}, the ith observation in the jth treatment group, compute

$$Z_{ij}=|X_{ij}-M_j|$$

and

$$W=A/B$$

where

$$A=\Sigma_j n_j(\bar{Z}_j-\bar{Z})^2/(J\ 1),\quad B=\Sigma\Sigma(Z_{ij}-\bar{Z}_j)^2/(N-J),$$

$$N=\Sigma n_j,\quad \bar{Z}_j=\Sigma_i Z_{ij}/n_j,\text{ and }\bar{Z}=\Sigma_j \bar{Z}_j/J$$

If $W>f$, where f is the $1-\alpha$ quantile of the F distribution with $J-1$ and $N-J$ degrees of freedom, reject (8.5.1) and conclude that the variances are unequal. In other words, perform an F test on the Z_{ij} values.

Table 8.5.2

How to Compute the Median

Let $X_1, \ldots, X_n$ be n observations, and let $X_{[1]} \leq \ldots \leq X_{[n]}$ be the observations written in ascending order. That is, $X_{[1]}$ is the smallest, $X_{[2]}$ is the second smallest, etc. If n is odd, the median is

$$M = X_{[(n+1)/2]}.$$

If n is even,

$$M = \{X_{[n/2]} + X_{[(n+2)/2]}\}/2.$$

For example, if the observations are 3, 9, 20, 17, 7, then M=9. If the observations are 24, 10, 7, and 12, the median is M=(10+12)/2=11.

O'Brien (1978) compared the Brown-Forsythe procedure to the Box-Scheffe test, which is not described in this chapter, and his results indicate that the Brown-Forsythe procedure has more power. While it cannot be stated unequivocally that the Brown-Forsythe procedure is better than the Box-Scheffe test, the Brown-Forsythe test seems to be better for general use. Evidently Kirk (1982) prefers the Box-Scheffe test, but he gave no reasons for his choice (cf. Martin and Games, 1977). Conover, Johnson, and Johnson (1981) compared sixty tests for equal variances, and the Brown-Forsythe procedure performed about as well or better than the others.

Still another robust test for equal variances was proposed by O'Brien (1979), but (for the moment at least) there appears to be no strong reason for preferring it over the Brown-Forsythe procedure, and so O'Brien's test is not described. For still another robust test, see Levene (1960). For references to related work, see O'Brien (1979) and Tan (1982).

8.6 MODIFICATIONS OF THE F TEST WHEN THE VARIANCES ARE UNEQUAL

This section describes four approximate solutions to the problem of testing for equal means when the variances are unequal. The first stems from Welch (1951), the second was suggested by Brown and Forsythe(1974a) and follows from the work of

Satterthwaite (1941), the third is based on an extension of results in Stein (1945), and the fourth was proposed by James (1951).

Before continuing, an important warning should be made. It is tempting to test for equal variances using the Brown-Forsythe procedure described above, and test for equal means with the F test if the test for equal variances is not significant; otherwise use the procedures described here. However, THIS PROCEDURE IS NOT RECOMMENDED because the test for equal variances may not have enough power to detect unequal variances in situations where the equal variance assumption should be abandoned. This point is illustrated below.

Welch's Method

Let

$$N=\Sigma n_j,$$

$$\bar{X}_j=\Sigma_i X_{ij}/n_j,$$

$$\bar{X}=\Sigma_i \Sigma_j X_{ij}/N,$$

$$s_j^2=\Sigma_i (X_{ij}-\bar{X}_j)^2/(n_j-1),$$

$$w_j=n_j/s_j^2,$$

$$u=\Sigma w_j,$$

$$\tilde{X}=\Sigma w_j \bar{X}_j/u,$$

$$A=\Sigma w_j (\bar{X}_j-\tilde{X})^2/(J-1),$$

$$B=2(J-2)\{\Sigma(1-w_j/u)^2/(n_j-1)\}/(J^2-1),$$

and

$$W=A/[1+B]. \qquad (8.6.1)$$

When the population means are equal--regardless of whether the variances are equal--W is approximately distributed as an F statistic with $\nu_1=J-1$ and

$$\nu_2=[(3/(J^2-1))\Sigma_j (1-w_j/u)^2/(n_j-1)]^{-1}$$

degrees of freedom. Thus, if $W>f$, where f is the $1-\alpha$ quantile of an F distribution with ν_1 and ν_2 degrees of freedom, reject H_0.

The Brown-Forsythe Method

The second procedure uses the statistic

$$F^{*}=C/D \qquad (8.6.2)$$

where

$$C=\Sigma_j n_j(\bar{X}_j-\bar{X})^2$$

and

$$D=\Sigma_j(1-n_j/N)s_j^2.$$

F^* also has approximately an F distribution with ν_1=J-1, but this time

$$\nu_2=[\Sigma_j c_j^2/(n_j-1)]^{-1}$$

where

$$c_j=(1-n_j/N)s_j^2/\{\Sigma_k(1-n_k/N)s_k^2\}.$$

The result that both W and F^* are approximately distributed as an F distribution is based on an asymptotic argument (i.e., assuming n_j is large). Let θ be the ratio of the largest population standard deviation (the largest σ_j value) to the smallest. For $\theta<3$, results in Brown and Forsythe (1974a) suggest that both W and F^* give good results when the n_j's are as small as 10, and reasonable results are obtained when the n_j's are as small as 5. However, for larger values of θ, both W and F^* may be unsatisfactory. This point is illustrated in Table 8.6.1 with some monte carlo results reported by Wilcox, Charlin, and Thompson (1986). Table 8.6.1 also shows what happens if the F test is used provided the Brown-Forsythe test for equal variances is nonsignificant; otherwise the W or F^* statistics are used. The notation W_{25} in Table 8.6.1 means that if the Brown-Forsythe test for equal variances is significant at the .25 level, W is used to test for equal means, otherwise the F test is used to test for equal means instead. The notation W_{10}, F^*_{25}, and F^*_{10} is defined in a similar manner. As can be seen, testing for equal variances gives better control over the Type I error probability, but a simpler method that is equally effective or better is to just abandon the F test and use F^* or W. Also, according to Bradley's criterion, even W and F^* are not always robust to unequal variances when θ=4 although they are substantially better than F. It appears that for equal sample sizes W is robust for θ as large as 4. In contrast, F^* is not robust and should be avoided. However, an argument in favor of F^* is that if the variances are equal, W tends to exceed the nominal α level while F^* does not. For unequal samples sizes, the actual signficance level of W can exceed .08

when testing at the α=.05 level.

Unfortunately the power of both F^* and W is difficult to determine (cf. Lee & Gurland, 1975). Whenever possible it is recommended that both power and Type I errors be controlled with the procedure in section 8.12. It is also noted that Clinch and Keselman (1982) have compared F^* to the F test as well as a procedure proposed by Welch (1951). They considered the effects of both unequal variances and nonnormality and concluded that F^* gave the best results, but the results in Table 8.6.1 indicate that F^* can exceed .075 with a nominal α level of .05. Of course the actual value of θ might exceed 4, in which case it may be that both W and F^* are even less robust.

Table 8.6.1

Actual Type I Error Probabilities, α=.05

Sample Sizes	Standard Deviations	F	F^*	W	F^*_{25}	F^*_{10}	W_{25}	W_{10}
4,8,10,12	2,2,1,1	.125	.059	.084	.079	.094	.104	.114
	4,3,2,1	.173	.065	.086	.076	.093	.096	.112
	4,1,1,1	.279	.081	.082	.103	.127	.113	.137
21,21,21,21	4,1,1,1	.097	.084	.055	.084	.084	.055	.055
50,50,50,50	4,1,1,1	.088	.084	.044	.084	.084	.044	.044
6,10,15,18,21,25	2,2,2,1,1,1	.150	.062	.079	.065	.072	.082	.089
	4,4,4,1,1,1	.234	.069	.080	.069	.069	.080	.080
	1,1,1,1,1,4	.041	.100	.073	.100	.100	.073	.073
	4,3,3,1,1,4	.091	.062	.080	.062	.062	.080	.080

Values in this table are based on 10,000 iterations.

An Asymptotic Chi-Square Solution

The third method for testing the equality of J means is as follows. Let

$$u=\max(s_1^2/n_1,\ldots,s_J^2/n_J).$$

That is, u is the largest of the J sample variances divided by the respective sample size. For each of the J treatment groups, compute

$$b_j=\{1 + (1/s_j)[(n_j-1)(n_j u-s_j^2)]^{1/2}\}/n_j$$

and

$$T_j=\Sigma_{i=1}^{n_j-1} X_{ij} \qquad (j=1,\ldots,J).$$

T_j is just the sum of the first n_j-1 observations from the jth group.

Let

$$\tilde{X}_j=T_j(1-b_j)/(n_j-1) + b_j X_{n_j j}$$

and

$$\tilde{X}=\Sigma_j \tilde{X}_j/J.$$

It can be shown that when the means are equal,

$$H=\Sigma(\tilde{X}_j-\tilde{X})^2/u \qquad (8.6.3)$$

has, approximately, a chi-square distribution with J-1 degrees of freedom. That is, you reject if $H>c$ where c is the $1-\alpha$ quantile of a chi-square distribution with J-1 degrees of freedom.

James' Second Order Method

The fourth and final procedure was proposed by James (1951). James actually proposed two procedures, but Brown and Forsythe (1974a) found his simpler procedure to be unsatisfactory, and so it is not described. James' more complicated procedure is applied as follows.

Compute

$$X_w=\Sigma w_j \bar{X}_j/W_b$$

where $w_j=n_j/s_j^2$ and $W_b=\Sigma w_j$. Then

$$Q=\Sigma w_j(\bar{X}_j-X_w)^2$$

has, approximately, a chi-square distribution with J-1 degrees of freedom when the null hypothesis is true. However, using c, the $1-\alpha$ quantile of a chi-square distribution, as a critical value is unsatisfactory when the sample sizes are small or even moderately large. James suggested adjusting the critical value as follows.

For any integers r and s, let

$$R_{st}=\Sigma(w_j/W_b)^t/\nu_j^s.$$

and

$$\chi_{2s}=c^{s}/[(J-1)(J+1)\ldots(J+2s-3)]$$

where

$$\nu_j=n_j-1.$$

(The quantity R_{st} corresponds to the expression given by James, but it differs slightly from the one reported by Dijkstra an Werter, 1981.) James' adjusted critical value is

$$c_a=c + (1/2)(3\chi_4+\chi_2)\Sigma(1-w_j/W_b)^2/\nu_j +$$

$$\{(1/16)(3\chi_4+\chi_2)^2(1-(J-3)/c)(\Sigma(1-w_j/W_b)^2/\nu_j)^2 +$$

$$(1/2)(3\chi_4+\chi_2)[(8R_{23}-10R_{22}+4R_{21}-6R_{12}^2+8R_{12}R_{11}-4R_{11}^2)$$

$$+ (2R_{23}-4R_{22}+2R_{21}-2R_{12}^2+4R_{12}R_{11}-2R_{11}^2)(\chi_2-1)$$

$$+ (1/4)(-R_{12}^2+4R_{12}R_{11}-2R_{12}R_{10}-4R_{11}^2+4R_{11}R_{10}-R_{10}^2)$$

$$(3\chi_4-2\chi_2-1)] +$$

$$(R_{23}-3R_{22}+3R_{21}-R_{20})(5\chi_6+2\chi_4+\chi_2) +$$

$$(3/16)(R_{12}^2-4R_{23}+6R_{22}-4R_{21}+R_{20})(35\chi_8+15\chi_6+9\chi_4+5\chi_2) +$$

$$(1/16)(-2R_{22}+4R_{21}-R_{20}+2R_{12}R_{10}-4R_{11}R_{10}+R_{10}^2)(9\chi_8$$

$$-3\chi_6-5\chi_4-\chi_2) +$$

$$+ (1/4)(-R_{22}+R_{11}^2)(27\chi_8+3\chi_6+\chi_4+\chi_2) +$$

$$(1/4)(R_{23}-R_{12}R_{11})(45\chi_8+9\chi_6+7\chi_4+3\chi_2)\}$$

You reject if $Q>c_a$.

Popular computer software packages do not yet include James' procedure. This is unfortunate because all indications are that James' procedure provides the best control over the probability of a Type I error when the variances are unequal (Dijkstra and Werter, 1981; Wilcox, 1987b). The next best procedure is the asymptotic chi-square procedure. One exception is when $J \leq 4$ and the sample sizes are equal. Then Welch and the asymptotic chi-square procedures appear to have very similar Type I error probabilities, but Welch's procedure can have more power in certain situations, so Welch's procedure should be used. In terms of Type I errors, there seems to be at most a negligible difference between the asymptotic chi-square solution and James' technique when the sample sizes are greater than or equal to 10 in each group. The asymptotic chi-square procedure is slightly more conservative in terms of Type I errors, and James' procedure can exceed the nominal level by a slight amount. The actual probability of a Type I error using H, Q, F, W and F^* is shown in Table 8.6.2 for J=4,6,10, and various sample size and variance configurations. Usually there is little difference in power between Q and H, but when the treatment group with the largest mean has the smallest variance, James' procedure can have substantially more power, and so it is recommended that you use James' procedure whenever possible.

Table 8.6.2
Empirical Type I Error Probabilities, $\alpha=.05$

Sample Sizes	Standard Deviations	H	Q	F	F*	W
11,11,11,11	1,1,1,1	.045	.046	.048	.046	.055
	5,1,1,1	.048	.047	.115	.088	.055
	5,4,3,1	.047	.048	.071	.063	.059
	6,1,1,1	.048	.047	.120	.088	.055
4,8,12,20	1,1,1,1	.055	.053	.048	.046	.073
	4,3,2,1	.064	.057	.248	.064	.083
	6,1,1,1	.074	.056	.390	.075	.081
	1,1,1,6	.042	.050	.012	.086	.067
10,10,15,25	1,1,1,1	.050	.054	.051	.049	.063
	4,3,2,1	.051	.054	.161	.061	.065
	1,2,3,4	.045	.053	.023	.067	.062
	6,1,1,1	.053	.053	.213	.081	.061
	1,1,1,6	.046	.053	.023	.097	.060
21,21,21,21	1,1,1,1	.049	.051	.051	.050	.056
	6,1,1,1	.049	.050	.105	.088	.055
	6,3,2,1	.049	.050	.083	.075	.056
6,10,16,20	1,1,1,1	.050	.051	.053	.049	.065
	4,3,2,1	.054	.053	.194	.059	.070
	4,1,1,1	.057	.053	.027	.077	.062
	1,1,1,4	.046	.051	.275	.072	.068
11,11,11,11,11,11	1,1,1,1,1,1	.044	.051	.051	.049	.074
	4,3,3,2,1,1	.042	.052	.079	.070	.075
	6,1,1,1,1,1	.041	.051	.136	.101	.074
	6,3,3,2,1,1	.041	.052	.102	.085	.075
11,15,20,20,20,20	1,1,1,1,1,1	.047	.055	.050	.050	.069
	6,4,2,1,1,1	.049	.055	.206	.091	.069
	1,1,1,1,1,6	.043	.053	.105	.108	.067
	6,1,1,1,1,1	.049	.055	.249	.103	.070
10,10,10,10,10, 10,10,10,10,10	1,1,1,1,1, 1,1,1,1,1	.048	.055	.054	.053	.101
	6,1,1,1,1, 1,1,1,1,1	.042	.055	.164	.115	.103
	9,1,1,1,1, 1,1,1,1,1	.040	.055	.180	.115	.103

8.7 MEASURING THE DIFFERENCES AMONG POPULATION MEANS, AND MEASURES OF ASSOCIATION

There is a strong temptation to conclude that if the F statistic is significant, then the means are substantially different. But the F statistic is a highly unsatisfactory measure of the magnitude of the differences among the means. The reason, as was pointed out in section 8.3, is that the magnitude of F is a function of both the sample size and $\Sigma\alpha_j^2$. Thus, once a significant F has been obtained, the question arises as to whether the difference among the means is substantial rather than significant. Of course making a judgment about what constitutes a substantial difference is by no means an easy task. If, for example, $\Sigma\alpha_j^2$ is used to measure the differences among the population means, at what point is this value large, and when is it small? Here it is assumed that experts in the relevant field are able to specify what will be considered a substantial difference.

Another and more basic issue is deciding how to measure overall differences. A simple measure is just

$$\delta=\Sigma\alpha_j^2$$

which can be estimated with

$$(\text{MSBG}-\text{MSWG})(J-1)/n.$$

For unequal n's use

$$\Sigma(\bar{X}_j-\bar{X})^2.$$

Several measures have been proposed under the assumption that the variances are equal. The first of these is Hays' ω^2 given by

$$\omega^2=\{\Sigma\alpha_j^2/J\}/\{\sigma^2+\Sigma\alpha_j^2/J\} \qquad (8.7.1)$$

where σ^2 is the common variance. You can estimate ω^2 with

$$\{\text{SSBG}-(J-1)\text{MSWG}\}/\{\text{SST}+\text{MSWG}\}.$$

Hays (1973) describes the motivation for (8.7.1), but the details are not given here because of the criticism ω^2 has received. The first criticism is that ω^2 is only defined when the variances are equal. If the means are unequal, it seems reasonable to suspect that the variances are often unequal as well, in which case there seems to be little motivation for using ω^2. Of course you can test for equal variances. If the test for equal variances is not significant and the power of the test is reasonably high, ω^2 might be used. Another criticism is that ω^2 is a function of both $\Sigma\alpha_j^2$ and σ^2. For fixed values of $\Sigma\alpha_j^2$, ω^2 approaches one as σ^2 approaches zero. Thus, $\Sigma\alpha_j^2$, which is an overall measure of the differences of the means, can be small, but if simultaneously $\Sigma\alpha_j^2$ is large relative to σ^2, ω^2 can be large. This argument does not mean that ω^2 be abandoned, only that its value be considered in conjunction with the estimated value of $\Sigma\alpha_j^2$. Keppel (1973) also expressed some concerns about ω^2, pointing out that it can be large even when F is not significant. Still another criticsm is that it is difficult to make judgments about whether ω^2 is large. Hays discusses the interpretation of ω^2, but nevertheless it is generally easier to make judgments in terms of δ.

Another measure of treatment effects is

$$\eta^2=\{(J-1)F\}/\{(J-1)F+N-J\}$$

where F is the F statistic from an ANOVA (e.g., Cohen, 1966; cf. Friedman, 1968). Again equal variances are assumed, and so this measure must be used with caution. Still another measure, based on equal variances, was suggested by Cohen (1977). For J=2 it is

$$d=(\mu_1-\mu_2)/\sigma.$$

For results on how to estimate d, see Hedges (1981). As pointed out in chapter seven, d has been criticized because it implicitly assumes normality, because it is more difficult to make judgments about whether d is large as opposed to making judgments about $\mu_1-\mu_2$, and because it assumes equal variances. As a result, this measure should be used with caution. It is suggested that instead treatment effects be measured either with $\Sigma\alpha_j^2$, or $\mu_j-\mu_k$ for all $j<k$. For additional comments on measuring effect size, see O'Grady (1982).

8.8 PARAMETRIC FUNCTIONS AND LINEAR CONTRASTS: A CLOSER LOOK AT THE F TEST

Although the F test is usually associated with testing (8.1.1), it turns out that it actually tests much more. The purpose of this section is to describe this more general aspect of the F test when the equal variance assumption is met. Parts of this section assume the reader has a basic knowledge of matrix algebra. Readers who are more interested in applied problems, rather than theoretical results, may want to skip or only skim this section.

By definition, a parametric function of J treatment means is any linear combination of the means given by

$$\Psi=\Sigma c_j\mu_j \tag{8.8.1}$$

where the c_j's are constants chosen by the experimenter. If the restriction $\Sigma c_j=0$ is added, Ψ is called a linear contrast. For example, if

$$c_1=1,\ c_2=-1,\ \text{and}\ c_3=c_4=\ldots=c_J=0,$$

$\Psi=\mu_1-\mu_2$, and the hypothesis

$$H_0:\Psi=0$$

is just another way of writing

$$H_0:\mu_1=\mu_2.$$

It is noted that the unbiased estimate of Ψ is

$$\hat{\Psi}=\Sigma c_j\bar{X}_j.$$

Also, if $\Psi_1=\Sigma c_{1j}\mu_j$ and $\Psi_2=\Sigma c_{2j}\mu_j$ are any two linear contrasts, then the correlation between $\hat{\Psi}_1$ and $\hat{\Psi}_2$ is

$$\{\Sigma c_{1j}c_{2j}/n_j\}/\{[\Sigma c_{1j}{}^2/n_j][\Sigma c_{2j}{}^2/n_j]\}^{1/2}.$$

Consider any two parametric functions, say Ψ_1 and Ψ_2. By definition, if the vector

$$(c_{11},c_{12},\ldots,c_{1J})$$

is multiplied by a constant h, the result is a vector where the j<u>th</u> element is hc_{1j}. That is,

$$h(c_{11},\ldots,c_{1J})=(hc_{11},\ldots,hc_{1J}).$$

For example, 3(-2,1,3)=(-6,3,9). The vectors

$$\underline{d}_1=(c_{11},\ldots,c_{1J})\ \text{and}\ \underline{d}_2=(c_{21},\ldots,c_{2J})$$

are said to be linearly dependent if $\underline{d}_1=h\underline{d}_2$ for some constant h. For example, the vectors (1,3) and (2,6) are linearly dependent because (2,6)=2(1,3). If two vectors are not linearly dependent they are defined to be linearly independent. For example (1,0,1) and (3,2,1) are linearly independent because there does not exist a constant h such that h(1,0,1)=(3,2,1).

Now consider q vectors, say $\underline{d}_1,\ldots\underline{d}_q$. They are defined to be linearly dependent if $\underline{d}_1$ is a linear combination of $\underline{d}_2,\ldots,\underline{d}_q$. For example, if q=3, $\underline{d}_1=(1,-1,0)$, $\underline{d}_2=(0,4,8)$ and $\underline{d}_3=(1,1,4)$, then

$$\underline{d}_1=\underline{d}_3-(1/2)\underline{d}_2,$$

and so these three vectors are linearly dependent. If $\underline{d}_1$ cannot be written as a linear combination of $\underline{d}_2,\ldots\underline{d}_q$, the vectors are defined to be linearly independent.

Consider any set of q linearly independent vectors

$$\underline{d}_1=(c_{11},\ldots,c_{1J})$$

$$\underline{d}_2=(C_{21},\ldots,c_{2J})$$

$$\vdots$$

$$\underline{d}_q=(c_{q1},\ldots,c_{qJ})$$

and suppose you want to test

$$H_0:\Psi_1=\Psi_2=\ldots=\Psi_q=0 \qquad (8.8.2)$$

where $\Psi_i=\Sigma_j c_{ij}\mu_j$, i=1,...,q, and where the Type I error probability is to be α. This can be done using the results described below. For now attention is restricted to the important special case

$$\Psi_i=\mu_i-\mu_{1+1},\ i=1,\ldots,J-1. \qquad (8.8.3)$$

The contrast coefficients corresponding to the Ψ_i's are linearly independent, and the test of (8.8.2) is equivalent to testing (8.1.1).

Next suppose you want to test the hypothesis that for any q constants, say $h_1,\ldots h_q$, that

$$\Sigma_{i=1}^{J-1}h_i\Psi_i=0 \qquad (8.8.4)$$

where the Ψ_i's are given by (8.8.3) and q=J-1. It turns out that you would use the same F statistic used to test (8.1.1). That is, testing for equal means with the F statistic is equivalent to testing whether (8.8.4) is true for all possible h_i values (Scheffe, 1959, p. 70). Thus, in actuality, the F test answers the question "are there any differences?" within the restrictions just described.

Further Results on the F Test

It should be mentioned that even more results can be derived for testing parametric functions that are based on the "general linear model" which is examined in considerable detail by Scheffe (1959). For a more elementary introduction to the general model, see Kirk (1982). For those interested in this model, be certain to notice that the general linear model assumes equal variances among the J treatment groups. Only a brief description of the general linear model is given here.

Again let $\Psi_i=\Sigma_j c_{ij}\mu_j$ $(i=1,\ldots,q)$ be any q parametric functions of the μ_j's. Let C be a q by J matrix where the ith row is the vector

$$(c_{i1},\ldots,c_{iJ}),$$

and suppose the rows are linearly independent. Note that this does not necessarily mean that $\hat{\Psi}_i$ is independent of $\hat{\Psi}_k$, $i\neq k$, where

$$\hat{\Psi}_i=\Sigma c_{ij}\bar{X}_j .$$

Suppose you want to test

$$H_0:\Psi_1=\ldots=\Psi_q=0, \qquad (8.8.5)$$

and assume there are an equal number of observations per group. To do this you reject H_0 if

$$\hat{\underset{\sim}{\Psi}}'(CC')^{-1}\hat{\underset{\sim}{\Psi}} > qf \qquad (8.8.6)$$

where

$$\hat{\underset{\sim}{\Psi}}'=(\hat{\Psi}_1,\ldots,\hat{\Psi}_q),$$

and f is the $1-\alpha$ quantile of the F distribution with q and N-J degrees of freedom.

As an illustration, consider

$$\Psi_1=\mu_1-\mu_2,$$

$$\Psi_2=\mu_2-\mu_3$$

and suppose you want to test

$$H_0:\Psi_1=\Psi_2=0.$$

Thus, q=2, and this is the same as testing $H_0:\mu_1=\mu_2=\mu_3$.

First note that for this special case

$$C=\begin{bmatrix} 1 & -1 & 0 \\ 0 & 1 & -1 \end{bmatrix}$$

Then

$$CC'=\begin{bmatrix} 2 & -1 \\ -1 & 2 \end{bmatrix}$$

and so

$$(CC')^{-1}=\begin{bmatrix} 2/3 & 1/3 \\ 1/3 & 2/3 \end{bmatrix}$$

Additional computations show that

$$\hat{\underset{\sim}{\Psi}}'(CC')^{-1}\hat{\underset{\sim}{\Psi}}=(2/3)\Sigma_k\Sigma_j\bar{X}_k\bar{X}_j$$

which can be shown to equal

$$\Sigma(\bar{X}_j-\bar{X})^2.$$

This in turn reveals that

$$\{\hat{\underset{\sim}{\Psi}}'(CC')^{-1}\hat{\underset{\sim}{\Psi}}\}/(2MSWG)$$

is equal to MSBG/MSWG. Thus, (8.8.6) yields the same test as was obtained in section 8.3.

The point is that any set of q linearly independent sets of parametric functions can be tested which includes as a special case (8.1.1). If for instance there is interest in testing

$$2\mu_1+3\mu_2+\mu_3$$

and

$$\mu_1+5\mu_2-2\mu_3,$$

(8.8.6) can be applied and the probability of a Type I error will be α when the equal variance assumption is met.

It should be mentioned that similar results are available for the case of unequal sample sizes (Scheffe, 1959), but these results are not discussed here.

8.9 THE RANDOM EFFECTS MODEL

Suppose you want to conduct a study on the effect of classroom size on the achievement levels of children in grade 4. Further suppose that the range of classroom sizes that you want to consider is from 10 to 50. You might randomly assign some students to classrooms having 10 students, and others to classrooms having 50 students, and then apply the fixed effect model in section 8.3, but the results give you little indication about what would happen for all the other possible classroom sizes. The purpose of this section is to describe a technique that can be used to make certain inferences about all possible classroom sizes that are of interest. More generally, the goal is to consider ways of making inferences about a large number of populations without actually estimating each one. Another illustration is given at the end of this section.

In the fixed effect model the treatment groups actually used in the study were predetermined, and the means were designated as

$$\mu_1, \ldots, \mu_J.$$

In the random effects model studied here, the treatment groups are not predetermined but rather randomly selected from a population of possible treatment groups. Thus, in the illustration, the factor "classroom size" is of interest, and the levels of this factor, that is the actual classroom sizes used in your experiment, are randomly sampled from all possible classroom sizes that are being investigated. Next subjects are randomly assigned to the classrooms with the sizes just determined, and then their achievement is measured at the end of the instructional program.

Assumptions

The difference between the random effects model and the fixed effects model is that in the latter, $\mu_1, \ldots \mu_J$ are J unknown

constants, while in the random effects model the μ_j's are random variables. Let $a_j = \mu_j - \mu$ where $\mu = E(\mu_j)$ is the expected value of μ_j for a randomly sampled treatment group. The model for the i<u>th</u> observation from the j<u>th</u> randomly sampled treatment group is

$$X_{ij} = \mu + a_j + \epsilon_{ij}$$

where by assumption

1) X_{ij} is normally distributed with mean μ_j and

variance σ_x^2,

2) a_j is normally distributed with mean 0 and variance σ_a^2, and

3) ϵ_{ij} is normally distributed with mean 0 and variance σ^2, and

4) a_j and ϵ_{ij} are assumed to be independent.

This model is of course very similar to the fixed effect model, the only difference being that the unknown parameter α_j has been replaced with the random variable a_j.

Derivation of an F Test

Suppose that all of the population means being studied are equal in value. Another way of saying this is that $\sigma_a{}^2$, the variance of a_j, equals zero because there is no variation among the population means. The problem then is to test whether

$$H_0:\sigma_a^2=0 \tag{8.9.1}$$

is consistent with the observations in your study.

To derive a test of (8.9.1) consider again the expectation of SSBG and SSWG, only this time the expectations take into account the random sampling of the treatment levels. First consider the SSBG term, and let $\bar{a}=\Sigma a_j/J$. Then

$$E(SSBG)=E[n\Sigma(\bar{X}_j-\bar{X})^2)]$$

$$=nE[\Sigma(\mu+a_j+\bar{\epsilon}_j-\mu-\bar{a}-\bar{\epsilon})^2]$$

$$=nE[\Sigma(a_j-\bar{a})^2+2(a_j-\bar{a})(\bar{\epsilon}_j-\bar{\epsilon})+(\bar{\epsilon}_j-\bar{\epsilon})^2].$$

But $E(a_j-\bar{a})(\bar{\epsilon}_j-\bar{\epsilon})=0$ because a and ϵ_{ij} are assumed to be independent. Also,

$$E[\Sigma(a_j-\bar{a})^2=(J-1)\sigma_a^2.$$

Similarly,

$$E[\Sigma(\bar{\epsilon}_j-\bar{\epsilon})^2]=(J-1)\sigma^2/n,$$

so

$$E(SSBG)=n[(J-1)\sigma_a^2+(J-1)\sigma^2/n$$

$$=(J-1)n\sigma_a^2+(J-1)\sigma^2. \quad (8.9.2)$$

which implies that

$$E(MSBG)=n\sigma_a^2+\sigma^2. \quad (8.9.3)$$

Similar calculations show that

$$E(MSWG)=\sigma^2.$$

Thus, MSBG/MSWG measures the magnitude of $n\sigma_a^2$ relative to σ^2, and when H_0 is true MSBG/MSWG has an F distribution with J-1 and J(n-1) degrees of freedom. This means that the calculations made to test (8.9.1) are the same as those to test (8.1.1). The only difference is that in the random effects model, treatment levels are randomly sampled.

Example 8.9.1. As another illustration of when the random effects model might be used, suppose you want to study the effect that drug A has on the metabolism of rats. Because there are many different amounts of the drug that might be used, you decide to use a random effects model to test the hypothesis that the drug has no effect. Suppose you randomly sample J=5 dosage levels, and that for each level n=21 rats receive an injection. It is assumed that each rat receives only one injection, so a total of 105 rats are needed. If α=.05, SSBG=200, and SSWG=400, then F=12.5. With 4 and 100 degrees of freedom, you reject H_0.

8.10 A MEASURE OF ASSOCIATION FOR THE RANDOM EFFECTS MODEL

Just as in the fixed effect model, a large F is not necessarily an indication that the means are substantially different. The problem this time is that F measures the magnitude of $n\sigma_a^2$ relative to σ^2. If σ^2 is relatively small, or if n is large, F can be large even though σ_a^2 is nearly equal to zero. Thus, it is important to report n as well as estimating both σ_a^2 and σ^2. From (8.9.3) the estimate of σ_a^2--assuming equal variances --is

$$\hat{\sigma}_a^2=(MSBG-MSWG)/n, \quad (8.10.1)$$

and the estimate of σ^2 is again MSWG.

A measure of association similar to ω^2 is

$$\rho_I=\sigma_a^2/\sigma_x^2 \tag{8.10.2}$$

where $\sigma_x{}^2$=VAR(X_{ij}). The quantity given by (8.10.2) is often called the intraclass correlation coefficient. Since $X_{ij}=\mu+a_j+\epsilon_{ij}$, and because a_j and ϵ_{ij} are assumed to be independent, VAR(X_{ij})$=\sigma_a{}^2+\sigma^2$. Thus, the motivation for using ρ_I is that it is the proportion of observed variance that is due to $\sigma_a{}^2$. An estimate of ρ_I is

$$\hat{\rho}_I=\hat{\sigma}_a^2/(\hat{\sigma}_a^2+\text{MSWG}) \tag{8.10.3}$$

Unlike ω^2, it is possible to test hypotheses about ρ_I and to determine confidence intervals. The derivation of these procedures is based on the result that, regardless of whether H_0 is true, $\bar{X}_j=\mu+a_j+\bar{\epsilon}_j$, and VAR($\bar{X}_j$)$=\sigma_a{}^2+\sigma^2/n$. Thus,

$$\Sigma(\bar{X}_j-\bar{X})^2/(\sigma_a^2+\sigma^2/n)=\text{SSBG}/(n\sigma_a^2+\sigma^2)$$

has a chi-square distribution with J-1 degrees of freedom. Similarly, SSWG/σ^2 has a chi-square distribution, and so

$$\{\text{MSBG}/(n\sigma_a^2+\sigma^2)\}/\{\text{MSWG}/\sigma^2\} \tag{8.10.4}$$

has an F distribution with J-1 and J(n-1) degrees of freedom. But (8.10.4) can be written as

$$Y=\{\text{MSBG}/\text{MSWG}\}\{(1-\rho_I)/[1+(n-1)\rho_I]\}$$

and so

$$\Pr(F''\le Y\le F')=1-\alpha \tag{8.10.5}$$

where F'' is the $\alpha/2$ quantile, and F' is the $1-\alpha/2$ quantile of the F distribution with J-1 and J(n-1) degrees of freedom.

From (8.10.4), algebraic manipulations show that a $100(1-\alpha)$% confidence interval for ρ_I is obtained by computing

$$A=n^{-1}\{\text{MSBG}/[\text{MSWG}(F')] - 1\}$$

and

$$B=n^{-1}\{\text{MSBG}/[\text{MSWG}(F'')] - 1\}.$$

Then

$$\Pr\{A/(A+1)\le\rho_I\le B/(B+1)\}=1-\alpha.$$

For an even better confidence interval, see Donner and Wells (1986).

As an illustration, suppose α=.1, n=7, J=4, MSBG=60, and MSWG=10. From Table A3, F'=3.01, and so A=.14. The lower tail probability of the F distribution can be determined from Table A3 as described in chapter six. As a result, F''=1/8.64=.116 so B=7.25. Thus, (.123,.8790) is a 90% confidence interval for ρ_I.

Testing Hypotheses About ρ_I

Suppose you want to test

$$H_0: \rho_I \le \rho_0 \qquad (8.10.6)$$

where ρ_0 is some known constant with a value between zero and one. For example, if ρ_0 is .1, (8.10.6) is testing the hypothesis that σ_a^2 accounts for at most 10% of the total variance, σ_x^2.

For notational convenience, let

$$\theta = \rho_I/(1-\rho_I).$$

Then (8.10.6) is equivalent to

$$H_0: \theta \le \theta_0$$

where $\theta_0 = \rho_0/(1-\rho_0)$. H_0 is rejected if

$$(MSBG/MSWG) > (1+n\theta_0)f$$

where f is the 1-α quantile of the F distribution with J-1 and J(n-1) degrees of freedom.

8.11 DETERMINING SAMPLE SIZE AND POWER IN THE FIXED EFFECTS MODEL: THE EQUAL VARIANCE CASE

In the past there have been two approaches to determining sample sizes and power, both of which assume equal variances. The first is to decide how much power you want in terms of $\Sigma\alpha_j^2$. For example, if $\Sigma\alpha_j^2$=2, you might want the probability of rejecting (8.1.1) to be .8. Increasing n will increase power, but there is the practical problem that the power also depends on the unknown parameter σ^2. Historically the solution was to estimate σ^2 with MSWG, assume MSWG is indeed equal to σ^2, and then determine whether enough observations were sampled so that the power would be at least as large as desired. If not, additional observations would be sampled. Today it is realized that this approach can be highly unsatisfactory. In particular, many more observations may be sampled than are actually needed. When observations are expensive or difficult to obtain, this can be an important consideration. Another problem is that assuming equal variances may be untenable. An exact method for controlling power and handling unequal variances is described in the next section.

Here it is noted that if the amount of power desired can be expressed in terms of σ, the common standard deviation among all the treatment groups, the sample size, n, can be determined without collecting any data at all. More specifically, suppose a constant C has been specified with the idea that if the largest difference between any two means is $C\sigma$, the power should be at least as large as some predetermined level, say $1-\beta$. Tables for determining n given J, C, α, and β are reported by Bratcher, Moran, and Zimmer (1970). A portion of their tables can be found in Kirk (1982).

For J=2 groups, determining sample size and controlling power in terms of $(\mu_1-\mu_2)/\sigma$ has received considerable criticism for the reasons outlined in chapter seven. The same criticisms apply here, and so it is recommended that power be controlled with the procedure in section 8.12 whenever possible.

8.12 AN EXACT PROCEDURE FOR THE FIXED EFFECT MODEL THAT CONTROLS POWER AND HANDLES UNEQUAL VARIANCES

Suppose you want to determine the number of observations needed so that when testing for equal means, the power will be reasonably large, and suppose that you are unwilling to assume that the variances are equal. This section describes an exact solution to this problem that was proposed by Bishop and Dudewicz (1978). In contrast to previous sections, a two-stage procedure is used that is similar in nature to the two-stage procedures described in chapters six and seven.

In some situations a two-stage sampling scheme may be inconvenient, and some comments are made at the end of this section on how you might be able to avoid having to sample additional observations in the second stage. It should be noted, though, that there are many situations where a two-stage procedure can be used. For example, in psychology it is common for subjects to be tested sequentially. That is, the first subject comes into the lab and the experiment is conducted, the second subject comes into the lab and the experiment is conducted again, etc. Once a reasonble number of subjects is observed under all conditions (say at least 15 per group), the calculations described below can be made to determine how many additional observations are needed. As already pointed out, having both unequal n's and unequal variances can seriously affect the actual Type I and Type II error probabilities of the F test, and so the procedure described here can be important.

Description of the Procedure

An explanation of the procedure is explicated by describing the computational steps with some real data. Accordingly, suppose you have J=3 treatment groups with n=10 observations per group as shown in Table 8.12.1. (A simple method for handling unequal sample sizes in the first stage is described below.) The first step is determining how much power is desired. This is done in terms of $\delta=\Sigma\alpha_j^2$. For the sake of illustration, suppose you want the power to be at least .8 when $\alpha=.05$ and $\delta=2.0$. The next step is determining the critical value that will be used, and this is done by referring to Table A6. If the critical value you want is not in Table A6, refer to Table A2 and determine the $1-\alpha$ quantile of the chi-square distribution with J-1 degrees of freedom. In the illustration this value is

$$\chi^2_{1-\alpha,J-1}=5.99.$$

Then compute

$$c=[(n-1)/(n-3)]\chi^2_{1-\alpha,J-1} \qquad (8.12.1)$$

which is approximately equal to the critical value that is needed below. In the illustration,

$$c=(9/7)(5.99)=7.70.$$

Better but more complicated approximations of c are described in Bishop, Dudewicz, Juritz and Stevens (1978). As n gets large, the approximation in (8.12.1) improves, but for n small, the actual Type I error probability can be as high as .068 with a nominal level of $\alpha=.05$. If you want a more accurate approximation of c, the procedure proposed by Hochberg (1975) can be used. In particular, compute

$$\nu=n-1,$$

$$A=(J-1)\nu/(\nu-2),$$

$$B=(\nu^2/J)[(J-1)/(\nu-2)],$$

$$C=3(J-1)/(\nu-4),$$

$$D=(J^2-2J+3)/(\nu-2),$$

$$E=B(C+D),$$

$$M=(4E-2A^2)/(E-A-2A)$$

and

$$L=A(M-2)/M.$$

Then c is approximately equal to Lf where f is the 1-α quantile of an F distribution with L and M degrees of freedom. For example, if n=12, α=.05, and J=8, c=18.698.

Table 8.12.1

Sample Data for J=3 Treatment Groups

Group 1	Group 2	Group 3
3	4	6
2	4	7
2	3	8
5	8	6
8	7	7
4	4	9
3	2	10
6	5	9
1	8	11
7	2	9
$\bar{X}_1=4.1$	$\bar{X}_2=4.7$	$\bar{X}_3=8.2$
$s_1{}^2=5.43$	$s_2{}^2=5.12$	$s_3{}^2=2.84$

Second Stage Data

3	4	2	4	6	8	7
2	5	2	4	5	2	6
3	4	3	4	5	3	6
3	4	1	3	3		7
3	5		3	2		9
2	6		4	2		10
5	5		5	4		10
6	2		4	4		11
6	3		5	2		
10	3		7	3		

Before continuing, it might help to comment on how the constant δ might be chosen. In terms of making judgments about some appropriate value for δ, it might facilitate matters by considering the "slippage" configuration of the means. This just means that

$$\mu_1=\mu_2=\ldots=\mu_{J-1},$$

but that $\mu_J>\mu_{J-1}$. The point is that it might help to consider how much power you want for some value of $\mu_J-\mu_{J-1}$. If you want the power to be .8 say when $\mu_J-\mu_{J-1}=a$, where a is some constant you have picked, then

$$\delta=(J-1)(a/J)^2 + [(J-1)a/J]^2.$$

For instance, if the measurements you are taking have values between 0 and 10, and if a difference of 1 between the largest and second largest mean is judged to be important, you would set a=1, and so for J=3 treatment groups, $\delta=6/9$.

The next step is determining a constant d that determines how much power will be achieved when the null hypothesis is tested with equation (8.12.2) below. To determine d, let Z be a standard normal random variable and choose z such that

$$\Pr(Z\le z)=\beta.$$

Next compute

$$b=(n-3)c/(n-1),$$

$$A=\{-z(\sqrt{2}) + [2z^2+4(2b-J+2)]^{1/2}\}/2,$$

$$B=A^2-b.$$

Then d is given approximately by

$$d=(n-3)(\delta/B)/(n-1) \qquad (8.12.2)$$

(Wilcox, 1986b).

The Second Stage

Next you determine the total number of observations needed for the j<u>th</u> treatment group. This is

$$n_j=\max\{n+1,\ (s_j^2/d)^{\dagger}+1\} \qquad (8.12.3)$$

where $s_j{}^2$ is the sample variance for the j<u>th</u> treatment group, and

$(s_j^2/d)^\dagger$ is the integer portion of s_j^2/d. That is, $(s_j^2/d)^\dagger$ is always computed by rounding s_j^2/d down to the nearest integer. The term "max" means to use the larger of the quantities inside the braces. That is, n_j equals n+1 or $(s_j^2/d)^\dagger+1$, whichever is largest. The s_j^2 values in the illustration are reported in Table 8.12.1, and so for d=.16, $s_1^2/d=33.94$, in which case $(s_1^2/d)^\dagger=33$, and $n=\max\{11,34\}=34$. This says that a total of 34 observations are needed for the first treatment group. You already have n=10 observations, so an additional 34-10=24 observations are required. Similarly, $n_2=33$, $n_3=18$, and so 23 and 8 additional observations are sampled from the second and third treatment groups. The resulting observations used in the illustration are shown in the bottom of Table 8.12.1.

Let

$$T_j=\Sigma_{i=1}^{n}X_{ij}$$

be the sum of the observations in the first stage of the jth treatment group. In the illustration $T_1=41$, $T_2=47$, and $T_3=82$. Also let

$$U_j=\Sigma_{i=n+1}^{n_j}X_{ij}$$

be the sum of the observations in second stage for the jth group. From Table 8.12.1, $U_1=92$, $U_2=92$ and $U_3=66$. Next, for each j, j=1,...,J, compute

$$b_j=n_j^{-1}\{1+ (1/s_j)[n(n_jd-s_j^2)/(n_j-n)]^{1/2}\} \qquad (8.12.4)$$

$$\tilde{X}_j=T_j\{1-(n_j-n)b_j\}/n + b_jU_j \qquad (8.12.5)$$

$$\tilde{X}=\Sigma_j\tilde{X}_j/J \qquad (8.12.6)$$

and

$$\tilde{F}=\Sigma(\tilde{X}_j-\tilde{X})^2/d. \qquad (8.12.7)$$

Note that in equation (8.12.4), s_j^2 is the sample variance based on the first stage data only. That is,

$$s_j^2=\Sigma_{i=1}^{n}(X_{ij}-T_j/n)^2/(n-1).$$

You reject H_0 if

$$\tilde{F}>c \quad (8.12.8)$$

where c was previously determined from (8.12.1). For the case at hand calculations show that $b_1=.03$, $b_2=.034$, and $b_3=.058$. For d=.16, say, this leads to

$$\tilde{X}_1=3.91,\ \tilde{X}_2=4.15,\ \tilde{X}_3=5.44 \text{ and } \tilde{F}=72.8,$$

and since 72.8>c, reject H_0.

Unequal Sample Sizes in the First Stage

There is a simple yet accurate method for handling unequal sample sizes in the first stage (Wilcox, 1986a). Suppose that in the first stage you have n_{0j} observations sampled from the j<u>th</u> group. Let $\nu_j=n_{0j}-1$ and compute

$$\nu=\{J/\Sigma[1/(\nu_j-2)]\} + 2. \tag{8.12.9}$$

Then the critical value, c, is determined as before, assuming that in the first stage you have $n=\nu+1$ observations in each of the J groups. For example, if in the first stage you have J=8 groups with sample sizes 10,10,10,10,10,10,10,80, then $\nu=9.9$ and the critical value, for $\alpha=.05$, is approximately c=17.63 using the chi-square approximation, while Hochberg's procedure yields c=19.4. Once c is determined, you compute d using (8.12.2). For example, if $\delta=7/8$, d=.038.

You also compute $\tilde{F}$ in a slightly different fashion. Suppose that in the first stage you sample m_j observations from the j<u>th</u> group. Rather than using equations (8.12.4) and (8.12.5), you now use

$$b_j=n_j^{-1}\{1+ (1/s_j)[m_j(n_jd-s_j^2)/(n_j-m_j)]^{1/2}\}$$

$$\tilde{X}_j=T_j\{1-(n_j-m_j)b_j\}/m_j + b_jU_j.$$

That is, you simply replace n in equations (8.12.4) and (8.12.5) with m_j when computing $\tilde{X}_j$. Otherwise the calculations are the same.

Comments on Choosing n

In theory any value for n can be used in the first stage. However, the normality assumption will almost certainly be violated in most situations, at least to some extent, and to minimize the effects of violating this assumption you will not want n to be too small. Simulation studies indicate that a crude rule for choosing n is to use n=25 if you want the actual Type I error probability to be within .01 of the nominal α level for typical departures from normality. For n=15 the difference between actual and nominal levels will be more like .015 (Wilcox, 1985).

Moshman (1958) and Seelbinder (1953) consider the effect of n on the expected number of observations required in the second stage. Unfortunately the answer depends on the unknown variances, and so their results would seem to have more theoretical than practical value.

Some Practical Considerations When Using a Two-Stage ANOVA Procedure

Although the two-stage ANOVA procedure just described has the advantage of handling unequal variances and controlling power, in some situations it may be difficult to obtain an additional sample of subjects, and for the procedure given here at least one more observation must be sampled beyond the n subjects sampled in the first stage. A simple way to always include the possibility of not having to sample any more subjects is to simply analyze only the first n-1 subjects in the first stage, and reserve the last subject for the second stage. If it turns out that n_j=n, no additional subjects are needed. An obvious objection to this procedure is that it is inefficient in the sense that only n-1 subjects are used in the first stage to estimate σ_j^2 when in fact n subjects were available.

Summary of Calculations

The steps and calculations for the $\tilde{F}$ test are summarized as follows:

(1) Randomly assign n subjects to the J treatment groups and compute the sample variances for each group.

(2) Determine a critical value c using Table A6, or the Hochberg approximation, or (8.12.1), and choose a value for $\delta=\Sigma\alpha_j^2$. The constant δ is used when determining power. If there are unequal sample sizes in the first stage, determine c via (8.12.9)

(3) Determine d using (8.12.2).

(4) For the jth treatment group sample an additional n_j-n observations where n_j is determined from (8.12.3).

(5) Compute $\tilde{F}$ using equations (8.12.4) through (8.12.7).

(6) If $\tilde{F}$>c, reject.

Comments on Why the $\tilde{F}$ Test Works

A few brief comments will be made about the theory behind the $\tilde{F}$ test. Stein (1945) showed that the random variable

$$(\tilde{X}_j-\mu_j)/\surd d$$

has a Student's t distribution with n-1 degrees of freedom. Bishop and Dudewicz (1978) pointed out that as a result, $\tilde{F}$ is distributed as

$$\Sigma[T_j-\bar{T}-(\mu_j-\mu)/\surd d]^2$$

where T_j is a Student's t random variable with n-1 degrees of freedom, and $\bar{T}=\Sigma T_j/J$. When H_0 is true

$$\tilde{F}=\Sigma(T_j-\bar{T})^2.$$

The approximations used to determine the critical value c and the constant d are based on these results.

EXERCISES

8.1 Suppose you are considering three brands of ice cream, and you want to know whether the amount of fat differs among the three brands. To find out you take n=3 samples for each of the J=3 brands and observe

Brand A	Brand B	Brand C
28	34	20
18	33	24
30	38	26

Assume equal variances and test $H_0:\mu_1=\mu_2=\mu_3$ with the F test. Use $\alpha=.05$. What is the unbiased estimate of σ^2?

8.2 Using the data in problem 8.1, use the Brown-Forsythe procedure to test for equal variances. Use $\alpha=.05$.

8.3 Repeat 8.1, but use the statistics W, F^* AND H given by equations (8.6.1), (8.6.2) and (8.6.3). If you can, also use James' second order method.

8.4 Assume equal variances and compute ω^2 using the data in problem 8.1.

8.5 In problem 8.1, assume the three brands of ice cream have been randomly sampled from among a larger number of brands.

a) Would you conclude that there is difference among the brands?

b) Compute a 95% confidence interval for ρ_I.

8.6 If n=3 and J=5, what is the critical value for the Bishop-Dudewicz ANOVA procedure? Use α=.05

8.7 Suppose J=4, n=15, β=.15, α=.01 and δ=1.0.
a) Use equation (8.12.2) to determine the constant d in the Bishop-Dudewicz ANOVA.
b) If the sample variances are s_1^2=1.2, s_2^2=4.0, s_3^2=12.0, s_4^2=28, and d=.039, how many additional observations are needed from each treatment group when applying the Bishop-Dudewicz ANOVA?

8.8 Assume equal variances, SSBG=450, SSWG=700, J=3 and n=5. What is the unbiased estimate of σ^2?

8.9 You want to apply the Bishop-Dudewicz ANOVA. Your initial sample sizes are 10,10,20,20,40,40,80, and 80. Compute ν, the critical value using both the chi-square and Hochberg procedures, assuming α=.05, and compute d assuming δ=7/8.

References

Bishop, T. (1. (1976) Heteroscedastic ANOVA, MANOVA and multiple comparisons. Unpublished PhD thesis, The Ohio State University.

Bishop, T. & Dudewicz, E. (1978) Exact analysis of variance with unequal variances: Test procedures and tables. Technometrics, 20, 419-420.

Bishop, T., Dudewicz, E. Juritz, J. & Stevens, M. (1978) Percentage points of a quadratic form in Student t variates. Biometrika, 65, 435-439.

Box, G. E. P. (1954) Some theorems on quadratic forms applied in the study of analysis of variance problems, I. Effect of inequality of variance in the one-way model. The Annals of Mathematical Statistics, 25, 290-302.

Bradley, J. V. (1978) Robustness? Journal of Mathematical and Statistical Psychology, 31, 144-152.

Bradley, J. V. (1980) Nonrobustness in Z, t, and F tests at large samples. Bulletin of the Psychonomic Society, 16, 333-336.

Bratcher, T. L., Moran, M. A. & Zimmer, W. J. (1970) Tables of sample sizes in the analysis of variance. Journal of Quality Technology, 9, 391-401.

Brown, M. & Forsythe, A. (1974a) The small sample behavior of some statistics which test the equality of several means. Technometrics, 16, 129-132.

Brown, M. & Forsythe, A. (1974b) Robust tests for the equality of variances. Journal of the American Statistical Association,

69, 364-367.
Clinch, J. & Keselman H. (1982) Parametric alternatives to the analysis of variance. Journal of Educational Statistics, 7, 207-214
Cohen, J. (1966) Some statistical issues in psychological research In B. B. Wolman (Ed.) Handbook of Clinical Psychology. New York: McGraw-Hill.
Cohen, J. (1977) Statistical power analysis for the behavioral sciences. New York: Academic Press.
Conover, W., Johnson, M. & Johnson, M. (1981) A comparative study of tests for homogeneity of variances, with applications to the outer continental shelf bidding data. Technometrics, 23, 351-361.
Dijkstra, J. & Werter, P. (1981) Testing the equality of several means when the population variances are unequal. Communications in Statistics--Simulation and Computation, B10, 557-569.
Donner, A. & Wells, G. (1986) A comparison of confidence interval methods for the intraclass correlation coefficient. Biometrics, 42, 401-412.
Fenstad, G. U. (1983) A comparison between U and V tests in the Behrens-Fisher problem. Biometrika, 70, 300-302.
Friedman, H. (1968) Magnitude of experimental effect and a table for its rapid estimation. Psychological Bulletin, 86, 978-984.
Games, P., Keselman, H. & Clinch, J. (1979) Tests for homogeneity of variance in factorial designs. Psychological Bulletin, 86, 978-984.
Hays, W. (1973) Statistics for the social sciences. New York: Holt, Rinehart and Winston.
Hedges, L. (1981) Distribution theory for Glass's estimation of effect size and related estimators. Journal of Statistics, 6, 107-128.
Hochberg, Y. (1975) Simultaneous inference under Behrens-Fisher conditions a two sample approach. Coomunications in Statistics, 4, 1109-1119.
Hsu, P. (1938) Contribution to the theory of "Student's" t-test as applied to the problem of two samples. Statistical Research Memoirs, 2, 1-24.
James, G.S. (1951) The comparison of several groups of observations when the ratios of the population variances are unknown. Biometrika, 38, 324-329.
Keppel, G. (1973) Design and analysis: A researcher's handbook Englewood Cliffs, New Jersey: Prentice-Hall
Kirk, R. (1982) Experimental design: Procedures for the behavioral sciences Belmont: Brooks/Cole.
Lee, A. & Gurland, J. (1975) Size and power of tests for equality

of means of two populations with unequal variances. Journal of the American Statistical Association, 70, 933-941.

Levene, H. (1960) Robust tests for the equality of variances. In I. Olkin (Ed.) Contributions to probability and statistics Palo Alto, CA: Stanford University Press.

Martin, C. & Games, P. (1977) ANOVA tests for homogeneity of variance: Nonnormality and unequal samples. Journal of Educational Statistics, 2, 187-206.

Moshman, J. (1958) A method for selecting the size of the initial sample in Stein's two sample procedure. Annals of Mathematical Statistics, 29, 1271-1275.

O'Brien, R. (1978) Robust techniques for testing heterogeneity of variance effects in factorial designs. Psychometrika, 43, 327-342.

O'Brien, R. (1979) A general ANOVA method for robust tests of additive models for variances. Journal of the American Statistical Association, 74, 877-88-.

O'Grady, K. (1982) Measures of explained variance: Cautions and limitations. Psychological Bulletin, 92, 766-777.

Ramsey, P. (1980) Exact type I error rates for robustness of Student's t-test with unequal variances. Journal of Educational Statistics, 5, 337-349.

Rogan, J. & Keselman, H. (1977) Is the ANOVA F-test robust to variance heterogeneity when sample sizes are equal?: An investigation via a coefficient of variation. American Educational Research Journal, 14, 493-498.

Roth, A. J. (1983) Robust trend tests derived and simulated: Analogs of the Welch and Brown-Forsythe tests. Journal of the American Statistical Association, 78, 972-980.

Satterthwaite, F. (1941) Synthesis of variance. Psychometrika, 6, 309-316.

Scheffe, H. (1959) The analysis of variance New York: Wiley

Schrader, R. & Hettmansperger, T. (1980) Robust analysis of variance based upon a likelihood ratio criterion. Biometrika, 67, 93-101

Seelbinder, B. (1953) On Stein's two-stage sampling scheme. Annals of Mathematical Statistics, 24, 640-649.

Stein, C. (1945) A two-sample test for a linear hypothesis whose power is independent of the variance. Annals of Mathematical Statistics, 16, 243-258.

Still, A. & White (1981) The approximate randomization test as an alternative to the F test in analysis of variance. British Journal of Mathematical and Statistical Psychology, 34, 243-252.

Tan, W. (1982) Sampling distributions and robustness of t, F and variance-ratio in two samples and ANOVA models with respect to departure from normality. *Communications in Statistics--Theory and Methods*, 11, 2485-2511.

Tomarken, A. & Serlin, R. (1986) Comparison of ANOVA alternatives under variance heterogeneity and specific noncentrality structures. *Psychological Bulletin*, 99, 90-99.

Welch, B. (1951) On the comparison of several mean values: An alternative approach. *Biometrika*, 38, 330-336.

Wilcox, R. (1985) The effects of skewness and kurtosis on three heteroscedastic ANOVA procedures that control power. *Journal of Organizational Behavior and Statistics*, 2, 29-36.

Wilcox, R. (1986a) A heteroscedastic ANOVA procedure with specified power. *Journal of Educational Statistics*, to appear

Wilcox, R. (1986b) Controlling power in a heteroscedastic ANOVA procedure. *British Journal of Mathematical and Statistical Psychology*, 39, 65-68.

Wilcox, R., Charlin, V. & Thompson, K. (1986) New monte carlo results on the robustness of the ANOVA F, W and F^* statistics. *Communications in Statistics--Simulation and Computation*, 15, 933-944.

Wilcox, R. (1987a) New designs in analysis of variance. *Annual Review of Psychology*, 38, 29-60.

Wilcox, R. R. (1987b) A new solution to testing the equality of means when the variances are unequal. Unpublished technical report.

CHAPTER NINE

MULTIPLE COMPARISONS

Multiple comparison procedures are techniques for comparing the means of J normal distributions just as was the case for the F test in chapter eight. The difference is that the F test is used to make a single decision about whether an entire set of equalities is consistent with data, while multiple comparison procedures are used to make several (multiple) decisions, one corresponding to each equality of interest. For example, the F test is used to test whether all of the parametric functions (defined in chapter eight) $\Psi_1,\ldots,\Psi_q$ are equal to zero, while multiple comparison procedures are concerned with making a decision for each Ψ_j $(j=1,\ldots,q)$. Of particular of interest is the set of all pairwise comparisons where for each k<j a decision is made about whether $\mu_k=\mu_j$.

9.1 COMMENTS ON A TYPICAL PROCEDURE

It has been a common practice to apply multiple comparison procedures only if a significant F test has already been obtained. In fact many popular books still advocate this approach. However, this practice has certain consequences which need to be considered, and they are described and illustrated in section 9.5. For now simply note that you may want to apply multiple comparison procedures regardless of whether you have already obtained a significant F test, and in fact there may be situations where multiple comparison procedures are applied without applying the F test at all. Before describing why and when this might be done, it will help to first describe the procedures that are most likely to be used; this is done in section 9.3, but first some preliminary concepts are needed.

9.2 EXPERIMENTWISE TYPE I ERROR

As just indicated, chapter eight was concerned with performinging a single overall test of whether a certain set of equalities are reasonable in light of the observations you have. In particular there was

$$H_0:\mu_1=\ldots=\mu_J, \tag{9.2.1}$$

and the critical value of the resulting F test was chosen so that the Type I error probability would be exactly α under normality and equal variances. As was pointed out, the F test actually tests much more than (9.2.1), but the point is that a <u>single</u> test is performed, and the probability of a Type I error is α.

Suppose instead you want to make all pairwise comparisons of the means. That is, you want to make a decision about whether $\mu_1=\mu_2$, and then make a decision about $\mu_1=\mu_3$, etc. Thus, for all $k<j$ the goal is to test

$$H_0: \mu_k = \mu_j. \tag{9.2.2}$$

For example, if J=3, there are three hypotheses of interest, namely,

$$H_0: \mu_1 = \mu_2,$$

$$H_0: \mu_1 = \mu_3,$$

and

$$H_0: \mu_2 = \mu_3,$$

and a decision about each is to be made. When all pairwise comparisons are made among J means, (9.2.2) involves J(J-1)/2 comparisons. Pairwise comparison of means is frequently of interest, but of course testing and rejecting (9.2.1) does not tell you which means are unequal.

Let's suppose you have some procedure for making all J(J-1)/2 comparisons in (9.2.2). For example, the usual t test might be used. For each comparison made there is the possibility of making a Type I error, which will be called the pairwise Type I error probability. More generally you might have q parametric functions of interest, and so q comparisons or tests will be made. The experimentwise (sometimes called the familywise) Type I error probability is the probability of at least one Type I error among all the comparisons being made.

The general problem is that the more comparisons you make with the t-test, the larger will be the probability of at least one Type I error. This is illustrated in section 9.5. The practical implication is that if you perform enough tests, you will probably get a significant result even when all the means are equal. As a result, there has been a considerable effort by statisticians to determine and control the experimentwise Type I probability, and the best of these procedures are described in the next section. Whenever necessary, α_e is used to distinguish the experimentwise Type I error probability from α, the pairwise error rate. When there is no chance of confusion, α_e is written simply as α.

9.3 DESCRIPTION OF MULTIPLE COMPARISON PROCEDURES

The choice of a multiple comparison procedure is a fairly complex issue, which is discussed in sections 9.4 and 9.5. The only goal here is to simply describe the procedures that are most likely to be used.

Fisher's Least Significant Difference Test

The first multiple comparison procedure is Fisher's least significant difference (LSD) test (Fisher, 1949, pp. 56-58). The goal is to perform all pairwise comparisons of the means, as described in (9.2.2), and this is accomplished by simply performing a t-test for each of the pairwise comparisons being made, provided that a significant F test has already been obtained. Assuming equal variances and equal n's, simply compute

$$T_{kj}=|\bar{X}_k-\bar{X}_j|/[2MSWG/n]^{1/2}$$

for every k and j, where k<j. The degrees of freedom are $\nu=J(n-1)$, and if t is the $1-\alpha/2$ quantile of the t distribution with ν degrees of freedom, reject $H_0: \mu_k=\mu_j$ if $T_{kj}>t$. For unequal n's use

$$T_{kj}=|\bar{X}_k-\bar{X}_k|/[MSWG(1/n_k + 1/n_j)]^{1/2},$$

where now $\nu=N-J$, and $N=\Sigma n_j$. (As in the previous chapter, n_j is the number of observations sampled from the j<u>th</u> group.)

An important property of Fisher's multiple comparison procedure is that it does not give you control over α_e, the experimentwise Type I error probability, if J>2, and it is applied without first obtaining a significant F test. In fact, as indicated in section 9.5, α_e can be substantially larger than α for J as small as 4. You can easily avoid this problem by using Fisher's test only after a significant F test. In this case, simulation studies suggest that the experimentwise Type I error probability will be closer to α <u>if the variances are equal</u>, but results in Hayter (1986) show that Fisher's LSD procedure can still be unsatisfactory. Perhaps a more serious problem with Fisher's LSD test is that equal variances are assumed. As pointed out in the previous chapter, if the variances are unequal, the actual Type I error probability of the t-test can be substantially different from the nominal level, and unequal variances can affect power as well. Hayter (1986) proposed an improvement on Fisher's LSD test, but equal variances were assumed.

Dunn's Procedure

Consider any q linear contrasts

$$\Psi_k=\Sigma_j c_{jk}\mu_j,\ k=1,\ldots,q,$$

and suppose that for each contrast you want to make a decision about whether

$$H_0:\Psi_k=0 \tag{9.3.2}$$

is reasonable. Again equal variances are assumed. A solution, similar to Fisher's LSD test, is to compute

$$T_k=\hat{\Psi}/[\text{MSWG}\{\Sigma_j(c_{jk}^2/n_j)\}]^{1/2} \tag{9.3.3}$$

where

$$\hat{\Psi}_k=\Sigma c_{jk}\bar{X}_j$$

is the unbiased estimate of Ψ_k, and then compare $|T_k|$ to the $1-\alpha/2$ quantile of the t distribution with N-J degrees of freedom.

As noted in chapter eight, a proper choice of the c_{jk}'s reduces (9.3.3) to Fisher's LSD test. Again, though, there is the problem that the experimentwise Type I error probability will exceed α for $q>1$. Moreover, even if the $\hat{\Psi}_k$ random variables are independent of one another, the T_k's will be dependent because each is a function of MSWG. As a result, there is no simple way of determining or controlling α_e exactly, but it is a simple matter to ensure that $\alpha_e\le\alpha$. Applying the Bonferroni inequality, it can be seen that if (9.3.3) is rejected whenever

$$|T_k|>t_{\alpha/2q,\nu}, \tag{9.3.4}$$

the $\alpha/2q$ quantile of Student's t distribution with ν=N-J degrees of freedom, then $\alpha_e\le\alpha$. That is, the experimentwise Type I error probability will not exceed α if each test is performed at the α/q level. Moreover, this result is true regardless of whether the $\hat{\Psi}_k$'s are independent of one another. Experience with the Bonferroni inequality indicates that for small α, α_e will be nearly equal to α if each comparison is made at the α/q level, but as α increases, so will the discrepancy between α and α_e.

Dunn (1961) was the first to propose that the critical value be adjusted via the Bonferroni inequality, and she provided some adjusted critical values. (Her procedure is sometimes called the Bonferroni t-test.) An improved table of critical values can be found in Table A7. For a more extensive table, see Dayton and Schafer (1973).

Example 9.3.1 As a simple illustration, suppose you want to test q=3 linear contrasts, namely,

$$H_0: \Psi_1 = \mu_1 - \mu_2 = 0$$

$$H_0: \Psi_2 = \mu_1 - \mu_3 = 0$$

and

$$H_0: \Psi_3 = \mu_2 - (\mu_3 + \mu_4)/2 = 0$$

where there are four groups. The contrast coefficients are (1,-1,0,0), (1,0,-1,0), and (0,1,-1/2,-1/2). Suppose the observations yield the values shown in Table 9.3.1. Then

$$T_1 = \{(1)(4) + (-1)(5)\}/\{10[(1)^2/20 + (-1)^2/20]\}^{1/2}$$

$$= -1,$$

$$T_2 = \{(1)(4) + (-1)(7)\}/\{10[(1)^2/20 + (-1)^2/20]\}^{1/2},$$

$$= -3,$$

and

$$T_3 = \{(1)(5) + (-1/2)(7) + (-1/2)(8)\}/$$

$$\{10[(1)^2/20 + (-1/2)^2/20 + (-1/2)^2/20]\}$$

$$= -3.33.$$

Suppose you want α_e to be at most .05. Since there are q=3 comparisons, Table A7 says that the critical value is approximately 2.45, where $\nu = J(n-1) = 76$. Continuing the calculations, $|T_1| = 1$, $|T_2| = 3$, and $|T_3| = 3.33$, so reject H_0 for both Ψ_2 and Ψ_3.

Table 9.3.1
Sample Data for J=4 Treatment Groups

$\bar{X}_1 = 4$, $\bar{X}_2 = 5$, $\bar{X}_3 = 7$, $\bar{X}_4 = 8$

$s_1^2 = 6.3$, $s_2^2 = 13.7$, $s_3^2 = 4.1$, $s_4^2 = 15.9$

$n_1 = n_2 = n_3 = n_4 = 20$, MSWG=10.0

Dunn-Sidak Procedure

More recently Dunn (1974) improved upon the Bonferroni t-test by employing an inequality derived by Sidak (1967). Again the homogeneity of variance assumption is adopted. For $\alpha \leq .01$ the improvement is negligible, but otherwise it is preferable to Dunn's procedure based on the Bonferroni inequality. The calculations are exactly the same as in Dunn's test. The only difference between the two procedures is that the Dunn-Sidak procedure uses Table A10 rather than Table A7. (For a more extensive table of critical values, see Bechhofer & Dunnett, 1982.) Games (1977) also reported some critical values using a slightly different approach than the one used to derive Table A10, but the values in Table A10 are uniformly better.

Consider again example 9.3.1. From Table A10 the critical value is approximately 2.45, whereas before it was 2.46. Again the experimentwise Type I error probability is at most .05 (assuming equal variances). This illustrates that the Dunn-Sidak test will have more power than Dunn's test. An important point is that Table A10 can only be used to perform two-sided (two-tailed) tests. If you want to perform one-sided tests, the percentage points in Krishnaiah and Armitage (1966) should be used.

Scheffe's Test

Scheffe (1953) proposed still another method of testing linear contrasts. However, rather than testing q specific linear contrasts, as in the Dunn and Dunn-Sidak techniques, all possible linear contrasts can be tested with the property that the experimentwise Type I error probability will be α_e. As in previous procedures, equal variances are assumed.

This time you compute

$$S=\{(J-1)(f)(MSWG)\Sigma c_j^2/n_j\}^{1/2} \qquad (9.3.5)$$

where f is the $1-\alpha_e$ quantile of the F distribution with J-1 and N-J degrees of freedom. The quantity f is read from Table A3. The confidence interval for Ψ is

$$(\hat{\Psi}-S,\ \hat{\Psi}+S).$$

If this interval does not contain zero, reject $H_0:\Psi=0$.

The Kaiser-Bowden Procedure

Brown and Forsythe (1974) proposed a modification of Scheffe's procedure that is less sensitive to unequal variances, but Kaiser and Bowden (1983) found that the Brown-Forsythe procedure can exceed the nominal α level. Kaiser and Bowden (1983) proposed a simple modification of the Brown-Forsythe procedure that, from their simulation studies, appears to be more satisfactory. To apply it, compute

$$\nu_2'=[\Sigma c_j^2 s_j^2/n_j]^2/ [\Sigma c_j^4 s_j^4/(n_j^2(n_j-1))] \tag{9.3.5a}$$

$$A=(J-1)[1+(J-2)/\nu_2']f$$

where f is the 1-α quantile of the F distribution with ν_1 and ν_2' degrees of freedom where ν_1=J-1 and ν_2' is given by (9.3.5a). This is in contrast to Scheffe's procedure where the degrees of freedom were ν_1 and ν_2. The confidence interval for Ψ is

$$\Psi \pm \{A\Sigma c_j^2 s_j^2/n_j\}^{1/2}.$$

<u>Example 9.3.2</u>. Consider again $\Psi=\mu_2-\mu_3/2-\mu_4/2$, which was tested with Dunn's procedure, but this time suppose Scheffe's procedure is applied instead. For the data in Table 9.3.1 with α=.05, f=2.74 (ν_1=3 and ν_2=76), and so

$$\hat{\Psi}=5-(1/2)(7)-(1/2)(8)=-2.5,$$

and

$$S=\{3(2.74)[10((1)^2/20 + (-1/2)^2/20 + (-1/2)^2/20)]\}^{1/2}$$

$$=[(8.22)(.75)]^{1/2}$$

$$=2.483.$$

Thus, $\hat{\Psi}\pm S=-2.5\pm 2.483$, and the confidence interval is

(-4.983, -0.017).

If instead the Kaiser-Bowden procedure is used,

$$\nu_2'=B/C,$$

where

$$B=[1^2(13.7)+(1/2)^2(4.1)+(1/2)^2(15.91)]/20^2$$

$=(18.7025)^2/20^2$
$=.8744587$

$C=[1^4(13.7)^2+(1/2)^4(4.1)^2+(1/2)^4(15.91)^2]/[20^2(19)]$
$=.0269157$

so

$\nu_2'=32.49.$

Thus,

$A=3(1+2/32.49)(2.91)=9.2674,$

$[9.2674(18.7025)/20]^{1/2}=2.945$

and the confidence interval is

$(-5.4,\ 0.445).$

Dalal (1975) as well as Hochberg (1976) also proposed alternatives to Scheffe's procedure that handle unequal variances. The extent to which they give better solutions than the Kaiser-Bowden procedure is not known.

A Welch-Bonferroni Test for q Linear Contrasts

If Ψ_k (k=1,...,q) are q linear contrasts, and the variances are not equal, an approximate solution for testing $H_0:\Psi_k=0$ (k=1,...,q) can be obtained using Welch's adjusted degrees of freedom ν_2' given by equation (9.3.5a), and then testing each hypothesis at the α/q level. Note that the term c_j^2 in equation (9.3.5a) is replaced with c_{jk}^2. Once ν_2' is calculated, compute

$$T_k=\Sigma_j c_{jk}\bar{X}_k/[\Sigma_j c_{jk}^2 s_j^2/n_j]^{1/2}.$$

If $|T_k|>t$ where t is read from Table A7 with ν_2' degrees of freedom, reject $H_0:\Psi=0$. For an illustration of this procedure, see section 10.2. If you want to test $H_0:\Psi=0$, and for this specific contrast you want the probability of a Type I error to be exactly α, and the probability of a Type II error to be exactly β, the two-stage procedure described by Wilcox and Chao (1985) can be used. Except for Fisher's LSD test, all of the procedures described so far can be used to determine confidence intervals for any set of q linear contrasts.

Welch-Dunn-Sidak Procedure for q Linear Contrasts

The Welch-Dunn-Sidak procedure is applied in the same way as the Welch-Bonferroni procedure except that you use Table A10 rather than Table A7. From simulation results based on all pairwise comparisons, this procedure would seem to be better than the Welch-Bonferroni, but more research is needed to determine whether this is indeed the case.

A Modified Simes-Welch Procedure

Still another procedure can be used that is motivated by results in Simes (1986). Let

$$A_k = \Sigma_j c_{jk} \bar{X}_k / [\Sigma_j c_{jk}^2 s_j^2 / n_j]^{1/2},$$

and let

$$P_k = \Pr\{-A_k \le T \le A_k\} \qquad (k=1,\ldots,q)$$

where T is a Student's t random variable with ν_2' degrees of freedom. P_k is called the significance level (or p-value) of the test of $H_0:\Psi_k=0$. (As before, ν_2' is given by equation 9.3.5a.) Let

$$P_{(1)} \le P_{(2)} \le \ldots \le P_{(q)}$$

be the P_k values written in ascending order. Combining Simes results with the Welch adjusted degrees of freedom procedure indicates that $H_0:\Psi_m=0$ $(m=1,\ldots,q)$ is rejected if P_m is the k<u>th</u> largest significance level (i.e., $P_m=P_{(k)}$, and if

$$P_{(j)} \le j\alpha/q \text{ for } j=1,\ldots,k$$

where α is the experimentwise Type I error probability that you want. That is, you reject the hypothesis with the lowest significance level if the significance level is less than α/q. If you reject, go on to the hypothesis with the next lowest significance level and reject if it is significant at the $2\alpha/q$ level, etc. Once a nonsignificant result is obtained, you stop and fail to reject the remaining hypotheses. This procedure has more power than the Welch-Bonferroni procedure, and the actual experimentwise Type I error probability is generally closer to the nominal level. For alternatives to the modified Simes procedure described here, see Shaffer (1986) and Holm (1979). The modified Simes procedure can be shown to have more power than the procedure proposed by Holm. Comparisons with Shaffer's procedure have not been made.

The remainder of the procedures in this section were developed specifically for making all pairwise comparisons, i.e., for determining simultaneous 1-α confidence intervals for $\mu_j - \mu_k$, $k<j$, which can be used to test $H_0: \mu_k = \mu_j$ for all $k<j$.

Tukey's Procedure

In addition to equal variances, Tukey's procedure requires equal sample sizes per treatment group. It is applied by computing

$$T = q_{\alpha,J,\nu}[\text{MSWG}/n]^{1/2} \qquad (9.3.6)$$

where n is the number of observations per treatment group, $\nu = J(n-1)$, and $q_{\alpha,J,\nu}$ is read from Table A9. The confidence interval for $\mu_k - \mu_j$ is

$$(\bar{X}_k - \bar{X}_j - T,\ \bar{X}_k - \bar{X}_j + T).$$

If this interval does not contain zero, reject $H_0: \mu_k = \mu_j$.

A particularly important characteristic of this procedure is that it provides an exact 100(1-α)% simultaneous confidence interval for all pairs of means. That is,

$$\Pr(\bar{X}_k - \bar{X}_j - T \le \mu_k - \mu_j \le \bar{X}_k - \bar{X}_j + T) = 1 - \alpha$$

provided the variances are equal. This means that among all the pairwise comparisons, the experimentwise Type I error probability is exactly α. Thus, Tukey's procedure gives you better control over the Type I error probability than does Dunn's procedure or the Dunn-Sidak procedure, where all that could be said was that the experimentwise Type I error probability is at most α. The advantage of the Dunn and Dunn-Sidak procedures is that they are not restricted to pairwise comparisons. It should also be mentioned that when making pairwise comparisons, Tukey's procedure is clearly better than Scheffe's (Stoline, 1981; Scheffe, 1959).

Tukey-Kramer Procedure

Kramer (1956) proposed a modification of Tukey's procedure for handling unequal sample sizes. It is still assumed, though, that the variances are equal. Instead of computing T with equation (9.3.6), use

$$T=q_{\alpha,J,\nu}[MSWG(1/n_k + 1/n_j)/2]^{1/2} \qquad (9.3.7)$$

where again $q_{\alpha,J,\nu}$ is read from Table A9 and ν=N-J. Otherwise the computations are the same as for Tukey's procedure.

It should be mentioned that this is only an approximate solution for handling unequal sample sizes. Hayter (1984) has shown that the actual experimentwise Type I error probability rate will be smaller than α when the variances are equal.

Dunnett's T3 and C Procedures

Simulation studies by Dunnett (1980b) revealed that the Tukey-Kramer procedure is sensitive to unequal variances, and several approximate solutions for handling unequal variances have been proposed (e.g., Games & Howell, 1976; Tamhane, 1979; Dunnett, 1980b). In terms of ensuring that the experimentwise Type I error probability does not exceed α, Stoline (1981) recommends that either Dunnett's T3 or C procedure be used.

For Dunnett's C procedure, the confidence interval for $\mu_k-\mu_j$ is

$$(\bar{X}_k-\bar{X}_j)\pm Q/\sqrt{2}$$

where

$$Q=A/B$$

$$A=(q_{\alpha,J,\nu_k} s_k^2/n_k + q_{\alpha,J,\nu_j} s_j^2/n_j),$$

$$B=[s_k^2/n_k + s_j^2/n_j]^{1/2},$$

$$\nu_k=n_k-1,\ \nu_j=n_j-1,$$

and q_{α,J,ν_j} is read from Table A9. Note that q is the same q used in Tukey's procedure.

Suppose that for the observations in Table 9.3.1 you want to test $H_0:\mu_1=\mu_2$. If the experimentwise Type I error probability for all pairwise comparisons is to be α=.05, then $\nu_1=\nu_2=19$, q=3.98 (J=4 and α=.05), and so Q=3.98/1.0=3.98. Then for k=1 and j=2,

$$\bar{X}_1-\bar{X}_2-Q/\surd 2=4-5-2.81 \text{ and } \bar{X}_1-\bar{X}_2+Q/\surd 2=1.81.$$

Thus, (-3.81, 1.81) is the confidence interval for $\mu_1-\mu_2$, the interval contains zero, and so $H_0:\mu_1=\mu_2$ would not be rejected.

Dunnett's T3

As for Dunnett's T3 procedure, the confidence interval is given by

$$\bar{X}_k-\bar{X}_j \pm V_{\alpha,C,\nu_{kj}}\{s_k^2/n_k + s_j^2/n_j\}^{1/2}$$

where V is read from Table A10, $C=(J^2-J)/2$ is the number of comparisons, and the degrees of freedom are

$$\nu_{kj}=[s_k^2/n_k + s_j^2/n_j]^2/ \{s_k^4/(n_k^2\nu_k) + s_j^4/(n_j^2\nu_j)\}$$

where again $\nu_k=n_k-1$, and $\nu_j=n_j-1$.

The choice between T3 and C depends on whether the degrees of freedom are large or small. For small degrees of freedom, use T3. There are no exact guidelines for deciding whether the degrees of freedom are small, but from Dunnett (1980b), if J=4, a rough guideline is to use T3 when the degrees of freedom are less than 50 for any treatment group; otherwise use Dunnett's C. The same recommendation applies for J=8, but other values of J were not considered in Dunnett's simulation study. Thus, it is tentatively recommended that T3 be used whenever $\nu_j<50$ for any j; otherwise use the C procedure or the Games-Howell procedure described below.

Games-Howell Procedure

The Games-Howell procedure uses the confidence interval

$$\bar{X}_k-\bar{X}_j \pm q_{\alpha,J,\nu_{kj}}\{[(s_j^2/n_j) + (s_k^2/n_k)]/2\}^{1/2}$$

where $q_{\alpha,J,\nu_{kj}}$ is read from Table A9, and where the degrees of freedom ν_{kj} are the same as they were in Dunnett's T3 procedure. As usual, if this interval does not contain zero, reject $H_0:\mu_k=\mu_j$.

A criticism of the Games-Howell procedure is that it can exceed the nominal α level. However, the simulation results reported by Dunnett (1980b) indicate that this only happens when the degrees of freedom are small. Stoline (1981) prefers Dunnett's C procedure to the Games-Howell procedure, but Dunnett's results suggest that when the observations are at least 50 in each group, the Games-Howell procedure does not exceed the nominal α, and is closer to the nominal α level than is Dunnett's C.

9.4 GUIDELINES FOR CHOOSING A MULTIPLE COMPARISON PROCEDURE

The first step in choosing a multiple comparison procedure is deciding whether your interest is restricted to all pairwise comparisons of the means, or whether other linear contrasts or even parametric functions are to be included. When attention is restricted to all pairwise comparisons, the following recommendations are made based on the information currently available.

Equal Variances

Suppose you want the experimentwise Type I error to be equal to α. If the sample sizes are equal, and if the homogeneity of variance assumption is met, use Tukey's procedure. If the sample sizes are not equal, use the Tukey-Kramer procedure. Stoline reports that the Tukey-Kramer procedure always gives shorter confidence intervals than the procedure proposed by Spjotvoll and Stoline (1973), and it compares favorably to a procedure proposed by Hunter (1976). For this reason, the Spjotvol-Stoline procedure and Hunter's procedure were not included in this chapter. The Tukey-Kramer test generally gives shorter confidence intervals than the Bonferroni t-test or Scheffe's test, but these latter two procedures can be useful when contrasts other than just pairwise comparisons are of interest. The most important point is that equal variances are being assumed, and simply testing for equal variances may not give a satisfactory indication of whether the Tukey or Tukey-Kramer procedure should be used. The problem is that tests for equal variances may not have enough power to detect unequal variances in situations where the assumption of unequal variances should be abandoned. A similar problem is associated with the F test as illustrated in chapter eight. For results indicating that the Tukey-Kramer procedure is sensitive to unequal variances, see Keselman and Rogan (1978) and Dunnett (1980b). In general it is recommended that multiple comparison procedures based on the assumption of equal variances never be used, and that procedures for unequal variances always be used instead.

Unequal Variances

Several approximate solutions have been proposed for handling unequal variances (Games & Howell, 1976; Tamhane, 1979; Dunnett, 1980b), and an exact two-stage solution is described in section 9.6. Among the procedures described above, when the sample sizes are equal, the best choices seem to be Dunnett's T3, C, or the Games-Howell procedure. T3 is generally better than the C or Games-Howell procedure when the degrees of freedom are less than or equal to 50; otherwise use the C procedure or the Games-Howell procedure. The Games-Howell procedure seems slightly preferable to Dunnett's C procedure when the degrees of freedom are large although an argument can be made for using Dunnett's C.

For unequal sample sizes there is less evidence about which procedure is best, but all indications are that the same advice applies that was given for the equal sample size case.

Example 9.4.1. To illustrate that different procedures can yield different results when using real data, consider the following data taken from Guthrie, Seifert, and Kirsch (1986). In one instance they reported the following results for J=4 treatment groups.

n_j:	18	33	30	19
$\bar{X}_j$:	27.06	30.37	18.40	15.84
s_j:	42.42	38.39	29.60	11.11

The Tukey-Kramer confidence interval for $\mu_1-\mu_3$ is (1.578, 15.742). Thus, you would reject $H_0:\mu_1=\mu_3$. However, using Dunnett's T3 the confidence interval is (-24.68, 42.00). For $\mu_1-\mu_4$, Tukey-Kramer gives (5.978, 17.962) while Dunnett's T3 gives (-11.41, 35.35).

Testing Parametric Functions

For linear contrasts and parametric functions other than all pairwise comparisons of the means, the Scheffe, Dunn, Dunn-Sidak, and Kaiser-Bowden procedures should be used. For unequal variances, use either the Simes-Welch, Welch-Bonferroni, the Welch-Dunn-Sidak, or the Kaiser-Bowden procedure. When the number of contrasts, q, is small, the Simes-Welch would seem to be best based on the information presently available, but for q large enough the Kaiser-Bowden procedure will give shorter confidence intervals. Perhaps there are situations where the Welch-Bonferroni is preferable to the Welch-Dunn-Sidak, but this hasn't been established.

For equal variances, the Dunn and Dunn-Sidak procedures will give shorter confidence intervals (and hence more power) than Tukey's or Scheffe's procedure when q, the number of contrasts, is small relative to J, the number of treatment groups. In practice these procedures should probably be avoided because they are sensitive to violations of the equal variance assumption. However, Dunn's procedure will be seen to play an important role in chapter eleven where repeated measures designs are discussed.

Effects of Non-normality

As was the case for the F test, multiple comparison procedures seem to be robust to departures from normality (Dunnett, 1982). For extreme departures from normality, see Dunnett (1982) and Ringland (1983).

9.5 THE EFFECT OF USING MULTIPLE COMPARISON PROCEDURES ONLY AFTER A SIGNIFICANT F TEST

As mentioned in section 9.1, it has been a common practice to apply multiple comparison procedures only if a significant F test has already been obtained. If your goal is to have the experimentwise Type I error rate exactly equal to α, or as close to α as possible, this practice may be highly unsatisfactory. There are two aspects to the problem. To describe the first, suppose observations are indeed sampled from normal distributions having equal variances, and suppose equal sample sizes are used. From the derivation of Tukey's test (e.g., Scheffe, 1959), it can be seen that the experimentwise Type I error probability is exactly α. But there is nothing in the derivation of Tukey's test that assumes you have already gotten a significant F test. That is, the experimentwise Type I error probability of Tukey's procedure is exactly α if you perform it regardless of whether the F test is significant.

The second aspect is that if you perform any multiple comparison procedure only after a significant F test, the Type I error probability will generally be smaller than if you perform the multiple comparison procedure without first performing the F test. (A possible exception is Scheffe's procedure.) For example, if Tukey's test is performed only after a significant F test has been obtained, the experimentwise Type I error probability will be smaller than α, in some cases by a substantial amount. This point is illustrated with the simulation results reported by Bernhardson (1975). Table 9.5.1 shows the experimentwise Type I error probability for Fisher's LSD, Tukey's test, and Scheffe's test using α=.05 when the multiple comparisons are performed only after a significant F test. The results are labeled α_2. As can be seen, as the number of treatment groups, J, increases, α_2 decreases. For example, if J=8, α_2 is approximately equal to .034 for Tukey's test. This implies that there will be less power when multiple comparison procedures are used only after a significant F test. A particularly interesting result is that Fisher's LSD test has an experimentwise Type I error probability that is closest to the nominal α level when J is large. However, this does not suggest that Fisher's LSD should be used because equal variances were assumed by Bernhardson, and because more research is needed to determine how well Fisher's LSD test compares to Dunnett's T3 and C as well as the Games-Howell procedure.

Table 9.5.1

Experimentwise Type I Error Probabilities When α=.05

	J=2		J=4		J=8		J=10	
	α_1	α_2	α_1	α_2	α_1	α_2	α_1	α_2
Fisher	.055	.055	.211	.051	.500	.050	.591	.050
Tukey	.055	.055	.053	.046	.049	.034	.049	.034
Scheffe	.055	.055	.025	.025	.003	.003	.003	.003

The quantity α_1 is the experimentwise Type I error probability when the multiple comparison procedure is applied regardless of the outcome of the F test. The second entry, α_2, is the probability when the multiple comparison procedure is applied only after F is significant.

Table 9.5.1 also shows the experimentwise Type I error probability without first performing an F test (the quantity α_1). Theory tells us that Tukey's procedure will have an experimentwise Type I error probability that is exactly equal to the nominal α level, and this gives some indication of the accuracy of Bernhardson's simulation study. The experimentwise Type I error probability of Fisher's LSD procedure is considerably larger than the nominal α value of .05. For example, if J=8, α_1=.591, and even with J=4, α_1=.211. This illustrates that in studies where nothing but t-tests are used, there can be a high probability of getting at least one significant result when in fact all the means are equal. Smith and Han (1981) derived a method for approximating the Type I error probability when a single linear contrast is tested only after a significant F test, but the results are rather complicated. Of course, in practice several comparisons are made and methods for dealing with this problem have not been developed.

Recommendations for Using Multiple Comparison Procedures in Conjunction with the F Test

If your only concern is making all pairwise comparisons of the means, and if you want the experimentwise Type I error probability to be equal to α, it is perfectly legitimate to omit the F test and use one of the multiple comparison procedures already described; the actual procedure you use can be determined from section 9.4. As illustrated in the previous section, most multiple comparison procedures are NOT derived under the assumption that a significant F test has already been obtained. Moreover, applying multiple comparison procedures only after a significant F test reduces power, and it reduces α by an amount that is difficult to determine. You may also want to test the hypothesis that no linear contrasts are equal to zero, in which case the F test (or some appropriate modification for handling unequal variances) can be used, but in order to ensure that a multiple comparison procedure has an experimentwise Type I error probability that is close to α, you should apply the procedure regardless of whether the F was significant.

Comments on Other Multiple Comparison Procedures

Two popular multiple comparison procedures were not included in this chapter, and perhaps this should be explained. The first is the Newman-Keuls, and the second is due to Duncan. Miller (1966, pp. 81-90) describes the history of these techniques.

From Bernhardson (1975) it appears that the Newman-Keuls and Tukey procedures have virtually indistinguishable Type I error probabilities. However, the experimentwise Type I error probability of the Newman-Keuls procedure can exceed α (Hartley, 1955). For an improvement of the Newman-Keuls procedure, see Begun and Gabriel (1981). As for Duncan's procedure, it performed in the same manner as Fisher's test when both were applied only after a significant F test. When Duncan's procedure is applied regardless of the outcome of the F test, the experimentwise Type I error probability is smaller than Fisher's LSD, but it is considerably larger than α for $J>2$. For related results, see Ramsey (1981).

9.6 EXACT MULTIPLE COMPARISON PROCEDURES THAT ALLOW UNEQUAL VARIANCES, CONTROL POWER, AND CONTROL THE LENGTH OF CONFIDENCE INTERVALS

A common feature of all the multiple comparison procedures discussed so far is that you compute a confidence interval for each of q linear contrasts that have the general form

$$\hat{\Psi} \pm A$$

where A is a random variable that is a function of your data. For example, Tukey's procedure is given by

$$\bar{X}_k - \bar{X}_j \pm q_{\alpha,J,\nu}[MSWG/n]^{1/2}$$

for all k<j where $q_{\alpha,J,\nu}[MSWG/n]^{1/2}$ plays the role of A.

The length of the confidence interval is 2A and it reflects the accuracy of your estimate of $\mu_k - \mu_j$ using $\bar{X}_k - \bar{X}_j$. A problem is that A is a function of the sample variance, and the larger the variance, the poorer is your estimate of Ψ. For instance, in Tukey's test MSWG estimates σ^2 using an average of the sample variances, and of course for a fixed sample size you have no control over how large MSWG might be. Thus, the length of the confidence interval, 2A, can be large by chance, and so what would be useful is a procedure that yields a confidence interval having a length that is more within your control. That is, what is needed is a procedure where you specify in advance how long of a confidence interval you are willing to allow.

A related problem is that none of the procedures described above give you precise control over power, and indeed for many of these procedures there are no simple yet accurate single-stage procedures for even approximating how many observations are required so that power will be reasonably close to 1 for a given value of $\mu_k - \mu_j$.

This section describes exact two-stage procedures for controlling power and the length of the confidence intervals while having the additional advantage of allowing the variances to be unequal. The solutions are highly related to the two-stage procedures given in chapter eight. First attention is focused on making all pairwise comparisons, after which an analog of Scheffe's test is discussed.

It is noted that if a significant two-stage $\tilde{F}$ statistic is obtained with the Bishop-Dudewicz procedure, you could then apply the procedures proposed by Ghosh or Chapman that were described in chapter seven. This approach is similar to using Fisher's LSD test. However, the experimentwise Type I error probability is not known. From previous results it seems reasonable to speculate that the experimetwise Type I error probability would be close to the nominal α level, but this has not been established.

Tamhane's Procedure

In the first stage of Tamhane's (1977) procedure you randomly sample n_0 observations from each of the J treatment groups yielding X_{ij} $(i=1,\ldots,n_0;\ j=1,\ldots,J)$. Suppose that for every pair of means you want the length of the confidence interval to be 2m. Then set

$$d=(m/h)^2$$

where the constant h, which depends on α, J, and $\nu=n_0-1$, is read from Table A11. (For $\nu>60$, use Table A9.) Next compute

$$n_j=\max\{n_0+1,\ (s_j^2/d)^\dagger+1\} \quad (9.6.1)$$

where $(s_j^2/d)^\dagger$ is the integer portion of s_j^2/d.

In the second stage you sample an additional n_j-n_0 observations from the jth treatment group, and then you compute $\tilde{X}_j$ using equation (8.12.5). The $100(1-\alpha)$% confidence interval for $\mu_j-\mu_k$ is

$$(\tilde{X}_j-\tilde{X}_k)\pm m \quad (9.6.2)$$

Tamhane (1977) shows that if H_0 is rejected when the interval does not contain zero, the experimentwise Type I error probability is exactly α.

Tamhane only considered the case where n_0 observations are randomly sampled from each group in the first stage, but there is a simple approximation for handling unequal sample sizes. In particular, suppose that in the first stage, n_{0j} observations are randomly sampled from the jth group. To determine h, set $\eta_j=n_{0j}-1$, and compute

$$\nu=[J/\Sigma(1/\eta_j)]^\dagger,$$

where $[\ ]^\dagger$ means to round down to the nearest integer. Then the value of h is read from Table A11 with ν degrees of freedom.

As a simple example, suppose J=3, and that in the first stage you have $n_{01}=10$, $n_{02}=20$ and $n_{03}=40$ observations randomly sampled from the three groups. Then $\nu=[3/(.1+.05+.025)]^\dagger=[17.14]^\dagger=17$. If $\alpha=.05$, then from Table A11, h is approximately 3.79. Once h has been determined, you compute d, n_j and the confidence intervals as before.

Hochberg's Procedure

Hochberg (1975) derived a multiple comparison procedure that gives simultaneous confidence intervals for all parametric functions, but we first discuss how to apply the procedure when making pairwise comparisons of the means.

Again suppose n_0 observations are sampled from each of J treatment groups, compute

$$n_j=\max\{n_0,\ (s_j^2/d)^{\dagger}+1\} \qquad (9.6.3)$$

and sample an additional n_j-n_0 observations from the j<u>th</u> group. As in Tamhane's procedure, the constant d can be chosen to control the length of the confidence intervals. In particular, refer to Table A11 and find the value of h corresponding to the values α, J, and $\nu=n_0-1$, ν being the degrees of freedom. Then the length of the confidence interval for $\mu_k-\mu_j$ will be at most $2h(\sqrt{d})$. Thus, if you want the length to be at most 2m, use

$$d=(m/h)^2$$

as was done in Tamhane's procedure.

In contrast to Tamhane, you compute

$$\bar{X}_j=\Sigma_i X_{ij}/n_j,$$

the sample mean for the j<u>th</u> group based on all n_j observations. The $100(1-\alpha)$% confidence interval for $\mu_k-\mu_j$, $k\neq j$, is

$$(\bar{X}_k-\bar{X}_j)\pm h[\max\{s_k/\sqrt{n_k},\ s_j/\sqrt{n_j}\}]. \qquad (9.6.4)$$

An advantage of Hochberg's procedure over Tamhane's is that additional observations may not be necessary in the second stage, and generally the length of the confidence interval will be shorter. A disadvantage is that instead of the constant h in equation (9.6.4), another constant should be used, but this constant has never been computed exactly. Hochberg (1976) suggested that this constant be approximated with the h values in Table A11, and he indicated that this approximation should give good results, particularly when J and n are not too small and α is not too large. Tukey (1953) showed that for $J>2$, the approximation works well when $\alpha\leq.05$. Another difference from Tamhane's procedure is that when attention is restricted to all pairwise comparisons of the means, the experimentwise Type I error probability under

Hochberg's procedure is less than or equal to α, while in Tamhane's procedure it is exactly equal to α. Another disadvantage of Hochberg's procedure is that there are no results on how to handle unequal sample sizes in the first stage.

Next consider any parametric function $\Psi=\Sigma c_j \mu_j$. Recall that a parametric function puts no restriction on the contrast coefficients, c_j, and in particular it is not necessarily the case that $\Sigma c_j=0$. Let

$$b_j=c_j s_j/\sqrt{n_j} \tag{9.6.5}$$

and compute A, the sum of the positive b_j values, let C be the sum of the negative b_j values, and let

$$D=\max\{A,-C\}. \tag{9.6.6}$$

The confidence interval for Ψ is

$$\hat{\Psi}\pm hD \tag{9.6.7}$$

where h is again read from Table A11. As usual,

$$\hat{\Psi}=\Sigma c_j \bar{X}_j.$$

Hochberg shows that

$$H_0: \Psi=0$$

can be tested for all possible parametric functions, and the experimentwise Type I error probability will be almost exactly α. Again, though, the constant h is an approximation of the exact constant required, but as previously mentioned, the approximation works reasonably well when J and n are not too small and α is not too large. Because $s_j/\sqrt{n_j}\leq\sqrt{d}$, the length of the confidence interval cannot exceed 2hD' where D' is computed in the same manner as D except that $s_j/\sqrt{n_j}$ is replaced with $\sqrt{d}$.

Example 9.6.1. Suppose J=3 and you want to test, among other things,

$$H_0: \Psi=0$$

where $\Psi=2\mu_1-\mu_2-\mu_3$. Suppose $\alpha=.05$, $n_0=40$,

$$s_1^2=3.9,\ s_2^2=3.4,\ s_3^2=2.8,$$

and d=.1. From equation (9.6.3),

$$n_1=\max\{40,\ (3.9/.1)^{\dagger}+1\}=40.$$

Similarly, $n_2=n_2=40$, and so no additional observations are required for any of the treatment groups.

Next, referring to equation (9.6.5), compute

$$b_1=2s_1/\surd n_1=2\surd 3.9/\surd 40=.62.$$

Similarly, $b_2=-0.29$, and $b_3=-0.26$. Thus, A=.62, C=-0.55, and D=max{.62,.55}=.62. If the sample means happen to be

$$\bar{X}_1=10.5,\ \bar{X}_2=11.2,\ \text{and}\ \bar{X}_3=12.8,$$

the estimate of Ψ is

$$\hat{\Psi}=2(10.5)-11.2-12.8=-3.0.$$

From Table A11, h=3.42, so from (9.6.7) the confidence interval for Ψ is

$$-3\pm3.42(.62)$$

$$=-3\pm2.12.$$

Healy's Procedure

In contrast to the Hochberg and Tamhane procedures, Healy (1956) assumes

$$\sigma_1=\sigma_2=\ldots=\sigma_J.$$

Again in the first stage, n_0 observations are randomly sampled from each group. The goal is to obtain confidence intervals for each of the quantities $\mu_k-\mu_j$ with the property that each interval has length 2m, and the experimentwise Type I error probability is α. To solve this problem, refer to Table A9 and determine q, the same quantity used in Tukey's procedure, where the degrees of freedom are $\nu=J(n_0-1)$. Next compute

$$d=(m/q)^2$$

and

$$n=\max\{n_0,\ [s^2/d]^{\dagger}+1\}.$$

Then sample an additional $n-n_0$ observations from each group, and compute the sample means

$$\bar{X}_1,\ldots,\bar{X}_J$$

using all n observations. The confidence interval for $\mu_k-\mu_j$ is

$$(\bar{X}_k-\bar{X}_j)\pm m.$$

If this interval does not contain zero, reject $H_0:\mu_k=\mu_j$.

The advantage of Healy's procedure over Tamhane's and Hochberg's is that for Healy's the degrees of freedom are $J(n_0-1)$ while for the other two the degrees of freedom are only n_0-1. This means that the expected number of observations required in the second stage will be smaller under Healy's procedure.

9.7 COMPARING TREATMENTS TO A CONTROL

In many instances the goal is not to make all pairwise comparisons of J means, but rather to compare each of the J means to the mean of a control group. Suppose, for example, you are manufacturing widgets and the average quality of your widgets, as measured by some appropriately chosen index, is μ_0. Mr. Hammer suggests three different methods that might improve the quality of your widgets. If the average quality under the three new methods is μ_1, μ_2, and μ_3, your immediate concern might be testing

$$H_0:\mu_j=\mu_0 \tag{9.7.1}$$

for each j, j=1,2,3. If you fail to reject H_0, there is no point in considering whether $\mu_1=\mu_2=\mu_3$ because of the cost of installing the new manufacturing process. That is, you will want to adopt a new manufacturing process only if one of the new procedures is different and in fact better than the control.

As another example, suppose you want to study J=4 drugs for treating depression. You want to take into account the psychosomatic effects of receiving medication, and so a control group is given a placebo. To determine whether any of the drugs has an effect on depression, you compare the outcome measures for each treatment to the control receiving the placebo.

Notice that in both examples, if a treatment is indeed different from the control group, you would also like to determine whether any treatments are better than the control and indeed which is best. The obvious solution to this problem is if you reject H_0, choose the method with the highest mean as the one that is most effective. (This assumes of course that the best method corresponds to the one with the highest mean.) A practical difficulty with this procedure is that it does not tell you how certain you can be that the best method was indeed chosen. Methods for dealing with this problem are described in chapter twelve. For methods that are directly relevant to comparing treatments to a control when μ_0 is known, see Bechhofer and Turnbull (1978) and Wilcox (1984). Here attention is restricted to the more basic problem of testing

$$H_0: \mu_j = \mu_0 \ (j=1, \ldots, J) \tag{9.7.2}$$

It is evident that testing (9.7.2) is similar to previous multiple comparison procedures where the goal is to compare all pairs of means. Here the goal is to make only J comparisons, and Dunnett (1955, 1964) supplied the appropriate critical values assuming normality and equal variances. The confidence interval for $\mu_j - \mu_0$ is

$$(\bar{X}_j - \bar{X}_0) \pm D_{\alpha,p,\nu} [MSWG(1/n_j + 1/n_0)]^{1/2} \tag{9.7.3}$$

where p=J+1 is the number of means, including the control, and ν=N-J is the degrees of freedom of MSWG. The constant D is read from Table A15. For unequal variances the Welch-Dunn-Sidak or the Simes-Welch procedure can be used.

Solution for Unequal Variances

Dudewicz, Ramberg, and Chen (1975) derived a two-stage procedure for comparing means to a control that allows unequal variances and gives control over the length of the confidence intervals. (For related results on this problem, see Dudewicz & Dalal, 1983.) In contrast to Dunnett's procedure, one-sided intervals are obtained. This means that one-tailed (directional) tests are made. (See equation 9.7.6 below.)

In the first stage you randomly sample n' observations from each of the J+1 treatment groups, and you compute the sample variances s_j^2 (j=0,1,...,J). Next compute

$$n_j = \max\{n'+1, \ (s_j^2/d)^{\dagger}+1)\}, \ j=0,1,\ldots,J$$

where again $(s_j^2/d)^{\dagger}$ is the integer portion of s_j^2/d. The constant d is given by $d=(m/h)^2$, m is a constant that will be explained in equation (9.7.5), and h is read from Table A20 with ν=n'-1 degrees of freedom. More extensive tables can be found in Dudewicz et al. (1975).

In the second stage you randomly sample an additional $n_j - n'$ observations from the jth treatment group, and compute the generalized sample means $\tilde{X}_j$ using equation (8.12.5). Finally, compute

$$\tilde{X}_j-\tilde{X}_0+m,\ j=1,\ldots,J \qquad (9.7.4)$$

The h values were determined so that for all j, $1\le j\le J$, it will be simultaneously true that

$$\mu_j-\mu_0\le\tilde{X}_j-\tilde{X}_0+m$$

with probability $1-\alpha$. Thus, as in previous two-stage procedures, you choose m to control the accuracy of the estimate of $\mu_j-\mu_0$. Moreover, when testing

$$H_0:\ \mu_j\le\mu_0,\ j=1,2,\ldots,J \qquad (9.7.6)$$

if you reject whenever

$$\tilde{X}_j-\tilde{X}_0>m,$$

the experimentwise Type I error probability will be exactly α. Also note that m controls power. The smaller m is, the more power you will have. In fact, for $\mu_j-\mu_0=\delta$, the probability of rejecting $H_0:\mu_j\le\mu_0$ (for fixed j) is approximately

$$\Pr(Z\le a/\surd 2)-$$
$$[(a^3+10a)(32)^{-1}(\pi)^{-1/2}\exp(-a^2/4)] \qquad (9.7.7)$$

where Z is a standard normal random variable, and

$$a=(-m+\delta)/\surd d.$$

Example 9.7.1. Suppose there are J=3 treatment groups and a control and that n'=15 observations are randomly sampled from each. Further suppose that the sample variances are $s_0{}^2=5.4$, $s_1{}^2=3.1$, $s_2{}^2=4.2$, and $s_3{}^2=1.2$. If you want to compare each treatment group to the control by testing

$$H_0:\mu_j\le\mu_0,\ j=1,2,3;$$

and if you want the experimentwise Type I error probability to be $\alpha=.05$, then from Table A20, h=3.17. Consider d=.5 in which case $m=h\surd d=2.24$, and suppose you want to determine the probability of rejecting $H_0:\mu_j\le\mu_0$ when $\delta=\mu_j-\mu_0=3.0$. The constant a in equation (9.7.7) is

$$(-2.24+3.0)/\surd .5=1.07.$$

From equation (9.7.7), the power for each of the three comparisons is approximately

$$.9345-.1588=.7757.$$

To get more power, use a smaller value for d. The n_j values are all equal to 16, so one additional observation is sampled from each treatment group. If the $\tilde{X}_j$ values turn out to be

$$\tilde{X}_0=10.8,\ \tilde{X}_1=11.8,\ \tilde{X}_2=14.0, \text{ and } \tilde{X}_3=9.6,$$

then conclude that $\mu_2>\mu_0$, but otherwise H_0 would not be rejected.

Several other extensions of Dunnett's original procedure have been proposed, but they are not described here. The interested reader is referred to Shaffer (1977), Dudewicz and Dalal (1975), Chen and Pickett (1984), Fligner (1984), Edwards and Hsu (1983) and Dunn (1964). The paper by Edwards and Hsu (1983) may be of particular interest when measuring effect size. In particular, they show how the procedures in this section can be used to obtain simultaneous confidence intervals for the difference between the largest mean and the J-1 other means that are smaller. That is, the procedure can be used to measure the superiority of the "best" treatment group relative to the others being considered, and it can be used to determine the probability that the best treatment group was indeed selected.

EXERCISES

9.1 Suppose J=3, $\bar{X}_1=13$, $\bar{X}_2=16$, $\bar{X}_3=20$, $n_1=n_2=n_3=10$, $s_1{}^2=8$, $s_2{}^2=10$, and $s_3{}^2=6$. Assume $\sigma_1=\sigma_2=\sigma_3$.

a) Test $\mu_1=\mu_2$ and $\mu_1=\mu_3$ using Dunn's procedure. Use $\alpha=.05$

b) Test $\mu_1=\mu_2$, $\mu_1=\mu_3$, and $\mu_2=\mu_3$ using Tukey's procedure. Use $\alpha=.05$.

c) Test $\mu_1=\mu_2$ and $\mu_2=\mu_3$ using the Dunn-Sidak test. Use $\alpha=.05$.

d) Perform all pairwise comparisons of the means using both Dunnett's T3 and C procedures. Use $\alpha=.05$

e) Repeat part a, but use Scheffe's procedure and then the Kaiser-Bowden procedure.

9.2 Suppose J=4, the sample means are 26, 32, 24, and 18. The sample sizes are 15, 20, 20, 25, and MSWG=8. Let $\Psi_1=\mu_1-\mu_2$ and $\Psi_2=\mu_3-\mu_4$, and note that

$$\hat{\Psi}_1=\bar{X}_1-\bar{X}_2 \text{ and } \hat{\Psi}_2=\bar{X}_3-\bar{X}_4$$

are independent.

a) Assume equal variances and suppose you want to test both $H_0:\Psi_1=0$ and $H_0:\Psi_2=0$. If both hypotheses are tested with the t-test at the $\alpha=.05$ level, will the probability that both tests result in a Type I error be $(.05)^2=.025$? That is, can the binomial distribution be used? Explain.

b) In part a, suppose you want the experimentwise Type I error to be .05, would you use Dunn's procedure or the Dunn-Sidak? Why? Apply the procedure you choose.

c) Test all pairwise comparisons of the means using the Tukey-Kramer procedure. Use $\alpha=.05$

d) Suppose the sample variances are 8,20,7, and 5. Apply Dunnett's T3 and C procedures as well as the Games-Howell.

9.3 Suppose your only interest is to test $H_0:\mu_j=\mu_k$ for all j<k. Assume equal variances and equal sample sizes. Is it necessary to apply the F test first, or can you simply apply Tukey's procedure?

9.4 Given $\bar{X}_1=5$, $\bar{X}_2=8$, $\bar{X}_3=9$, $s_1{}^2=2$, $s_2{}^2=3$, $s_3{}^2=4$, $n_1=n_2=n_3=10$, MSWG=3, and $\alpha=.05$. Perform all pairwise comparisons using
a) Tukey's procedure
b) Dunn's procedure
c) Dunn-Sidak
d) Scheffe
e) Kaiser-Bowden
f) Dunnett's T3 and C
g) Games-Howell

9.5 Apply the Tukey-Kramer procedure to the data in 9.4, but assume $n_1=5$, $n_2=10$, $n_3=15$.

9.6 For the data in 9.4, assume equal variances and suppose you want to test $H_0:\Psi_1=0$ and $H_0:\Psi_2=0$ where $\Psi_1=\mu_1+\mu_2-2\mu_3$, $\Psi_2=\mu_1-2\mu_2+\mu_3$.
a) Which procedure would you use?
b) Perform the test with $\alpha=.05$
c) If you hadn't been told that the variances were equal, which procedure would you use?

9.7 Suppose you have J=3 treatment groups, $s_1{}^2=5$, $s_2{}^2=6$, $s_3{}^2=8$, $n_0=15$, and $\alpha=.05$.
a) If you apply Tamhane's procedure to obtain confidence intervals having length 3, how many more observations do you

need?

b) Assume the sums of the observations in the first stage for the three treatment groups are $T_1=10$, $T_2=12$, and $T_3=8$, while the sums of the observations in the second stage are $U_1=4$, $U_2=6$, and $U_3=5$. For each of the J groups, compute $\tilde{X}_j$

c) Compute the confidence intervals for $\mu_1-\mu_2$ using Hochberg's procedure.

9.8 Assume MSWG=8, $n_0=10$, $\alpha=.01$, and J=4.

a) For Healy's procedure, how many more observations are required if the length of the confidence intervals are to be 20?

b) Once the additional observations are available, assume $\bar{X}_1=14$, $\bar{X}_2=14$, $\bar{X}_3=10.5$, and $\bar{X}_4=16$. Would you reject $H_0:\mu_1=\mu_2$?

References

Bechhofer, R. & Dunnett, C. (1982) Multiple comparisons for orthogonal contrasts: Examples and tables. Technometrics, 24, 213-222.

Bechhofer, R. & Turnbull, B. (1978) Two (k+1)-decision selection procedures for comparing k normal means with a specified standard. Journal of the American Statistical Association, 73, 385-392.

Begun, J & Gabriel, K. (1981) Closure of the Newman-Keuls multiple comparison procedure. Journal of the American Statistical Association, 76, 241-245.

Bernhardson, C. (1975) Type I error rates when multiple comparison procedures follow a significant F test of ANOVA. Biometrics 31, 229-232.

Brown, M. B. & Forsythe A. (1974) The ANOVA and multiple comparisons for data with heterogeneous variances. Biometrics, 30, 719-724.

Chen, H. J. & Pickett, J. R. (1984) Selecting all treatments better than a control under a multivariate normal distribution and a uniform prior distribution. Communications in Statistics--Theory and Methods, 13, 59-80.

Dalal, S. (1975) Simultaneous confidence procedures for univariate and multivariate Behrens-Fisher type problems. Biometrika, 65, 221-225

Dayton, C. & Schafer W. (1973) Extended tables of t and chi-square for Bonferroni tests with unequal error allocation.

Journal of the American Statistical Association, 68, 78-83.

Dudewicz, E. & Dalal, S. (1983) Multiple comparisons with a control when the variances are unknown and unequal. American Journal of Mathematical and Management Sciences, 3, 275-298.

Dudewicz, E., Ramberg, J. & Chen, H. (1975) New tables for multiple comparisons with a control (unknown variances). Biometrische Zeitschrift 17, 13-26

Dunn, O. (1961) Multiple comparisons among means. Journal of the American Statistical Association, 56, 52-64.

Dunn, O. (1974) On multiple tests and confidence intervals Communications in Statistics, 3, 101-103.

Dunnett, C. (1955) A multiple comparison procedure for comparing several treatments with a control. Journal of the American Statistical Association, 50, 1096-1121.

Dunnett, C. (1980a) Pairwise multiple comparisons in the homogeneous variance, unequal sample size case. Journal of the American Statistical Association, 75, 789-795.

Dunnett, C. (1980b) Pairwise multiple comparisons in the unequal variance case. Journal of the American Statistical Association, 75, 796-800.

Dunnett, C. (1982) Robust multiple comparisons Communications in Statistics--Theory and Methods, 11, 2611-2629.

Edwards, D. & Hsu, J. (1983) Multiple comparisons with the best treatment. Journal of the American Statistical Association, 78, 965-971 (correction, 1984, p. 965)

Fisher, R. (1949) The design of experiments Edinburgh: Oliver and Boyd, Ltd.

Fligner, M. A. (1984) A note on two-sided distribution-free treatment versus control multiple comparisons. Journal of the American Statistical Association, 79, 208-211.

Games, P.(1977) An improved t table for simultaneous control on g contrasts. Journal of the American Statistical Association, 72, 531-534.

Games, P. & Howell, J. (1976) Pairwise multiple comparison procedures with unequal n's and/or variances: A monte carlo study. Journal of Educational Statistics, 1, 113-125.

Guthrie, J., Seifert, M. Kirsch, I. (1986) Effects of Education occupation and setting on reading practices. American Educational Research Journal, 23, 151-160.

Hartley, H. (1955) Some recent developments in analysis of variance. Communications in Pure and Applied Mathematics, 8, 47-72.

Hayter, A. (1984) A proof of a conjecture that the Tukey-Kramer multiple comparison procedure is conservative. Annals of

Statistics, 12, 61-75.

Hayter, A. (1986) The maximum familywise error rate of Fisher's least significant difference test. Journal of the American Statistical Association, 81, 1000-1004.

Healy, W. (1956) Two-sample procedures in simultaneous estimation. Annals of Mathematical Statistics, 27, 687-702

Hochberg, Y. (1975) Simultaneous inference under Behrens-Fisher conditions--a two sample approach. Communications in Statistics, 4, 1109-1119.

Hochberg, Y. (1976) A modification of the T-method of multiple comparisons for a one-way layout with unequal variances Journal of the American Statistical Association, 71, 200-203.

Holm, S. (1979) A simple sequentially rejective multiple test procedure. Scandinavian Journal of Statistics, 6, 65-70.

Hunter, D. (1976) An upper bound for the probability of a union Journal of Applied Probability, 13, 597-603.

Kaiser, L & Bowden, D. (1983) Simultaneous confidence intervals for all linear contrasts of means with heterogeneous variances Communications in Statistics--Theory and Methods, 12, 73-88

Keselman, H. & Rogan, J. (1978) A comparison of the modified Tukey and Scheffe methods of multiple comparisons for pairwise contrasts Journal of the American Statistical Association, 73, 47-51

Kramer, C. (1956) Extension of multiple range test to group means with unequal number of replications. Biometrics, 12, 307-310.

Krishnaiah, P. R. & Armitage, P. V. (1966) Tables for multivariate t-distributions. Sankhya, Series B, 28, 31-56.

Miller, R. (1966) Simultaneous statistical inference. New York: McGraw-Hill.

Ramsey, P. (1981) Power of univariate pairwise multiple comparison procedures. Psychological Bulletin, 90, 352-366.

Ringland, J. (1983) Robust multiple comparisons Journal of the American Statistical Association, 78, 145-151.

Scheffe, H. (1953) A method of judging all contrasts in the analysis of variance. Biometrika, 40, 87-104.

Scheffe, H. (1959) The analysis of variance. New York: Wiley

Shaffer, J. P. Multiple comparisons emphasizing selected contrasts: An extension of generalization of Dunnett's procedure. Biometrics, 33, 293-303.

Shaffer, J. P. (1986) Modified sequentially rejective multiple test procedures. Journal of the American Statistical Association, 81, 826-831.

Sidak, Z. (1967) Rectangular confidence regions for the means of multivariate distributions. Journal of the American Statistical Association, 62, 626-633.

Simes, R. J. (1986) An improved Bonferroni procedure for multiple tests of significance. Biometrika, 73, 751-754.

Smith, W. C.& Han, C. (1981) Error rate for testing a contrast after a significant F test. Communications in Statistics--Simulation and Computation, B10, 546-556.

Spjotvoll, E. & Stoline, M. (1973) An extension of the T-method of multiple comparisons to include the case with unequal sample sizes. Journal of the American Statistical Association, 68, 975-978.

Stoline, M. (1981) The status of multiple comparisons: Simultaneous estimation of all pairwise comparisons in one-way ANOVA designs. The American Statistician, 35, 134-141.

Stoline, M. & Ury, H. (1979) Tables of the Studentized maximum modulus distribution and an application to multiple comparisons among means. Technometrics, 21, 87-93.

Tamhane, A. (1977) Multiple comparisons in model I one-way ANOVA with unequal variances. Communications in Statistics--Theory and Methods, A6, 15-32.

Tamhane, A. (1979) A comparison of procedures for multiple comparisons of means with unequal variances. Journal of the American Statistical Association. 74, 471-480.

Tukey, J. (1953) The problem of multiple comparisons. Unpublished manuscript.

Wilcox, R. (1984) Selecting the best population provided it is better than a standard: The unequal variance case. Journal of the American Statistical Association, 79, 887-891.

Wilcox, R. & Chao, E. (1985) Planned comparisons: Controlling power and determining sample sizes. British Journal of Mathematical and Statistical Psychology, 38, 216-221.

CHAPTER TEN

TWO-WAY ANOVA

Chapter eight dealt with the problem of testing

$$H_0: \mu_1 = \ldots = \mu_J$$

where the μ_j's are the population means of J independent treatment groups. Suppose you want to compare two methods of teaching statistics, and that you want to take into account whether a student has had strong training in mathematics prior to taking the course. In particular, suppose that each student in your study is classified as either having or not having a strong training in mathematics. Thus, there are four population means of interest:

μ_{11}=expected score on the final exam among the students having a strong background in mathematics and receiving method 1,
μ_{12}=expected score on the final exam among students having a strong background in mathematics and receiving method 2,
μ_{21}=expected score under method 1 and poor training in mathematics, and
μ_{22}=expected score under method 2 with poor training.

If you randomly sample students having a strong training in mathematics, and randomly assign them to method 1 or 2, and you do the same for students who do not have a strong training in mathematics, you will have four independent treatment groups, and you can test

$$H_0: \mu_{11} = \mu_{12} = \mu_{21} = \mu_{22}$$

using the techniques in chapter eight. However, alternative relationships among the means may be of interest. For example, if

$$\mu_{11} > \mu_{12}, \text{ but } \mu_{21} < \mu_{22},$$

this indicates that method 1 is better than method 2 among students having a strong background in mathematics, while for the other students, method 2 is better than method 1. This is an example of what is called a disordinal interaction. An ordinal interaction means that

$$\mu_{11}-\mu_{21}>\mu_{12}-\mu_{22}>0 \text{ or } \mu_{11}-\mu_{21}<\mu_{12}-\mu_{22}<0.$$

There is said to be an interaction among the means if

$$\mu_{11}-\mu_{12}\neq\mu_{21}-\mu_{22}.$$

Another potential question of interest is whether there is a difference between the two methods if the mathematics background of the students is ignored. One approach to this problem is to test

$$(\mu_{11}+\mu_{21})/2=(\mu_{12}+\mu_{22})/2.$$

A more detailed discussion of this problem is given in section 10.3.

10.1 THE MODEL AND ITS ASSUMPTIONS

The situation described above is a special case of a two-way analysis of variance. The term "two-way" means that there are two _factors_ or independent variables that are being investigated. In the illustration the two factors are method of teaching and training in mathematics. The _levels_ of a factor refer to a value or category of the factor. In the example, the factor "method of teaching" has two levels, namely method 1 and method 2. The other factor has two levels as well. More generally, the first factor might have J levels, and the second might have K. In this case the experimental design is often called a J by K design indicating that there are two factors with J and K levels, respectively. For convenience the first factor is called factor A and the second factor B.

Suppose n examinees are randomly sampled and assigned to the j_th_ level of factor A and the k_th_ level of factor B, let X_{ijk} be the observed outcome of the i_th_ examinee in the (j,k)_th_ level, and let

$$\mu_{jk}=E(X_{ijk}).$$

The general goal is to make inferences about μ_{jk} (j=1,...,J; k=1,...,K).

Let

$$\mu=\Sigma\Sigma\mu_{jk}/JK,$$

$$\bar{\mu}_{j.}=\Sigma_k\mu_{jk}/K \quad (j=1,\ldots,J),$$

and

$$\bar{\mu}_{.k}=\Sigma_j\mu_{jk}/J \quad (k=1,\ldots,K).$$

where the "dot" notation means summation is over the indicated subscript. For example $\bar{\mu}_j.$ indicates that summation is over the second subscript. The quantities

$$\mu, \ \alpha_j=\bar{\mu}_{j.}-\mu \text{ and } \beta_k=\bar{\mu}_{.k}-\mu$$

are called the grand mean, the main effects for factor A and the main effects for factor B, respectively.

It should be mentioned that in some situations a more general definition of main effects is used (e.g., Kendall & Stuart, 1973. Also see Scheffe, 1959, section 4.1). For instance, let w_{jk} be weights or constants chosen by the experimenter with the property that $w_{jk}\geq 0$ and $\Sigma_k w_{jk}=1$ for any j. The mean for the j<u>th</u> level of factor A is now defined to be

$$A_j=\Sigma_k w_{jk}\mu_{jk},$$

and the main effect for the j<u>th</u> level of factor A is

$$A_j-\mu.$$

A similar definition applies to the main effects for factor B using a possibly different set of weights, say v_{jk}. In <u>survey</u> studies it is common to set

$$w_{jk}=n_{jk}/n_{j.}$$

when defining main effects for factor A, where n_{jk} is the number of observations in the (j,k)<u>th</u> group, and

$$n_{j.}=\Sigma_k n_{jk}.$$

In contrast, <u>experimental</u> studies use

$$w_{jk}=1/K.$$

The point is that the choice of weights has implications about how the $\mu_j.$'s are estimated.

To clarify this point, consider a situation where methods of teaching are compared, and suppose factor A is concerned with two computer software packages for teaching statistics, while method B refers to different books that might be adopted. If there are two computer software packages and three different books, you have a 2 by 3 design. Suppose the number of subjects and resulting sample sizes are as follows.

		B		
		1	2	3
A	1:	$n_{11}=5$ $\bar{X}_{11}=70$	$n_{12}=10$ $\bar{X}_{12}=90$	$n_{13}=20$ $\bar{X}_{13}=40$
	2:	$n_{21}=15$ $\bar{X}_{21}=40$	$n_{22}=20$ $\bar{X}_{22}=110$	$n_{23}=25$ $\bar{X}_{23}=90$

If the weights $w_{jk}=n_{jk}/n_{j.}$ are used, this suggests that you estimate the population mean of the jth level of factor A with

$$\Sigma_k n_{jk}\bar{X}_{jk}/n_{j.}$$

This is equivalent to simply ignoring factor B. That is, this last expression is equal to

$$\Sigma_i \Sigma_k X_{ijk}/n_{j.}\,.$$

For example, in the illustration for the first level of factor A you have a total of 5+10+20=35 observations, and the mean of the first level of factor A is just the average of these 35 observations. This is in contrast to using equal weights where the population mean of the jth level of factor A is estimated with

$$\Sigma_k \bar{X}_{jk}/K.$$

In the illustration the mean of the first level of factor A, using equal weights, is

$$(70+90+40)/3=66.7$$

The weighted mean is

$$[5(70)+10(90)+20(40)]/35=58.75.$$

Both are reasonable estimates of $\bar{\mu}_{j.}$, but except for the case of equal sample sizes per group, they generally give different results. For $w_{jk}=n_{jk}/n_{j.}$, treatment groups having a relatively large number of observations provide a bigger contribution to the estimate of $\bar{\mu}_{j.}$ while for equal weights the means corresponding to the treatment groups contribute equally.

Referring to the illustration, there may be various reasons why it was impractical to assign an equal number of subjects to the six conditions, and if the levels of the factor "computer software packages" are compared using weights $w_{jk}=n_{jk}/n_{j.}$, $\bar{X}_{11}$ does not contribute as much to the estimate of the mean of the jth level of factor A as does $\bar{X}_{12}$ and $\bar{X}_{13}$ even though this was not intended. In this case you may want to use equal weights instead. The decision about which weights to use plays an important role when performing multiple comparisons, which are discussed in the next section. For convenience, the remainder of this section assumes equal weights are used.

If for some j, h, k, and m,

$$\mu_{jk}-\mu_{hk}\neq\mu_{jm}-\mu_{hm},\ j\neq h,\ k\neq m,$$

it is said that an interaction exists among the means. This is, of course, a slight generalization of the notion of an interaction in a 2 by 2 design. If

$$\mu_{jk}>\mu_{jm} \text{ and } \mu_{hk}<\mu_{hm}, \text{ or if } \mu_{jk}<\mu_{jm} \text{ and } \mu_{hk}>\mu_{hm},$$

the interaction is called disordinal. If there is an interaction and $\mu_{jk}-\mu_{jm}$ and $\mu_{hk}-\mu_{jm}$ are both positive or both negative, the interaction is called ordinal.

As another illustration of interactions, suppose you have K=3 teaching methods and you want to consider whether the effects are related to gender. Suppose the means are

			B	
		1	2	3
A	male	89	106	50
	female	44	100	93

There is a disordinal interaction because 89>44 while 50<93. Thus, for methods 1 and 3, males are better off receiving method 1, while females perform better under method 3. There is also an ordinal interaction because 89-44≠106-100. Thus, males do better under method 1, while under method 2 the means are more nearly equal. The grand mean is μ=80.335. The main effects for factor B (assuming equal weights) are

$$\beta_1=\{(89+44)/2\}-80.335=-13.835,\ \beta_2=22.665,\ \text{and } \beta_3=-8.835$$

For factor A the main effects are

$$\alpha_1=81.67-80.335=1.335 \text{ and } \alpha_2=-1.335.$$

Because method 2 yields the best results, regardless of gender, the interactions would not seem to be overly interesting because it does not influence your choice of method--method 2 should always be used. Of course, if instead μ_{12}=50 and μ_{22}=36, the disordinal interaction takes on more significance since method 1 is best for males, while method 3 is best for females.

The immediate goal is to extend the results in chapter eight to provide an F test for

$$H_0:\alpha_1=\alpha_2=\ldots=\alpha_J \tag{10.1.1}$$

$$H_0:\beta_1=\ldots=\beta_K \tag{10.1.2}$$

and

H_0: there are no interactions.

As was the case for the one-way model, the F tests about to be derived are exploratory in nature. That is, they test a large family of equalities that include the above null hypotheses as a special case. To test specific hypotheses, multiple comparison procedures can be used, as discussed below.

Let X_{ijk} be as defined above. Extending the one-way model, it is assumed that

$$X_{ijk}=\mu+\alpha_j+\beta_k+\gamma_{jk}+\epsilon_{ijk} \tag{10.1.3}$$

where α_j and β_k were defined in the introduction to this chapter, where

$$\gamma_{jk}=\mu_{jk}-\alpha_j-\beta_k-\mu$$

$$=\mu_{jk}-\bar{\mu}_{j.}-\bar{\mu}_{.k}+\mu$$

and ϵ_{ijk} is normally distributed with mean zero and variance σ^2. Thus, the observations X_{ijk} are assumed to be normally distributed with mean μ_{jk}. Until stated otherwise, all JK treatment groups are assumed to have a common variance σ^2.

It is noted that

$$\Sigma\alpha_j=0,\ \Sigma\beta_k=0 \text{ and } \Sigma_j\gamma_{jk}=\Sigma_k\gamma_{jk}=0.$$

If there are no interaction effects, all of the γ_{jk} values are equal to zero. Thus, testing for interactions reduces to testing

$$H_0:\gamma_{11}=\gamma_{12}=\ldots=\gamma_{JK}=0.$$

It will help later on to note that an alternative way of writing the null hypotheses is

$$H_0:\ \Sigma\alpha_j^2=0 \qquad (10.1.4)$$

$$H_0:\ \Sigma\beta_k^2=0 \qquad (10.1.5)$$

and

$$H_0:\ \Sigma\Sigma\gamma_{jk}^2=0. \qquad (10.1.6)$$

An important point is that if the null hypotheses in (10.1.4) and (10.1.5) are true, there still might be an interaction effect. For instance, if the population means in a 2 by 2 design are $\mu_{11}=10$, $\mu_{12}=16$, $\mu_{21}=16$ and $\mu_{22}=10$, then $\mu=13$, $\alpha_1=\alpha_2=\beta_1=\beta_2=0$, but there is an interaction effect. If instead $\mu_{11}=10$, $\mu_{12}=20$, $\mu_{21}=30$, and $\mu_{22}=40$, there is a main effect for factor A since $10+20\neq30+40$, and there is also a main effect for factor B, but there is no interaction since $\mu_{11}-\mu_{21}=\mu_{12}-\mu_{22}$.

The derivation of the F test in the two-way model is similar to the derivation of the F test in the one-way model. In particular, the total sum of squares,

$$\Sigma\Sigma\Sigma(X_{ijk}-\bar{X}_{...})^2,$$

is partitioned into quantities that can be used to test the null hypotheses. The "dot" notation used in this last expression indicates summation over the corresponding subscript. For instance

$$\bar{X}_{...}=\Sigma\Sigma\Sigma X_{ijk}/nJK,$$

$$\bar{X}_{..k}=\Sigma_i\Sigma_j X_{ijk}/nJ,$$

and

$$\bar{X}_{.jk}=\Sigma_i X_{ijk}/n.$$

In this section it is assumed that all JK treatment groups have an equal number of observations, namely n.

First note that the unbiased estimate of the main effects and interaction terms are

$$\hat{\alpha}_j=\bar{X}_{.j.}-\bar{X}_{...},\ j=1,\ldots,J; \qquad (10.1.7)$$

$$\hat{\beta}_k=\bar{X}_{..k}-\bar{X}_{...},\ k=1,\ldots,K; \qquad (10.1.8)$$

and

$$\hat{\gamma}_{jk}=\bar{X}_{.jk}-\bar{X}_{.j.}-\bar{X}_{..k}+\bar{X}_{...}$$

Omitting the algebra, it can be shown that

$$\Sigma\Sigma\Sigma(X_{ijk}-X_{...})^2=nK\Sigma\hat{\alpha}_j^2+nJ\Sigma\hat{\beta}_k^2\ +$$

$$n\Sigma\Sigma\hat{\gamma}_{jk}^2+\Sigma\Sigma\Sigma(X_{ijk}-\bar{X}_{.jk})^2. \qquad (10.1.9)$$

The quantities in this last equation have special names. They are

$$SSTOT=\Sigma\Sigma\Sigma(X_{ijk}-\bar{X}_{...})^2,$$

$$SSA=nK\Sigma\hat{\alpha}_j^2$$

$$SSB=nJ\Sigma\hat{\beta}_k^2$$

$$SSINTER=n\Sigma\Sigma\hat{\gamma}_{jk}^2$$

$$SSWG=\Sigma\Sigma\Sigma(X_{ijk}-\bar{X}_{.jk})^2$$

where the term "SS" stands for sum of squares. Thus, equation (10.1.9) can be written as

$$SSTOT=SSA+SSB+SSINTER+SSWG. \qquad (10.1.10)$$

From (10.1.3) it can be seen that

$$X_{ijk}-\bar{X}_{.jk}=\epsilon_{ijk}-\bar{\epsilon}_{.jk},$$

where

$$\bar{\epsilon}_{.jk}=\Sigma_i\,\epsilon_{ijk}/n.$$

Thus,

$$SSWG=\Sigma\Sigma\Sigma(\epsilon_{ijk}-\bar{\epsilon}_{.jk})^2.$$

Because the ϵ_{ijk}'s are independent standard normal random variables, results in chapter 6 tell us that for any j and k,

$$\Sigma_i(\epsilon_{ijk}-\bar{\epsilon}_{.jk})^2/\sigma^2$$

has a chi-square distribution with n-1 degrees of freedom. But the sum of independent chi-square distributions is again a chi-square distribution and so $SSWG/\sigma^2$ has a chi-square distribution with JK(n-1) degrees of freedom, in which case

$$E(SSWG)=JK(n-1)\sigma^2. \qquad (10.1.11)$$

This result holds regardless of whether the null hypothesis is true. Consequently, an unbiased estimate of σ^2 is

$$MSWG=SSWG/JK(n-1) \tag{10.1.12}$$

Using the same procedure that was used in the one-way model, it can be seen that when

$$H_0:\Sigma\alpha_j^2=0$$

is true, SSA/σ^2 has a chi-square distribution with J-1 degrees of freedom, and so

$$MSA=SSA/(J-1) \tag{10.1.13}$$

is an unbiased estimate of σ^2. However, when H_0 is false,

$$E(MSA)=\sigma^2+nK\Sigma\alpha_j^2/(J-1) \tag{10.1.14}$$

Similarly, when $H_0:\Sigma\beta_k{}^2=0$ is true, SSB/σ^2 has a chi-square distribution with K-1 degrees of freedom and

$$MSB=SSB/(K-1) \tag{10.1.15}$$

is an unbiased estimate of σ^2. When H_0 is false,

$$E(MSB)=\sigma^2+Jn\Sigma_k\beta_k^2/(K-1). \tag{10.1.16}$$

As for SSINTER, it can be shown that when $H_0:\Sigma\Sigma\gamma_{jk}{}^2=0$ is true, $SSINTER/\sigma^2$ has a chi-square distribution with (J-1)(K-1) degrees of freedom, and

$$MSINTER=SSINTER/[(J-1)(K-1)]$$

is an unbiased estimate of σ^2. When H_0 is false

$$E(MSINTER)=\sigma^2+\Sigma\Sigma n\gamma_{jk}^2/[(J-1)(K-1)]. \tag{10.1.17}$$

Referring to the definition of the F distribution, it is seen that when

$$H_0:\Sigma\alpha_j^2=0$$

is true,

$$F=MSA/MSWG$$

has an F distribution with ν_1=J-1 and ν_2=JK(n-1) degrees of freedom. You reject H_0 if $F>f$ where f is the $1-\alpha$ quantile of the F distribution, which is read from Table A3. As in the one-way model you use a one-tailed test because a large F value suggests that $\Sigma\alpha_j{}^2>0$. Similarly, you test $H_0:\Sigma\beta_k{}^2=0$ with MSB/MSWG where now the degrees of freedom are $\nu_1=K-1$ and $\nu_2=JK(n-1)$. To test

$$H_0:\Sigma\gamma_{jk}^2=0,$$

use

$$F=MSINTER/MSWG$$

with $\nu_1=(J-1)(K-1)$ and $\nu_2=JK(n-1)$ degrees of freedom.

Computational Steps

When computing the sum of squares terms, the following formulae are easier to use. Let

$$A=(\Sigma\Sigma\Sigma X_{ijk})^2/N,$$

where $N=JKn$ is the total number of observations. It is assumed that equal samples per group are being used. Next compute

$$B=\Sigma\Sigma\Sigma X_{ijk}^2.$$

Then

$$SSTOTAL=B-A$$

$$SSA=[\Sigma_j(\Sigma_i\Sigma_k X_{ijk})^2/Kn]-A,$$

$$SSB=[\Sigma_k(\Sigma_i\Sigma_j X_{ijk})^2/Jn]-A,$$

$$SSWG=B-\Sigma_j\Sigma_k(\Sigma_i X_{ijk})^2/n,$$

and

$$SSINTER=SSTOT-SSA-SSB-SSWG$$

It is noted that unequal sample sizes can be handled using results in Scheffe (1959, section 4.4), and a solution is also possible using the "general linear model" as described, for example, by Kirk (1982) or Neter and Wasserman (1974).

Example 10.1.1. Suppose you want to compare two methods of treating a particular psychological disorder. Further suppose that you suspect that the effectiveness of the treatments might be influenced by the cultural background of the patients, and so you want to take into account whether a patient is Asian, Hispanic, or Caucasian. Thus, you have a 2 by 3 design.

Suppose the ratings on the effectiveness of the methods are:

	Treatment 1	Treatment 2
Asian	45	53
	50	67
Hispanics	60	36
	61	35
Caucasian	53	36
	63	65

Thus, there are n=2 observations per group, N=12,

$A=(45+50+...+65)^2/12=32,448$,

$B=45^2+...+65^2=33,964$,

$\Sigma_k(\Sigma_i \Sigma_j X_{ijk})^2/Kn=[(45+...+63)^2+(53+...+65)^2]/6$
$=32,581.3$,

$\Sigma_j(\Sigma_k \Sigma_i X_{ijk})^2/Kn=[(45+...+67)^2+...+(53+...+65)^2]/4$
$=32,544.5$,

$\Sigma_j \Sigma_k(\Sigma_i X_{ijk})^2/n=33,382$,

SSTOT=1,516,

SSA=96.5

SSB=133.3

SSWG=582

and

SSINTER=704.2.

The results are typically reported as follows.

Source	SS	DF	MS	F
A	96.5	2	48.25	.50
B	133.3	1	133.3	1.37
INTER	704.2	2	352.1	3.62
WITHIN	582	6	97	
TOTAL	1,516			

With 2 and 6 degrees of freedom, and $\alpha=.05$, the critical F value is, from Table A3, 5.14, and so the test for interactions is not significant. The tests for main effects are not significant as well.

10.2 MULTIPLE COMPARISONS

Because JK independent treatment groups are being investigated, all of the multiple comparison procedures described in chapter nine can be applied. However, some care must be taken when choosing the set of linear contrast coefficients that will be used. Consider, for example, the j levels of factor A. One approach is to just pool the observations, as discussed in the previous section, and apply the procedures described in chapter nine. In effect you ignore the levels of factor B and treat the data as if you had a one-way ANOVA design. Alternatively, you may want to perform all pairwise comparisons of the $\mu_j.$'s where the $\mu_j.$'s are estimated using the approach described in the previous section based on equal weights. It is this latter approach which is the focus of attention here.

Example 10.2.1. To illustrate the way multiple comparisons might be performed, consider a 2 by 3 design with the following results.

Table 10.2.1

	Factor B		
Factor A	$\bar{X}_{11}=50$, $s_{11}^2=20$	$\bar{X}_{12}=60$, $s_{12}^2=10$	$\bar{X}_{13}=70$, $s_{13}^2=15$
	$\bar{X}_{21}=70$, $s_{21}^2=25$	$\bar{X}_{22}=50$, $s_{22}^2=14$	$\bar{X}_{23}=40$, $s_{23}^2=16$

Also suppose $n_{11}=n_{12}=n_{13}=n_{21}=n_{22}=n_{23}=10$. For notational convenience $\bar{X}_{.jk}$ is written simply as $\bar{X}_{jk}$. Also let

$$\mu._1=\mu_{11}+\mu_{21},\quad \mu._2=\mu_{12}+\mu_{22},\text{ and }\mu._3=\mu_{13}+\mu_{23},$$

and suppose that $H_0:\mu._k=\mu._m$ is to be tested for all k<m. That is, you want to perform all pairwise comparisons of the main effects of factor B. Also suppose the experimentwise Type I error probability is to be $\alpha=.05$. Let $\bar{Y}_k=\bar{X}_{1k}+\bar{X}_{2k}$ (k=1,2,3) and assume the variances are equal. Note that $\bar{Y}_k$ is an unbiased estimate of $\mu._k$, the $\bar{Y}_k$'s have equal sample sizes, and they have equal variances as well. This means that Tukey's procedure can be used. In particular, MSWG=16.67, $\nu=54$, and because there are three means being compared, you refer to Table A9 and find q=3.41. Compute

$$T=q[J(MSWG)/n]^{1/2}=6.23.$$

The confidence interval for $\mu_{\cdot k}-\mu_{\cdot m}$ is

$$(\bar{Y}_k-\bar{Y}_m)\pm T$$

For $\mu_{\cdot 1}$ and $\mu_{\cdot 2}$, the confidence interval is

$$(120-110)\pm 6.23=(3.77,\ 16.23).$$

Thus, reject $H_0:\mu_{\cdot 1}=\mu_{\cdot 2}$.

More generally, if you have a J by K design with equal variances and equal sample sizes, and you want to perform all pairwise comparisons of the main effects of factor B, compute

$$\bar{Y}_k=\Sigma_j \bar{X}_{jk} \qquad (k=1,\ldots,K)$$

and

$$T=q_{\alpha,K,\nu}[J(MSWG)/n]^{1/2}$$

where $q_{\alpha,K,\nu}$ is read from Table A9 with $\nu=JK(n-1)$ degrees of freedom. Note that the second subscript on q is K, not JK. That is, when referring to Table A9, the number of means being compared is K. Let $\mu_{\cdot k}=\Sigma_j \mu_{jk}$. The confidence interval for $\mu_{\cdot k}-\mu_{\cdot m}$ is

$$(\bar{Y}_k-\bar{Y}_m-T,\ \bar{Y}_k-\bar{Y}_m+T).$$

If this interval does not contain zero, reject $H_0:\mu_{\cdot k}=\mu_{\cdot m}$.

If you prefer formulating the null hypothesis in terms of

$$H_0:\bar{\mu}_{.k}=\bar{\mu}_{.m}$$

rather than

$$H_0:\mu_{.k}=\mu_{.m},$$

then

$$T=q_{\alpha,K,\nu}[MSWG/(Jn)]^{1/2},$$

and the confidence interval for $\bar{\mu}_{\cdot k}-\bar{\mu}_{\cdot m}$ is

$$(\bar{X}_{..k}-\bar{X}_{..m})\pm T.$$

Factor A is handled in a similar manner. Compute

$$\bar{Z}_j = \Sigma_k \bar{X}_{jk} \qquad (j=1,\ldots,J)$$

and

$$T = q_{\alpha,J,\nu}[K(MSWG)/n]^{1/2}$$

in which case you reject $H_0: \mu_{j.} = \mu_{m.}$ if

$$(\bar{Z}_j - \bar{Z}_m - T,\ \bar{Z}_j - \bar{Z}_m + T)$$

does not contain zero.

For unequal sample sizes, assuming equal variances, the Tukey-Kramer procedure can be used. For factor B you compute

$$\nu = (\Sigma\Sigma n_{jk}) - JK,$$

$$MSWG = \Sigma\Sigma\Sigma(X_{ijk} - \bar{X}_{.jk})^2/\nu$$

$$B_k = \Sigma_j 1/n_{jk} \qquad (k=1,\ldots,K)$$

and

$$T = q_{\alpha,K,\nu}[MSWG(B_k + B_m)/2]^{1/2}$$

For example, if you want to compare $\mu_{.1}$ and $\mu_{.2}$ and the sample sizes are $n_{11}=5$, $n_{12}=15$, $n_{13}=25$, $n_{21}=10$, $n_{22}=15$, and $n_{23}=20$, then $B_1=.3$ and $B_2=.133$. If MSWG=18,

$$T = 3.37[(18)(.3+.133)/2]^{1/2} = 6.66.$$

If $\bar{Y}_1=120$ and $\bar{Y}_2=110$, the confidence interval for $\mu_{.1}-\mu_{.2}$ is

$$(120-110) \pm 6.66 = (3.34, 16.66).$$

This interval does not contain zero so you reject H_0.

As for factor A, compute

$$A_j = \Sigma_k 1/n_{jk} \qquad (j=1,,,.J)$$

$$T = q_{\alpha,J,\nu}[MSWG(A_j + A_m)/2]^{1/2},$$

and the confidence interval for $\mu_{j.} - \mu_{m.}$ is

$$(\bar{Z}_j - \bar{Z}_m) \pm T$$

where $\bar{Z}_j = \Sigma_k \bar{X}_{jk}$.

Welch-Bonferroni

For unequal variances the modified Simes-Welch, the Welch-Bonferroni or the Welch-Dunn-Sidak procedure can be used. First consider the Welch-Bonferroni--suppose you want to compare the main effects of levels k and m of factor B, and let

$$\Psi_{km}=[\Sigma_j \mu_{jk}]-[\Sigma_j \mu_{jm}]=\mu_{.k}-\mu_{.m}.$$

Then $H_0:\mu_{.k}=\mu_{.m}$ is the same as $H_0:\Psi=0$. Let $s_{jk}{}^2$ be the sample variance for the observations in the j<u>th</u> level of factor A and the k<u>th</u> level of factor B. The contrast coefficients are

$$c_{1k}=c_{2k}=\ldots=c_{Jk}=1 \text{ and } c_{1m}=c_{2m}=\ldots=c_{Jm}=-1.$$

To test H_0, compute

$$\hat{\Psi}_{km}=\Sigma_j(\bar{X}_{jk}-\bar{X}_{jm})$$

and

$$T=\hat{\Psi}/[\Sigma_j s^2_{jk}/n_{jk}+\Sigma_j s^2_{jm}/n_{jm}]^{1/2}.$$

The degrees of freedom are

$$\nu=E^2/D$$

where

$$E=\Sigma_j(s^2_{jk}/n_{jk}+s^2_{jm}/n_{jm})$$

and

$$D=\Sigma_j[(s^2_{jk}/n_{jk})^2/(n_{jk}-1)+(s^2_{jm}/n_{jm})^2/(n_{jm}-1)].$$

If all pairwise comparisons are to be made, there are $C=(K^2-K)/2$ null hypotheses. If $|T|>t$, where t is read from Table A7, reject H_0.

As for factor A, to compare levels j and m, let

$$\Psi_{jm}=\Sigma_k(\mu_{jk}-\mu_{mk})=\mu_{j.}-\mu_{m.},$$

$$\hat{\Psi}_{jm}=\Sigma_k(\bar{X}_{jk}-\bar{X}_{mk}),$$

and

$$T=\hat{\Psi}_{jm}/[\Sigma_k(s^2_{jk}/n_{jk}+s^2_{mk}/n_{mk}]^{1/2}.$$

The degrees of freedom are

$$\nu=E^2/D$$

where

$$E=\Sigma_k (s_{jk}^2/n_{jk} + s_{mk}^2/n_{mk})$$

and

$$D=[\Sigma_k (s_{jk}^2/n_{jk})^2/(n_{jk}-1) + (s_{mk}^2/n_{mk})^2/(n_{mk}-1)].$$

The critical value is again read from Table A7, but this time the number of comparisons (assuming all pairwise comparisons are to be performed) is $C=J(J-1)/2$.

Welch-Dunn-Sidak

As indicated in chapter nine, the Welch-Dunn-Sidak procedure is used in the same manner as the Welch-Bonferroni procedure, using Table A10 rather than Table A7. All indications are that the Welch-Dunn-Sidak procedure is better than the Welch-Bonferroni.

Modified Simes-Welch

All indications are that the modified Simes-Welch procedure is better than the Welch-Bonferroni or Welch-Dunn-Sidak. The degrees of freedom are the same as in the Welch-Bonferroni. The modified Simes-Welch procedure is applied as outlined in section 3 of chapter nine.

Example 10.2.2. The Welch-Bonferroni procedure is illustrated with the data in Table 10.2.1. Suppose all pairwise comparisons of the main effects for factor B are to be made and that $\alpha=.05$. Then C=3 comparisons are to be made, since you have a 2 by 3 design (i.e., K=3). First consider the main effects of levels 1 and 2. Then

$$E=(20/10 + 25/10 + 10/10 +14/10)=6.9$$

$$D=20^2/[10^2(10-1)] + \ldots + 14^2/[10^2(10-1)]$$

and

$$\nu=E^2/D=32.4.$$

From Table A7, the critical value is approximately t=2.54. Continuing the calculations,

$$\hat{\Psi}=50+70-60-50=10,$$

and

$$T=10/[20/10 + 25/10 + 10/10 + 14/10]^{1/2} = 3.81$$

so $H_0:\mu_{.1}=\mu_{.2}$ is rejected. The other main effects are tested in the same manner.

Interactions

The techniques in chapter nine can also be used to test for both ordinal and disordinal interactions. For instance, you can test $H_0:\mu_{11}=\mu_{12}$ and $H_0:\mu_{21}=\mu_{22}$. If both tests are significant, and if $\bar{X}_{11}-\bar{X}_{12}$ and $\bar{X}_{21}-\bar{X}_{22}$ have opposite signs, you would conclude that there is a disordinal interaction. It should be noted that for the equal variance case, some caution must be used when interpreting the results. Suppose you estimate the common variance with MSWG. When performing the t-tests you might be tempted to assume that because $\bar{X}_{11}-\bar{X}_{12}$ and $\bar{X}_{21}-\bar{X}_{22}$ are independent, the event of a Type I error for the first t-test is independent of the event of a Type I error for the second. However, because each t-test has MSWG in its denominator, these events are not independent. By using the critical values in Table A10, the experimentwise Type I error probability will be exactly α. As noted in chapter nine, if the linear contrasts are correlated, the critical values in Table A10 ensure that the experimentwise Type I error will not exceed α. Of course in most situations equal variances should not be assumed, and the procedures for unequal variances in chapter nine should be used instead.

The Extended Tukey-Kramer Test for Disordinal Interactions

Although the procedures in chapter nine can be used to test for disordinal interactions, even better procedures can be applied. First consider the case of equal variances and equal sample sizes, and suppose you want to perform all pairwise comparisons of the means in each of the J rows in a J by K ANOVA. That is, you want to test

$$H_0:\mu_{jk}=\mu_{jm}$$

for j=1,...,J and all k<m. If, for example, you reject $H_0:\mu_{24}=\mu_{25}$ as well as $H_0:\mu_{34}=\mu_{35}$, and if $\bar{X}_{24}-\bar{X}_{25}>0$ while $\bar{X}_{34}-\bar{X}_{35}<0$, you would conclude that there is a disordinal interaction.

Note that a total of C=JK(K-1)/2 comparisons are made. For all pairwise comparisons in the first row, the experimentwise Type I error probability will be α if Tukey's procedure is applied. The same is true for all pairwise comparisons in the second row, etc. But how do you control the experimentwise Type I error probability among all JK(K-1)/2 comparisons? To solve this problem, you again apply Tukey's procedure, but instead of reading the critical value q from Table A9, you read q from Table A13. For unequal sample sizes you simply apply the Tukey-Kramer procedure and again q is read from Table A13. An important point is that when using Table A13, it is assumed that you are performing all pairwise comparisons in each of the J rows. If instead you want to perform all pairwise comparisons in each column, you reverse the roles of J and K when referring to Table A13.

Example 10.2.3. Suppose you have a 3 by 4 ANOVA and you want to perform all pairwise comparisons in each of the 3 rows. That is, there are a total of $3(4)(4-1)/2=18$ comparisons to be made. If the degrees of freedom are $\nu=10$, Table A13 says that $q=5.19$. If instead you want to perform all pairwise comparisons in each of the $K=4$ columns, then you are performing $KJ(J-1)/2=4(3)(3-1)/2=12$ comparisons, and the critical value is read from Table A13 with $J=4$ and $K=3$. If again $\nu=10$, the critical value q is now 4.95 rather than 5.19.

Example 10.2.4. Suppose you have three methods of teaching reading and you want to also compare males versus females. Further suppose that the results of your experiment are given in Table 10.2.1 and that you are interested in whether there is a disordinal interaction. To find out, you decide to perform all pairwise comparisons in the first row (say males), and you also want to perform all pairwise comparisons in the second row (females). Thus, $J=2$ and $K=3$. Note that it is assumed that your primary goal is to compare methods of teaching, and that comparing males versus females is of interest only to the extent that a disordinal interaction exists. In some situations you may be interested in all pairwise comparisons of all JK means in which case the Tukey or Tukey-Kramer procedure can be used as described in chapter nine. The advantage of limiting the number of hypotheses being tested to only those that are of interest is that you will have more power than you would if additional tests are performed. This is assuming, of course, that if additional tests are performed, the experimentwise Type I error probability is not to exceed α.

Continuing the example, there are $n=10$ observations in each group, so $\nu=56$, and from Table A13, with $\alpha=.05$, q is approximately equal to 3.80. (For $\nu=40$, $q=3.85$ while for $\nu=60$, $q=3.78$.) Thus, when applying the Tukey-Kramer procedure procedure, you get

$$T=q[MSWG(1/n_{11} + 1/n_{12})/2]^{1/2}$$

$$=3.80[16.67(1/10 + 1/10)/2]^{1/2}$$

$$=4.91.$$

This is the same equation for T as given by (9.3.7). Thus, the confidence interval for $\mu_{11}-\mu_{12}$ is

$$(50-60)\pm4.91,$$

and so you reject. Next consider $H_0:\mu_{21}=\mu_{22}$. Again T=4.91, the confidence interval for $\mu_{21}-\mu_{22}$ is

$$(70-50)\pm4.91,$$

and again you reject. Because 50-60<0 and 70-50>0, you conclude that there is a disordinal interaction, and in particular method 1 is best for females while the reverse is true for males.

Another way of studying interactions is with linear contrasts. For example, you might test

$$H_0: \Psi=(\mu_{11}-\mu_{12})-(\mu_{21}-\mu_{22})=0.$$

However, this approach, by itself, does not tell you whether an interaction is ordinal or disordinal. For instance, suppose you reject H_0 and conclude that $\Psi<0$. This does not tell you whether you can reject $\mu_{11}=\mu_{12}$ or $\mu_{21}=\mu_{22}$. In order to conclude that you have a disordinal interaction, you must reject both $H_0:\mu_{11}=\mu_{12}$ and $H_0:\mu_{21}=\mu_{22}$.

Disordinal Interactions and Unequal Variances

As for handling unequal variances, an extension of Dunnett's T3 or C can be used. For J>1 these procedure are called method ET3 (for extended T3), and method EC (for extended C).

Suppose that all pairwise comparisons are to be made in each of the J rows. That is, you want simultaneous confidence intervals for $\mu_{jk}-\mu_{jm}$ for j=1,...,J and all k≠m. The confidence interval for $\mu_{jk}-\mu_{jm}$, using method EC, is given by

$$(\bar{X}_{jk}-\bar{X}_{jm})\pm Q/\surd 2$$

where

$$Q = A/B,$$

$$A = q_{\alpha,\nu_{jk}}s^2_{jk}/n_{jk} + q_{\alpha,\nu_{jm}}s^2_{jm}/n_{jm},$$

$$B = [s^2_{jk} + s^2_{jm}]^{1/2},$$

$$\nu_{jk} = n_{jk}-1 \text{ and } \nu_{jm} = n_{jm}-1$$

The quantity q is read from Table A13. When J=1, the procedure reduces to Dunnett's C, in which case q is read from Table A9.

As for method ET3, the confidence interval is given by

$$(\bar{X}_{jk}-\bar{X}_{jm})\pm V_{\alpha,C,\nu_{jkm}}[s_{jk}^2/n_{jk} + s_{jm}^2/n_{jm}]^{1/2}$$

where V is read from Table A10, and where C=JK(K-1)/2 is the number of comparisons being performed. The degrees of freedom for method ET3 are

$$\nu_{jkm} = E^2/D$$

where

$$E=(s_{jk}^2/n_{jk} + s_{jm}^2/n_{jm})$$

and

$$D=(s_{jk}^2/n_{jk})^2/(n_{jk}-1) + (s_{jm}^2/n_{jm})^2/(n_{jm}-1).$$

Again it should be stressed that if all JK(JK-1)/2 pairwise comparisons are to be made, you do not use Table A13. Instead you use the procedures in chapter nine. The point here is that you may not want to do all pairwise comparisons, but rather restrict your attention to all pairwise comparisons within each of the J rows. In this case Table A13 will give you shorter confidence intervals.

It should be noted that for J>2, a similar extension of the Games-Howell procedure can be derived, but it is not recommended. If $n_{jk}>50$ for all j and k, method EC seems to be best, while for small degrees of freedom in any treatment group, method ET3 is preferred.

<u>Example 10.2.5</u>. Again consider the data in Table 10.2.1. Because the number of observations per group is only 10, method ET3 should be used. The degrees of freedom for testing $H_0:\mu_{11}=\mu_{12}$ are

$$(2.0+1.0)^2/(4/9 + 1/9)=16.2.$$

There are C=2(3)(3-1)/2=6 comparisons, and so referring to Table A10, V=2.97 (assuming α=.05). The confidence interval for $\mu_{11}-\mu_{12}$ is

$$(50-60)\pm2.97[2+1]^{1/2}=-10\pm5.14.$$

Again you reject. If instead you had used method EC, the confidence interval for $\mu_{jk}-\mu_{jm}$ is

$$(\bar{X}_{jk}-\bar{X}_{jm})\pm Q/\surd 2.$$

For $\mu_{11}-\mu_{12}$,, $\nu_{11}=\nu_{12}=9$, q=4.52 (for α=.05, J=2 and K=3), so

$$Q=[4.52(2) +4.52(1)]/[2 + 1]^{1/2}.$$

10.3 CONTROLLING POWER AND HANDLING UNEQUAL VARIANCES

Section 8.12 described an exact two-stage procedure that guarantees that the probability of a Type I error will be exactly α in the one-way ANOVA, and the procedure also gives you control over power in terms of $\Sigma\alpha_j{}^2$. This section describes an extension of those results to the two-way model.

As before, the first stage consists of randomly sampling n observations from each of the JK treatment groups. The observations are represented by X_{ijk} (i=1,...,n; j=1,...,J; k=1,...,K). First consider factor A and suppose you want to reject $H_0:\Sigma\alpha_j{}^2=0$ when $\Sigma\alpha_j{}^2=\delta>0$, where δ is some number you have picked. The first step is determining the critical value that is needed. If the type I error probability is to be α, the critical value is approximately equal to c, where c is chosen so that

$$\Pr\{\chi^2_{J-1}\le(n-3)c/(n-1)\}=1-\alpha, \tag{10.3.1}$$

where χ^2_{J-1} is a chi-square random variable with J-1 degrees of freedom. The constant c can be determined from Table A2. For example, if J=4 and α=.05, from Table A2

$$\Pr\{\chi^2_3\le 7.81\}=.95.$$

If, for example, n=12, 9c/11=7.81, and so c=9.55.

Next you determine the constant d by referring to Table A1 and determining z such that $\Pr(Z\le z)=\beta$, computing

$$b=(n-3)c/(n-1),$$

$$A=(1/2)\{-z(\surd 2) + [2z^2+4(2b-\eta+1)]^{1/2}\} \tag{10.3.2}$$

where η=J-1, in which case

$$d=[\delta/(A^2-b)](n-3)/(n-1). \tag{10.3.3}$$

Then you compute

$$n_{jk}=\max\{n+1,\ (s_{jk}^2/d)^{\dagger}+1\}$$

where

$$s_{jk}^2=\Sigma(X_{ijk}-\bar{X}_{.jk})^2/(n-1)$$

is the sample variance for the (j,k)th treatment group based on the initial n observations. The quantity $(s_{jk}^2/d)^{\dagger}$ is the integer portion of s_{jk}^2/d.

The second stage consists of randomly sampling an additional $n_{jk}-n$ observations from the (j,k)th treatment group. Once these observations are available, you compute

$$D=n(n_{jk}d-s_{jk}^2),$$

$$E=(n_{jk}-n)s_{jk}^2$$

$$b=\{1+[D/E]^{1/2}\}/n_{jk}$$

and

$$a=[1-(n_{jk}-n)b]/n.$$

Note that both a and b have different values across the JK treatment groups. That is, for j=1 and k=1 the values for a and b will be different from, say j=1 and k=2, etc.

Next compute

$$\tilde{X}_{jk}=\sum_{i=1}^{n} aX_{ijk} + \sum_{i=n+1}^{n_{jk}} bX_{ijk}.$$

Once $\tilde{X}_{jk}$ has been determined for all JK groups, compute

$$\tilde{X}_{j.}=\Sigma_k\tilde{X}_{jk}/K,$$

$$\tilde{X}_{.k}=\Sigma_j\tilde{X}_{jk}/J,$$

$$\tilde{X}_{..}=\Sigma\Sigma\tilde{X}_{jk}/(JK)$$

and

$$\tilde{F}=K\Sigma_j(\tilde{X}_{j.}-\tilde{X}_{..})^2/d. \qquad (10.3.4)$$

If $\tilde{F}>c$, reject H_0: $\Sigma\alpha_j^2=0$.

Factor B

As for factor B, compute

$$\tilde{F}=J\Sigma_k(\tilde{X}_{.k}-\tilde{X}_{..})^2/d$$

and reject H_0 if $\tilde{F}>c$. Note that if $J\neq K$, a new critical value must be determined. This time you choose c so that

$$\Pr\{\chi^2_{K-1}<(n-3)c/(n-1)\}=1-\alpha.$$

The power is again controlled through the choice of d, which is given approximately by equation (10.3.3) where now $\delta=\Sigma\beta_k^2$ is some alternative value that you have chosen, and $\eta=K-1$.

Interactions

As for interactions, compute

$$\tilde{F}=\Sigma\Sigma(\tilde{X}_{jk}-\tilde{X}_{j.}-\tilde{X}_{.k}+\tilde{X}_{..})^2/d.$$

An approximate critical value is the constant c such that

$$\Pr\{\chi^2_L<(n-3)c/(n-1)\}=1-\alpha \qquad (10.3.5)$$

where $L=(J-1)(K-1)$. This approximation seems to work well when n is at least 10, and it improves as n gets large. Again the power is controlled through the choice of d. If the power is to be $1-\beta$ for

$$\delta=\Sigma\Sigma\gamma^2_{jk}>0,$$

first determine c using (10.3.5), set $\eta=(J-1)(K-1)$, compute A using (10.3.2), and then d using (10.3.3).

When making judgments about what value of δ to use when testing for interactions, it may help to consider the value of δ for a particular configuration of means. For instance, if $J=K=2$, you might want the power to be reasonably high when $\mu_{11}=10$, $\mu_{12}=6$, $\mu_{21}=6$, and $\mu_{22}=10$. Then $\mu=\mu_{1.}=\mu_{.1}=\mu_{2.}=\mu_{.2}=8$, and since $\gamma_{jk}=\mu_{jk}-\mu_{j.}-\mu_{.k}+\mu$, $\gamma_{11}=10-8-8+8=2$, $\gamma_{12}=-2$, $\gamma_{21}=-2$, $\gamma_{22}=2$, and $\Sigma\Sigma\gamma_{jk}^2=16$. It might be difficult to assign actual numbers to the μ_{jk}'s but the only thing that really matters is the values of the differences $\mu_{11}-\mu_{12}$ and $\mu_{21}-\mu_{22}$. The reason is that if you add the constant a to every μ_{jk} value, $\Sigma\Sigma\gamma_{jk}^2$ remains the same. For example, if $a=-6$, $\mu_{11}=\mu_{22}=4$, $\mu_{12}=\mu_{21}=0$, and again $\Sigma\Sigma\gamma_{jk}^2=16$.

Example 10.3.1. Suppose that when testing for an interaction effect you want the power to be $1-\beta=.8$ when $\delta=16$. To keep the illustration simple, suppose $J=K=2$, $s_{11}^2=10$, $s_{12}^2=12$, $s_{21}^2=9$,

$s_{22}{}^2=9$, and n=17. Then L=1. If $\alpha=.05$, the critical value is chosen so that

$$\Pr\{\chi_1^2 \le 14c/16\}=.95.$$

From Table A2, 14c/16=3.84, and so c=4.39.

As for d, from Table A1, $\Pr(Z\le -.84)=.2$, so z=-.84. Then b=3.84, $\eta=(J-1)(K-1)=1$, and from (10.3.2),

$$A=(1/2)\{.84(\surd 2) + [2(.84)^2 + 4(2(3.84)-1+1)]^{1/2}$$

$$=3.428.$$

Since $\delta=16$,

$$d=\{16/[3.428^2-3.84]\}(14/16)=1.77$$

Thus,

$$n_{11}=\max\{17+1, (10/1.77)^{\dagger}+1\}=18.$$

Similarly, $n_{21}=n_{12}=n_{22}=18$ and so only one additional observation is required for each treatment group.

10.4 RANDOM EFFECTS MODEL

In the one-way random effects model described in section 8.9, the J levels were chosen at random. The goal in this section is to consider the two-way model when the levels of both factors are chosen at random. That is, you randomly sample J levels for factor A and K levels for factor B, and then you randomly sample n subjects from each of the JK independent treatment groups.

Generalizing the one-way model, the two factor model is

$$X_{ijk}=\mu+a_j+b_k+c_{jk}+\epsilon_{ijk} \qquad (10.4.1)$$

where μ is the grand mean while a_j, b_k, c_{jk}, and ϵ_{ijk} are independent normally distributed random variables with means all equal to zero and variances $\sigma_a{}^2$, $\sigma_b{}^2$, $\sigma_c{}^2$, and σ^2, respectively. In contrast to the fixed effect two-way model, it is not assumed that $\Sigma a_j=\Sigma b_k=\Sigma_j c_{jk}=\Sigma_k c_{jk}=0$. The goal is to derive F tests for

$$H_0:\sigma_a{}^2=0,$$

$$H_0:\sigma_b{}^2=0,$$

and

$$H_0:\sigma_c{}^2=0.$$

Using techniques similar to those used in chapter eight, it can be shown that

$$E(SSB)=(K-1)Jn[\sigma_b^2 + \sigma_c^2/J + \sigma^2/(nJ)]$$

where as before

$$SSB=\Sigma_k Jn(\bar{X}_{..k}-\bar{X}_{...})^2. \quad (10.4.2)$$

Again MSB is defined to be SSB/(K-1), and so

$$E(MSB)=Jn\sigma_b^2+n\sigma_c^2+\sigma^2. \quad (10.4.3)$$

Also

$$E(MSA)=Kn\sigma_a^2+n\sigma_c^2+\sigma^2 \quad (10.4.4)$$

and

$$E(MSWG)=\sigma^2. \quad (10.4.5)$$

Therefore, MSA/MSWG measures the effect of both σ_a^2 and σ_c^2. Consequently, you cannot use MSA/MSWG to test $H_0:\sigma_a^2=0$. However, it can be shown that

$$E(MSINTER)=\sigma^2+n\sigma_c^2 \quad (10.4.6)$$

and so MSA/MSINTER measures the extent to which $\sigma_a^2>0$. It can also be shown that MSA/MSINTER has an F distribution with J-1 and (J-1)(K-1) degrees of freedom. Thus, if

$$MSA/MSINTER>f$$

where f is the 1-α quantile of the F distribution with ν_1=J-1 and ν_2=(J-1)(K-1) degrees of freedom, which is read from Table A3, reject $H_0:\sigma_a^2=0$.

For similar reasons you reject $H_0:\sigma_b^2=0$ if

$$MSB/MSINTER>f,$$

only now the degrees of freedom are K-1 and (J-1)(K-1). As for testing $H_0:\sigma_c^2=0$, use

$$F=MSINTER/MSWG$$

with (J-1)(K-1) and JK(n-1) degrees of freedom. In summary, the calculations for the sum of squares are exactly the same as in the fixed effect model, but the F tests are different.

Measuring Treatment Effects

Treatment effects can be measured in much the same way as they were for the one-way model. In particular, since the variance of the X_{ijk}'s is

$$\sigma_x^2=\sigma_a^2+\sigma_b^2+\sigma_c^2+\sigma^2,$$

$$\rho_a=\sigma_a^2/\sigma_x^2$$

is the proportion of total variance accounted for by factor A. That is, ρ_a measures the treatment effect of factor A. For factor B and interactions you would use

$$\rho_b=\sigma_b^2/\sigma_x^2$$

and

$$\rho_c=\sigma_c^2/\sigma_x^2.$$

From equations (10.4.3)-(10.4.6), unbiased estimates of $\sigma_a{}^2$, σ_b, $\sigma_c{}^2$, and σ^2 are

$$\hat{\sigma}_a{}^2=(\text{MSA-MSINTER})/(nK),$$

$$\hat{\sigma}_b{}^2=(\text{MSB-MSINTER})/(nJ)$$

$$\hat{\sigma}_c{}^2=(\text{MSINTER-MSWG})/n$$

and

$$\hat{\sigma}^2=\text{MSWG}.$$

Thus, to estimate ρ_a for example, you would use

$$\hat{\rho}_a=\hat{\sigma}_a{}^2/[\hat{\sigma}_a{}^2+\hat{\sigma}_b{}^2+\hat{\sigma}_c{}^2+\hat{\sigma}^2].$$

The Mixed Model

Next suppose that the levels of factor A are fixed but that the levels of factor B are sampled at random. Now the model is

$$X_{ijk}=\mu+\alpha_j+b_k+c_{jk}+\epsilon_{ijk}$$

where $\Sigma\alpha_j=\Sigma_j c_{jk}=0$. The random variables b_k, c_{jk}, and ϵ_{ijk} are assumed to be independent and normally distributed with means all equal to zero and variances $\sigma_b{}^2$, $\sigma_c{}^2$, and σ^2. Proceeding as was done in the previous model, it can be shown that

$$E(MSA)=\sigma^2+n\sigma_c^2+nK\Sigma\alpha_j^2/(J-1),$$

$$E(MSB)=\sigma^2+nJ\sigma_b^2,$$

$$E(MSINTER)=\sigma^2+n\sigma_c^2$$

and

$$E(MSWG)=\sigma^2.$$

To test $H_0:\Sigma\alpha_j^2=0$ use

$$F=MSA/MSINTER$$

with J-1 and (J-1)(K-1) degrees of freedom. For $H_0:\sigma_b^2=0$ use

$$F=MSB/MSWG$$

with K-1 and JK(n-1) degrees of freedom. For $H_0:\sigma_c^2=0$ use

$$F=MSINTER/MSWG$$

with (J-1)(K-1) and JK(n-1) degrees of freedom.

EXERCISES

10.1 Suppose you have a 2 by 3 design with the following observations.

		Factor B	
	1	2	3
Factor 1:	5,4,1,8	6,2,12,9	10,15,16,2
A 2:	9,18,20,10	15,9,2,3	12,14,16,9

a) Assume equal variances and perform the F tests for main effects and interactions using $\alpha=.05$. What is the unbiased estimate of σ^2?

b) Perform all pairwise comparisons of the main effects for factor B using Tukey's procedure. Use $\alpha=.01$

c) Test $H_0:\mu_{11}=\mu_{13}$ and $H_0:\mu_{21}=\mu_{23}$ assuming equal variances and that the experimentwise Type I error is to be at most $\alpha=.05$. Do the results indicate that there is a disordinal interaction?

d) Repeat part c but do not assume equal variances.

e) Assume equal variances and use Dunn's procedure to test

$$H_0: \mu_{11} - \mu_{12} = \mu_{21} - \mu_{22} \text{ and } H_0: \mu_{11} - \mu_{13} = \mu_{21} - \mu_{23}.$$

The experimentwise Type I error is to be at most .05.

f) Assume equal variances and estimate $\Sigma\alpha_j^2$ and $\Sigma\beta_k^2$.

g) In 10.1e, should you use the Dunn-Sidak procedure rather than Dunn's?

h) Repeat part e but do not assume equal variances.

10.2 For the data in problem 10.1, suppose the levels of both factors A and B were sampled at random.

a) Perform the appropriate F tests using α=.05. Assume equal variances.

b) Estimate σ_a^2.

10.3 For the data in 10.1, suppose you want to test

$$H_0: \mu_{.1} = \mu_{.2} = \mu_{.3}$$

and that the power is to be at least .90 when $\Sigma\beta_k^2$=10.

a) If α=.05, what is the critical value?

b) How many observations are required from each group?

c) Suppose that in part b only one additional observation is sampled from each group and that the observed values are

		B		
		1	2	3
A	1:	10	4	12
	2:	13	14	10

Compute $\tilde{X}_{jk}$ for all six groups assuming d=8.0

d) Assuming $\tilde{X}_{11}$=8, $\tilde{X}_{12}$=10, $\tilde{X}_{13}$=9, $\tilde{X}_{21}$=14, $\tilde{X}_{22}$=16, and $\tilde{X}_{23}$=9, test $H_0: \mu_{.1} = \mu_{.2} = \mu_{.3}$ using α=.05 and d=8.0.

e) Test $H_0: \Sigma\Sigma\gamma_{jk}^2 = 0$ using the results from part d. Use α=.01 and assume d=3.0

References

Kendall, M. G. & Stuart, A. (1973) The advanced theory of statistic.s Vol. 2. New York: Hafner

Kirk, R. (1982) Experimental design: procedures for the behavioral sciences Monterey aAliforni: Brooks/Cole.

Neter, J & Wasserman, W (1974) Applied linear statistical models Homewood, Illinois: Irwin

Scheffe, H. (1959) The analysis of variance New York: Wiley.

CHAPTER ELEVEN

REPEATED MEASURES AND RANDOMIZED BLOCKS DESIGNS

An important feature of the ANOVA model in chapter eight is that the J treatment groups are independent. In chapter seven it was noted that for J=2 groups it can be advantageous to test $H_0:\mu_1=\mu_2$ using dependent groups. For example, suppose you conduct an experiment on mice in which the goal is to determine whether two different conditions affect learning. You could randomly assign some mice to one condition and randomly assign a different (independent) sample of mice to the other and test $H_0:\mu_1=\mu_2$, where μ_j is the average learning occurring under the j<u>th</u> condition. Alternatively, you could randomly sample n pairs of litter mates and assign one litter mate to each of the two treatment groups. If X_{ij} (i=1,...,n; j=1,2) are the n pairs of observations, you can test $H_0:\mu_1=\mu_2$ with

$$T=(\sqrt{n})(\bar{X}_1-\bar{X}_2)/s_D \tag{11.0.1}$$

where

$$s_D^2=\Sigma(D_i-\bar{D})^2/(n-1)$$

and

$$D_i=X_{i1}-X_{i2}.$$

T has a Student's t distribution with ν=n-1 degrees of freedom.

The experiment on pairs of litter mates is an example of what is called a randomized block design. As another example, suppose you want to investigate the effects of a particular diet on cholesterol levels. If you measure a subject's cholesterol level at four different times, say every six weeks, and you want to compare cholesterol levels at the four different times, you have a randomized block design. This latter design is commonly called a repeated measures design because you repeatedly measure the same subjects.

The essential feature of a completely randomized block design is that you have n independent random vectors of observations, say

$$(X_{i1},\ldots,X_{iJ}),\ i=1,2,\ldots,n.$$

If in the mice experiment there are three mice per litter and each is assigned to one of three treatment groups, the length of the vector is J=3. As in chapter eight, $X_{1j},\ldots,X_{nj}$ is assumed to be a random sample from a normal distribution. The goal is to test

$$H_0:\mu_1=\ldots=\mu_J,$$

but X_{ij} and X_{ik}, $j \neq k$, are dependent observations, and so the procedures in chapter eight do not necessarily apply.

11.1 THE HUYNH-FELDT PROCEDURE

For the j<u>th</u> and k<u>th</u> blocks (or the j<u>th</u> and k<u>th</u> times a subject is measured), let

$$s_{jk}=\Sigma_i (X_{ij}-\bar{X}_j)(X_{ik}-\bar{X}_k)/(n-1). \qquad (11.1.1)$$

Note that for j=k,

$$s_{jk}=s_j^2=\Sigma(X_{ij}-\bar{X}_j)^2/(n-1)$$

which is the usual sample variance for the j<u>th</u> treatment group. The statistic s_{jk} is an estimate of

$$\sigma_{jk}=E(X_j-\mu_j)(X_k-\mu_k)$$

which is called the covariance between the j<u>th</u> and k<u>th</u> treatment groups. For $j \neq k$, s_{jk} is called the sample covariance between the j<u>th</u> and k<u>th</u> measures.

Let

$$SSB=J\Sigma(\bar{X}_{i.}-\bar{X})^2,$$

$$SSE=\Sigma\Sigma(X_{ij}-\bar{X}_{i.}-\bar{X}_{.j}+\bar{X}_{..})^2,$$

where

$$\bar{X}_{i.}=\Sigma_j X_{ij}/J$$

and

$$\bar{X}_{.j}=\Sigma_i X_{ij}/n$$

$$\bar{X}_{..}=\Sigma\Sigma X_{ij}/(Jn).$$

Under certain circumstances the hypothesis of equal means can be tested with

$$F=MSB/MSE \qquad (11.1.2)$$

where

$$MSB=SSB/(J-1)$$

and

$$MSE=SSE/[(J-1)(n-1)].$$

In particular, F will have an F distribution with J-1 and (J-1)(n-1) degrees of freedom if the variances and covariances satisfy certain conditions. These conditions are not described here because if these conditions are not met, the statistic F does not have an F distribution. (For a description of these conditions, see Huynh & Feldt, 1970.) These restrictions can be tested (e.g., Anderson, 1958), but the test of these restrictions is not robust to violations of the normality assumption (Keselman, Rogan, Mendoza & Breen, 1980). Even under normality, this test is useful only if its power is reasonably high. Simulation studies indicate that a better approach is to use the procedure described below, which deals more directly with these restrictions.

Box (1954) showed that the degrees of freedom of the F statistic can be adjusted so that F will have, approximately, an F distribution when the variances and covariances are known. Of course they are not known, but they can be estimated using the sample variances and covariances. In fact two methods, based on the sample variances and covariances, have been proposed for adjusting the degrees of freedom, and they are described below.

Let

$$\bar{\sigma}^2=\Sigma_j \sigma_j^2/J$$

and

$$\bar{s}^2=\Sigma_j s_j^2/J$$

be the average sample variances, let

$$\tilde{s}=\Sigma\Sigma s_{jk}/J^2$$

be the average of all of the s_{jk}'s, and compute

$$\bar{s}_j=\Sigma_k s_{jk}/J$$

$$\hat{A}=J^2(\bar{s}^2-\tilde{s})^2/(J-1)$$

$$\hat{B}=[\Sigma\Sigma s_{jk}^2]-[2J\Sigma_j \bar{s}_j^2]+[J^2\tilde{s}^2]$$

$$\hat{\epsilon}=\hat{A}/\hat{B}$$

and

$$\tilde{\epsilon}=[n(J-1)\hat{\epsilon}-2]/\{(J-1)[n-1-(J-1)\hat{\epsilon}]\}.$$

Let A and B be the quantities where the sample variances and covariances in the expressions for $\hat{A}$ and $\hat{B}$ are replaced with the corresponding parameters. That is, the statistic s_{jk} is replaced by σ_{jk} for all j and k. Then $\hat{\epsilon}$ and $\tilde{\epsilon}$ are estimates of the parameter ϵ=A/B. The parameter ϵ is sometimes referred to as Box's correction factor.

To test H_0, you compute the F statistic using equation (11.1.2). You then adjust the degrees of freedom based on the estimate of ϵ. If ϵ were known, F would have, approximately, an F distribution with $\nu_1=\epsilon(J-1)$ and $\nu_2=\epsilon(J-1)(n-1)$ degrees of freedom. Because ϵ is not known, Huynh and Feldt (1976) suggest estimating ϵ with $\tilde{\epsilon}$, in which case the degrees of freedom are

$$\nu_1=\tilde{\epsilon}(J-1) \text{ and } \nu_2=\tilde{\epsilon}(n-1)(J-1).$$

The parameter ϵ can also be estimated with $\hat{\epsilon}$, and Huynh and Feldt report simulation results indicating that $\tilde{\epsilon}$ generally gives more satisfactory results. However, when $\tilde{\epsilon}$ is used, the actual significance level can exceed the nominal α level, but for α=.05 the actual significance level never exceeded .06 in the simulations reported by Huynh and Feldt. Also, it can be shown that

$$\tilde{\epsilon} \geq \hat{\epsilon}$$

which means that an F test based on $\hat{\epsilon}$ will always have a lower Type I error probability (cf. Collier, Baker, Mandeville & Hayes, 1967). For the moment it seems that $\hat{\epsilon}$ should be used because it gives more conservative results. If, however, it is known that ϵ>.75, $\tilde{\epsilon}$ is recommended by Huynh and Feldt as well as Barcikowski and Robey (1984). Huynh and Feldt argue that ϵ>.75 is fairly common in educational studies, but nevertheless, ϵ is an unknown parameter.

Accordingly, $\hat{\epsilon}$ should probably be used in most situations unless you are willing to use a procedure that is slightly liberal (i.e., exceeds the nominal α level).

As a final note, it can be shown that

$$1/(J-1) \leq \epsilon \leq 1,$$

but citing an unpublished dissertation by H. E. Gary, Kirk (1982) notes that $\tilde{\epsilon}$ can exceed one. If this happens, you should estimate ϵ to be one.

11.2 PAIRWISE MULTIPLE COMPARISONS

Next attention is turned to testing $H_0:\mu_j=\mu_k$ for all $j<k$. Because observations are dependent, many of the multiple comparison procedures in chapter nine cannot be used unless certain assumptions are made (Scheffe, 1959). Although these assumptions can be tested, the power of the test of these assumptions may not be high enough for many practical situations, and so for the moment it is suggested that you simply follow the procedure described below.

Maxwell (1980) compared four multiple comparison procedures and concluded that the best procedure is to use the paired (or correlated) t-test with the significance level adjusted according to the Bonferroni inequality. More specifically, let

$$D_{ijk}=X_{ij}\ X_{ik}\quad (i=1,\ldots,n;\ j<k)$$

and compute

$$\bar{D}_{jk}=\Sigma D_{ijk}/n,$$

and

$$s_{jk}^2=\Sigma(D_{ijk}-\bar{D}_{jk})^2/(n-1).$$

The critical value is read from Table A7. (This is the same table used in Dunn's procedure.) Assuming all pairwise comparisons are to be made, the total number of comparisons is $C=(J(J-1)/2$, and the degrees of freedom are $\nu=n-1$. If, for example, $\alpha=.05$, $J=4$, and $n=11$, the critical value is $c=3.28$.
If

$$|(\sqrt{n})\bar{D}_{jk}/s_{jk}|>c,$$

reject $H_0:\mu_j=\mu_k$. From the Bonferroni inequality, the experimentwise Type I error probability will not exceed α.

It is noted that a slightly better and more extensive table of critical values is available (Wilcox, 1985). Wilcox's table is better in the sense that the experimentwise Type I error probability is always as close or closer to the nominal α level, but again the actual α level never exceeds the nominal level. If the number of comparisons, C, is even, Wilcox showed that if each hypothesis is tested at the

$$1-[1-2\alpha/C]^{1/2}$$

level, the experimentwise Type I error probability will be less than or equal to α. This is in contrast to using the Bonferroni inequality where each hypothesis is tested at the α/C level. For small α there is a negligible difference in the resulting critical values, but the difference in the critical values increases as α gets large. Also, for large C, the Bonferroni inequality gives better results. Thus, use the procedure that gives the shortest confidence intervals. For C odd, Wilcox showed that the nominal α level will not be exceeded if you perform the tests at the

$$1 - \{-1+[1-4d(\alpha-1-d)]^{1/2}\}/(2d)$$

level, where $d=(C-1)/2$.

An improvement on the Bonferroni procedure was recently proposed by Simes (1986), and all indications are that it gives better results. A description of Simes' procedure is given in the next section. (See equation 11.3.2.)

11.3 LINEAR CONTRASTS

If desired, any set of linear contrasts can also be tested. As in chapter nine, let

$$c_{1k},\ldots,c_{Jk} \quad (k=1,\ldots,C)$$

be C sets of J linear contrast coefficients, let

$$\Psi_k=\Sigma_j c_{jk}\mu_j \quad (k=1,\ldots,C)$$

and

$$\hat{\Psi}_k=\Sigma_i \Sigma_j c_{jk}X_{ij}/n.$$

Compute

$$\hat{\sigma}_k^2=\Sigma_i (\Sigma_j c_{jk}X_{ij}-\hat{\Psi}_k)^2/(n-1),$$

and reject $H_0:\Psi_k=0$ if

$$(\sqrt{n})|\hat{\Psi}_k/\hat{\sigma}_k|>c,$$

where the critical value c is read Table A7 with $\nu=n-1$ degrees of freedom. Again the table of critical values in Wilcox (1985) can be used.

Modified Simes' Procedure

More recently, Simes (1986) proposed a modification of the Bonferroni procedure that can used for the problem at hand. Let

$$A_k=(\sqrt{n})\hat{\Psi}_k/\hat{\sigma}_k$$

and let

$$P_k=\Pr(-A_k \le T_\nu \le A_k),\ k=1,\ldots,C \qquad (11.3.1)$$

where T_ν is a Student's t random variable with ν=n-1 degrees of freedom.

(That is, you use Table A14 to evaluate 11.3.1.)
P_k is called the significance level of the kth test. If you had set c=A_k, you would reject $H_0:\Psi_k=0$, and the probability of a Type I error would have been P_k. Let

$$P_{(1)}\le P_{(2)}\le\ldots\le P_{(C)}$$

be the P_k values written in ascending order. Following Simes' suggestion, reject $H_0:\Psi_k=0$ if $P_k=P_{(j)}$, that is, P_k is the jth largest significance level, and

$$P_{(m)} \le m\alpha/C \quad (m=1,,,j) \qquad (11.3.2)$$

where, as usual, α is the experimentwise Type I error probability you desire. In other words, reject H_0: $\Psi_k=0$ if

$$P_{(m)} \le m\alpha/C,$$

and if all previous tests with lower significance levels were also rejected. That is, you reject the hypothesis with the smallest significance level if it is less than α/C. If you reject, continue on to the next highest significance level and reject if it is less than $2\alpha/C$, etc. Once you fail to reject, do not perform any more hypotheses and fail to reject those that have not been tested. All indications are that for most practical situations, the modified Simes procedure is conservative (the actual experimentwise Type I error probability will not exceed α), and it generally gives better results than the Bonferroni inequality. In particular, it has more power than the Bonferroni procedure, and in some cases the power is considerably higher.

11.4 EFFICIENCY

A basic issue when designing an experiment is deciding whether a randomized block design should be used, or whether independent groups would provide more power. In many situations an investigator has no choice about which design should be used, but if a choice is possible, how does one decide?

Vonesh (1983) compared the length of the confidence intervals based on the Bonferroni inequality for independent versus dependent groups. He found that as n increased, with the correlations fixed, the length of the confidence intervals for repeated measures designs became shorter relative to the length for independent groups. That is, the ratio of the lengths got smaller with a ratio less than one indicating that a repeated measures design is better than using independent groups. In contrast, as the number of comparisons increased, with n and the correlations fixed, the ratio increased.

Let ρ_m be the minimum correlation among all the correlations between random variables. That is, if ρ_{jk} is the correlation between X_{ij} and X_{ik}, $\rho_m = \min\{\rho_{jk}\}$ where the minimum is over all j<k. Vonesh's results were limited to J=4 and 5, but the results suggest that for $n \geq 20$ and $\rho_m > .25$, repeated measures designs provide better results (shorter confidence intervals) than independent groups. For n=10 and $\rho_m < .25$ independent groups are slightly better. To complicate matters, it appears that the advantage of repeated measures designs decreases as J gets large. An added difficulty is that the correlations are not known, and in most situations the best you can do is to use a randomized block design if you suspect <u>all</u> of the correlations are greater than .25.

11.5 TESTS FOR EQUAL VARIANCES

Again it is assumed that you have J dependent treatment groups with variances

$$\sigma_1^2, \ldots, \sigma_J^2.$$

In various situations it is important to be able to test

$$H_0: \sigma_1^2 = \ldots = \sigma_J^2.$$

For example, you might have J forms of a particular psychological test, and want to know whether the forms have equal variances. This is a particularly important question in classical test theory where the assumption of parallel tests needs to be verified (Lord & Novick, 1968). The issue of equal variances also might arise in learning experiments (Levy, 1976). For independent treatment groups the Brown-Forsythe procedure can be used as described in chapter eight. For dependent groups, procedures have been proposed that may be robust to non-normality, but more research is needed to determine how well these procedures perform.

For J=2 groups the Sandvik-Olson procedure is especially easy to use, but it is based on the Wilcoxon signed rank test, and so a description of this procedure is reserved until chapter fifteen. For J>2 groups, Harris (1985) proposed two procedures that are asymptotically robust. That is, they can be expected to give good control over Type I errors under non-normality provided the sample sizes are not too small. Unfortunately it is not known just how large a sample size is needed, and it is not known how these procedures compare to the Sandvik-Olson procedure when J=2.

The first procedure proposed by Harris (1985) is based on

$$W_r=[(n-1)s'H'(H\hat{\Psi}H')^{-1}Hs]/[1-s'H'(H\hat{\Psi}H')^{-1}Hs$$

where

$$s=(s_1^2,\ldots,s_J^2)'$$

is the J by 1 vector of sample variances,

$$\hat{\Psi}_{jk}=\Sigma_i(X_{ij}-\bar{X}_j)^2(X_{ik}-\bar{X}_k)^2/(n-1),$$

$\hat{\Psi}$ is a J by J matrix where the (j,k)th element is $\hat{\Psi}_{jk}$, and H is a (J-1) by J matrix given by

$$H=\begin{bmatrix} -1 & 1 & 0 & \ldots & 0 \\ -1 & 0 & 1 & \ldots & 0 \\ \vdots & & & & \vdots \\ -1 & 0 & 0 & \ldots & 1 \end{bmatrix}$$

You reject H_0 when $W_r>c$ where c is the 1-α quantile of the chi-square distribution with J-1 degrees of freedom (i.e., use Table A2).

Harris' second test for equal variances is based on

$$W_g=(n-1)v'H'(HQH')^{-1}Hv$$

where

$$v=(\log s_1^2,\ldots,\log s_J^2)$$

and where the (j,k)th element of the J by J matrix Q is

$$q_{jk}=\hat{\Psi}_{jk}/(s_j^2 s_k^2).$$

The statistic $\hat{\Psi}_{jk}$ is defined as before, and again when H_0 is true, W_g has, approximately, a chi-square distribution with J-1 degrees of freedom. That is, reject if $W_g>c$ where c is read from Table A2.

Cohen (1986) argues that W_r is inferior to W_g and shows that in terms of controlling Type I errors, W_g may require at least n=100 and perhaps even n=150 observations. That is, for smaller sample sizes, Harris' W_g may not be robust to non-normality. Cohen proposes an alternative solution that gives better control over Type I errors, but for nonnormal distributions it can be unsatisfactory. In terms of controlling Type I errors, Levy's (1976) procedure is best, but it has the disadvantage of having low power. It seems that more research is needed to determine a truly satisfactory method for comparing the variances of dependent groups. Five new procedures are being investigated, but unfortunately no results are available at this time.

EXERCISES

11.1 You perform a repeated measures ANOVA with J=5 treatment groups. Suppose the variances and covariances for the jth and kth treatment group are given by the following matrix.

1.00	.62	.62	.54	.29
.62	1.00	.67	.53	.38
.62	.67	1.00	.62	.48
.54	.53	.62	1.00	.62
.29	.38	.48	.62	1.00

That is s_{jk} is the value in the jth and the kth column. For example, $s_{24}=.53$ while $s_{43}=.62$. The sample variances in this example are all equal to one. Compute $\hat{\epsilon}$ and $\tilde{\epsilon}$.

11.2 Suppose you have J=4 treatment groups. Assume $\epsilon=1$ and test $H_0:\mu_1=\ldots=\mu_J$ using the following data.

J: 1	2	3	4
5	1	8	9
1	3	8	7
9	2	7	8
9	5	4	7
8	3	5	13
7	2	7	15
3	5	3	8
6	8	6	12

11.3 Perform multiple comparisons on the data in problem 11.2 using paired t-tests.

References

Anderson, T. W. (1958) An introduction to multivariate statistical analysis. New York: Wiley.

Barcikowski, R. & Robey, R. (1984) Decisions in single group repeated measures analysis: statistical tests and three computer packages. The American Statistician, 38, 148-150.

Box, G. E. P. (1954) Some theorems on quadratic forms applied in the study of analysis of variance problems: II Effect of inequality of variance and correlation of errors in the two-way classification. Annals of Mathematical Statistics, 25, 484-498.

Cohen, A. (1986) Comparing variances of correlated variables. Psychometrika, 51, 379-391.

Collier, R., Baker, F., Mandeville, G. & Hayes, T. (1967) Estimates of test size for several test procedures based on conventional variance ratios in the repeated measures design. Psychometrika, 32, 339-353.

Harris, P. (1985) Testing for variance homogeneity of correlated variables. Biometrika, 72, 103-107.

Huynh, H. & Feldt, L. (1970) Conditions under which mean square ratios in repeated measurements designs have exact F-distributions. Journal of the American Statistical Association, 65, 1582-1589.

Huynh, H. & Feldt, L. (1976) Estimation of the Box correction for degrees of freedom from sample data in randomized block and split-plot designs. Journal of Educational Statistics, 1, 69-82.

Keselman, H. J., Rogan, J. C., Mendoza, J. L. & Breen, L. J. (1980) Testing the validity conditions of repeated measures F tests. Psychological Bulletin, 87, 479-481.

Kirk, R. (1982) Experimental Design: Procedures for the

behavioral sciences Belmont CA: Brooks/Cole.
Levy, K. (1976) A procedure for testing the equality of p correlated variances. British Journal of Mathematical and Statistical Psycology, 29, 89-93.
Lord, F. & Novick, M. (1968) Statistical theories of mental test scores. Reading MA: Addison-Welsey.
Maxwell, S. E. (1980) Pairwise multiple comparisons in repeated measures designs. Journal of Educational Statistics, 5, 269-287.
Scheffe, H. (1959) The analysis of variance. New York: Wiley
Simes, R. (1986) An improved Bonferroni procedure for multiple tests of significance. Biometrika, 73, 751-754.
Vonesh, E. (1983) Efficiency of repeated measures designs versus completely randomized designs based on multiple comparisons. Communications in Statistics--Theory and Methods, 12, 289-302.
Wilcox, R. (1985) An extended and slightly improved table of critical values for testing q linear contrasts in a repeated measures design. Communications in Statistics--Simulation and Computation, 14, 55-70.

CHAPTER 12

SELECTION TECHNIQUES

Hypothesis testing procedures are a common way of comparing random variables, but in many situations these procedures provide only the first step in addressing the issues that are important. For instance, suppose you have three methods for treating schizophrenia, and that the average or expected effectiveness of the j<u>th</u> method is μ_j. Further suppose that you test and reject $H_0:\mu_1=\mu_2=\mu_3$. In fact, suppose you conclude that $\mu_1\neq\mu_2\neq\mu_3$. What do you do now? A likely response might be to choose the method that appears to be most effective. If the higher the μ_j the better the method, the natural thing to do is to choose the method associated with the largest sample mean, and this is exactly what is done in practice. However, this procedure leaves an important issue unresolved--how certain can you be that the best treatment yielded the highest sample mean? Put another way, how certain can you be that the best treatment was indeed selected? If $\mu_2>\mu_1$ and $\mu_2>\mu_3$, and if $\bar{X}_2>\bar{X}_1$, and $\bar{X}_2>\bar{X}_3$, a correct selection is made because you would choose method 2. But of course there is some chance that you might observe $\bar{X}_2<\bar{X}_1$ or $\bar{X}_2<\bar{X}_3$, in which case an inferior method would be selected.

The procedures in this chapter are somewhat related to power. You may have noticed that power can be controlled when comparing any two independent treatment groups, but in terms of all pairwise comparisons, power has been virtually ignored. That is, the notion of a Type I error for one comparison was extended to $C>1$ comparisons via the concept of the familywise Type I error probability, but a similar extension for power was not described. For instance, suppose you compare $J=4$ groups and you fail to reject using Dunnett's T3 procedure. How certain can you be that none of the four treatment groups has a substantially higher mean than the others? Also, how certain can you be that if one method is substantially better than the others, it will be selected as being the best? The purpose of this chapter is to describe methods for addressing this last question. The solutions described here are based on what are called "ranking and selection" techniques.

There are two general approaches to ranking and selection problems: 1) determine a procedure so that, regardless of what the means might actually be, the probability of selecting the best procedure will be close to 1, and 2) estimate the probability of a correct selection once the experiment is complete and the data is available for analysis. The first approach has, by far, received the most attention by statisticians, although some results on the latter approach are available. (Ranking and selection procedures are also divided according to whether an "indifference zone" is used, or a "subset selection" procedure is employed, but this distinction is not discussed here.)

It might be mentioned that some researchers have suggested that in some situations, ranking and selection techniques are more important than testing hypotheses. For example, in the illustration, the goal is to choose one of the three methods for general use in treating schizophrenia. If the three methods are equally effective, and their costs are about the same, it makes little difference which method is chosen. The important issue is that if there is a difference among the means, you want to be reasonably certain of choosing the best one. The argument goes that if $H_0:\mu_1=\mu_2=\mu_3$ is true, you may still want to choose a method for general use, assuming the methods are better than no treatment at all, and of course the one that yielded the largest sample mean would be chosen. On the other hand, this argument is not always a compelling reason to abandon hypothesis testing. For instance, one of the treatment groups might be a control group that receives no treatment at all. In this case it would seem that a treatment should be selected only if its mean is different, and in fact larger, than the mean of the control. Thus, it is not being suggested that hypothesis testing be abandoned. The only point being made is that there are different views on how statistical problems should be approached. The point of view taken here is that testing for equality among population means is often an important goal, but many other goals arise in practice in such that an alternative or complementary procedure might be considered. Ranking and selection is one such family of techniques.

12.1 SOLUTION FOR NORMAL DISTRIBUTIONS HAVING A COMMON KNOWN VARIANCE

To help fix ideas, first consider J independent normal distributions with unknown means $\mu_1,\ldots,\mu_J$ and <u>known</u> variances $\sigma_1^2,\ldots,\sigma_J^2$. Also assume that $\sigma_1=\ldots=\sigma_J=\sigma$, say. Let $\mu_{[1]}\leq\ldots\leq\mu_{[J]}$ be the J means written in ascending order. The problem is to determine which treatment group has the largest mean $\mu_{[J]}$.

The general procedure is quite simple. You randomly sample n subjects from each treatment group, where n is to be determined, and compute the sample means, say $\bar{X}_j$, j=1,...,J. Let

$$\bar{X}_{[1]}\leq\ldots\leq\bar{X}_{[J]}$$

be the J sample means written in ascending order. For example, if $J=3$, $\bar{X}_1=2$, $\bar{X}_2=6$, and $\bar{X}_3=3$,

$$\bar{X}_{[1]}=2,\ \bar{X}_{[2]}=3,\ \text{and}\ \bar{X}_{[3]}=6.$$

Next you simply decide that the treatment group yielding $\bar{X}_{[J]}$ has mean $\mu_{[J]}$. In the example, the second treatment group has the largest sample mean, so you decide that it has the largest population mean. In symbols, you decide that $\mu_{[3]}=\mu_2$.

A correct selection (CS) is said to have been made if the treatment group with mean $\mu_{[J]}$ yields $\bar{X}_{[J]}$. That is, the treatment group with the largest population mean yields the largest sample mean.

One problem is that Pr(CS), the probability of a correct selection, depends on what the actual means happen to be. If $J=3$, $\mu_1=1$, $\mu_2=2$, and $\mu_3=10$, there is a higher probability of a correct decision than if $\mu_1=\mu_2=9$ and again $\mu_3=10$. In fact, as the μ_j's get closer in value, with n fixed, Pr(CS) approaches 1/J no matter how large n might be. To accomodate this problem, an indifference zone is used. This just means that you specify a positive constant, say δ_0, with idea that if

$$\delta=\mu_{[J]}-\mu_{[J-1]}\geq\delta_0,$$

you want to be reasonably certain of selecting the treatment group having the largest mean, $\mu_{[J]}$. If, however, $\delta<\delta_0$, the means are said to be similar in value, and so it makes little difference whether the treatment group having mean $\mu_{[J]}$ or $\mu_{[J-1]}$ is selected. In fact, when $\mu_{[J]}-\mu_{[j]}<\delta$ for all $j<J$, it is common practice to define the probability of a correct selection to be one. The term "indifference zone" refers to the open interval $(0,\delta_0)$. If δ is in the indifference zone, you are indifferent as to which of the two treatment groups associated with $\mu_{[J]}$ and $\mu_{[J-1]}$ is selected. But if $\delta\geq\delta_0$, you want to be reasonably certain of selecting the treatment group associated with $\mu_{[J]}$. The constant δ_0 is chosen by the experimenter, and it represents what is judged to be a substantial difference between two treatment groups. In some cases you might want δ_0 to be small,

but you should keep in mind that as δ_0 gets closer to zero, and if for instance you want PR(CS)≥.8, the required sample size approaches infinity. This will become evident from equation (12.2.2) given below.

To determine how large of a sample size you need, you first choose a constant, P_0, $1/J<P_0<1$, with the idea that you want

$$\Pr(CS)\geq P_0 \tag{12.1.1}$$

whenever $\mu_{[J]}-\mu_{[J-1]}>\delta_0$. It is assumed that sampling is from normal distributions. The reason for requiring $P_0>1/J$ is that you can guarantee $\Pr(CS)\geq 1/J$ without sampling any observations at all--you simply choose a treatment group at random.

Next you compute

$$n=(\tau\sigma/\delta_0)^2 \tag{12.1.2}$$

where τ is read from Table A18. Then you randomly sample n subjects from each group, compute the sample means, and select the group having the largest sample mean as the one having mean $\mu_{[J]}$.

Bechhofer (1954) showed that this procedure guarantees $\Pr(CS)\geq P_0$ for any δ not in the indifference zone.

<u>Example 12.1.1</u> Suppose you have three methods for reducing the weight of obese individuals, and you want to select one method for general use. Let μ_j be the expected weight loss under method j, and for illustrative purposes, suppose $\sigma=10$, $P_0=.95$, and $\delta_0=5$. Thus, if under the best treatment method, subjects lose five pounds or more, on the average, than subjects who receive some other method, you want to choose the best treatment group with probability at least .95. From Table A18, $\tau=2.7101$, and so

$$n=(2.7107(10)/5)^2=29.38.$$

Thus, you need to randomly assign n=30 subjects to each treatment group.

12.2 SOLUTION FOR NORMAL DISTRIBUTIONS HAVING A COMMON UNKNOWN VARIANCE

Again consider J independent normal distributions having a common variance, but this time it is assumed that σ is unknown. As before, it is desired to satisfy (12.1.1) whenever

$$\mu_{[J]}-\mu_{[J-1]}\geq\delta_0.$$

To solve this problem, a two-stage procedure is required that is similar to the two-stage procedures in chapters 7-10.

To apply the procedure, first randomly sample n subjects from each of the J treatment groups, and compute

$$s^2=\Sigma\Sigma(X_{ij}-\hat{\mu}_j)^2/[(n-1)J]$$

where $\hat{\mu}=\Sigma_i X_{ij}/n$. In the terminology of chapter eight, s^2 is MSWG, the mean squares within groups based on Jn observations. The degrees of freedom are $\nu=J(n-1)$.

Next, compute

$$N=\max\{n,[(2s^2h^2/(\delta_0)^2]^+\}$$

where h is read from Table A19, and $(2s^2h^2/(\delta_0)^2)^+$ means that the quantity $2s^2h^2/(\delta_0)^2$ is rounded up to the nearest integer. The quantity N is the total sample size needed from each group. Thus, you randomly sample N-n additional observations from each group. Once the observations are available, compute

$$\bar{X}_j=\Sigma_i X_{ij}/N,$$

and select the treatment group associated with $\bar{X}_{[J]}$, the largest sample mean, as the one having mean $\mu_{[J]}$. Bechhofer, Dunnett, and Sobel (1954) showed that the values of h in Table A19 guarantee $\Pr(CS)\geq P_0$ whenever $\delta\geq\delta_0$.

Example 12.2.1. Consider example 12.1.1, but this time suppose that for each group you already have observations on n=11 subjects, σ is unknown, and $s^2=100$. With J=3, $\nu=3(10)=30$, and so for $P_0=.95$, Table A19 says that h=1.99. Thus, because $\delta_0=5$,

$$N=\max\{11,\ [2(100)(1.99)^2/5^2]^+\}$$

$$=31.69^+$$

$$=32.$$

Consequently, N-n=21 additional observations are randomly sampled from each group. Once these additional observations are available, if

$\bar{X}_1=12$, $\bar{X}_2=24$, and $\bar{X}_3=8$,

method 2 is selected as the best method for reducing weight.

Note that N=n is possible, meaning that sampling additional observations from each group is unnecessary.

It is noted that simultaneous 1-α confidence intervals for

$$\mu_{[J]} - \mu_j$$

can be obtained using the single-stage procedure developed by Edwards and Hsu (1983). That is, you can obtain confidence intervals for the difference between the "best" treatment group and the others which are "inferior". In many situations these confidence intervals may provide a more meaningful measure of "effect size" than the measures discussed in chapter eight.

12.3 SOLUTION FOR J INDEPENDENT NORMAL DISTRIBUTIONS HAVING UNKNOWN AND UNEQUAL VARIANCES

If J independent normal distributions have different variances, a slightly different procedure must be used to select the distribution having the largest mean. Two solutions for handling unequal variances have been proposed (Dudewicz & Dalal, 1975; Rinott, 1978), but only the procedure proposed by Rinott is described here. As in the previous section, you first randomly sample n observations from each group. Let

$$s_j^2=\Sigma_i(X_{ij}-\hat{\mu}_j)^2/(n-1)$$

be the sample variance for the j<u>th</u> group, where $\hat{\mu}_j=\Sigma_i X_{ij}/n$, j=1,...,J. Again the goal is to have $\Pr(CS)\ge P_0$ whenever $\delta\ge\delta_0$. Now, however, you compute

$$N_j=\max\{n,\ [(h/\delta_0)^2 s_j^2]^+\}$$

where $[\ ]^+$ means you round up to the nearest integer, and where the constant h is read from Table A16.

Finally, you randomly sample an additional N_j-n observations from the j<u>th</u> group, compute $\bar{X}_j=\Sigma_i X_{ij}/N_j$ where the summation is over all N_j observations in the j<u>th</u> group, and select the treatment group corresponding to $\bar{X}_{[J]}$, the largest sample mean, as the one having mean $\mu_{[J]}$.

<u>Example 12.3.1</u>. Suppose J=3, n=11, P_0=.95, δ_0=5,

$s_1^2=108.2$, $s_2^2=109.8$, and $s_3^2=140$.

From Table A16, h=3.118, and

$$N_1=\max\{11,[(3.118/5)^2(108.2)]^+\}=43.$$

Similarly, $N_2=43$ and $N_3=55$. Thus, an additional 43-11=32 observations are needed from the first two groups, while the third needs 44.

12.4 SOLUTION FOR J INDEPENDENT BINOMIAL DISTRIBUTIONS

To illustrate how ranking and selection techniques might be used in terms of the binomial distribution, suppose you have J=4 methods for treating alcoholism, and that your measure of success is whether the patient is drinking one year after the treatment is completed. Let p_j be the probability that a randomly sampled subject, who receives method j, is not drinking alcohol after one year. If n subjects are randomly assigned to the jth treatment, and X_j is the number of subjects who are not drinking after one year, then from chapter 4, X_j has a binomial distribution with probability of success p_j. It is assumed that different subjects are assigned to the treatment groups, and so there are a total of nJ subjects, and the X_j's are independent. Of course the "best" treatment is the one with the largest probability of success. If

$$p_{[1]}\leq\ldots\leq p_{[J]}$$

are the p_j's written in ascending order, the method having probability of success $p_{[J]}$ is best. A natural "distance" measure is $\delta=p_{[J]}-p_{[J-1]}$, the difference between the largest and second largest p_j values. If δ is large, you will want to be reasonably certain of choosing the method associated with $p_{[J]}$. In fact, it is assumed that when $\delta\geq\delta_0$, you want $Pr(CS)\geq P_0$ where δ_0 and P_0 are constants that you have chosen, and CS again stands for correct selection.

In terms of deciding which method is best, you use the "obvious" procedure and decision rule. In particular, you randomly sample n subjects from each treatment group, and let

$$X_{[1]}\leq\ldots\leq X_{[J]}$$

be the observed number of successes written in ascending order. A method for determining how large n should be is given below by equation (12.4.1). The treatment group yielding $X_{[J]}$ is selected as being best. In case of ties, you choose at random from among the methods having the highest number of observed successes. For instance, if J=4, X_1=20, X_2=40, X_3=30, and X_4=38, method 2 is selected as being the best. If instead X_4=40, you must choose either method 2 or 4. Thus, you choose method 2 with probability 1/2; otherwise method 4 is selected. If k methods are tied for best, one of these methods is selected at random for general use, and so each method has probability 1/k of being chosen.

Determining n

The one remaining problem is determining how large n should be. Some exact sample sizes are reported by Sobel and Huyett (1957), but they are not given here. Instead a normal approximation is used, namely

$$n=(\tau/2\delta_0)^2 \qquad (12.4.1)$$

where τ is read from Table A18.

Example 12.4.1 Continuing the illustration, suppose you have four methods of treating alcoholism, and you want to be 95% certain of selecting the best treatment whenever $\delta \geq .05$. Then P_0=.95, δ_0=.05, and from Table A18, τ=2.916. Thus,

$$n=(2.916/.10)^2=850.4.$$

Hence, you need 851 subjects for each treatment group. One reason n is so large is that δ_0 is relatively small. If instead δ_0=.10, n=213. If P_0=.9 and δ_0=.1, then n=151.

As a final comment, numerous procedures have been proposed that are extensions of the techniques described in this chapter. Many of the these procedures are summarized in the books by Gibbons, Olkin and Sobel (1977) as well as Gupta and Panchapakesan (1979)

EXERCISES

1. Describe how the procedures in this chapter supplement the multiple comparison procedures in chapter 9.

2. You have five methods for helping subjects maintain their body weight after having lost weight through dieting. Let μ_j be the average number of pounds gained under method j. Then the most

effective method is $\mu_{[1]}$. Suppose that with probability at least .95, you want to select the most effective method if $\mu_{[2]}-\mu_{[1]}\geq 8$. Assume normality and that $\sigma=4$. How many subjects should you sample from each treatment group?

3. Solve problem 2, but this time assume you have an initial sample of 15 subjects from each group, and that MSWG=14. How many more subjects should be sampled from each group? (Assume equal variances.)

4. Solve problem 2 but without assuming equal variances. Assume that the sample variances are 8, 12, 18, 13, and 18.

References

Bechhofer, R. (1954) A single-sample multiple decision procedure for ranking means of normal populations with known variances. _Annals of Mathematical Statistics_, 25, 16-39.

Bechhofer, R., Dunnett, C,. & Sobel, M. (1954) A two-sample multiple decision porcedure for ranking means of normal populations with a common unknown variance. _Biometrika_, 41, 170-176.

Dudewicz, E. J. & Dalal, S. R. (1975) Allocation of observations in ranking and selection with unequal variances. _Sankhya_, series B, 37, 28-78.

Edwards, D. G. & Hsu, J. C. (1983) Multiple comparisons with the best treatment. _Journal of the American Statistical Association_, 78, 965-971 (Correction, 1984, 79, 965).

Gibbons, J., Olkin, I. & Sobel, M. (1977) _Selecting and Ordering Populations_: _A New Statistical Methodology_. New York: Wiley.

Gupta, S. & Panchapakesan, S. (1979) _Multiple Decision Procedures: Theory and Methodology of Selecting and Ranking Populations._ New York: Wiley

Rinott, Y. (1978) On two-stage selection procedures and related probability inequalities. _Communications in Statistics--Theory and Methods_, A7, 799-811.

Sobel, M. & Huyett, M (1957) _Bell System Technical Journal_, 36, 537-576.

CHAPTER 13

CORRELATION AND REGRESSION

Regression has been one of the most rapidly growing fields in statistics. In fact this area has grown so enormously that there is no hope of including in a single chapter all of the important results that have emerged in recent years. Accordingly, this chapter introduces the most basic results, and describes some of the issues that have practical importance. An important feature of this chapter is that it includes some new results on the analysis of covariance as well as some heteroscedastic procedures that are not available in existing books. Readers interested in learning more about regression might consult the books by Draper and Smith (1981), Edwards (1979), and Neter and Wasserman (1974).

13.1 CORRELATION

Consider two random variables, say X and Y. These random variables might be height and weight, or perhaps number of pounds overweight and blood pressure, etc. The correlation coefficient, ρ, is a measure that indicates the extent to which X and Y are linearly related. In terms of population parameters, ρ is defined by

$$\rho=COV(X,Y)/(\sigma_x\sigma_y)$$

where COV(X,Y) is the "covariance" of X and Y, which is defined by

$$COV(X,Y)=E\{(X-\mu_x)(Y-\mu_y)\}=E(XY)-\mu_x\mu_y.$$

It can be shown that $-1\leq\rho\leq1$. The value of ρ is related to the extent to which X and Y have a linear relationship, but ρ by itself does not tell you much about what this relationship is. (X and Y are linearly related if Y=bX+a where the constant b is the slope and the constant a is the intercept.) When Y=bX+a and b>0, $\rho=1$, and when b<0, $\rho=-1$.

An important property of ρ is that when X and Y are independent, $\rho=0$. To verify this, note that from the rules of expectation, when X and Y are independent,

$$COV(X,Y)=E(XY)-\mu_x\mu_y$$

$$=\mu_x\mu_y-\mu_x\mu_y$$

$$=0.$$

However, $\rho=0$ does not imply that X and Y are independent unless certain restrictions are imposed. Among these is the assumption that both X and Y have a normal distribution. (An additional restriction is that the joint distribution of X and Y be bivariate normal. Assuming that the marginal distributions of X and Y are normal does not necessarily mean that the joint distribution is bivariate normal. See Broffitt, 1986.) There is nothing obvious about this result, and no proof is given.

For those unfamiliar with the theory behind the correlation coefficient, there is often a strong temptation to interpret ρ in ways that are highly inappropriate. For instance, if $\rho=0$, you might think that X and Y are not related in any way at all. Suppose though that $Y=\surd(1-X^2)$, $-1\leq X\leq 1$. Then X and Y have an exact relationship since given X, Y is determined exactly, yet $\rho=0$. The correct interpretation of $\rho=0$ is that there might be an exact relationship between X and Y, but this relationship is as far away from being linear as it can be.

Another common mistake is to conclude that if $\rho=1$, a large increase in X will mean a large increase in Y. Suppose $Y=.000001X$. (That is, $b=.000001$ and $a=0$.) Then $\rho=1$, but if X is increased from 0 to 100, y only increases from 0 to .0001.

Still another common mistake is to conclude that if ρ is close to 1, X causes Y or Y causes X. It may be that X causes Y, but such a relationship cannot be proven with the correlation coefficient. For a more detailed discussion of the properties of ρ, see Carroll (1961).

Estimating ρ

Let $(X_1,Y_1),\ldots,(X_n,Y_n)$ be the observations for n randomly sampled subjects. Then

$$r=[\Sigma(X_i-\bar{X})(Y_i-\bar{Y})]/[\Sigma(X_i-\bar{X})^2\Sigma(Y_i-\bar{Y})^2]^{1/2} \qquad (13.1.1)$$

is the most common estimate of ρ. It should be noted, however, that when n is small, say less than or equal to 20, this estimate of ρ might be seriously biased. An estimate of ρ that is more nearly unbiased is

$$\tilde{\rho}=r(1+[1-r^2]/[2(n-3)]) \qquad (13.1.2)$$

(Olkin & Pratt, 1958).

Testing Hypotheses about ρ

A common practice is to test $H_0:\rho=0$. You might suspect that X and Y are independent, in which case you can test your suspicion with the procedure about to be described. However, as previously indicated, concluding that $\rho=0$ does not mean X and Y are independent unless you also assume normality.

To test $H_0:\rho=0$, in addition to having a random sample of n subjects, you must assume that either X or Y is normally distributed. Some books claim that both X and Y have to be normally distributed, but Hogg and Craig (1970) show that this is not true.

To perform the test, you first compute r using equation (13.1.1), and then

$$T=r(n-2)^{1/2}/(1-r^2)^{1/2}.$$

When H_0 is true, T has a Student's t distribution with $\nu=n-2$ degrees of freedom. If the probability of a Type I error is to be α, reject H_0 if $|T|>t$ where t is the $1-\alpha/2$ quantile of Student's t distribution which is read from Table A14.

<u>Example 13.1.1</u> Suppose that for n=5 randomly sampled subjects you measure stress, X, and performance, Y, on some task. Suppose the observations are:

X	Y
15	30
18	35
24	28
12	28
20	36
$\Sigma X=89$	$\Sigma Y=157$

Then r=.49. Suppose you want to test the hypothesis that stress, X, and performance, Y, are independent, or that the relationship between X and Y is as far away from being linear as is possible. This means that you want to test $H_0:\rho=0$, and so you compute

$$T=.49\sqrt{3}/\sqrt{(1-.49^2)}$$
$$=.97$$

With $\alpha=.05$ and $\nu=3$ degrees of freedom, $1-\alpha/2=.975$ and the critical value is t=3.182. Thus, you do not reject H_0.

If in your report you wanted to provide an estimate of ρ, you could use r=.49, but referring to equation (13.1.2), a less biased estimate of ρ is $\tilde{\rho}=.58$. It might be tempting to test $H_0:\rho=0$ using

$\tilde{\rho}$ rather than r, but this is inappropriate based on the results reported here.

Testing $H_0:\rho=\rho_0$, ρ_0 a known constant

In some situations, previous investigations, or theoretical considerations, might give you some indication of what the value of ρ should be. If, for example, previous investigations indicate that that the correlation between X=anxiety and Y=blood pressure is $\rho=.5$, you may want to test $H_0:\rho=.5$ to see whether your data is consistent with previous findings. More generally, you may want to test $H_0:\rho=\rho_0$, $-1\leq\rho_0\leq 1$, where ρ_0 is a known constant. To perform the test you compute

$$Z=[\ln\{(1+r)/(1-r)\}]/2,$$

where ln is the natural logarithm. R. A. Fisher showed that Z has, approximately, a normal distribution with mean ρ and variance $1/(n-3)$. Thus, when H_0 is true,

$$(n-3)^{1/2}(Z-\rho_0)$$

has a standard normal distribution, and so you reject H_0 if

$$|(n-3)^{1/2}(Z-\rho_0)|>z_{1-\alpha/2}$$

where $z_{1-\alpha/2}$ is the $1-\alpha/2$ quantile of the standard normal

distribution which is read from Table A1. For a table of exact critical values, see Odeh (1982).

Example 13.1.2 Continuing example 13.1.1, suppose you want to test $H_0:\rho=.3$ with $\alpha=.05$. Because r=.49, it is seen that Z=.536, and

$$|(5-3)^{1/2}(.536-.3)|=.334.$$

From Table A1, the critical value is 1.96, and so you do not reject the hypothesis that the correlation between stress and performance is .3.

Testing Whether Two Correlations are Equal

Suppose you are interested in the correlation between two variables in which case you may want to know whether the correlation differs for two populations of subjects. For example, you might be interested in the severity of a phobia, X, and the number of hours treating the phobia, Y. Furthermore, you might be interested in whether the correlation is the same for Hispanics and Blacks.

Let ρ_1 and ρ_2 be the population correlations for the two groups, and let r_1 and r_2 be the corresponding estimates based on n_1 and n_2 subjects, respectively. Because, by assumption, different random samples of subjects are used to compute r_1 and r_2, the statistics r_1 and r_2 are independent. Consequently,

$$Z_i=[\underline{\ln}\{(1+r_i)/(1-r_i)\}]/2 \quad (i=1,2)$$

are also independent random variables, and $H_0:\rho_1=\rho_2$ can be tested with

$$Z=(Z_1-Z_2)/\sqrt{B},$$

where

$$B=1/(n_1-3) + 1/(n_2-3).$$

If $|Z|>z_{1-\alpha/2}$, where $z_{1-\alpha/2}$ is read from Table A1, reject H_0.

Unfortunately this procedure is not robust to nonnormality (Yu & Dunn, 1982). For dependent groups, Yu and Dunn recommend a procedure based on Kendall's tau, which is described at the end of section 15.4. For independent groups, see Duncan and Layard (1973).

Example 13.1.3. For n_1=15 Hispanics, you estimate the correlation between a phobia and number of hours treating the phobia to be r_1=.35, while for n_2=20 Blacks the correlation is r_2=.45. To test the assumption that the two groups have the same correlation, compute $Z_1=\underline{\ln}\{1.35/.65\}/2=.365$, $Z_2=.485$, $B=(1/12)+(1/17)=.1422$, and $Z=-.318$. If α=.05, you do not reject, because $.318<1.96$.

13.2 LINEAR REGRESSION USING A SINGLE PREDICTOR

Again suppose that for each subject in a population of subjects you are interested in two variables, say X and Y. For example, Y might be a subject's score on the verbal section of the SAT test, and X might be the number of hours spent training for the test. A common goal is to devise a rule for predicting the value of Y, given an observed value for X. In the example you might want to know the score you could expect if a subject had no special training in preparation for the SAT test as opposed to studying say 20 hours. The simplest approach to this problem is to randomly sample n subjects, observe the values $(X_1,Y_1),\ldots,(X_n,Y_n)$, and then search for a linear rule that in some sense gives you an optimal estimate of the value of Y_i based on the value of X_i. That is, the problem is to find constants, say b_0 and b_1 such that

$$Y_i'=b_1X_i+b_0 \tag{13.2.1}$$

is reasonably close to the value of Y_i $(i=1,\ldots,n)$. That way, when you observe a new subject and you are told the value of X, but not the value of Y, equation (13.2.1) can be used to predict his or her SAT score.

The quantity

$$Y_i-Y_i'$$

is called a residual, which measures the discrepancy between the observed Y_i value and predicted Y_i value based on (13.2.1). A common approach to choosing b_1 and b_0 is to choose them with the goal of minimizing

$$\Sigma(Y_i-Y_i')^2.$$

That is, the sum of the squares of the residuals is to be as small as possible. This approach is based on what is called the least squares criterion.

Substituting b_1X+b_0 for Y_i', the goal is to choose b_1 and b_0 so that

$$\Sigma(Y_i-b_1X_i-b_0)^2 \tag{13.2.2}$$

is as small as possible. Without assuming anything about the distribution of X and Y, the solution can be shown to be

$$b_1=[\Sigma(X_i-\bar{X})(Y_i-\bar{Y})]/[\Sigma(X_i-\bar{X})^2]$$

$$=[(\Sigma X_iY_i)-n\bar{X}\bar{Y}]/[(\Sigma X_i^2)-n\bar{X}^2] \tag{13.2.3}$$

and

$$b_0=\bar{Y}-b_1\bar{X} \tag{13.2.4}$$

The resulting regression equation, $Y'=b_1X+b_0$, is called the least squares regression of Y on X.

Notice that the expressions for b_1 and b_0 were derived in terms of the n observations that were available. That is, b_1 and b_0 determine the "best" linear estimate of Y, given X, for the n observations in your sample. In terms of parameters, a similar result is obtained. In particular, suppose X and Y are indeed linearly related, and that

$$Y=\beta_1X+\beta_0 \tag{13.2.5}$$

where β_1 and β_0 are unknown parameters. If equation (13.2.5) is assumed to be true, β_1 and β_0 can be determined from the variances and covariances of X and Y without assuming anything about the shape of the distribution of X or Y. Applying the rules of expectation to (13.2.5),

$$\mu_y=\beta_1\mu_x+\beta_0 \tag{13.2.6}$$

where μ_y=E(Y), and μ_x=E(X). Thus, subtracting (13.2.6) from (13.2.5),

$$\beta_1X+\beta_0-\beta_1\mu_x-\beta_0=Y-\mu_y,$$

and so $\beta_1(X-\mu_x)=Y-\mu_y$. Multiplying both sides of this last equation by $X-\mu_x$ yields

$$\beta_1(X-\mu_x)^2=(Y-\mu_y)(X-\mu_x).$$

Taking expectations of both sides yields

$$\beta_1\sigma_x^2=COV(X,Y).$$

Thus,

$$\beta_1=COV(X,Y)/\sigma_x^2 \tag{13.2.7}$$

and

$$\beta_0=\mu_y-\beta_1\mu_x. \tag{13.2.8}$$

If you estimate COV(X,Y) with $\Sigma(X_i-\bar{X})(Y_i-\bar{Y})/(n-1)$, and σ_x^2 with

$$\Sigma(X_i-\bar{X})^2/(n-1),$$

then substitute these values for the corresponding parameters in equations (13.2.7) and (13.2.8), you get b_1 and b_0 as the estimates of β_1 and β_0. Put another way, if you assume $Y=\beta_0+\beta_1X$, the estimates of the parameters β_0 and β_1 are b_0 and b_1.

From equation (13.2.7) it can be seen that $\beta_1=\rho\sigma_y/\sigma_x$, and this reveals how the correlation coefficient is related to finding a linear estimate of Y given X. It should be noted that it is common to write the regression equation as

$$Y' = \rho(\sigma_y/\sigma_x)X + \mu_y - \rho(\sigma_y/\sigma_x)\mu_x$$

$$= \rho(\sigma_y/\sigma_x)(X - \mu_x) + \mu_y.$$

$$= \beta_1(X - \mu_x) + \mu_y$$

where $\beta_1 = \rho\sigma_y/\sigma_x$.

It should also be noted that in many situations, Y is dichotomous, in which case the regression model described here should not be used. For a description of the difficulties associated with predicting a dichotomous variable, and a solution to these difficulties, see for example, Agresti (1984, chapter 6).

Confidence Intervals for β_1, β_0 and μ_y

To obtain confidence intervals for β_1, β_0 and μ_y it is necessary, in contrast to previous results in this section, to make assumptions about the distribution of Y, but no assumption about the distribution of X is required. In particular, it is assumed that the conditional distribution of Y given $X_1, \ldots, X_n$ is normal with mean $\mu_y + \beta_1(X_i - \bar{X})$ (or $\beta_1 X + \beta_0$) and variance σ^2. The estimate of μ_y is simply

$$\hat{\mu}_y = \bar{Y}$$

while the estimates of β_1 and β_0 are given by (13.2.3) and (13.2.4) above.

Notice that for any value of X, it is assumed that the Y_i's have a common variance. For instance, if the observed values of the X_i's are 8, 15, 21, and 36, it is assumed that the variance of the Y's corresponding to X=8 is σ^2, the variances of the Y's corresponding to X=15 is σ^2, etc. (Unequal variances is a complicated problem, and considerably more research is needed in this area. For some interesting possibilities on how to deal with unequal variances, see Wu, 1986.) Thus, the situation is similar to the one-way ANOVA model in chapter eight, only here it is assumed that the means of the Y's are linearly related to the value of X, while in ANOVA the goal was to determine whether the Y's have the same means regardless of what the X values might be. Note that if the means of the Y's are equal, regardless of what the X values happen to be, they are also linearly related. In the context of ANOVA, the X values correspond to levels of the factor being studied. In fact, an ANOVA can be performed using regression techniques in conjunction with what are called "dummy" variables. For further details, see Draper and Smith (1981).

From theorem 4.5.2, it is seen that b_1, b_0, and $\bar{Y}$ have normal distributions with means β_1, β_0, and μ_y, and variances

$$\sigma^2/\Sigma(X_i-\bar{X})^2,\ \sigma^2\Sigma X_i^2/\{n\Sigma(X_i-\bar{X})^2\},\ \text{and } \sigma^2/n,$$

respectively. An unbiased estimate of σ^2 is

$$\hat{\sigma}^2=\Sigma(Y_i-\bar{Y}-b_1(X_i-\bar{X}))^2/(n-2) \qquad (13.2.9)$$

Moreover, it can be shown that

$$T_1=(\bar{Y}-\mu_y)/[\hat{\sigma}^2/n]^{1/2}$$

$$T_2=(b_1-\beta_1)/[\hat{\sigma}^2/\Sigma(X_i-\bar{X})^2]^{1/2}$$

and

$$T_3=(b_0-\beta_0)/[\hat{\sigma}^2\Sigma X_i^2/\{n\Sigma(X_i-\bar{X})^2\}]^{1/2}$$

each have a t distribution with n-2 degrees of freedom. Consequently, confidence intervals can be obtained for β_1, β_0 and μ_y as is illustrated below.

Example 13.2.1 Suppose that for a random sample of n=10 subjects you find that

$$\bar{Y}=10,\ b_1=.45,\ \hat{\sigma}^2=4.0,\ \text{and } \Sigma(X_i-\bar{X})^2=50.$$

From Table A14 the .975 quantile of the t distribution with n-2=8 degrees of freedom is 2.306, and so

$$\Pr\{-2.306<(.45-\beta_1)/[4.0/50]^{1/2}<2.306)=.95.$$

Rearranging terms, it is seen that

$$.45\pm 2.306\{4.0/50\}^{1/2}$$

is a 95% confidence interval for β_1. In general, if $\Pr(T\le t)=1-\alpha/2$, where T is a Student's t random variable with n-2 degrees of freedom,

$$b_1\pm t\{\hat{\sigma}^2/[(\Sigma(X_i-\bar{X})^2]\}^{1/2} \qquad (13.2.10a)$$

is a $1-\alpha$ confidence interval for β_1. The quantity t is read from Table A14. The $1-\alpha$ confidence interval for μ_y is

$$\bar{Y} \pm t[\hat{\sigma}^2/n]^{1/2} \quad (13.2.10b)$$

while the confidence interval for β_0 is

$$b_0 \pm t\{\hat{\sigma}^2 \Sigma X_i^2/[n\Sigma(X_i-\bar{X})^2]\}^{1/2} \quad (13.2.10c)$$

<u>Controlling the Experimentwise Type I Error Probability</u>

It should be noted that $\bar{Y}$ and $\hat{\beta}_1$ can be shown to be independent, but the statistics T_1 and T_2 are <u>not</u> independent because each has σ^2 in its denominator. The joint distribution of T_1 and T_2 is the Studentized maximum modulus distribution. Some percentage points of this distribution are in Table A10. The important point here is that you can get exact simultaneous confidence intervals for both β_1 and μ_y. In particular, by reading t from Table A10, rather than Table A14, the probability is exactly $1-\alpha$ that the confidence interval given by (13.2.10a), and the confidence interval given by (13.2.10b), contain β and μ_y, respectively. Put another way, if you wanted to test $H_0:\beta_1=0$, and you wanted to also test $H_0:\mu_y=0$, the experimentwise Type I error probability would be exactly α if the confidence intervals for β_1 and μ_y are based on t read from Table A10 (with C=2), as opposed to reading t from Table A14.

Similarly, if you test the hypothesis $H_0:\beta_1=0$ using equation (13.2.10a), the probability of a Type I error is exactly α, and if you test $H_0:\beta_0=0$ using equation (13.2.10c), the probability of a Type I error is again α. But suppose you want the experimentwise Type I error to be at most α when testing both $H_0:\beta_1=0$ and $H_0:\beta_0=0$. To do this, simply replace t in equations (13.2.10a) and (13.2.10c) with the critical value read from Table A10 with C=2.

It is noted that the covariance of b_1 and b_0 is

$$\mathrm{COV}(b_1,b_0) = -\sigma^2 \Sigma X_i/\Sigma(X_i-\bar{X})^2,$$

and that b_1 and b_0 have a multivariate t distribution. These results can be used to get confidence intervals for β_1 and β_0 such that the experimentwise Type I error probability is exactly α (Wilcox, 1986).

<u>Example 13.2.2</u> Suppose you want to test $H_0:\beta_1=0$ and $\beta_0=0$, and you want the experimentwise Type I error probability to be at most $\alpha=.05$. If $\nu=24$, then t=2.38.

Interpretation of r^2

As in the ANOVA, it is useful to partition the total sum of squares, $SSTOT=\Sigma(Y_i-\bar{Y})^2$, into two parts. In the present context,

$$Y_i-\bar{Y}=Y_i-Y_i'+Y_i'-\bar{Y},$$

and it can be shown that

$$\Sigma(Y_i-\bar{Y})^2=\Sigma(Y_i-Y_i')^2+\Sigma(Y_i'-\bar{Y})^2. \tag{13.2.11}$$

As previously noted, the quantity $e_i=Y_i-Y_i'$ is called a residual, and

$$SSRES=\Sigma(Y_i-Y_i')^2$$

is called the residual sum of squares. The quantity

$$SSREG=\Sigma(Y_i'-\bar{Y})^2$$

is called the regression sum of squares, and so equation (13.2.11) can be written as

$$SSTOT=SSRES+SSREG.$$

Consider the ratio SSREG/SSTOT. This is the proportion of the total sum of squares that corresponds to SSREG. If there is an exact linear relationship between the observed Y_i's and X_i's, $Y_i'=Y_i$ $(i=1,\ldots,n)$, and so SSRES=0, in which case SSREG/SSTOT=1. When X_i gives a poor indication of the value of Y_i, SSRES will be large, and when SSRES=SSTOT, the regression estimate of Y_i, namely Y_i', is as poor an estimate as it can be. Of course SSREG=0 means that SSREG/SSTOT=0 as well. It turns out that

$$SSREG/SSTOT=r^2. \tag{13.2.12}$$

Thus, r^2, which is known as the coefficient of determination, measures the proportion of total sum of squares that can be accounted for by the linear regression of Y on X. Notice that if you divide both sides of equation (13.2.11) by n-1, the sample variance of the Y_i's, namely SSTOT/(n-1), has been partitioned into two quantities. From (13.2.12), $r^2=[SSREG/(n-1)]/[SSTOT/(n-1)]$, and so r^2 can also be interpreted as the proportion of the sample variance of the Y_i's that is accounted for by a linear rule and X. For a description of some possible difficulties with r^2, see Weisberg (1985, pp. 73-76 and 106-109).

Handling Unequal Variances

An important feature of the procedure just described is that the confidence intervals were derived under the assumption that for any value of X, the Y_i's have a common variance. One approach to handling unequal variances is to use weighted least squares (Draper & Smith, 1981). The purpose of this section is to describe a method for obtaining a confidence interval for β_1 when the variances are unequal and when there is more than one observed Y value corresponding to each X value in your experiment. This situation might occur, for example, when n_j subjects receive a certain dosage X_j of a drug where there are k dosage levels of interest, and your goal is to investigate a linear regression model for predicting Y from the dosage level X. The procedure described here was proposed by Tan (1986).

For notational convenience the model is written in a slightly different form than was done above. In particular, the model is

$$Y_{ij}=\beta_0+\beta_1X_j+\epsilon_{ij} \quad (13.2.13)$$

where Y_{ij} is the observed value of Y for the i<u>th</u> subject corresponding to the j<u>th</u> value of X, where $i=1,\ldots,n_j$; $j=1,\ldots,k$ and $n_j>1$ Thus, it is assumed that there are k values of X in your experiment and that for j<u>th</u> value of X you observe $n_j>1$ subjects. Furthermore, it is assumed that the ϵ_{ij}'s are normally distributed with $E(\epsilon_{ij})=0$ but with

$$\mathrm{Var}(\epsilon_{ij})=\sigma_j^2.$$

If $\sigma_1=\ldots=\sigma_k$, the model reduces that considered above.

Let

$$\bar{Y}_j=\Sigma_i Y_{ij}/n_j,\ \hat{\sigma}_j^2=\{\Sigma_i(Y_{ij}-\bar{Y}_j)^2\}/(n_j-1),$$

$$\hat{\lambda}_j=n_j/\hat{\sigma}_j^2,\ j=1,\ldots,k;$$

$$\hat{X}=[\Sigma_j\hat{\lambda}_jX_j]/[\Sigma_j\hat{\lambda}_j],$$

$$SXY=\Sigma_j\hat{\lambda}_j(X_j-\hat{X})\bar{Y}_j,$$

and

$$SXX=\Sigma_j\hat{\lambda}_j(X_j-\hat{X})^2.$$

The unbiased estimator of β_1 proposed by Tan is

$$\tilde{\beta}_1 = SXY/SXX. \qquad (13.2.14)$$

(For results on estimating β_1 with weighted least squares, versus ordinary least squares, see Jacquez, Mather and Crawford, 1968.)

Next consider the problem of obtaining a 1-α confidence interval for β_1. Tan solves this problem by first approximating the α quantile of the statistic

$$(SXX)^{1/2}(\tilde{\beta}_1 - \beta_1).$$

The approximation is given by

$$h = z + h_1 + h_2$$

where

$$\Pr(Z \le z) = 1 - \alpha,$$

Z is a standard normal random variable (i.e., z is read from Table A1),

$$h_1 = \Sigma_j (z/4f_j)\{(z^2-7)A_j^2 + 8q_jA_j\},$$

$$q_j = 1 - p_j,$$

$$p_j = \hat{\lambda}_j/(\Sigma_m \hat{\lambda}_m)$$

$$A_j = \hat{\lambda}_j(X_j - \hat{X})^2/SXX,$$

$$h_2 = .5zh_1^2 + \Sigma\{(1/4f_j)g_{1j} - (1/f_j^2)(g_{2j}/6 + g_{3j}/32)\}$$

$$-\Sigma_{m \ne j} g_{4mj}/(32 f_m f_j),$$

$$f_j = n_j - 1,$$

$$g_{1j} = (-1/4)\{A_j h_1 [A_j(7 - 10z^2 + z^4) - 8q_j(1 - z^2)] +$$

$$4A_j a_{1j}(1 - z^2) + 4a_{2j}\},$$

$$a_{1j}=(z/2)\Sigma_m(1/f_m)\{[(z^2-7)A_m+4q_m][A_m(A_j-\delta_{jm})+2C_{mj}] +$$
$$4p_mA_m(\delta_{mj}-p_j)\},$$

$\delta_{mj}=1$ if $m=j$; otherwise $\delta_{mj}=0$,

$$C_{mj}=\hat{\lambda}_m p_j(X_m-\hat{X})(X_j-\hat{X})/SXX,$$

$$a_{2j}=(z/2)\Sigma_m(1/f_m)\{2[(z^2-7)A_m+4q_m][A_j(A_j-1+p_j)(A_m-\delta_{mj}) +$$
$$p_mp_jA_j+C_{mj}(2A_j-2q_j-\delta_{mj})] \quad +$$
$$(z^2-7)[A_j(A_m-\delta_{mj})+2C_{mj}]^2 + 8p_j(\delta_{mj}-p_m)[A_j(A_m-\delta_{mj})$$
$$+ 2C_{mj}] - 8A_m(\delta_{mj}-p_m)p_j(1-p_j)\}$$

$$g_{2j}=zA_j\{A_j^2(75-22z^2+z^4)-24q_jA_j(6-z^2)+72q_j^2\},$$

$$q_{3j}=zA_j\{A_j^3(1089-489z^2+45z^4-z^6)-48A_j^2q_j(61-20z^2+z^4)$$
$$+96A_jq_j^2(27-5z^2)-768q_j^3\}$$

$$q_{4mj}=z\{A_mA_j[A_mA_j(1089-489z^2+45z^4-z^6) + 32p_mp_j(17-3z^2) +$$
$$64q_mq_j(5-z^2)] - 8(A_mq_j+A_jq_m)[A_mA_j(61-$$
$$20z^2+z^4)+16p_mp_j + 4C_{mj}(17-3z^2)] +$$
$$32C_{mj}[A_mA_j(61-20z^2+z^4)+8p_mp_j+8q_mq_j$$
$$+ 4C_{mj}(5-z^2)]\}.$$

The $1-\alpha$ confidence interval for β_1 is

$$[\tilde{\beta}_1 - (SXX)^{-1/2}h_{\alpha/2},\ \tilde{\beta}_1 + (SXX)^{-1/2}h_{1-\alpha/2}]$$

where h_α is the α quantile approximated as described above. For a brief illustration of this procedure, see Tan (1986).

13.3 MULTIPLE REGRESSION

Again it is assumed n subjects are randomly sampled. This time, for the ith subject, you observe the quantities Y_i, $X_{i1},\ldots,X_{ik}$. That is, you have k predictor variables rather than just one. Generalizing results in the previous section, the goal is to find a linear rule for determining Y_i based on the values X_{ij} $(j=1,\ldots,k)$. That is, the regression estimate of Y_i is to have the form

$$Y_i'=b_0+\Sigma_j b_j X_{ij}.$$

Consistent with the previous section, a least squares criterion is used. Thus, b_0, $b_1,\ldots,b_k$ are to be chosen so as to minimize

$$SSRES=\Sigma(Y_i-Y_i')^2,$$

the residual sum of squares. It can be shown that the b_j values that minimize SSRES are the values that are the solution of the equations

$$b_1\Sigma x_{i1}^2 + b_2\Sigma x_{i1}x_{i2} + \ldots + b_k\Sigma X_{i1}x_{ik}=\Sigma x_{i1}y_i$$

$$b_1\Sigma x_{i2}x_{i1} + b_2\Sigma x_{i2}^2 + \ldots + b_k\Sigma x_{i2}x_{ik}=\Sigma x_{i2}Y_i$$

$$\vdots$$

$$b_1\Sigma x_{ik}x_{i1} + b_2\Sigma x_{ik}x_{i2} + \ldots + b_k\Sigma x_{ik}^2=\Sigma x_{ik}Y_i,$$

where $x_{ij}=X_{ij}-\bar{X}_j$, $y_i=Y_i-\bar{Y}$, $\bar{X}_j=\Sigma_i X_{ij}/n$, $\bar{Y}=\Sigma Y_i/n$, and $b_0=\bar{Y}-\Sigma b_j\bar{X}_j$.

These equations are called "normal" equations.

Example 13.3.1 Suppose you observe

Subject	Y	X_1	X_2
1	10	1	4
2	18	9	3
3	12	9	3
4	20	13	10
	$\bar{Y}=15$	$\bar{X}_1=8$	$\bar{X}_2=5$

To determine a linear regression equation for predicting Y from X_1 and X_2, first compute the y_i, x_{i1}, and x_{i2} values. These are

y	x_1	x_2
-5	-7	-1
3	1	-2
-3	1	-2
5	5	5

Thus, $\Sigma x_{i1}^2=(-7)^2+\ldots+5^2=76$, $\Sigma x_{i2}^2=34$, $\Sigma x_{i1}x_{i2}=7-2-2+25=28$,

$\Sigma x_{i1}y_i=35+3-3+25=60$, and $\Sigma x_{i2}y_i=30$. So

$$76b_1+28b_2=60$$

and

$$28b_1+34b_2=30.$$

Solving for b_1 and b_2 yields $b_1=.67$ and $b_2=.33$, and so $b_0=15-.67(8)-.33(5)=7.99$. Therefore, the regression equation is

$$Y'=.67X_1+.33X_2+7.99.$$

Thus, if you observe $X_1=1$ and $X_2=2$, the predicted Y value is $.67(1)+.33(2)+7.99=9.32$.

As in the previous section, the total sum of squares, $SSTOT=\Sigma(Y_i-\bar{Y})^2$ can be partitioned into two parts, namely,

$$SSRES=\Sigma(Y_i-Y_i')^2 \text{ and } SSREG=\Sigma(Y_i'-\bar{Y})^2.$$

Again it turns out that SSTOT=SSREG+SSRES, and so SSREG/SSTOT

gives you a measure of how well Y′ predicts Y. Also, SSREG/SSTOT is the proportion of the variance of the Y_i's that is accounted for by X_1, X_2 and a linear regression equation.

<u>Definition 13.3.1</u> The multiple correlation coefficient is the correlation between Y′ and Y.

It can be shown that an estimate of the squared multiple correlation is

$$R^2=SSREG/SSTOT,$$

but the details of the derivation are omitted. (For alternative estimates, see Lucke & Embretson, 1984.) It is noted that the parameter corresponding to R^2 can be derived in terms of the variances and covariances of Y, $X_1,\ldots,X_k$. The interested reader is referred to Wilks (1962, p. 91). When there are two predictor variables, i.e., k=2,

$$R^2=(r_{y1}^2+r_{y2}^2-2r_{y1}r_{y2}r_{12})/(1-r_{12}^2) \tag{13.3.2}$$

where r_{12}=CORR(X_1,X_2), where CORR means correlation, and

$$r_{yi}=\text{CORR}(Y,X_i),\ i=1,2.$$

It is also of interest to note that for the special case k=2,

$$b_1=[s_y(r_{y1}-r_{y2}r_{12})]/[s_1(1-r_{12}^2)]$$

and

$$b_2=[s_y(r_{y2}-r_{y1}r_{12})]/[s_2(1-r_{12}^2)]$$

where $s_y^2=\Sigma(Y_i-\bar{Y})^2/(n-1)$, and $s_j^2=\Sigma_i(X_{ij}-\bar{X}_j)^2/(n-1)$, j=1,2.

The test of $H_0:\rho=0$ can be extended to the problem of testing the hypothesis that the multiple correlation coefficient is equal to zero. To apply the test, compute SSRES and SSREG as described above, and then compute

MSRES=SSRES/(n-k-1)

MSREG=SSREG/k

and

F=MSREG/MSRES.

The F statistic has an F distribution with k and n-k-1 degrees of freedom when H_0 is true, and so you reject H_0 if F>f where f is the 1-α quantile of the F distribution. As usual, f is read from Table A3. The justification of the test is similar to the justification of the test of $H_0:\rho=0$, which was described in section 13.1. It should be pointed out that the usual homogeneity of variance assumption is required.

It is also possible to test $H_0:\beta_j=0$ for each j, j=1,...,k, where β_j is the parameter corresponding to b_j. To do this, you compute

$$T_j=b_j/\sqrt{A}$$

where $A=(1-R^2)/[(1-R_j^2)(n-k-1)]$, and R_j^2 is the squared

multiple correlation coefficient for the regression of Y on

$$X_1,\ X_2,\ldots,X_{j-1},\ X_{j+1},\ldots,X_k.$$

That is, R_j^2 is the squared multiple correlation coefficient when the jth predictor variable is omitted from the regression analysis. The statistic T_j has a Student's t distribution with n-k-1 degrees of freedom. Again the homogeneity of variance assumption is required, and the Y's are assumed to have a normal distribution. If $|T_j|>t$ reject H_0 where t is the $1-\alpha/2$ quantile of Student's t distribution which is read from Table A14. Note that for each j, the test of $H_0:\beta_j=0$ will have a Type I error probability equal to α, but the experimentwise Type I error will exceed α. To ensure that the experimentwise Type I error does not exceed α, you can apply the Dunn-Sidak multiple comparison procedure which was described in chapter 9. This just means that instead of reading the critical value t from Table A14, read the critical value from Table A10.

It is noted that you can also test hypotheses such as

$$H_0:\beta_1=\ldots=\beta_k=0$$

rather than performing multiple comparisons on each of the β's (e.g., Neter & Waserman, 1974). As was the case in the analysis of variance model, the results for multiple comparisons on the β's can lead to different conclusions than those obtained when testing $H_0:\beta_1=\ldots=\beta_k=0$. That is, you might reject $H_0:\beta_1=\ldots=\beta_k=0$ but not reject $H_0:\beta_j=0$ for any j, j=1,...,k. For an illustration of this point, see Fairly (1986).

Improved Simultaneous Regression Parameters

The remainder of this section describes a method for obtaining simultaneous $1-\alpha$ confidence intervals for regression parameters that in some cases yields substantially shorter confidence intervals than those obtained with Table A10, particularly when the number of predictors, k, is small. It is assumed that the reader is familiar with basic matrix algebra, and so some readers may want to skim or skip the remainder of this section. For convenience the regression model is written in a slightly different fashion, namely

$$Y_i=\beta_1X_{i1}+\ldots+\beta_kX_{ik}+e_i \quad (i=1,\ldots n)$$

where Y_i is the dependent variable, $X_{i1}=1$, and $X_{i2},\ldots,X_{ik}$ are the known values of the k-1 independent variables, and the e_i are independently normally distributed random variables with mean 0 and common variance σ^2 Let

$$\underset{\sim}{X}=(x_{ij})$$

be the n by k matrix of X values, and let s^2 be the usual estimate of σ^2 in which case $\nu s^2/\sigma^2$ has a chi-square distribution with ν=n-k-2 degrees of freedom. Let u_{ij} be the (i,j)th element of the matrix

$$(\underset{\sim}{X}'\underset{\sim}{X})^{-1}.$$

Then s is independent of the Y_i's, and the b_i's have a multivariate t distribution with correlation matrix

$$\rho_{ij}=(u_{ii}u_{jj})^{-1/2}u_{ij}$$

which is known. It can be shown (Wilcox, 1986) that

$$b_i \pm h(u_{ii})^{1/2}s \quad (i=1,\ldots,k)$$

provides conservative simultaneous confidence intervals for the parameters β_i where h is read from Table 21 with

$$\rho=\max_{i\neq j}(u_{ii}u_{jj})^{-1/2}u_{ij}.$$

That is, the probability is at least 1-α that these k confidence intervals contain the β_i's. Put another way, if you test $H_0:\beta_i=0$ (i=1,...,k), the experimentwise Type I error probability is at most α. For ρ=0, this procedure reduces to using the percentage points of the Studentized maximum modulus distribution, which are the percentage points reported in Table A10. The confidence intervals just described are uniformly shorter than those obtained with Table A10. When k is not too large, the confidence intervals can be substantially shorter, but for k>8 there is no advantage to using this more complicated procedure.

13.4 POLYNOMIAL REGRESSION

Again consider the situation where two observations, say X and Y, are taken on every subject, but this time suppose you want to include the possibility that X and Y have a curvilinear relationship. One approach to this problem is to determine a regression equation of the form

$$Y=\beta_0+\Sigma_{j=1}^{k}\beta_j x^j \qquad (13.4.1)$$

for some integer k. The quantity k is called the degree of the polynomial in equation (13.4.1). If you choose k=1, equation (13.4.1) reduces to $Y=\beta_0+\beta_1 X$, which is the linear equation in section 13.2. The idea is that you might get a better prediction of the estimate of Y by choosing k>1. If you choose k=2,

$$Y=\beta_0+\beta_1X+\beta_2X^2 \qquad (13.4.2)$$

and this is called a quadratic regression equation. The previous section described how to estimate the regression coefficients when $Y=\beta_0+\beta_1X_1+\beta_2X_2$, and the same procedure is used to estimate the regression coefficients in equation (13.4.2). That is, you treat X as being the first predictor variable, X_1, and you treat X^2 as the second predictor variable X_2. The point is that in the equation

$$Y=\beta_0+\Sigma\beta_iX_i,$$

the X_i's can be any variable at all. In particular, you can set $X_1=X$, $X_2=X^2$, $X_3=X^3$, etc., and apply the procedures described in the previous section. Thus, even though you have only two measures for each subject, you have k predictor variables, namely, X, $X^2,\ldots,X^k$.

<u>Example 13.4.1</u> Suppose you have the observations

Y	X	X^2
1	-1	1
7	4	16
.		
.		
.		
5	-3	9.

To determine the least squares quadratic regression equation of Y on X and X^2, compute

$$\bar{X}_1=\Sigma X_i/n=(-1+4+\ldots-3)/n,\ \bar{X}_2=\Sigma X_i^2/n=(1+16+\ldots+9)/n,$$

$$A=\Sigma(X_i-\bar{X}_1)^2,\ B=\Sigma(X_i^2-\bar{X}_2)^2,\ C=\Sigma(X_i-\bar{X}_1)(X_i^2-\bar{X}_2),$$

$$D=\Sigma(X_i-\bar{X}_1)(Y_i-\bar{Y}),\ E=\Sigma(X_i^2-\bar{X}_2)(Y_i-\bar{Y}).$$

Then you solve the normal equations

$$b_1A+b_2C=D$$

$$b_1C+b_2B=E$$

for b_1 and b_2. Then $b_0=\bar{Y}-b_1\bar{X}_1-b_2\bar{X}_2$, and

$$Y' = b_0 + b_1 X + b_2 X^2.$$

If, for example, A=4, B=36, C=72, D=100, and E=118, then

$$4b_1 + 72b_2 = 100$$

$$72b_1 + 36b_2 = 118$$

which yields $b_1 = 136/140 = .971$, and $b_2 = 1.335$.

An important point is that in theory, any degree polynomial can be used, but in practice third degree polynomials and higher can lead to computational difficulties (Weisberg, 1985). Accordingly, it is recommended that you generally use polynomials having degree at most 2.

As a final note, there are many other ways in which you might derive a curvilinear relationship between Y and X. For example, you might consider the model

$$Y' = \beta_0 + \underline{\ln}(X),$$

or some other function of X might be used instead. For an alternative approach to deriving regression equations, see Hastie and Tibshirani (1986).

13.5 ORTHOGONAL POLYNOMIALS

With the polynomial regression equation of the previous section, you might test the hypothesis $\beta_2 = \beta_3 = \ldots = \beta_k = 0$, and if you fail to reject, use the regression equation $Y = \beta_0 + \beta_1 X$. If you conclude that $\beta_2 \neq 0$ and $\beta_1 \neq 0$, you might use a quadratic equation, etc. These hypotheses can be tested using the results in section 13.3. The goal in this section is to provide a simpler method for testing these hypotheses.

It should be stressed that the procedure about described in the following can only be used when the X values are equally spaced. For instance, if the observed values are 4, 6, 8, and 10, the values are equally spaced because 4-6=6-8=8-10. Of course, in many cases, the observed X values are not equally spaced, but there are situations where they are. For instance, X might be different dosages of a drug, in which case equally spaced values of X could be used in an experiment.

Suppose the only values of the variable X in your experiment are

$$x_1, \ldots, x_J.$$

For example, you might want to study the effect of J=4 amounts of a drug, X, on some variable Y, and the amounts might be $x_1=100$, $x_2=200$, $x_3=300$, and $x_4=400$ milligrams.

Consider the polynomial regression equation

$$Y'=\beta_0+\beta_1X+\beta_2X^2+\beta_3X^3.$$

As indicated in the previous section, you could, for each m, (m=1,...,k) test $H_0:\beta_m=0$. For equally spaced x_j values, however, a simpler method for testing these hypotheses can be used.

Let $\mu_j=E(Y|X=x_j)$. That is, μ_j is the mean of Y given that the value of X is x_j. For instance, in the illustration, for j=2, μ_2 is the mean of Y when 200 milligrams of the drug are being used. It can be shown that for a proper choice of the constants

$$c_1,...,c_J,$$

you can test $H_0:\beta_m=0$ by testing $H_0:\Psi=0$ where $\Psi=\Sigma c_j\mu_j$. Put another way, there is a linear contrast of the J means that allows you to test $H_0:\beta_m=0$ for any m, m=1,...,J-1. The required contrast coefficients are reported in Table A8. These constants are called coefficients of orthogonal polynomials. The coefficients for testing $H_0:\beta_1=0$ are the coefficients in Table A8 corresponding to a "linear" contrast. To test $H_0:\beta_2=0$, you use the coefficients in Table A8 corresponding to quadratic contrasts, etc.

<u>Example 13.5.1</u> Continuing the illustration, suppose you have J=4 levels of drug X, and you want to consider the regression equation

$$Y'=\beta_0+\beta_1X+\beta_2X^2+\beta_3X^3.$$

To test $H_0:\beta_1=0$, it is seen from Table A8 that the appropriate contrast coefficients are -3, -1, 1, and 3. Thus, testing $H_0:\beta_1=0$ can be accomplished by testing

$$H_0:\ -3\mu_1-\mu_2+\mu_3+3\mu_4=0,$$

and this can be done using the procedures described in chapter 9. For instance, if corresponding to the J=4 levels of the drug, the sample means of the Y's are $\bar{Y}_1=15$, $\bar{Y}_2=20$, $\bar{Y}_3=18$, and $\bar{Y}_4=24$, then you compute

$$T=[-3(15)-20+18+3(24)]/[MSWG\Sigma c_j^2/n_j]^{1/2}$$

where

$$MSWG=\Sigma\Sigma(Y_{ij}-\bar{Y}_j)^2/(N-J)$$

is the usual mean square within groups, the c_j's are the contrast coefficients, and Y_{ij} is the ith observation of Y corresponding to the jth value of X. For the case at hand, $c_1=-3$, $c_2=-1$, $c_3=1$, and $c_4=3$. Of course, n_j is the number of Y values corresponding to $X=x_j$. If instead you want to test $H_0:\beta_2=0$, you refer to Table A8 and find that $c_1=1$, $c_2=-1$, $c_3=-1$, and $c_4=1$. Otherwise the calculations are exactly the same. Note that $\beta_m=0$ is a reasonable conclusion if you do not reject H_0 and the power of the test is reasonably large.

Partial Correlation

Consider three random variables, say Y_1, Y_2, and Y_3, and let

$$Y_1'=b_{01}+b_{11}Y_3 \text{ and } Y_2'=b_{02}+b_{12}Y_3$$

be the least squares regression equation of Y_1 on Y_3 and Y_2 on Y_3, respectively. The correlation between

$$Y_1-Y_1' \text{ and } Y_2-Y_2', \text{ say } \rho_{12.3},$$

is called the partial correlation between Y_1 and Y_2 with Y_3 held constant. Let ρ_{ij} be the correlation between Y_i and Y_j. It can be shown that

$$\rho_{12.3}=[\rho_{12}-\rho_{13}\rho_{23}]/[(1-\rho_{13}^2)(1-\rho_{23}^2)]^{1/2}.$$

To clarify the term "with Y_3 held constant," suppose Y_1, Y_2, and Y_3 are normally distributed with correlations ρ_{ij}. It can be shown that the conditional distributions of Y_1 and Y_2, given Y_3, are normal, and that the correlation between Y_1 and Y_2 is $\rho_{12\cdot3}$. Thus, if you restrict your attention to the Y_1 and Y_2 values corresponding to any particular value of Y_3, the resulting correlation between Y_1 and Y_2 is $\rho_{12\cdot3}$ regardless of what the value of Y_3 might be.

Estimating $\rho_{12\cdot3}$ can be accomplished by simply estimating ρ_{ij} in the usual way with r_{ij}, and computing

$$r_{12.3}=[r_{12}-r_{13}r_{23}]/[(1-r_{13}^2)(1-r_{23}^2)]^{1/2}.$$

13.6 ANALYSIS OF COVARIANCE

In chapter 11 it was pointed out that repeated measures designs, or more generally randomized block designs, may be useful in terms of reducing experimental error, and thus increasing power. An alternative way of possibly reducing the error variance is to take into account the value of some variable that is related to the variable that you are investigating. For example, suppose you have two methods of teaching statistics, and you want to compare the methods in terms of the score on the final exam. You could, of course, use a t-test. But suppose that for each subject in your study you are told the number of college mathematics courses taken prior to taking statistics. You suspect that previous training in mathematics is related to the effectiveness of the two teaching methods, and so it is only natural to try to take this information into account when comparing the two methods. Analysis of covariance (ANCOVA) is a technique for accomplishing this goal. In the illustration, number of previous mathematics courses is an example of what is called a covariate or concomitant variable.

Continuing the illustration, suppose that for each treatment group there is a linear relationship between Y, the score on the final exam, and X, the number of previous mathematics courses. Also assume that the regression equation for the two groups is

$$Y_{ij}=\beta(X_{ij}-\bar{X})+\mu_j+\epsilon_{ij} \tag{13.6.1}$$

where $\bar{X}=\Sigma\Sigma X_{ij}/N$, $N=\Sigma n_j$, n_j is the number of observations sampled from the jth group, and ϵ_{ij} is a normal random variable with mean zero and variance σ^2. The X_{ij}'s are viewed as constants. Thus,

$$E(Y_{ij})=\mu_j+\beta(X_{ij}-\bar{X}) \tag{13.6.2}$$

and the variance of Y_{ij} is σ^2. Note that the model assumes equal variances for both groups, and it also assumes that both treatment groups have identical slopes. That is, the regression lines are assumed to be parallel. Methods for dealing with the violation of these two assumptions are described below. Also note that the model says that the expected value of Y_{ij} is a function of the treatment group to which a subject belongs, as well as the value of X_{ij}.

It is common to write (13.6.1) as

$$Y_{ij}=\mu+\alpha_j+\beta(X_{ij}-\bar{X})+\epsilon_{ij} \tag{13.6.2a}$$

where μ is the grand mean, and $\alpha_j=\mu_j-\mu$. This is, of course, a generalization of the one-way ANOVA model in chapter eight.

To provide a little more insight into how ANCOVA can affect your conclusions, suppose that the two regression lines corresponding to the two treatment groups in the illustration are identical with positive slopes. That is, $\mu_1=\mu_2$, in which case $\mu+\alpha_j=0$, and so $E(Y_{ij})=\beta(X_{ij}-\bar{X})$. In fact, suppose $\beta=13$ and $\bar{X}=1$. Then for an examinee who has X=2 mathematics courses prior to taking statistics, the expected score on the final exam is 13(2-1)=13 regardless of whether the subject is a man or woman. If X=6, E(Y)=13(6-1)=65. Now suppose that by chance, all the subjects in group 1 (women) have X=2, while for group 2 (men) X=6. Then the men will do better on the final exam even though for men and women who have the same number of prior mathematics courses, their expected scores on the final exam are the same. Thus, if by chance method 1 has a preponderance of subjects with low X values, while method 2 has subjects with high X values, method 2 will generally appear to be superior to method 1 even though there is no difference among subjects having equal X values. In fact it is possible to ignore the X values and conclude that method 1 is better than method 2 using the usual t-test, but come to the opposite conclusion when the regression of Y on X is taken into account.

Before continuing, it is noted that there is a vast amount of literature on ANCOVA, and it is impossible to cover all of the relevant literature in a single chapter. Readers interested in this topic might consult the book by Huitema (1980), which is devoted solely to ANCOVA, and a special issue of Biometrics (1982, vol. 38, no. 3) on this subject might be consulted as well.

Importance of the Assumptions

ANCOVA is more sensitive to violations of the underlying assumptions than is ANOVA, even when equal sample sizes are used (Atiqullah, 1964). In particular, if X is normally distributed, it appears that ANCOVA is robust to nonnormality in the Y scores. However, departures from normality in the X scores affects the robustness of ANCOVA to departures from normality in the Y scores. Even if X is normally distributed, ANCOVA may not be robust to non-normality in the Y scores (Conover & Iman, 1982). It is noted, though, that Conover and Iman's results were limited to n=10 observations per treatment group. As in ANOVA, unequal variances can also have an adverse effect on the Type I error probability. Methods for dealing with these problems are described below as are methods for dealing with non-parallel regression slopes. Another potential problem is that if the regression equation is actually quadratic, but is assumed to be linear, this has a serious effect on the F test given in equation (13.6.3) below. For further comments on the robustness of ANCOVA, see Elashoff (1969).

Computational Steps

To test $H_0:\mu_1=\ldots=\mu_J$ (assuming there are n observations per group) under the assumptions described above, you perform the following computations:

$$YSQ=(\Sigma\Sigma Y_{ij})^2/nJ,$$

$$ASY=\Sigma\Sigma Y_{ij}^2,$$

$$AY=\Sigma_j(\Sigma_i Y_{ij})^2/n,$$

$$XSQ=(\Sigma\Sigma X_{ij})^2/Jn$$

$$ASX=\Sigma_i\Sigma_j X_{ij}^2,$$

$$AX=\Sigma_j(\Sigma_i X_{ij})^2/n,$$

$$PXY=(\Sigma\Sigma X_{ij})(\Sigma\Sigma Y_{ij})/nJ$$

$$ASXY=\Sigma\Sigma X_{ij}Y_{ij},$$

$$AXY=\Sigma_j(\Sigma_i X_{ij})(\Sigma_i Y_{ij})/n$$

TYY=ASY-YSQ,
AYY=AY-YSQ,
SYY=ASY-AY,
TXX=ASX-XSQ,
AXX=AX-XSQ,
SXX=ASX-AX,
TXY=ASXY-PXY,
SXY=ASXY-AXY,
TADJ=TYY - $(TXY)^2$/TXX,
SADJ=SYY - $(SXY)^2$/SXX,
AADJ=TADJ-SADJ

and

$$F=[AADJ/(J-1)]/[SYY/(nJ-J-1)] \quad (13.6.3)$$

The degrees of freedom are J-1 and nJ-J-1, and the critical value is read from Table A3. If F exceeds the critical value, reject $H_0:\mu_1=\ldots=\mu_J$.

Tests For Equal Slopes

There is a test for equal slopes that can be applied under the assumption of equal variances (e.g., Huitema, 1980), but this test should not be used when the equal variance assumption is violated, and so it is not described here. It is recommended that the following test for equal slopes be used instead.

Tan's Test for Equal Slopes

For the case of unequal variances, Tabatabai and Tan (1985) examined the following procedure (which they call Tan's test) based on the model

$$Y_{ij}=\mu+\alpha_j+\beta_j(X_{ij}-\bar{X}_j)+\epsilon_{ij}, \tag{13.6.4}$$

where μ is the grand mean, the intercepts α_j satisfy $\Sigma n_j\alpha_j=0$,

$$\bar{X}_j=\Sigma_i X_{ij}/n_j$$

and n_j is, as usual, the number of observations sampled from the jth group. In contrast to the model in (13.6.2a), the β's are not assumed to be equal, and the variances of the error terms,

$\sigma_j^2=\mathrm{VAR}(\epsilon_{ij})$, are not assumed to be equal as well.

To test $H_0:\beta_1=\ldots=\beta_J$, compute

$$N=\Sigma n_j,\ \bar{Y}_j=\Sigma_i Y_{ij}/n_j,\ \bar{Y}=\Sigma_j n_j\bar{Y}_j/N,\ s_{xxj}=\Sigma_i(X_{ij}-\bar{X}_j)^2,$$

$$s_{xyj}=\Sigma_i(X_{ij}-\bar{X}_j)Y_{ij},$$

$$\hat{\sigma}_j^2=\{\Sigma_i[(Y_{ij}-\bar{Y}_j)-\hat{\beta}_j(X_{ij}-\bar{X}_j)]^2\}/\nu_j$$

$$\nu_j=n_j-2,\ \hat{\beta}_j=s_{xyj}/s_{xxj},$$

$$\hat{\beta}=\Sigma_j n_j\hat{\beta}_j/N,$$

$$M_1=\Sigma_j n_j(\hat{\beta}_j-\hat{\beta})^2,$$

$$M_2=\Sigma_j\{n_j\hat{\sigma}_j^2(1-n_j/N)/s_{xxj}\},$$

and

$$F=M_1/M_2. \tag{13.6.5}$$

The degrees of freedom are J-1 and

$$\hat{d}=M_2^2/\{\Sigma_j n_j^2(1-n_j/N)^2\hat{\sigma}_j^4/[\nu_j s_{xxj}^2]\}.$$

The critical value f is read from Table A3, and as usual, you reject H_0 if F>f. This procedure has also been shown to be robust to nonnormality. It is tempting to test for equal variances and use (13.6.4) if you fail to reject, but from results reported in chapter eight, it seems better to simply abandon (13.6.4) and always use (13.6.5).

It is noted that Potthoff (1965) proposed a test for parallel regression lines that also allows unequal variances. Potthoff's procedure has the advantage of handling more than one predictor, but the solution is limited to J=2 groups. For some nonparametric tests that two regression lines are parallel, see Potthoff (1974), Hollander (1970), Conover (1980, section 5.5), Sen (1972), and Adichie (1974, 1975). Perhaps there are situations where these alternative procedures compare favorably to Tan's solution, but this has not been established.

Multiple Comparisons

Next the problem of pairwise multiple comparisons among the μ_j's is considered. The procedure described here was suggested by Hochberg and Varon-Salomon (1984) and is an extension of Tukey's procedure that was described in chapter nine. For the moment, it is assumed that there are equal sample sizes per group as well as equal variances. That is, each group has n subjects. Again the model is

$$Y'=\mu_j+\beta(X_{ij}-\bar{X}).$$

where $\bar{X}=\Sigma\bar{X}_j/J$. Sometimes the model is written as

$$E(Y_{ij}|X_{ij})=\mu_j+\beta(X_{ij}-\bar{X}).$$

(Another way of thinking about regression is to think of Y' as the expected value of Y given X.) Note that the model assumes equal slopes, and this assumption can be tested with Tan's procedure given above. However, unless you are reasonably certain that Tan's test has an acceptably high power level, it is recommended that you do not assume parallel slopes, that you avoid the procedure described in this section, and that you compare the regression lines using equation (13.6.7) below.

Before continuing, first consider the problem of estimating the μ_j's. From (13.6.2)

$$\mu_j=E(Y_{ij})-\beta(X_{ij}-\bar{X}),$$

and so a natural estimate of μ_j is

$$\hat{\mu}_j = \bar{Y}_j - \hat{\beta}(\bar{X}_j - \bar{X}),$$

where $\hat{\beta}$ is an estimate of β which is given below. The quantity $\hat{\mu}_j$ is the estimate of what is called the adjusted effect. That is, $\hat{\mu}_j$ is the estimate of the average Y's in group j adjusted for the effect of the covariate X. To compute the adjusted effects you first estimate β by computing

$$SXX = \Sigma\Sigma(X_{ij} - \bar{X}_j)^2,$$

$$SYY = \Sigma\Sigma(Y_{ij} - \bar{Y}_j)^2,$$

$$SXY = \Sigma\Sigma(X_{ij} - \bar{X}_j)(Y_{ij} - \bar{Y}_j),$$

and

$$\hat{\beta} = SXY/SXX.$$

The resulting values of $\hat{\mu}_j$ are unbiased estimates of μ_j, the adjusted effects. It is also noted that in this notation, an estimate of the common variance is

$$s^2 = (SYY - \hat{\beta}^2 SXX)/\nu, \qquad (13.6.6)$$

where $\nu = nJ - J - 1$.

Having computed the adjusted effects, $\hat{\mu}_j$, the confidence intervals are given by

$$\hat{\mu}_j - \hat{\mu}_k \pm s q_{\alpha,J,\nu} [(1/n) + (\bar{X}_j - \bar{X}_k)^2/2SXX]^{1/2},$$

where $q_{\alpha,J,\nu}$ is read from Table A9.

It should be noted that applying a Tukey-Kramer procedure to adjusted means, as is done here, has met with some criticism. A brief discussion of this issue can be found in Huitema (1980). However, the more recent work by Hochberg and Varon-Salomon (1984) suggests that a Tukey-Kramer procedure should be used whenever the variances are equal, and results reported by Bryant and Fox (1985) confirm this view.

Crossing Regression Lines and Unequal Variances.

There are two practical problems with the Tukey-Kramer multiple comparison procedure given above. First, it assumes the regression lines are parallel. Although Tan's procedure can be used to test this assumption, Tan's procedure may not have enough power to detect unequal slopes in situations where this assumption should be abandoned. A better approach would seem to be to apply a procedure that does not require the assumption of equal slopes. Second, the procedure just described assumes equal variances among the J treatment groups. All indications are that it is best to simply abandon procedures that assume equal variances, and wherever possible, use a procedure that does not require this assumption.

Determining whether two regression lines cross is an important practical problem. Suppose that two regression lines cross at $X=c$. Then one of the treatment groups, say group 1, has a higher expected Y value for $X<c$. That is, for $X<c$, $E(Y_1|X)>E(Y_2|X)$. But for $X>c$, treatment group 2 has a higher average value. That is $E(Y_2|X)>E(Y_1|X)$. Put another way, for $X<c$, method 1 tends to be better than method 2, while for $X>c$, the reverse is true.

Of course if you reject the hypothesis that two regression lines are parallel using say Tan's test, you would conclude that the regression lines cross at some value of X. However, this leaves open the issue of whether the distance between the regression lines is large at any X value that might occur in practice. The procedure about to be described is better able to deal with this issue.

First attention is given to the problem of testing for crossing regression lines with the assumption that the treatment groups have equal variances. A solution for unequal variances is described momentarily. It should be noted that when equal variances can be assumed, the Johnson-Neyman (1936) procedure is a well known technique that can be used to determine where regression lines cross for the case $J=2$ groups. For $J>2$ the procedure is easily extended via the Bonferroni inequality (Potthoff, 1964). A summary of these procedures can be found in Huitema (1980). Here an alternative procedure is described that takes advantage of Sidak's multiplicative inequality, and then the procedure is extended to the case of unequal variances.

Consider any two X values, say $X=c_1$ and $X=c_2$, $c_1<c_2$. The values c_1 and c_2 might be the smallest and largest X values observed in your study, but they can be any X values that are of interest to you. The immediate goal is to decide whether any pair of regression lines cross somewhere in the interval $c_1<X<c_2$. Once this is done, the Johnson-Neyman procedure will be modified to handle unequal variances. To accomplish this goal, assume that for

the j<u>th</u> group

$$E(Y_j|X)=\beta_{0j} + \beta_{1j}X,$$

and let

$$\tau_{ijk}=(\beta_{0j}-\beta_{0k})+[\beta_{1j}c_i-\beta_{1k}c_i].$$

The quantity τ_{ijk} is the distance between the two regession lines at $X=c_i$ $(i=1,2)$. For the j<u>th</u> group, β_{1j} and β_{0j} are estimated with b_{1j} and b_{0j}, which are computed using equations (13.2.3) and (13.2.4), respectively. The unbiased estimate of τ_{ijk} is

$$D_{ijk}=(b_{0j}-b_{0k})+[b_{1j}c_i-b_{1k}c_i].$$

The variance of D_{ijk} is $q_{ijk}\sigma^2$ where

$$q_{ijk}=(n_j+n_k)/(n_jn_k) + (\bar{X}_j-c_i)^2/C_j + (\bar{X}_k-c_i)^2/C_k,$$

and $C_j=\Sigma_i(X_{ij}-\bar{X}_j)^2$.

Let

$$s^2=\Sigma_j\Sigma_i(Y_{ij}-b_{0j}-b_{1j}X_{ij})^2/\nu$$

where

$$\nu=\Sigma(n_j-2).$$

The hypothesis that the j<u>th</u> and k<u>th</u> regression lines are identical is $H_0:\tau_{1jk}=\tau_{2jk}=0$. When this hypothesis is true,

$$T_{ijk}=D_{ijk}/(s\sqrt{q_{ijk}}),\ i=1,2$$

has a Student's t distribution with ν degrees of freedom. Under the assumption that the variances are equal across all J groups, the Dunn-Sidak procedure can be used to get simultaneous confidence intervals for the τ_{1jk}'s as well as for the τ_{2jk}'s. For the τ_{ijk}'s, the $1-\alpha$ joint confidence intervals are given by

$$D_{ijk}\pm hs\sqrt{q_{ijk}},\ i=1,2;\ j<k, \tag{13.6.7}$$

where h is read from Table A10 with C=J(J-1) being the number of comparisons. If this interval does not include zero, reject $H_0:\tau_{ijk}=0$. If you reject both $H_0:\tau_{1jk}=0$ and $H_0:\tau_{2jk}=0$, and if D_{1jk} and D_{2jk} have opposite signs, you conclude that the j<u>th</u> and k<u>th</u> regression lines cross. That is, decide they cross if $D_{1jk}<0$ and $D_{2jk}>0$, or if $D_{1jk}>0$ and $D_{2jk}<0$. If $D_{1jk}>0$ and $D_{2jk}>0$, group 1 is better (has higher expected Y values) than group 2 for all X in the interval (c_1,c_2). If $D_{1jk}<0$ and $D_{2jk}<0$, the reverse is true. This procedure guarantees that the experimentwise Type I error will be at most $1-\alpha$.

An important feature of this procedure is that it tells you something about the magnitude of the distance between the regression lines. This is important even when the regression lines do not cross. Suppose J=2 and that for $X=c_1$ the confidence interval given by (13.6.7) is (-10,-1) while at $X=c_2$ the confidence interval is (.5, 8). Thus, you would conclude that the regression lines cross. At $X=c_1$ it appears that the distance between the regression lines is at least 1 unit, while at $X=c_2$ the distance is at least .5. Suppose instead that the confidence intervals at $X=c_1$ and c_2 are (-18, -9) and (12, 22). Again you would conclude that the regression lines cross, but this time the magnitude of the distance between the two lines is much greater within the range of X values that are of interest in your study. The latter case might represent a much more important finding than the former where the lines are much closer together over the range of possible X values. Of course, rejecting the hyothesis that the lines are parallel tells you nothing about the magnitude of the distance between the lines for the X values that are of practical interest. Some researchers might want confidence intervals at all the possible X values with the property that the experimentwise Type I error probability is α. For results on this problem see Potthoff (1964).

Unequal Variances

The procedure just described is based on Sidak's inequality, which assumes equal variances, and so the next goal is to describe approximate solutions for situations where the assumption of equal variances may not be true. The procedures described here are based on an extension of Dunnett's T3 and C procedures as well as an extension of the Games-Howell technique (Wilcox, in press).

An Extended Dunnett's C Procedure

Let

$$s_j^2=\Sigma_i[Y_i-b_{0j}-b_{1j}(X_{ij}-\bar{X}_j)]^2/(n_j-2) \qquad (13.6.8)$$

be the estimate of σ_j^2, the variance associated with the j*th* group. Because the D_{1jk}'s are independent, Dunnett's C procedure can be applied to test

$$H_0:\tau_{1jk}=0,\ j<k,$$

and of course the same can be done for $H_0:\tau_{2jk}=0$, $j<k$. (Note, however, that D_{1jk} is not independent of D_{2jk}, as pointed out above.) Here the variance of $b_{0j}+b_{1j}(\bar{X}_j-c_i)$ is

$$u_{ij}\sigma_j^2,$$

where

$$u_{ij}=(1/n_j)+(\bar{X}_j-c_i)^2/C_j,\ j=1,\ldots,J.$$

As before, $C_j=\Sigma_i(X_{ij}-\bar{X}_j)^2$.

To apply Dunnett's C procedure, compute

$$D_{1jk}\pm[h_j u_{1j}s_j^2 + h_k u_{1k}s_k^2]/[2(u_{1j}s_j^2 + u_{1k}s_k^2)]^{1/2}. \tag{13.6.9}$$

If this confidence interval does not contain zero, reject $H_0:\tau_{1jk}=0$. The constant h_j is the $1-\alpha$ percentage point of the "bivariate" Studentized range distribution which is read from Table A13 with $\nu_j=n_j-2$ degrees of freedom. When referring to Table A13, the quantity K in the table refers to the number of treatment groups, and you always set J=2. (You use J=2 because you are comparing the regression lines at two points, namely c_1 and c_2.) For example, if there are 5 groups, $\alpha=.05$ and the degrees of freedom are 10, $h_j=5.19$. The procedure can be applied again to test $H_0:\tau_{2jk}=0$ for all $j<k$. If you reject $H_0:\tau_{1jk}=0$ as well as $H_0:\tau_{2jk}=0$, and if D_{1jk} and D_{2jk} have different signs, conclude that the regression lines cross.

Dunnett's T3 Procedure

Dunnett's T3 procedure extends immediately to the problem at hand. You test $H_0:\tau_{ijk}=0$ by computing

$$D_{ijk}\pm V_{jk}(u_{ij}s_j^2+u_{ik}s_k^2)^{1/2}, \tag{13.6.10}$$

where V_{jk} is read from Table A10 with $C=J(J-1)$ comparisons and degrees of freedom

$$\nu_{jk}=(u_{ij}s_j^2+u_{ik}s_k^2)^2/[(u_{1j}s_j^2)^2/\nu_j+(u_{1k}s_k^2)^2/\nu_k]. \tag{13.6.11}$$

If for all i and j, $1/u_{ij}$ is large, say greater than 50, the extended Dunnett's C procedure should be used over Dunnett's T3.

For $1/u_{ij}$ small for any i or j, use Dunnett's T3.

An Extended Games-Howell

The degrees of freedom are the same as in Dunnett's C procedure, and the u_{ij}'s are defined as before. The confidence interval for τ_{ijk} is

$$D_{ijk} \pm h_{jk}\{[(u_{ij}s_j^2 + u_{ik}s_k^2)]/2\}^{1/2}$$

where h_{jk} is read from Table A13 with degrees of freedom given by (13.6.11). As in Dunnett's C procedure, you apply the procedure at $X=c_1$, and then you apply it again at $X=c_2$. Again the quantity K in Table A13 refers to the number of groups and the quantity J in the table is always J=2. For example, if $\alpha=.05$, the degrees of freedom are 9 and there are 3 groups, $h_{jk}=4.52$. If $1/u_{ij}$ is large for all i and j, Dunnett's C and the extended Games-Howell procedures perform about equally well.

Comments about the Johnson-Neyman Procedure

The procedures just described can be used to improve upon the Johnson-Neyman procedure, which is commonly used to determine an interval, say (c_b, c_u), with the property that two regression lines cross inside this interval. The derivation of the Johnson-Neyman procedure is briefly described, and then it is modified to handle unequal variances. For further details of the derivation, see Wilcox (in press).

First consider a specific value for X, say X=c, let $D_{jk}=(b_{0j}-b_{0k})+[b_{1j}+b_{1k}]c$ be the estimated distance between the jth and kth regression lines at X=c. That is, D_{jk} is just the value of D_{ijk} with $c_1=c_2=c$, say. The statistic D_{jk} estimates τ_{jk}, the actual distance between the regression lines at X=c. Let

$$u_j=(1/n_j) + (\bar{X}_j-c)^2/C_j.$$

The problem of obtaining simultaneous confidence intervals for τ_{jk} for all j<k, is just the problem of obtaining simultaneous confidence intervals for all pairwise differences of the means of J independent normal distributions. Thus, for the equal variance case, results in chapter nine indicate that the Tukey-Kramer procedure is best. In particular the confidence interval for τ_{jk} is

$$D_{jk} \pm q_{\alpha,J,\nu}s[(u_j + u_k)/2]^{1/2},$$

where s^2 is the estimate of the common variance σ^2, and $q_{\alpha,J,\nu}$

is the 1-α quantile of the Studentized range distribution with $\nu=\Sigma(n_j-2)$ degrees of freedom. Proceeding as was done by Johnson and Neyman (1936), who restricted their attention to J=2 groups, two values of c are determined, say c_b and c_u, so that either the upper or lower end of the confidence interval is equal to zero. That is, the goal is to find the smallest and largest X values for which the hypothesis $H_0:\tau_{jk}=0$ would be rejected. Setting

$$q=q_{\alpha,J,\nu},$$

the values of c_b and c_u are

$$c_b=\{-B-[B^2-4AC]^{1/2}\}/2A$$

and

$$c_u=\{-B+[B^2-4AC]^{1/2}\}/2A,$$

where

$$A=(b_{1j}-b_{1k})^2 - (q^2s^2/2)(1/C_j + 1/C_k),$$

$$B=2(b_{1j}-b_{1k})(b_{0j}-b_{0k})+q^2s^2(\bar{X}_j/C_j + \bar{X}_k/C_k)$$

$$C=(b_{0j}-b_{0k})^2 - E - (q^2s^2/2)[\bar{X}_j^2/C_j + \bar{X}_k^2/C_k],$$

and

$$E=(q^2s^2/2)(1/n_j + 1/n_k).$$

Thus, it would be concluded that the j<u>th</u> and k<u>th</u> regression lines cross somewhere in the interval (c_b, c_u), and of course this process can be applied for all j<k.

The unequal variance case

As noted in chapter nine, it is known that the Tukey-Kramer procedure is not robust to unequal variances. Also, the derivation of c_b and c_u ignores the fact that an attempt is being made to obtain confidence intervals at two X values. To deal with these problems, first compute c_b and c_u replacing the expressions for A, B, C, and E with

$$A=(b_{1j}-b_{1k})^2 - (q^2/2)(s_j^2/C_j + s_k^2/C_k),$$

$$B=2(b_{1j}-b_{1k})(b_{0j}-b_{0k})+q^2(s_j^2\bar{X}/C_j + s_k^2\bar{X}/C_k)$$

$$C=(b_{0j}-b_{0k})^2 - E -$$

$$q^2/2)[(s_j^2\bar{X}_j^2/C_j + (s_k^2\bar{X}_k^2/C_k)],$$

and

$$E=(q^2/2)(s_j^2/n_j + s_k^2/n_k),$$

where q is chosen according to whether you are using the extended Games-Howell, or the extended T3. (The extension of Dunnett's C is not considered.) For the extended Games-Howell procedure, $q=h$ where h is read from Table A13 with degrees of freedom

$$\eta_{jk}=(u_j s_j^2+u_k s_k^2)^2/$$
$$[(u_j s_j^2)^2/\nu_j+(u_k s_k^2)^2/\nu_k].$$

For the extended T3 procedure, $q=(J?)h_{jk}$, where h_{jk} is read from Table A10 again with η_{jk} degrees of freedom and where the number of comparisons (when referring to Table A10) is J^2-J. Note that in both cases, the value of q depends on which two treatment groups are being compared.

For technical reasons, the resulting values for c_b and c_u may not be correct because the degrees of freedom, η, is only an approximation of the degrees of freedom actually required. As a result, both c_b and c_u may need to be adjusted and this must be done iteratively. As a check on the value for c_b, compute the $1-\alpha$ confidence interval for the distance between the regression lines at $X=c_b$. If one end of the interval is close to zero, c_b is correct because for $X<c_b$, you would reject $H_0:\tau_{jk}=0$. If one end of the confidence interval is not zero, the value for c_b may have to be adjusted as illustrated below. A similar procedure is applied to the point $X=c_u$.

<u>Example 13.6.1</u> Suppose there are J=3 groups with $s_1=2$, $s_2=1$, $s_3=4$, and $n_1=n_2=n_3=15$. For convenience only the first two regression lines are compared, and it is assumed that $C_1=130$, $C_2=99.23$, $\bar{X}_1=5.8$, $\bar{X}_2=5.533$, $b_{01}=9.857$, $b_{02}=3.155$, $b_{11}=.209$, and $b_{12}=1.237$. If equal variances are assumed, the estimate of the common variance is $s^2=7$, and the resulting Johnson-Neyman interval, with $\alpha=.05$, is $c_b=2.7$ and $c_u=25.76$. That is, the lines cross somewhere in the interval (2.7, 25.76). Next suppose that without assuming equal variances, you compute the .95 confidence interval for the distance between the regression lines at X=2.7 using the extended T3 procedure. The result is (1.72, 6.12). But c_b is supposed to be the value of X such that for $X>c_b$ you would not reject $H_0:\tau_{12}=0$ while for $X<c_b$ you would reject. Thus, $c_b=2.7$ is too small. Similarly, the confidence interval at X=25.76 is (-30.4,-9.2) which indicates that c_u is less than 25.76. That is,

the Johnson-Neyman interval (2.7, 25.76), based on the equal variance assumption, is too large.

To adjust the Johnson-Neyman interval for unequal variances, first compute η_{12} yielding $\eta_{12}=19$ degrees of freedom. For the problem at hand you would use the extended T3 procedure when computing c_b and c_u, and this yields $c_b=4.5$ and $c_u=8.8$. (The value for h is 2.92.) As indicated above, this is only an approximation of the values for c_b and c_u, and you must check the accuracy of this approximation by computing the confidence intervals for τ_{12} at X=4.5 and X=8.8. For X=4.5 the confidence interval is (0.33,4.02) and this suggests that c_b should be slightly higher. At X=4.8 the confidence interval is (0.005,3.5) and so you are closer to accepting $H_0:\tau_{12}=0$ than you were at X=4.4. Thus, a better value for c_b is 4.8. Similarly, the confidence interval for the distance between the lines at X=8.8 is (-4.8,0.11) while at X=9 it is (-5.09,.-0.007), and so a better value for c_u is X=9. The conclusion is that the lines appear to cross somewhere in the interval (4.8,9.0), and this interval is considerably smaller than the Johnson-Neyman interval obtained under the assumption of equal variances.

In closing it is noted that there are nonparametric analogs of ANCOVA such as the procedures proposed by Quade (1967) or Conover and Iman (1982). If the goal is to compare the distribution of the Y's, given an X, Quade's test might be used. A description of this procedure is given by Huitema (1980). While nonparametric procedures have great appeal, application of these procedures does not necessarily mean that no restrictive assumptions are required. For example, Quade (1967) assumes that the distribution of X is the same among all the treatment groups. The extent to which violating this assumption causes practical difficulties is not known. In general, ANCOVA is a complex problem, and the various procedures available must be used with caution.

EXERCISES

13.1 Consider the following data.

X	Y
12.2	1.8
41.0	7.8
5.4	0.9
13.0	2.6
22.6	4.1
35.9	6.4
7.2	1.3
5.2	0.9
55.0	9.1

2.4	0.7
6.8	1.5
29.6	4.7
58.7	8.2
$\Sigma X=295.0$	$\Sigma Y=50.0$

a) Determine the least squares linear regression of Y on X.
b) Determine a 90% confidence interval for β_1.
c) Determine joint 95% confidence intervals for both β_0 and μ_y. That is, determine two intervals such with probability at least .95, the first interval contains μ_y and the second contains β_0.
d) Compute the correlation between X and Y.
e) Test $H_0: \rho=0$. Use $\alpha=.05$.

13.2 You have the following data
X: 50 56 62 70 80
Y: 0 4 5 6 9
Determine the regression equation for predicting Y from X.

13.3 Suppose that for equally spaced X values you observe
$\bar{Y}_1=20$, $\bar{Y}_2=23$, $\bar{Y}_3=30$, $\bar{Y}_4=34$, and $\bar{Y}_5=40$.
Assume equal variances and equal sample sizes of 16 observations per group. Also assume MSWG=36, and test for both a linear and quadratic trend using the appropriate linear contrasts. Assume that the experimentwise Type I error probability is to be at most .05.

13.4 Suppose you apply Tan's test for equal slopes and fail to reject. Is it reasonable to proceed with ANCOVA assuming parallel regression lines?

13.5 Suppose $\bar{Y}=36$, $\bar{X}_1=48$, $\bar{X}_2=24$, $240b_1+480b_2=1{,}200$, and $480b_1+120b_2=880$. What is the linear regression equation for predicting Y from X_1 and X_2.

13.6 You perform an ANCOVA with n=20 observations per group with J=2 groups. Assume equal variances, $s^2=4$, $D_{112}=4.0$, $q_{112}=.03$, $D_{212}=-6.0$, $q_{212}=.06$, and $\alpha=.05$. Is it reasonable to assume that the regression lines do not cross?

13.7 Suppose $s_1{}^2=1.5$, $s_2{}^2=4.9$, $\bar{X}_1=10$, $\bar{X}_2=15$, $C_1=C_2=680$, $D_{112}=6$, $D_{212}=18$, $c_1=2$, $c_2=25$, $n_1=20$, and $n_2=10$. Apply the extensions of the Games-Howell as well as the extensions of Dunnett's T3 and C procedure for comparing regression lines.

References

Adichie, J. N. (1974) Rank score comparison of several regression parameters. The Annals of Statistics, 2, 396-402

Adichie, J. N. (1975) On the use of ranks for testing the coincidence of several regression lines. The Annals of Statistics, 3, 521-527.

Agresti, A. (1984) Analysis of ordinal categorical data New York: Wiley.

Atiqullah, M. (1964) The robustness of the covariance analysis of a one-way classification. Biomertrika, 51, 365-372.

Broffitt, J. D. (1986) Zero correlation, independence, and normality. The American Statistician, 40, 276-277.

Bryant, J. & Fox, G. (1985) Some comments on a class of simultaneous inference procedures in ANCOVA. Communications in Statistics--Theory and Methods, 14, 2511-2530.

Carroll, J. (1961) The nature of the data, or how to choose a corrlation coefficient. Psychometrika, 26, 347-372.

Conover, W. (1980) Practical nonparametric statistics, New York: Wiley.

Conover, W. & Iman, R. (1982) Analysis of covariance using the rank transformation. Biometrics, 38, 715-724.

Duncan, G. & Layard M. (1973) A monte-carlo study of asymptotically robust tests for correlation coefficients. Biometrika, 60, 551-558.

Draper, N. & Smith, H. (1981) Applied regression analysis New York: Wiley.

Edwards, A. (1979) Multiple regression and the analyis of covariance San Francisco: W. H. Freeman.

Elashoff, J. (1969) Analysis of covariance: A delicate instrument. American Educational Research Journal, 6, 383-401

Fairly, D. (1986) Cherry trees with cones? The American Statistician, 40, 138-139.

Hastie, T. & Tibshirani, R. (1986) Generalized additive models Statistical Science, 1, 297-318.

Hochberg, Y. & Varon-Salomon, Y. (1984) On simultaneous comparisons in analysis of covariance. Journal of the American Statistical Association, 79, 863-866.

Hogg, R. & Craig, A. (1970) Introduction to mathematical statistics. New York: Macmillan.

Huitema, B. (1980) The analysis of covariance and alternatives New York: Wiley.

Jacquez, J. A., Mather, F. J. & Crawford, C. R. (1968) Linear regression with non-constant, unknown error variances: Sampling experiments with least squares, weighted least squares and maximum likelihood estimators.

Biometrics, 24, 607-626.
Johnson, P. & Neyman, J (1936) Tests of certain linear hypotheses and their application to some educational problems. Statistical Research Memoirs, 1, 57-93.
Lucke, J. F. & Embretson, S. (1984) The biases and mean squared errors of estimators of multinomial squared multiple correlation. Journal of Educational Statistics, 9, 183-192.
Neter, J. & Wasserman, W. (1974) Applied linear statistical models. Homewood Illinois: Irwin.
Odeh, R. (1982) Critical values of the sample product-moment correlation coefficient in the bivariate normal distribution Communications in Statistics--Simulation and Computation, 11, 1-26.
Olkin, I. & Pratt J. (1958) Unbiased estimation of certian correlation coefficients. Annals of Mathematical Statistics, 29, 201-211.
Potthoff, R. (1964) On the Johnson-Neyman technique. Psychometrika 29, 241-256.
Potthoff, R. (1965) Some Scheffe-type tests for some Behrens-Fisher type regression problems.
Potthoff, R. (1974) A non-parametric test of whether two simple regression lines are parallel. The Annals of Statistics, 2, 295-310.
Quade, D. (1967) Rank analysis of covariance. Journal of the American Statistical Association, 62, 1187-1200.
Sen, P. K. (1972) On a class of aligned rank order tests for the identity of the intercepts of several regession lines. The Annals of Statistics, 43, 2004-2012.
Tabatabai, M. & Tan, W. (1985) Some comparative studies on testing parallelism of several straight lines under heteroscedastic variances. Communications in Statistics--Simulation and Computation, 14, 837-844.
Tan, W. (1986) Inferences on regression coefficients in a regression model under heteroscedasticity and robustness with respect to departure from normality. Communications in Statistics--Simulation and Computation, 15, 35-60.
Weisberg, S. (1985) Applied linear regression. New York: Wiley.
Wilcox, R. (1986) Improved simultaneous confidence intervals for regression parameters and linear contrasts. Communications in Statistics--Simulation and Computation, 15, 917-932.
Wilcox, R. (in press) Pairwise comparisons of J independent regression lines over a finite interval, simultaneous pairwise comparisons of the parameters, and the Johnson-Neyman technique. British Journal of Mathematical and Statistical Psychology.

Wilks, S. (1962) Mathematical statistics. New York: Wiley

Wu, C. F. J. (1986) Jacknife, bootstrap and other resampling methods in regression analysis. Annals of Statistics, 1261-1294.

Yu, M. C. & Dunn, O. J. (1982) Robust tests for the equality of two correlation coefficients: A monte carlo study. Educational and Psychological Measurement, 42, 987-1004.

CHAPTER FOURTEEN

CATEGORICAL DATA

The goal in this chapter is to cover some of the more basic issues relevant to analyzing categorical data, and to indicate some of the practical problems that you might encounter. For further information on analyzing categorical data, the excellent books by Agresti (1984), Fleiss (1973), and Fienberg (1980) can be consulted.

14.1 GOODNESS OF FIT TESTS

The simplest situation to be examined is where each subject can be described as belonging to one of k mutually exclusive groups or categories. If n subjects are randomly sampled and there are only k=2 groups, the resulting probability function is the binomial that was discussed in chapter four. For n randomly sampled subjects where each subject belongs to $k\geq 2$ categories, the resulting probability function is the multinomial given by

$$[n!/(n_1!n_2!\ldots n_k!)][p_1^{n_1}\ldots p_k^{n_k}],$$

where n_j is the number of subjects observed in the jth category $(j=1,\ldots,k)$, $\Sigma n_j=n$ and $\Sigma p_j=1$.

Example 14.1.1. Suppose n=30 randomly sampled subjects are asked whether they agree, have no opinion, or disagree that nuclear power plants should not be used. Assume that every subject gives a response, and that each subject belongs to one and only one of the k=3 categories. If the probabilities associated with these three categories are $p_1=.2$, $p_2=.5$, and $p_3=.3$, the probability that exactly $n_1=10$ subjects agree, $n_2=15$ subjects have no opinion, and $n_3=5$ subjects disagree is

$$[30!/(10!15!5!)][.2^{10}.5^{15}.3^5].$$

It is noted that in some situations, n is viewed as a random variable in which case the multinomial model is no longer appropriate. Situations where n is random results in what is called the Poisson model. If you condition on n, that is, you consider the distribution of $n_1,\ldots,n_k$ given n, the Poisson model reduces to the multinomial model described above. Only the multinomial model is considered here.

The goal in the remainder of this section is to test certain hypotheses about the p_j's. Initially attention is focused on testing

$$H_0: p_1=p_{01},\ p_2=p_{02}, \ldots,\ p_k=p_{0k} \tag{14.1.1}$$

where $p_{01}, \ldots, p_{0k}$ are known constants that are of interest to you. An important special case is $p_{01}=p_{02}=\ldots=p_{0k}=1/k$. For k=2 you can test this hypothesis with the sign test described in chapter five. For k>2 you can test

$$H_0: p_1=\ldots=p_k=1/k \tag{14.1.2}$$

with

$$X^2=\Sigma(n_i-n/k)^2/(n/k) \tag{14.1.3}$$

It can be shown that as n gets large, X^2 approaches a chi-square distribution with k-1 degrees of freedom. You reject H_0 if $X^2>c$ where c is read from Table A2 and satisfies

$$\Pr(\chi^2_{k-1} \le c)=1-\alpha,$$

where χ^2_{k-1} is a chi-square random variable with k-1 degrees of freedom. Notice that X^2 is a discrete random variable, and the distribution of X^2 is being approximated by a chi-square distribution that is continuous. Several alternative methods for testing H_0 have been proposed (Sobel & Uppuluri, 1974; Young, 1962; Smith, Rae, Manderscheid & Silbergeld, 1979; and Wilcox, 1982), and exact critical values for the statistic X^2 have been tabled (Smith et al., 1979; Katti, 1973). Whenever possible it is recommended that the exact critical values be used since the chi-square approximation can be inadequate when n is small or even moderately large.

From Smith et al. (1979) a simple improvement to the X^2 statistic is to reject H_0 if

$$X^2 > c - (k/n) \tag{14.1.4}$$

where c is again the $1-\alpha$ quantile of a chi-square distribution with k-1 degrees of freedom. However, for k=2, (14.1.4) gives poor results and should not be used. From Koehler and Larntz (1980) it appears that the chi-square approximation of the distribution of X^2 will be reasonably accurate when $n/k \ge .25$, $k \ge 3$, $n \ge 10$, and $n^2/k \ge 10$.

It can be shown that the minimum possible value of X^2 is

$$L=(k/n)[n(2v+1) - kv(v+1)] - n,$$

where v is the largest integer such that $vk \le n$. The largest possible value is

$$M=n(k-1).$$

Let

$$r=[A^2(1-A)/B^2]-A,$$

$$s=[A(1-A)^2/B^2]+A-1,$$

where

$$A=(k-1-L)/(M-L)$$

and

$$B=2(k-1)(1-1/n)/(M-L)^2.$$

Then (14.1.4) can be generally improved upon by rejecting H_0 if

$$(X^2-L)/(M-L)>c$$

where now c is the $1-\alpha$ quantile of a beta distribution with parameters r and s. Methods for determining the percentage points of the beta distribution are described in chapter 15. Although computer subroutines are available for evaluating the beta distribution, (14.1.4) has the advantage of being relatively simple to use. As a final note, if X^2 is written as

$$-n+(k/n)\Sigma n_i^2,$$

the exact distribution of X^2 can be computed using results in Alam and Mitra (1981). However, the computations require a computer.

Example 14.1.2. Consider the data in example 14.1.1 and suppose you want to test $H_0:p_1=p_2=p_3$. Then

$$X^2=[(10-10)^2+(15-10)^2+(5-10)^2]/10=5.$$

With $k-1=2$ degrees of freedom and $\alpha=.05$, Table A2 gives a critical value of $c=5.99$. Thus, do not reject.

Example 14.1.3. Another example is given involving a study that was actually conducted. Thirty multiple-choice test items were given to 206 males and 180 females. All of the subjects were approximately 14 years old. Each item was intended to measure the spatial abilities of the examinees. Each subject was shown a picture of two flags, and they had to indicate how they would alter their position relative to the first flag so that they would see the flag as shown in the second picture. Each item had one correct response and four distractors, and the items were scored according to an answer-until-correct scoring procedure. That is, an examinee chose a response by erasing a shield on an answer sheet that indicated whether the correct response was selected. If an incorrect response was chosen, the examinee chose another response, and this process continued until the correct response was chosen. Let p_i be the probability of a correct response on the <u>ith</u> try of the first item among all the examinees who did not get the correct response on the first try. Thus, every examinee belongs to one of four mutually exclusive categories (according to whether they required two, three, four, or five attempts), and the number of subjects falling into these four categories were

20 16 12 2.

If these examinees were choosing responses at random, the probabilities associated with these four categories should all be equal to 1/4. To test the hypothesis that this is indeed the case, compute

$$X^2=(4/50)(56.25+12.15+0.25+110.25)=14.31.$$

With $\nu=4-1=3$ degrees of freedom and $\alpha=.05$, $c=7.81$. Consequently, you reject H_0.

It is noted that under the multinomial model being considered here, $E(n_i)=np_i$ $(i=1,\ldots,k)$. Next suppose you want to test (14.1.1). This time you use

$$X^2=\Sigma(n_i-np_i)^2/np_i. \qquad (14.1.5)$$

This illustrates a more general form of the chi-square test, namely

$$X^2=\Sigma(\text{observed-expected})^2/\text{expected}$$

which was proposed by Karl Pearson. Again the degrees of freedom are $\nu=k-1$, and you reject H_0 if $X^2>c$ where c is read from Table A2.

Smith et al. (1981) proposed another method of testing (14.1.1) that is based on the "likelihood ratio" statistic

$$G^2=2\Sigma n_i\log(n_i/np_{0i}) \qquad (14.1.6)$$

You determine the critical value, c, exactly as you did for the X^2 statistic, only this time you reject if

$$G^2 > cq$$

where

$$q = 1 + AB,$$

$$A = 1/[6n(k-1)],$$

and

$$B = -1 + \Sigma(1/p_{0i}) + (1/n)\Sigma[(1/p_{0i}) - (1/p_{0i})^2].$$

It appears that testing H_0 with G^2 rather than X^2 generally gives you better control over the probability of committing a Type I error, but it seems that more research is needed to completely resolve this issue.

Still another approach to testing (14.1.1) is to use the Freeman-Tukey procedure, but results in Larntz (1978) indicate that X^2 gives better results.

Example 14.1.4. The G^2 statistic is illustrated with the data in example 14.1.3. Then A=.0011111, B=15.96, q=1.0177326, cq=7.948, and G^2=7.95, so you reject H_0.

14.2 TESTS FOR INDEPENDENCE AND COMPARING BINOMIALS

In the previous section a single variable with k possible values was considered. This section begins a description of basic procedures for analyzing the relationship between two or more variables. It will help to consider a specific case, so suppose each of n randomly sampled subjects is classified according to whether they are happily married, and whether they have a low or high income. Thus, there are two variables of interest, namely marital satisfaction and income, and each subject is assumed to belong to one of four mutually exclusive categories. The probabilities associated with these four categories are shown in Table 14.2.1

Table 14.2.1

		INCOME	
		<u>high</u>	<u>low</u>
HAPPILY	yes:	p_{11}	p_{12}
MARRIED	no:	p_{21}	p_{22}

As already explained in chapter three, this is an example of a two-way contingency table. The two-way table in the example is sometimes called a fourfold table, meaning that there are four cells. This table is also called a 2 x 2 table, meaning that the row variable (marital satisfaction) has two possible values (yes and no) as does the column variable. When the row variable has R possible values, and the column variable has C, you have what is sometimes called an R x C table. In the illustration, the quantity p_{11} is the joint probability that a randomly sampled subject is happily married <u>and</u> has a high income. The quantity p_{12} is the probability that a randomly sampled subject is happily married and has a low income, etc. In the more general case where the first variable has R possible values and the second has C, p_{ij} is the probability that a randomly sampled subject has the i<u>th</u> value of the first variable and the j<u>th</u> value of the second.

The notation

$$p_{+j}=\Sigma_i p_{ij}$$

and

$$p_{i+}=\Sigma_j p_{ij}$$

will be used where the "+" indicates summation over the corresponding subscript. These two quantities are called marginal probabilities. In the example, $p_{1+}=p_{11}+p_{12}$ is the marginal probability that a randomly sampled examinee is happily married. As explained in chapter three, two categorical variables are independent if

$$p_{ij}=p_{i+}p_{+j}$$

In the example, if

$$p_{1+}=.6,\ p_{2+}=.4,\ p_{+1}=.3, \text{ and } p_{+2}=.7$$

then marital satisfaction and income are independent if

$$p_{11}=p_{1+}p_{+1}=.18,$$

$$p_{12}=p_{1+}p_{+2}=.42,$$

$$p_{21}=p_{2+}p_{+1}=.12,$$

and

$$p_{22}=p_{2+}p_{+2}=.28.$$

In the example, p_{1+} is the probability that a randomly sampled subject is happily married, p_{2+} is the probability that the subject is not happily married, etc.

To test the hypothesis that the two random variables are independent, compute

$$X^2=\{n(n_{11}n_{22}-n_{12}n_{21})^2\}/\{n_{1+}n_{2+}n_{+1}n_{+2}\} \tag{14.2.1}$$

When H_0 is true, X^2 has, approximately, a chi-square distribution with 1 degree of freedom. You reject H_0 if $X^2>c$ where c is the $1-\alpha$ quantile of the chi-square distribution which is read from Table A2.

An alternative method of testing for independence is

$$X^2=\{n[\,|n_{11}n_{22}-n_{12}n_{21}| - (n/2)]^2\}/$$

$$\{n_{1+}n_{2+}n_{+1}n_{+2}\}$$

The term n/2 in this last equation is called the Yates' correction for continuity. Many books omit this term, which is consistent with the advice given by Plackett (1964), Grizzle (1967) and Conover (1974). Mantel and Greenhouse (1968) disagreed with their argument, but more recently Conover (1974) has argued that Yate's correction should only be used when marginal frequencies satisfy

$$n_{1+}=n_{2+} \text{ and } n_{+1}=n_{+2}$$

and when the marginal frequencies are fixed in advance. That is, the correction should not be used when you randomly sample n subjects, and then determine to which of the four cells the subject belongs. In the illustration this corresponds to sampling n subjects and determining whether they are happily married and whether they have a high income. This is in contrast to situations where you randomly sample say 50 subjects who are happily married, and 50 subjects who are not, in which case n_{1+} and n_{2+} are fixed.

Example 14.2.1. Consider the following data for n=100 randomly sampled subjects.

		INCOME	
		high	low
HAPPILY	yes	10	30
MARRIED	no	20	40

Thus,

$$n_{1+}=40,\ n_{2+}=60,\ n_{+1}=30,\ n_{+2}=70,\ n=100$$

and

$$X^2=100[10(40) - 20(30)]^2/\{40(60)(30)(70)\}$$

$$=.794$$

With $\alpha=.05$, c=3.84, and so you do not reject.

The test for independence can be extended to an R by C table. This time you compute

$$X^2=\Sigma_i \Sigma_j (n_{ij} - n_{i+}n_{+j}/n)^2/[n_{i+}n_{+j}/n],$$

and the degrees of freedom are $\nu=(R-1)(C-1)$. Again the critical value, c, is read from Table A2, and you reject if $X^2>c$. Various improvements on this test for independence were considered by Hosmane (1986), but Hosmane's results suggest that the test just presented generally works well in practice. One possible exception is a situation where there are small cell frequencies, that is, some of the n_{ij}'s are small, and where $\alpha\le.01$

Comparing Binomials: Purposive Sampling

An important feature of the 2 x 2 table described above is that n subjects are randomly sampled, and each can be categorized into one of four mutually exclusive groups. In contrast is the sampling method where M subjects are sampled who have characteristic A, and you observe whether they have characteristic C. You then randomly sample M' subjects who do not have characteristic A and observe how many have characteristic C. Fleiss (1973) calls this purposive sampling. In effect you have two binomial probability functions with probabilities of success p_1 and p_2, respectively. The goal now is to test

$$H_0: p_1=p_2. \tag{14.2.2}$$

Every subject falls into one of four categories, and the notation used above is used again here.

Continuing the illustration, suppose you have two groups of subjects, the first is happily married while the second is not. That is, marital satisfaction is characteristic A. Suppose you randomly sample M=50 subjects who are happily married and determine whether they have high incomes. The number having a high income will be denoted by n_{11}, and the number having a low income will be denoted by n_{12}. The random variable n_{11} has a binomial probability function. That is,

$$f(n_{11}) = \{M!/[n_{11}!(M-n_{11})!]\}p_1^{n_{11}}(1-p_1)^{M-n_{11}}$$

is the probability of observing n_{11} subjects with high incomes among the $M=n_{11}+n_{12}$ subjects randomly sampled from the population of subjects who are happily married.

Next you sample say $M'=30$ subjects who are not happily married, and you determine their incomes as well. This time let n_{21} (n_{22}) be the number who have high (low) incomes. The random variable n_{21} has a binomial probability function with probability of success p_2. To test the hypothesis that $p_1=p_2$, compute

$$\hat{p}_1=n_{11}/M$$

$$\hat{p}_2=n_{21}/M'$$

$$\bar{p}=(n_{11}+n_{21})(M+M'),\ \bar{q}=1-\bar{p},$$

$$Z=|\hat{p}_1-\hat{p}_2|/[\bar{p}\bar{q}(1/M + 1/M')]^{1/2} \tag{14.2.3}$$

When M and M' are large, Z has, approximately, a standard normal distribution. Thus, reject H_0 if $Z > z$ where z is the $1-\alpha/2$ quantile of the standard normal distribution which is read from Table A1. As noted by Sathe (1982) as well as Eberhardt and Fligner (1977), it is possible to derive procedures having more power than (14.2.3), but these procedures have a higher probability of committing a Type I error. For large enough sample sizes these alternative procedures give better results, but it is not clear just how large of a sample size is needed for this to be the case.

Recall from chapter six that if Z has a standard normal distribution, Z^2 has a chi-square distribution with 1 degree of freedom. It can be shown (Fleiss, 1973) that if you square the statistic in equation (14.2.3), you get the X^2 statistic given by (14.2.1). Thus, even though different sampling methods were used, the calculations and approximation to the null distribution are the same as before.

Again there is the issue of whether the Yates' continuity correction should be used. Garside and Mack (1976) computed the exact Type I error probabilities of the chi-square statistic when testing H_0: $p_1=p_2$ with Z^2 where Z is given by (14.2.3), and the critical value is read from the chi-square distribution with 1 degree of freedom. They also did this with Yates' correction. For convenience, let p be the common value of p_1 and p_2 under the assumption that H_0 is true. For $M=M'=40$, the Z^2 statistic yielded type I error probabilities closer to the nominal $\alpha=.05$ level than those obtained using the Yates' continuity correction. Using Z^2 the actual Type I error probability exceeded .05. The worst case was p=.1 where the actual Type I error rate was .0544. However, using the continuity correction, the Type I error rate was .0193.

Having $M\neq M'$ can greatly affect the Type I error probability. For example, if M=30 and M'=10, the probability of a Type I error using Z^2 is .0448 when p=.2, but it is only .0068 using the continuity correction. For p=.1 the two probability rates are now .009 and .0002.

To get a confidence interval for p_2-p_1, let c be the $1-\alpha$ quantile of the chi-square distribution with 1 degree of freedom and compute

$$\Delta=[\hat{p}_2-\hat{p}_1]/[1+c/M'] - [(\hat{p}_1-1/2)c/M']/[1+c/M']$$

$$A=[c/M']/\{1+c/M'\}^2$$

and

$$L^2=A[\{1+c/M'\}\{.25(1 + M'/M) - (M'/M)(\hat{p}_1-.5)^2\}-(.5-\hat{P}_2)^2].$$

The confidence interval is

$$(\Delta-|L|,\ \Delta+|L|)$$

Anbar (1983).

Anbar (1983) shows that it is possible to design an experiment so that an even better confidence interval for p_2-p_1 is obtained.

In particular, suppose you have N subjects, you want to assign some of the subjects to treatment group 1, and the rest to treatment group 2, and you want to get a confidence interval for $p_2 - p_1$. Suppose that among the N subjects available you assign a subject to treatment group 1 with probability 1/2. That is, with probability 1/2 you assign the first subject to group 1, otherwise you assign the subject to group 2. Then with probability 1/2 you assign the second subject to group 1, etc. The assignment of subjects to treatment groups can be done with a table of random numbers.

As before, let n_{11} be the number of successes in group 1 and n_{21} be the number of successes in group 2. The confidence interval is

$$\Delta_1 \pm L_1$$

where

$$\Delta_1 = \{(n_{11} + M' - n_{21})/(.5N) - 1\}/[1+c/N]$$

and

$$L_1^2 = \Delta^2 - [\Delta^2 - c/N]/[1+c/N].$$

where c is the $1-\alpha$ quantile of the chi-square distribution with 1 degree of freedom.

Power

Suppose you want to test H_0: $p_1 = p_2$ and you want the power to be $1-\beta$ for some value of $p_1 - p_2$ you have chosen. Let

$$\bar{P} = (p_1 + p_2)/2, \ \bar{Q} = 1 - \bar{P}, \ q_1 = 1 - p_1, \ q_2 = 1 - p_2,$$

let z be the $1-\alpha/2$ quantile of the standard normal distribution, and let b be chosen so that $\Pr\{Z > b\} = 1-\beta$ where as usual, Z is a standard normal random variable. That is, b is read from Table A1. Then the required sample size you need for each group is approximately

$$M = [z(2\bar{P}\bar{Q})^{1/2} - b(p_1 q_1 + p_2 q_2)^{1/2}]^2/[p_1 - p_2]^2.$$

For a table of sample sizes needed to achieve a desired power level, see Fleiss (1973).

14.3 MEASURES OF ASSOCIATION

If two categorical variables are dependent, a practical issue is measuring the strength of their relationship. Many measures have been proposed, but many of these are unsatisfactory. For reviews of measures of association, see Goodman and Kruskal (1954,

1959) as well as Harris and Pearlman (1977). Only a few of the more important measures are discussed here, and attention is restricted to 2 x 2 tables.

An obvious approach to measuring association is to use X^2 because the higher X^2 is, the "more significant" is the test for independence. However, this approach is generally regarded as inadequate (Goodman & Kruskal, 1954). Still another approach is to simply compute the correlation between the categorical variables being studied. This leads to

$$\phi=[X^2/n]^{1/2}$$

which is called the phi coefficient. Of course this is just a simple function of X^2, and it seems that all functions of X^2 have little value as measures of association. Fleiss (1973, p. 43) suggests that the phi coefficient is useful in psychometrics, in particular factor analysis, but in recent years the phi coefficient has fallen from favor in this area as well.

The Odds Ratio

One of the more useful measures of association is the odds ratio (sometimes called the cross-product ratio). For the moment it is assumed that subjects are sampled according to the multinomial model.

For a 2 x 2 table, the odds ratio is defined by

$$\theta=[p_{11}p_{22}]/[p_{12}p_{21}].$$

It can be shown that $0\le\theta<\infty$. When $\theta=1$, the two variables are independent.

An important point about the odds ratio is that it can be interpreted in terms of ratios of conditional probabilities. Referring to example 14.2.1, let X be the row variable (marital satisfaction in the example), and let Y be the column variable (income). For notational convenience suppose the possible values for both X and Y are 1 and 2. In the example, X=1 means a subject is happily married, etc.

Let

$$R_1=Pr(Y=1|X=1)/Pr(Y=2|X=1).$$

This quantity is called the odds of observing Y=1, instead of Y=2, when X=1. The estimate of R_1 is

$$\hat{R}_1=n_{11}/n_{12}$$

In example 14.2.1, the estimate of R_1 is 10/30=1/3. In words, given that a subject is happily married, the probability of having a low income is three times the probability that the subject's income is high. The quantity

$$R_2=\Pr(Y=1|X=2)/\Pr(Y=2|X=2)$$

is the odds that Y=1 when X=2. In the example, among the subjects who are not happily married, the probability of observing a subject with a high income is R_2 times the probability of having a low income. If $\Pr(Y=1|X=1) > \Pr(Y=1|X=2)$, $\theta > 1$, while if $\Pr(Y=1|X=1) < \Pr(Y=1|X=2)$, $\theta < 1$.

The odds ratio is just the ratio R_1/R_2, the ratio of the odds. The estimate of the odds ratio is

$$\hat{\theta}=[n_{11}n_{22}]/[n_{12}n_{21}].$$

The standard deviation of the statistic $\hat{\theta}$ is approximately

$$\hat{\theta}n^{-1/2}[1/p_{11} + 1/p_{12} + 1/p_{21} + p_{22}]^{1/2}.$$

This last equation is useful in judging the precision of the estimate of θ, but it is not useful when testing $H_0:\theta=1$ (i.e., testing the hypothesis that X and Y are independent). To test for independence, use the chi-square test given by (14.2.1). It is also noted that procedures for testing the equality of the odds ratio among J fourfold tables are available. The interested reader is referred to Hauck (1984) and the papers he cites.

An important property of the odds ratio is that if you interchange both the rows and columns of the table, θ remains unchanged. Also, the risks R_1 and R_2 were defined in terms of the conditional probabilities of Y given X, but you get the same value for θ if R_1 and R_2 are defined in terms of the conditional probability of X given Y. In fact, when interpreting θ, this latter approach may be more useful. In the illustration, you may want to interpret θ in terms of the probability of being happily married, given a high income, as opposed to the probability of having a high income given that a subject is happily married.

Example 14.3.1. For the data in example 14.2.1, the estimated odds ratio is [10(40)]/[20(30)]=2/3. In words, the odds of being happily married, given a high income, are two-thirds the odds of being happily married when income is low.

The Odds Ratio in Purposive Sampling

Rather than multinomial sampling, suppose observations are obtained through purposive sampling that was described above. That is, two binomials are to be compared. Thus, for subjects having characteristic A, say, you sample M subjects and observe how many do or do not have characteristic B. You then sample M′ subjects who do not have characteristic A and again determine which have characteristic B. For example, characteristic A might be families where one or both parents are obese, and B might be the event that the oldest offspring is obese by the age of 25. The results of the study can be recorded as shown in the table.

		Obese Offspring yes	no
Parents	yes	p_{11}	p_{12}
Obese	no	p_{21}	p_{22}

The odds ratio for this model is

$$\theta=\{Pr(B=yes|A=yes)Pr(B=no|A=no)\}/$$

$$\{Pr(B=no|A=yes)Pr(B=yes|A=no)\}$$

where B refers to obese offspring and A refers to obese parents. If the observations for the four cells are n_{11}, n_{12}, n_{21}, and n_{22}, the estimate of the odds ratio is

$$\hat{\theta}=[n_{11}n_{22}]/[n_{12}n_{21}].$$

The estimated standard error of this statistic is

$$\hat{\theta}[1/n_{11} + 1/n_{12} + 1/n_{21} + 1/n_{22}]^{1/2}.$$

It is noted that other measures of association have been proposed that are functions of the conditional probabilities. One such measure, proposed by Yule (1900), is

$$Q=[R_1-R_2]/[R_1+R_2].$$

It can be seen that in terms of the odds ratio, θ,

$$Q=(\theta-1)/(\theta+1).$$

Criticism of the Odds Ratio

While the odds ratio is useful, some caution must be used in its application. In particular, the odds ratio may not reflect certain characteristics of the data that are important in a given study. This point was raised by Berkson (1958). Fleiss (1973, p. 60) illustrates Berkson's point with the following data.

Table 14.3.1

Mortality rates per 100,000 person-years from lung cancer and coronary artery disease.

	Smokers	Nonsmokers	$\hat{\theta}$	Difference
Lung Cancer	48.33	4.49	10.8	43.84
Coronary Artery Disease	294.67	169.54	1.7	125.13

The odds ratio suggests that the effects of smoking on lung cancer is greater than it is on coronary artery disease. However, the difference in the mortality rates suggests that the reverse is true. Berkson pointed out that the odds ratio does not reflect the number of deaths due to either cause. Berkson went on to argue that "it is only the total number of increased deaths that matters."

Kappa and the Proportion of Agreement

Another measure of association is the proportion of agreement given by

$$P=p_{11}+p_{22}$$

where the multinomial model is being assumed. This simple measure might be useful in the following situation. Suppose n examinees are given a pass/fail test, and these same examinees are given another form of the test that is intended to measure the same psychological construct. It may be of interest to know whether agreement between the two test forms is obtained in the sense that if a subject passes (fails) the first test, the same subject passes (fails) the second. The probabilities associated with the four possible outcomes are

		TEST 1	
		Pass	Fail
TEST 2	Pass	p_{11}	p_{12}
	Fail	p_{21}	p_{22}

Thus, the probability that a randomly sampled examinee is classified in the same manner by both tests is P.

As another example, suppose two judges are asked to rate n subjects according to whether they exhibit some psychological disorder. Suppose a rating of 1 means the subject has the disorder, while a rating of 2 means the disorder is absent. Then P is the probability that the two raters will agree for a randomly sampled subject.

The estimate of P is

$$\hat{P}=(n_{11}+n_{22})/n.$$

Moreover, the statistic $m=n_{11}+n_{22}$ has a binomial probability function. That is, the probability of exactly m agreements among the n observations is

$$f(m) = \binom{n}{m}P^m(1-P)^{n-m},$$

and so results on the binomial probability function can be applied to the estimate of P.

Cohen (1960) pointed out that there will be some agreement between two raters, say, even when the two raters are acting independently of one another. In fact, the proportion of agreement expected by chance alone is

$$P_c=p_{1+}p_{+1}p_{2+}p_{+2}.$$

Thus, $P-P_c$ is the amount of agreement beyond chance. Cohen suggested that $P-P_c$ be rescaled so that the resulting index would have a value of 1 when there is perfect agreement. The result is

$$\kappa=(P-P_c)/(1-P_c).$$

When there is less than chance agreement, $P < P_c$ in which case $\kappa<0$. When there is only chance agreement, $P=P_c$ in which case $\kappa=0$. If P=1 there is perfect agreement and $\kappa=1$.

The estimate of P_c is just

$$\hat{P}_c=[n_{1+}n_{+1}n_{2+}n_{+2}]/n^2,$$

and the estimate of κ is

$$\hat{\kappa}=(\hat{P}-\hat{P}_c)/(1-\hat{P}_c).$$

An important point is that κ treats the variables as being nominal (Agresti, 1984). For ordinal variables, Fleiss, Cohen, and Everitt (1969) suggest using a weighted version of κ. In particular, replace P and P_c with

$$P=\Sigma\Sigma w_{ij}p_{ij}$$

and

$$P_c=\Sigma\Sigma w_{ij}p_{i+}p_{+j}$$

where w_{ij} are weights chosen by the experimenter. One choice for the weights is

$$w_{ij}=1-|i-j|,$$

while for an r x r table you might use

$$w_{ij}=1-|i-j|/r.$$

The idea is to weight the observations according to how far away they are from the main diagonal. If, for example, two raters agree to categorize a subject as belonging to the j<u>th</u> class of r categories, that is X=Y=j, there is exact agreement and the observation would be recorded along the diagonal of the r x r table. The more unequal X and Y are, the more disagreement there is, and this is reflected through w_{ij} because the more unequal i and j are, the smaller is w_{ij}.

One concern over Kappa has been the "base rate problem". That is, the value kappa is function of the number of passes and fails. The practical ramification of this problem is that the magnitude of kappa is difficult to interpret. (See Sptiznagel and Helzer, 1985, for further details.) Kappa is often recommended when measuring interrater agreement, but other approaches to measuring interrater agreement might be used (e.g., Uebersax, 1987).

14.4 LOGLINEAR MODELS

The goal in this section is to provide a very brief glimpse of loglinear models. Attention is primarily restricted to R x C tables and multinomial sampling, but some comments on more complicated tables are provided.

Let

$$\mu_{ij}=\log p_{ij}$$

where p_{ij} is defined as before. Also let

$$\mu_{i.}=\Sigma_j\mu_{ij}/c,\ \mu_{.j}=\Sigma_i\mu_{ij}/r,\ \mu=\Sigma\Sigma\mu_{ij}/(rc)$$

$$\alpha_i=\mu_{i.}-\mu,\ \beta_j=\mu_{.j}-\mu,\ \text{and}\ \gamma_{ij}=\mu_{ij}-\alpha_i-\beta_j+\gamma_{ij}.$$

A little algebra yields

$$\mu_{ij}=\mu + \alpha_i + \beta_j + \gamma_{ij}. \quad (14.4.1)$$

It can be seen that

$$\Sigma\alpha_i = \Sigma\beta_j = \Sigma_i\gamma_{ij} = \Sigma_j\gamma_{ij} = 0.$$

Notice the close resemblance between (14.4.1) and the two-way ANOVA model in chapter ten.

When there is independence it can be seen that $\gamma_{ij}=0$ for all i and j. For a 2 x 2 table

$$\gamma_{11}=\gamma_{22}=-\gamma_{12}=-\gamma_{21},$$

and

$$\gamma_{11}=(1/4)\log\theta$$

where as before, θ is the odds ratio. The γ_{ij}'s are "association parameters" that measure departure from independence. The main point is that for higher dimensional tables, additional "interaction terms" can be added to reflect different types of associations that might exist among the variables. For example, in addition to being interested in marital satisfaction and income, you might also want to take into account level of education. For instance, you might be interested in couples where both husband and wife have at least a college diploma as opposed to couples where one or both did not complete college. Now you might want to know whether marital satisfaction is independent of both income and education, whether the joint distribution of marital satisfaction and income is independent of education, etc. More generally, for three characteristics, say A, B, and C, you might want to know whether Pr(A=i,B=j|C=k)=Pr(A=i,B=j), i.e., A and C are jointly independent of C, whether Pr(A=i|B=j,C=k)=Pr(A=i), i.e., the probability of observing A=i is unaffected by the values of B and C, etc. Each of the possible models can be represented by a loglinear model where an appropriate "interaction" term is set equal to zero. This can be helpful when analyzing complicated contingency tables, but the details are not given here. Further information about this topic can be found in Fienberg (1980), Bishop, Fienberg, and Holland (1975) and Agresti (1984).

EXERCISES

14.1 You randomly sample n=54 subjects and ask them whether they agree, disagree, or have no opinion that persons with a college education feel more satisfied with their lives. Let p_i (i=1,2,3) be the probabilities associated with these three responses, and suppose you observe $n_1=9$, $n_2=30$, and $n_3=15$. Test $H_0: p_1=p_2=p_3$. Use equation (14.1.3) and $\alpha=.05$.

14.2 Suppose $n_1=9$, $n_2=2$, and $n_3=4$. Test $H_0: p_1=p_2=p_3$ using both equations (14.1.3) and (14.1.4). Also use $\alpha=.05$. Can you expect the chi-square approximation of X^2 to be reasonably accurate?

14.3 Suppose $n_1=10$, $n_2=20$, $n_3=30$. Test $H_0: p_1=.5$, $p_2=.2$, and $p_3=.3$ using equation (14.1.5) and $\alpha=.05$.

14.4 Suppose $n_{11}=7$, $n_{12}=40$, $n_{21}=12$, and $n_{22}=46$. Test for independence using $\alpha=.05$.

14.5 You have two methods for curing a certain psychological disorder. You randomly sample M=20 subjects having the disorder and you get 5 cures under method one. You randomly sample another M'=24 subjects and get 4 cures. Test H_0: $p_1=p_2$ using $\alpha=.05$.

14.6 Compute the odds ratio, the proportion of agreement, and kappa for the data in exercise 14.4.

References

Agresti, A. (1984) Analysis of ordinal categorical data New York: Wiley.

Alam K. & Mitra, A. (1981) Polarization test for the multinomial distribution. Journal of the American Statistical Association, 76, 107-109.

Anbar, D. (1983) Estimating the difference between two probabilities, with special reference to clinical trials. Biometrics, 39, 257-262.

Berkson, J. (1958) Smoking and lung cancer: Some observations on two recent reports. Journal of the American Statistical Association, 53, 28-38.

Bishop, Y., Fienberg, S. & Holland , P. (1975) Discrete multivariate analysis: Theory and Practice. Cambridge:

MIT Press.

Cohen, J (1960) A coefficient of agreement for nominal scales. Educational and Psychological Measurement, 20, 37-46.

Conover, W. J. (1974) Some reasons for not using the Yates continuity correction for 2 x 2 tables (with comments). Journal of the American Statistical Association, 69, 374-382

Eberhardt, K. R. & Fligner, M. A. (1977) A comparison of two tests for equality of two proportions. American Statistician, 31-151-155.

Fienberg, S. (1980) The analysis of cross-classified data, 2nd Edition. Cambridge: MIT Press.

Fleiss, J. L. (1973) Statistical methods for rates and proportions New York: Wiley.

Fleiss, J., Cohen, J. & Everitt, B. (1969) Large sample standard errors for kappa and weighted kappa. Psychological Bulletin, 72, 323-327.

Garside, G. R. & Mack C. (1976) Actual Type 1 error probabilities for various tests in the homogeneity case of the 2 x 2 contingency table. The American Statistician, 30, 18-21.

Goodman, L. A. & Kruskal, W. H. (1954) Measures of association for cross-classifications. Journal of the American Statistical Association, 49, 732-76

Goodman, L. A. & Kruskal, W. H. (1959) Measures of Association for cross-classifications. II Journal of the American Statistical Association, 54, 123-163.

Grizzle, J. E. (1967) Continuity correction in the χ^2-test for 2 x 2 tables. American Statistician, 21, 28-32.

Harris, C. W. & Pearlman, A. (1977) Conventional significance tests and indices of agreement or association. In C. Harris, A. Pearlman and R. Wilcox, (Eds.) Achievement test items--methods of study. Center for the Study of Evaluation monograph no. 6. Los Angeles: UCLA graduate school of education

Hauck, W. W. (1984) A comparative study of conditional maximum likelihood estimation of a common odds ratio. Biometrics, 40, 1117-1123.

Hosmane, B. S. (1986) Improved likelihood ratio tests and Pearson chi-square tests for independence in two dimensional tables. Communications in Statistics--Theory and Methods, 15, 1875-1888.

Katti, S. K. (1973) Exact distribution for the chi-square test in the one way table. Communications in Statistics, 2, 435-447

Koehler, K. & Larntz, K. (1980) An empirical investigation of goodness-of-fit statistics for sparse multinomials. Journal of the American Statistical Association, 75, 336-344.

Larntz, K. (1978) Small-sample comarisons of exact levels for

chi-squared goodness-of-fit statistics. Journal of the American Statistical Association, 73, 253-263.
Mantel, N. & Greenhouse, S. (1968) What is the continuity correction? American Statistician, 22, 27-30.
Plackett, R. L. (1964) The continuity correction in 2 x 2 tables Biometrika, 51, 327-337.
Sathe, Y. S. (1982) Another test for equality of two proportions Communications in Statistics--Simulation and Computation, 11, 373-375.
Sobel, M. & Uppuluri, V. (1974) Sparse and crowded cells and Dirichlet distributions. The Annals of Statistics, 2, 977-987.
Smith, P. Rae, D., Manderscheid, R. & Silbergeld, S. (1979) Exact and approximate distributions of the chi-square statistic for equiprobability. Communications is Statisitcs--Simulation and Computation, B8, 131-149.
Smith, P., Rae, D., Manderscheid, R. & Silbergeld, S. (1981) Approximating the moments and distribution of the likelihood ratio statistic for multinomial goodness of fit. Journal of the American Statistical Association, 76, 737-740.
Spitznagel, E. L. & Helzer, J. E. (1985) A proposed solution to the base rate problem in the kappa statistic. Archives of General Psychiatry, 42, 725-728
Uebersax, J. S. (1987) Diversity of decision-making models and the measurement of interrater agreement. Psychological Bulletin, 101, 140-146.
Wilcox, R. R. (1982) A comment on approximating the X^2 distribution in the equiprobable case. Communications in Statistics--Simulation and Computation, 11, 619-623.
Young, D. H. (1962) Two alternatives to the standard χ^2 test of the hypothesis of equal cell frequencies. Biometrika, 49, 107-116.
Yule, G. U. (1900) On the association of attributes in statistics. Philos. Trans. roy. Soc., Series A, 194, 257.

CHAPTER 15

NONPARAMETRIC PROCEDURES

Most of the hypothesis testing procedures described in this book assume sampling is from a normal distribution. In contrast, the procedures in this chapter make no assumptions about the form of the distribution from which you are sampling--the only assumption is that you are sampling from a continuous distribution. However, the procedures described in this chapter are not necessarily intended to be substitutes for the techniques designed to make inferences about population means. Instead, these procedures are intended for making inferences about other properties of a distribution. This point will be clearer when the null hypotheses are described.

Statistical techniques, where nothing is assumed about the shape of the distribution, are called distribution-free procedures. Many books use the term nonparametric to mean distribution-free, but some authorities (e.g. Kendall & Buckland, 1982) object to this practice and prefer to reserve the term "nonparametric" to refer to hypotheses which do not explicitly make an assertion about a parameter. The emphasis in this chapter is on nonparametric procedures although some distribution-free procedures are included as well.

As with so many areas in statistics, results on nonparametric procedures have grown enormously. Accordingly, the emphasis here is on basic results, but some recent developments are covered, including a new procedure for comparing medians. For additional information on nonparametric techniques, see Conover (1980).

15.1 MANN-WHITNEY TEST FOR TWO INDEPENDENT GROUPS

Consider two independent groups, and let $F_j(x)$ be the distribution function corresponding to the j<u>th</u> group. For the Mann-Whitney U test, also known as the Mann-Whitney-Wilcoxon test, the null hypothesis is

$$H_0: F_1(x)=F_2(x) \text{ for any } x.$$

That is, if X_j is the random variable associated with the j<u>th</u> group, j=1,2, $Pr(X_1 \le x)=Pr(X_2 \le x)$ for any x, which means that the distributions are identical. An equivalent way of stating the null hypothesis is

$$H_0: Pr(X_1 < X_2)=1/2,$$

while the alternative hypothesis is

$$H_1: \Pr(X_1 \le X_2) \ne 1/2.$$

Some books suggest that you can test $H_0: \mu_1 = \mu_2$ using the Mann-Whitney test, but you should keep in mind that $\mu_1 \ne \mu_2$ implies that $F_1(x) \ne F_2(x)$, but that $F_1(x) \ne F_2(x)$ does not necessarily mean that $\mu_1 \ne \mu_2$. For instance, if X_1 is normally distributed with $\mu_1=10$ and variance $\sigma_1{}^2=5$, and X_2 is normally distributed with mean $\mu_2=10$ and variance $\sigma_2{}^2=10$, $F_1(x) \ne F_2(x)$ for every value of x except x=10. Thus, $H_0: F_1(x)=F_2(x)$ should be rejected, but if it is rejected, it would be incorrect to conclude that $\mu_1 \ne \mu_2$. In order to use the Mann-Whitney procedure to test $H_0: \mu_1 = \mu_2$, you must be able to assume that the distributions may have different means, but that otherwise they have exactly the same shape. This is the same as assuming that if there is any difference between the two distributions, it is that there exists some constant c such that $\Pr(X_1 \le x) = \Pr(X_2 \le x+c)$.

To apply the Mann-Whitney procedure, let X_{ij} ($i=1,\ldots,n_j$; $j=1,2$) be a random sample from the j<u>th</u> group, and compute

$$Z_{ik}=1, \text{ if } X_{i1} < X_{k2}$$

and

$$Z_{ik}=0, \text{ if } X_{i1} > X_{k2}.$$

In other words, if the i<u>th</u> subject in the first group has a lower score than the k<u>th</u> subject in the second group, set $Z_{ik}=1$; otherwise set $Z_{ik}=0$. The procedure assumes that there are no ties among the n_1+n_2 scores. Methods for dealing with ties are described below.

Next, for the i<u>th</u> subject in the first group, compute

$$S_i = \Sigma_k Z_{ik}$$

which is the number of observations from the second group that exceeds X_{i1}, the i<u>th</u> observation from the first group. For instance, if you observe

Group 1:	8	9.5	10	7
Group 2:	12.2	9.4	7.4	

the value of the first subject in the first group, $X_{11}=8$, is smaller than two of the observations in the second group, namely, 12.2 and 9.4. Thus, $S_1=2$, and similarly, $S_2=1$, $S_3=1$, and $S_4=3$.

Next compute

$$U=\Sigma S_i \tag{15.1.1}$$

In the illustration, U=7. The smallest possible value for U is always zero, and the largest possible value is n_1n_2. If H_0 is true,

$$Pr(Z_{ik})=P(X_{i1}<X_{k2})=1/2.$$

This means that

$$E(Z_{ik})=(1)Pr(X_{i1}<X_{k2})+(0)Pr(X_{i1}>X_{k2})$$

$$=1/2$$

which can be used to show that

$$E(U)=n_1n_2/2 \tag{15.1.2}$$

The variance of U is

$$\sigma_u^2=n_1n_2(n_1+n_2+1)/12. \tag{15.1.3}$$

When U is close to n_1n_2, this suggests that $F_1(x)\le F_2(x)$ for all x, while U close to zero suggests that $F_1(x)\ge F_2(x)$. It can be shown that when n_1 and n_2 are large, and H_0 is true, U has, approximately, a normal distribution with mean $n_1n_2/2$ and variance $\sigma_u{}^2$ given by equation (15.1.3). Thus, reject H_0 if

$$|(U-n_1n_2/2)/\sigma_u|>c,$$

where c is the usual critical value for a two-sided test associated with the standard normal distribution. That is, perform a Z-test where c is read from Table A1. For n_1 and n_2 small, the exact critical values have been computed by Milton (1964) for $n_1\le 20$ and $n_2\le 40$, and by Verdooren (1963) for n_1 and $n_2\le 25$.

An alternative way of computing U is to first combine the observations into one group, and write the values in ascending order. For instance, for the data given above, you get

	7	7.4	8	9.4	9.5	10	12.2
Rank:	1	2	3	4	5	6	7.

Underneath these values are the ranks of the observations. The smallest value gets a rank of 1, the second smallest a rank of 2, etc. Finally, let S be the sum of the ranks corresponding to the observations from the second group. In the illustration

S=2+4+7=13. Next compute

$$U=S-n_2(n_2+1)/2. \quad (15.1.4)$$

For the sample data, U=13-3(4)/2=7, which agrees with the previous calculations.

Handling Ties

In theory there is a zero probability that among the observed values of a continuous variable, there will be two or more identical values in a given experiment. In practice ties do indeed occur, and this problem is handled by averaging the ranks of the tied values, and adjusting the expression for σ_u^2. In particular, equation (15.1.3) becomes

$$\sigma_u^2=n_1n_2\{n_1+n_2+1-\Sigma[(b_i^3-b_i)(n_1+n_2)^{-1}(n_1+n_2\ 1)^{-1}]\}/12$$

where the summation is over the G distinct sets of tied observations, and b_i represents the number of tied observations in the ith set, i=1,...,G.

Example 15.1.1 Consider the following data.

Group 1: 7 8 7. 9 7.5
Group 2: 8 8.5 11 11 11.

Pooling the observations and writing them in ascending order yields

7 7.5 7.5 8 8 8.5 9 11 11 11.

Thus, the second and third values are equal, and so their ranks are both equal to (2+3)/2=2.5. Similarly, the rank corresponding to the two values of 8 are (4+5)/2=4.5, and the rank of the last three values is (8+9+10)/3=9. Thus, the ranks corresponding to the pooled data are

1 2.5 2.5 4.5 4.5 6 7 9 9 9.

There are G=3 distinct sets of tied values, namely, {7.5,7.5}, {8,8} and {11,11,11}. Then

S=4.5+6+9+9+9=37.5,

U=37.5-5(6)/2=22.5,

$b_1=2$, $b_2=2$, $b_3=3$, and

$$\sigma_u^2=5(5)[5+5+1-36/(10(9))]/12=22.08.$$

Assuming normality, you then compute

$$Z=(22.5-12.5)/(22.08)^{1/2}$$

$$=2.13.$$

With $\alpha=.02$ Table A1 says that the critical value is $c=2.05$, and so you would reject H_0 and accept the alternative hypothesis that $F_1(x)\le F_2(x)$ since $U>n_1n_2/2$.

Measuring Treatment Effects.

For the two group t-test in chapter 7, it was pointed out that testing and rejecting H_0 does not give you a very good indication about whether $\mu_1-\mu_2$ is large. To address this issue you need to estimate $\mu_1-\mu_2$ in a more direct fashion. A similar problem arises for the Mann-Whitney test, but this time the issue is not whether the means are nearly equal, but whether the distributions are substantially different. A simple way of comparing two distributions is to use

$$p=\Pr(X_1<X_2),$$

the probability that a randomly sampled observation from group 1 will be less than a randomly sampled observation from group 2. An unbiased estimate of p is

$$\hat{p}=U/(n_1n_2),$$

and the variance of $\hat{p}$ is $\sigma_u^2/(n_1n_2)^2$.

15.2 THE KRUSKAL-WALLIS NONPARAMETRIC ANOVA

The Mann-Whitney test was extended by Kruskal and Wallis (1952) to situations where J independent treatment groups are being compared. This time you are testing

$$H_0: F_1(x)=F_2(x)=\ldots=F_J(x), \text{ for all } x.$$

The data is arranged in the same way as in the one-way ANOVA. That is, X_{ij} is the ith observation from the jth group ($i=1,\ldots,n_j$;

$j=1,\ldots,J$). Let $N=\Sigma n_j$ be the total number of observations. As in the Mann-Whitney test, you combine all N observations into one group and assign ranks. Let $R(X_{ij})$ be the resulting rank of the ith observation from the jth group, and let

$$R_j=\Sigma_i R(X_{ij})$$

be the sum of the ranks in the jth group. In case of ties, the ranks are averaged as they were in the Mann-Whitney test.

To test H_0, compute

$$S^2=(N-1)^{-1}[\Sigma\Sigma(R(X_{ij}))^2-N(N+1)^2/4] \tag{15.2.1}$$

and

$$T=S^{-2}[\Sigma R_j^2/n_j-N(N+1)^2/4] \tag{15.2.2}$$

If there are no ties, S^2 simplifies to

$$S^2=N(N+1)/12 \tag{15.2.3}$$

and T becomes

$$T=\{12/[N(N+1)]\}\Sigma R_j^2/n_j-3(N+1).$$

For small sample sizes, exact critical values are available from Iman, Quade, and Alexander (1975). For large sample sizes, the critical value is approximately equal to c where

$$\Pr(\chi^2_{J-1}\le c)=1-\alpha$$

and where χ^2_{J-1} is a chi-square random variable with J-1 degrees of freedom. That is, c is read from Table A2. If $T>c$, reject H_0.

Example 15.2.1 Suppose the observed values for J=3 independent groups are:

Group 1	Group 2	Group 3
40 (1)	45 (3)	61 (9)
56 (6)	58 (7)	65 (10)
42 (2)	60 (8)	55 (5)
		47 (4)

The ranks of the pooled observations are indicated in parentheses. For example, the rank of $X_{12}=45$ is 3. Thus, $R_1=(1+6+2)=9$, $R_2=18$, and $R_3=28$. Because there are no ties,

$$T=\{12/(10(11))\}[9^2/3+18^2/3+28^2/4] - 3(10+1)$$

$$=3.109.$$

The approximate critical value, with 2 degrees of freedom and $\alpha=.05$, is $c=5.99$. Because $3.109 < 5.99$, you do not reject H_0.

Multiple Comparisons

Conover (1980, p. 231) describes a multiple comparison procedure that reportedly would be used only if the Kruskal-Wallis test is significant. In particular, reject $H_0:F_j(x)=F_k(x)$ if

$$|R_j/n_j - R_k/n_k|>$$

$$t_{1-\alpha/2}[S^2(N-1-T)/(N-J)]^{1/2}(1/n_j + 1/n_k)^{1/2} \qquad (15.2.5)$$

where $t_{1-\alpha/2}$ is the $1-\alpha/2$ quantile of a Student's t distribution with N-J degrees of freedom.

Example 15.2.2 Because you did not get a significant result in example 15.2.1, the multiple comparison procedure should not be applied. However, to illustrate the computations, suppose a significant result was obtained. Then with $\alpha=.05$ and $\nu=10-3=7$ degrees of freedom, Table A14 says that $t_{1-\alpha/2}=2.365$. Consider the first two groups. Because there are no ties, from example 15.2.1, $S^2=9.167$, and so the right side of equation 15.2.5 is

$$2.365[(9.167)(10-1-3.109)/(10-3)]^{1/2}(1/3+1/3)^{1/2}$$

$$=5.27.$$

Because

$$|R_1/n_1 - R_2/n_2|=3 < 5.27,$$

you do not reject $H_0:F_1(x)=F_2(x)$. Of course, the other pairs of distributions can be compared in a similar manner.

15.3 WILCOXON SIGNED RANK TEST FOR DEPENDENT GROUPS

Unlike the Mann-Whitney and Kruskal-Wallis tests, the Wilcoxon signed rank test can be used when you have two dependent groups. Thus, it is assumed that you have a random sample, say $X_{ij}(i=1,\ldots,n_j;\ j=1,2)$ where X_{i1} and X_{i2} are dependent random variables. As explained in chapter 7, one of the simplest situations where this type of experimental design occurs is where you have two observations for each of n randomly sampled subjects. Using the same illustration used in chapter 7, you might be interested in whether a particular training program affects a subject's endurance, and so X_{ij} might be a measure of the i<u>th</u> subject's endurance before training, and X_{i2} the same subject's endurance after the training is complete.

<u>Assumptions</u>

As indicated by Conover (1980, p. 281), the assumptions under the null hypothesis are:

1) The distribution of $D_i=X_{i1}-X_{i2}$ is symmetric,
2) The D_i's are mutually independent,
3) The D_i's have the same median, and
4) The measurement scale of the D_i's is at least interval.

Let μ_m be the population median of the D_i's. The null hypothesis is

$$H_0:\mu_m=0.$$

Put another way, the null hypothesis is that the probability of having an observation from the first group greater than the corresponding observation from the second is 1/2. If $\mu_m>0$, this indicates that the observations in the first group tend to be larger than the observations in the second, and if $\mu_m<0$, the reverse is true. For this reason, the Wilcoxon signed rank test is often described as a test of whether the distributions of the two groups are identical.

To apply the procedure, first throw out any observations where $X_{i1}=X_{i2}$, and then rank the $|D_i|$ values that remain. That is, the smallest value of $|D_i|$ receives a rank of 1, the second smallest a rank of 2, etc. As in the Mann-Whitney test, if there are ties, the corresponding ranks are averaged.

Let U_i be the rank of $|D_i|$. If $D_i>0$, set

$$R_i=U_i \tag{15.3.1}$$

and if $D_i<0$, set

$$R_i=-U_i. \tag{15.3.2}$$

If n is large or there are ties, compute

$$W=\Sigma R_i/[\Sigma R_i^2]^{1/2} \quad (15.3.3)$$

If there are no ties, (15.3.3) simplifies to

$$W=\Sigma R_i/[n(n+1)(2n+1)/6]^{1/2} \quad (15.3.4)$$

If n is small and there are no ties, let $V_i=U_i$ if $D_i>0$, and $V_i=0$ if $D_i<0$, and compute

$$W=\Sigma V_i. \quad (15.3.5)$$

When W is computed with (15.3.3) or (15.3.4), W has, approximately, a standard normal distribution and so you reject H_0 if $|W|>c$ where c is the $1-\alpha/2$ quantile of the standard normal distribution which is read from Table A1. If instead you computed W using equation (15.3.5), the critical value is read from Table A17. Table A17 only gives the lower percentage points of the distribution of W. That is, the tabled value is w_α where $Pr(W\leq w_\alpha)=\alpha$. The upper percentage point is given by

$$w_{1-\alpha}=\{n(n+1)/2\}-w_\alpha.$$

If the Type I error is to be α, reject H_0 if $W>w_{1-\alpha/2}$ or if $W<w_{\alpha/2}$.

Example 15.3.1 If the observations are

Group 1:	15	45	60	43	72
Group 2:	8	50	50	40	74

then

$\lvert D_i\rvert$:	7	5	10	3	2
U_i:	4	3	5	2	1
R_i:	4	-3	5	2	-1

Because n is small, and there are no ties, equation (15.3.5) is used, yielding W=11. From Table A17, with $\alpha=.05$, the critical values are

$$w_{.025}=0, \text{ and } w_{.975}=5(6)/2 - 0=15.$$

Thus, you do not reject.

Testing For Equal Variances in Dependent Groups

In various situations it is desired to test whether two dependent groups have equal variances. This problem arises, for example, in mental test theory where the reliability of an instrument or test is to be estimated. The question of equal variances also arose in connection with a procedure in chapter 7 for testing $H_0:\mu_1=\mu_2$ where μ_1 and μ_2 are the means of two independent normal random variables. When there are missing observations, one of these procedures was based on the assumption that $\sigma_1=\sigma_2$.

Let (X_i, Y_i), i=1,...,n, be the n pairs of observations where there are no missing observations. Sandvik and Olsson (1982) suggest testing $H_0:\sigma_1=\sigma_2$ by computing

$$D_i=|X_i-M_1|-|Y_i\ M_2|,\quad i=1,\ldots,n$$

where M_1 and M_2 are the sample medians corresponding to the two groups. A method for computing the sample median was described in Table 8.5.2 in chapter 8. Next you apply the Wilcoxon signed rank test to the D_i values. When $\sigma_1>\sigma_2$, the D_i's will tend to be positive.

Example 15.3.2 Suppose that for two dependent groups you observe

Group 1:	10	12	20	18	17
Group 2:	12	14	25	24	20.

Then $M_1=17$, $M_2=20$, and you compute

D_i: -1 -1 -2 -3 0.

Because $D_5=0$, it is thrown out, and so the ranks of $|D_i|$ are

U_i: 1.5 1.5 3 4,

and the R_i values are

R_i: -1.5 -1.5 -3 -4.

Because there are ties, equation (15.3.3) is used yielding

$$W=-10/\sqrt{29.5}=-1.84.$$

With $\alpha=.10$, Table A1 yields c=1.64, and since $|-1.84|>1.64$, reject $H_0:\sigma_1=\sigma_2$ and conclude that the variances are not equal.

15.4 MEASURES OF ASSOCIATION

As pointed out in chapter 13, the correlation coefficient measures the extent to which two random variables, say X and Y, are linearly related, and it can be used to test the assumption that X and Y are independent. This section describes two related measures of association that measure the extent to which X and Y are monotonically related. That is, they measure the extent to which Y is an increasing or decreasing function of X. If for any two randomly sampled subjects you observe the pairs of values (X_j, Y_j) and (X_k, Y_k), $j \neq k$, X and Y have a positive monotonic relationship if $X_j < X_k$ implies that $Y_j < Y_k$, and a negative relationship if $X_j < X_k$ implies that $Y_j > Y_k$. For example, if $Y = X^2$, and $X \geq 0$, X and Y have a positive monotonic relationship because Y is an increasing function of X. Of course, $\rho \neq 1$ because even though X and Y are related to each other in an exact fashion, this relationship is not linear. The two coefficients described in this section measure the extent to which two random variables have a monotonic relationship, and they can be used to test the assumption that X and Y are independent.

Spearman's Rho

The idea behind Spearman's rho is very simple. You have a random sample of n pairs of observations, say $(X_1, Y_1), \ldots (X_n, Y_n)$. To compute Spearman's rho, you simply write the X_i values in ascending order and assign ranks in the usual manner. That is, the smallest value gets a rank of 1, etc. Next you assign ranks to the Y_i values in the same manner. Let $R(X_i)$ be the rank assigned to X_i, and $R(Y_i)$ the rank assigned to Y_i. Spearman's rho is just the correlation between these ranks, which can be seen to equal

$$r_s = A/B \qquad (15.4.1)$$

where $A = [\Sigma R(X_i) R(Y_i)] - n(n+1)^2/4$ and

$$B = [\Sigma R^2(X_i) - n(n+1)^2/4)]^{1/2} [\Sigma R^2(Y_i) - n(n+1)^2/4\}]^{1/2}.$$

If there are no ties,

$$r_s = \{\Sigma [R(X_i) - (n+1)/2][R(Y_i) - (n+1)/2]\} / [n(n^2-1)/12], \qquad (15.4.2)$$

which can be shown to equal

$$1-\{6\Sigma[R(X_i)-R(Y_i)]^2\}/[n(n^2-1)] \qquad (15.4.3)$$

Equation (15.4.3) is usually easier to evaluate than (15.4.2)

Let ρ_s be the population parameter corresponding to r_s. Because ρ_s is a correlation, $-1 \le \rho_s \le 1$. It is also observed that $\rho=1$ implies $\rho_s=1$, and $\rho=-1$ implies $\rho_s=-1$. In addition, if X and Y are independent, $\rho_s=0$. However, $\rho_s=1$ does not necessarily mean that $\rho=1$, and $\rho_s=-1$ does not necessarily mean that $\rho=-1$.

Example 15.4.1 Suppose you want to determine whether there is a monotonic relationship between introversion, X, and incidence of insomnia, Y, during a particular month. If you randomly sample n=5 subjects and observe

X:	14	28	15	23	36
Y:	0	3	6	12	18

the ranks of these scores are

R(X):	1	4	2	3	5
R(Y):	1	2	3	4	5

and so

$$r_s=1-6[(1-1)^2+(4-2)^2+...+(5-5)^2]/[5(5^2-1)]$$
$$=.7.$$

To test the hypothesis that X and Y are independent, versus $H_1:\rho_s\neq 0$, compute

$$T=r_s[(n-2)/(1-r_s^2)]^{1/2}. \qquad (15.4.4)$$

For n large, T has, approximately, a Student's t distribution with n-2 degrees of freedom. If $|T|>t$ where t is the $1-\alpha/2$ quantile of the Student's t distribution which is read from Table A14, reject H_0. For critical values when n is small, see Glasser and Winter (1961). According to Hays (1981), equation (15.4.4) can be used when n is as small as 10.

Kendall's tau

Kendall's tau is another measure that indicates the extent to which X and Y are monotonically related. Many researchers prefer Kendall's tau to Spearman's rho on the grounds that Kendall's tau is easier to interpret.

Again you randomly sample n subjects and observe the pairs of values (X_i,Y_i), $i=1,...,n$. Kendall's tau is based on the notion of concordance. Two pairs of observations, say (X_i,Y_i) and (X_j,Y_j) are defined to be concordant if $X_i>X_j$ and $Y_i>Y_j$, or if $X_i<X_j$ and

$Y_i<Y_j$. The two pairs of observations are discordant if $X_i<X_j$ and $Y_i>Y_j$, or if $X_i>X_j$ and $Y_i<Y_j$. The maximum number of concordances among the observations is the number of ways of having i<j which is n(n-1)/2.

Let

$$Z_{ij}=1,$$

if (X_i, Y_i) a) and (X_j, Y_j) are concordant, and set

$$Z_{ij}=-1$$

if they are discordant. Define

$$N=\Sigma_{i<j}Z_{ij}.$$

In other words, sum Z_{ij} over all i<j. N is the number of concordant pairs minus the number of discordant pairs. The estimate of Kendall's tau is

$$\hat{\tau}=N/[n(n-1)/2] \qquad (15.4.5)$$

As with Spearman's rho, $-1\le\tau\le1$. When X and Y are independent, $\tau=0$, and when there is a perfect monotonic relationship between X and Y, τ equals 1 or -1.

To test $H_0:\tau=0$, compute

$$Z=\hat{\tau}/\hat{\sigma}_\tau$$

where

$$\hat{\sigma}_\tau^2=2(2n+5)/[9n(n-1)].$$

Z has, approximately, a standard normal distribution. If

$$|Z|>z_{1-\alpha/2},$$

$z_{1-\alpha/2}$ being read from Table A1, reject H_0. Note that if X and Y are independent, $\tau=0$, but $\tau=0$ does not necessarily mean that X and Y are independent. For additional information about Kendall's tau and related topics, see Kendall (1970).

Comparing Correlations on Dependent Measures

Let $(X_{i1}, X_{i2}, X_{i3}, X_{i4})$, i=1,...,n, be four measures on each of n subjects. Let ρ_{jk} be the correlation between X_{ij} and X_{ik}, and let

r_{jk} be the estimate of ρ_{jk}. (See equation 13.1.1.) Note that because the same subjects are used to compute both r_{12} and r_{34}, r_{12} and r_{34} are dependent statistics. Chapter thirteen described a method for testing $H_0:\rho_{12}=\rho_{34}$, but unfortunately the method is not robust to nonnormality. Yu and Dunn (1982) recommend the following procedure based on Kendall's tau, which can also be used to test $\rho_{12}=\rho_{13}$.

For fixed i and j, let $Z_{12ji}=1$ if (X_{j1},X_{j2}) and (X_{i1},X_{i2}) are concordant. If they are discordant, set $Z_{12ji}=-1$. Define Z_{34ji} in a similar manner, only now you work with the observations (X_{j3},X_{j4}) and (X_{i3},X_{i4}). Let

$$D_{12i}=\Sigma_j Z_{12ji},$$

$$D_{34i}=\Sigma_j Z_{34ji},$$

$$D_i=D_{12i}-D_{34i},$$

$$K_{12}=[n(n-1)]^{-1}\Sigma_i D_{12i},$$

$$K_{34}=[n(n-1)]^{-1}\Sigma_i D_{34i},$$

and

$$s^2=\{4/[n(n-1)^3]\}^{-1}\Sigma(D_i-\bar{D})^2.$$

Then

$$K=(K_{12}-K_{34})/s$$

has, approximately, a standard normal distribution, and you reject $H_0:\rho_{12}=\rho_{34}$ if $|K|>c$ where c is the $1-\alpha/2$ quantile of the standard normal distribution.

15.5 THE QUADE TEST

The Quade test (Quade, 1979) is an extension of the Wilcoxon signed rank test to J treatment groups. As in chapter 11, it is assumed that you have a random sample of n sets of related observations called blocks, and that each of the J observations within a block are the results corresponding to the J treatments. For example, you might be interested in J=3 methods of treating hypertension in dogs, and a block might be the dogs from the same litter. Thus, the observations within a block may be dependent, but by randomly sampling litters, the observations in different blocks (i.e., across litters) will be independent. It is also assumed that subjects within a block are randomly assigned to the J treatments, and that every subject within a block receives only one of the treatments.

To illustrate the computational steps of Quade's test, consider the following data:

Block	Treatment A	B	C
1	53	48	63
2	19	26	36
3	47	40	52
4	55	56	42

First you assign ranks to the observations in the first block. The smallest value among the three observations in the first block is 48, and so it receives a rank of 1, 53 gets a rank of 2 and 63 a rank of 3. You repeat this process for each block. For the data given above, the values of $R(X_{ij})$, the rank of the jth observation in the ith block are:

Block	Treatment A	B	C
1	2	1	3
2	1	2	3
3	2	1	3
4	2	3	1

Next, for the ith block, you compute D_i, say, the difference between the largest and smallest X_{ij} values, That is,

$$D_i = \max_j\{X_{ij}\} - \min_j\{X_{ij}\}$$

where $\max_j\{X_{ij}\}$ is largest of the J observations in the ith block, and $\min_j\{X_{ij}\}$ is the smallest. For the sample data, the D_i values are $D_1=15$, $D_2=17$, $D_3=12$, and $D_4=14$.

Next rank the D_i values, and let $R(D_i)$ be the rank of the ith value. As usual, if there are ties, their ranks are averaged. In the illustration, $R(D_1)=3$, $R(D_2)=4$, $R(D_3)=1$, and $R(D_4)=2$. Finally, compute

$$S=\Sigma_j[(\Sigma_i R(D_i)R(X_{ij})]^2$$

$$W=\{72S/[J(J+1)n(n+1)(2n+1)]\} - \{9(J+1)n(n+1)/[2(2n+1)]\}$$

$$A=1 - \{6(3n^2+3n-1)/[5n(n+1)(2n+1)]\}$$

$$B=3A-2+ \{72(3n^4+6n^3-3n+1)/[7n^2(n+1)^2(2n+1)^2]\}$$

$\nu=(J-1)A^3/B^2$

$X=\{[W-J+1]A/B\} + \nu.$

When H_0 is true, X has a chi-square distribution with ν degrees of freedom. Thus, reject H_0 if $X>c$ where c is the $1-\alpha$ quantile of the chi-square distribution with ν degrees of freedom which is read from Table A2.

When n is not too small, H_0 can be tested with W rather than X. In particular, reject H_0 if $W>c$ where now the degrees of freedom are J-1 rather than ν. Unfortunately, Quade (1979) does not indicate just how large n must be before the simpler version of the test, based on W, can be used.

Continuing the illustration,

$$S=[3(2)+4(1)+1(2)+2(2)]^2$$
$$+[3(1)+4(2)+1(1)+2(3)]^2$$
$$+[3(3)+4(3)+1(3)+2(1)]^2$$

$$=1256,$$

$$W=41.7-40=1.7$$

$$A=1-[6(48+12-1)]/[5(4)(4+1)(8+1)]$$
$$=.606$$

$$B=.18$$

$$\nu=13.73$$

and

$$X=(1.7-3+1)(.606)/(.18)+13.73$$
$$=-1.01+13.73$$
$$=12.72.$$

With $\nu=13.73$ degrees of freedom, and $\alpha=.05$, c is approximately 23.3, and since $X<c$, do not reject H_0.

Measuring Treatment Effects

Measuring treatment effects can be accomplished with the same techniques for measuring treatment effects in Friedman's test, which is described in the next section.

15.6 THE FRIEDMAN TEST

Suppose you have two dependent treatment groups and you want to test the hypothesis that the probability is 1/2 that an observation from the first group will be greater than the corresponding observation from the second. For example, if each block contains two dogs from the same litter, if X_1 is the effect of drug A on blood pressure for the first dog, and X_2 is the effect of drug B on the second dog, then you can test $H_0:Pr(X_1>X_2)=1/2$ as follows. Let X_{ij} be the i<u>th</u> observation (block) from the j<u>th</u> treatment group, and let $Y_i=1$ if $X_{i1}-X_{i2}>0$; otherwise $Y_i=0$. The Y_i's have a binomial probability function, and you can test the null hypothesis with the sign test which was described in chapter 5. Friedman (1937) devised a generalization of the sign test to J>2 dependent treatment groups.

As with Quade's test, the null hypothesis is that

$$F_1(x)=F_2(x)=\ldots=F_J(x).$$

Thus, the null hypothesis is that the cumulative probability functions for each of the J treatments are identical. Both Quade's and Friedman's test assume blocks are randomly sampled, but in contrast to Quade's test, Friedman's test does not use the quantities $\max_j\{X_{ij}\}-\min_j\{X_{ij}\}$.

To apply Friedman's procedure, for each block you rank the observations. Call these ranks $R(X_{ij})$ and note that the $R(X_{ij})$ values are the same quantities used in Quade's procedure. Next compute

$$A=\Sigma\Sigma[R(X_{ij})]^2,$$

$$R_j=\Sigma_i R(X_{ij})$$

and

$$B=\Sigma R_j^2/n.$$

If there are no ties, A simplifies to

$$A=nJ(J+1)(2J+1)/6.$$

When H_0 is true,

$$F=(n-1)[B-\{nJ(J+1)^2/4\}]/(A-B) \qquad (15.6.1)$$

has, approximately, an F distribution with $\nu_1=J-1$ and $\nu_2=(n-1)(J-1)$ degrees of freedom. Thus, if F>f, where f is the $1-\alpha$ quantile of an F distribution, which is read from Table A3, you reject H_0.

There is also a version of Friedman's test that is based on the chi-square distribution, but from Iman and Davenport (1980), the test based on (15.6.1) appears to give better results.

Multiple comparisons.

Conover (1980) recommends the following multiple comparison procedure. If Friedman's test is significant, treatment groups j and k are declared to be different if

$$|R_j - R_k| > t_{1-\alpha/2}\{2n(A-B)/[(J-1)(n-1)]\}^{1/2}$$

where t is the $1-\alpha/2$ quantile of Student's t distribution with $(n-1)(J-1)$ degrees of freedom.

Evidently, when $J<5$, Quade's test has more power than Friedman's, but for $J\geq5$ treatment groups, the reverse may be true (Iman, Hora & Conover, 1984).

Example 15.6.1 Friedman's test is illustrated with the same data used to illustrate Quade's test. From the ranked values, $R_1=2+1+2+2=7$, and similarly $R_2=7$, and $R_3=10$. Then $A=2^2+1^2+\ldots+1^2=56$, $B=(7^2+7^2+10^2)/4=49.5$, and

$$F=3[49.5-4(3)(3+1)^2/4]/(56-49.5)$$
$$=.69.$$

The degrees of freedom are $\nu_1=2$ and $\nu_2=6$, and so with $\alpha=.05$ you do not reject.

Measuring Treatment Effects

Treatment effects for treatment groups j and k can be measured with p=Pr(an observation from group j is greater than the corresponding observation in group k). The estimate of p is

$$\hat{p}=\Sigma Y_i/n,$$

where $Y_i=1$ if $X_{ij}-X_{ik}>0$; otherwise $Y_i=0$.

15.7 THE IMAN PROCEDURE

Still another approach to comparing J dependent treatment groups was proposed by Iman (1974) and studied by Iman, Hora and Conover (1984). Again the null hypothesis is

$$H_0: F_1(x)=F_2(x)=\ldots=F_J(x).$$

In contrast to the Friedman and Quade tests, you do not rank the observations within a block. Instead you rank all nJ observations so that the values of the ranks now range from 1 to nJ. As an illustration, consider the data used to demonstrate Quade's test that is given at the beginning of the previous section. The resulting ranks are:

Block	Treatment A	B	C
1	9	7	12
2	1	2	3
3	6	4	8
4	10	11	5

Next you simply perform an F test on these ranked values using the computational steps described in chapter eleven. That is, you apply the F test given by equation (11.1.2) with degrees of freedom J-1 and (J-1)(n-1).

Iman, Hora, and Conover (1984) compared the power of Iman's procedure to the power obtained using the Friedman and Quade tests. In most cases, Iman's approach had more power. However, Iman et al. do not recommend that the Friedman and Quade tests be abandoned. They suggest that all three procedures be applied, and that if there are any discrepancies among the results, you should try to ascertain why this occurred. Unfortunately, though, there are no exact guidelines on how any discrepancies should be resolved. However, it is clear from results in Agresti and Pendergast (1986) that if the number of observations per groups is as small as 10, the Friedman test should not be used because when testing at the .05 level the actual probability of a Type I error can be less than .02 or greater than .075. For $n \geq 30$ this difficulty did not occur, but even for n=30 there are situations where the Iman procedure can exceed .07 when J=5. For J=2 this difficulty did not occur. Agresti and Pendergast did not consider Quade's test, and so it is not known whether it has a similar problem.

15.8 THE AGRESTI-PENDERGAST PROCEDURE

Still another procedure was proposed by Agresti and Pendergast (1986) for comparing J distributions in a repeated measures design. Again let $R(X_{ij})$ be the rank of the i<u>th</u> observation in the j<u>th</u> group where all the observations are pooled. That is, X_{ij} gets the same rank as it did under the Iman procedure. For notational convenience let $R_{ij}=R(X_{ij})$ and set

$$\bar{R}_{.j}=\Sigma_i R_{ij}/n$$

and

$$s_{jk}=\Sigma(R_{ij}-\bar{R}_{.j})(R_{ik}-\bar{R}_{.k})/(n-J+1).$$

The vector $\bar{\underset{\sim}{R}}'$ having length J is defined by

$$\bar{\underset{\sim}{R}}'=(\bar{R}_{.1},\ldots,\bar{R}_{.J}),$$

and the J-1 by J matrix C is defined by

$$C=\begin{bmatrix}1 & -1 & 0\ldots 0 & 0\\ 0 & 1 & -1\ldots 0 & 0\\ \cdot & \cdot & \cdot & \cdot\\ 0 & 0 & \ldots 1 & -1\end{bmatrix}$$

The test statistic is

$$F=[n/(J-1)](C\underset{\sim}{R})'(CSC')^{-1}C\bar{\underset{\sim}{R}},$$

where $S=(s_{jk})$.

Under the null hypothesis of identical distributions, F has approximately an F distribution with $\nu_1=J-1$ and $\nu_2=(J-1)(n-1)$ degrees of freedom. Thus, the critical value is read from Table A3.

For J=2 groups, the Agresti-Pendergast procedure and the Iman procedure are identical. For J>5 there are situations where the Agresti-Pendergast procedure provides better control over Type I errors. For example, Agresti and Pendergast report a situation with n=50 observations and a nominal level of $\alpha=.05$ where the actual probability of Iman's procedure was .0705 while the Agresti-Pendergast procedure had an estimated level of .0465. All indications are that the Agresti-Pendergast procedure is better for J>2. While an actual level of .07 may not seem large, there are no guarantees that the Iman procedure will not have Type I error probabilities even higher.

Because researchers are usually interested in determining which distributions are different rather than stopping their investigation after rejecting the hypothesis that all of the distributions are identical, an easier way of performing the analysis is to simply apply the Iman procedure to every pair of distributions and adjust the α level using the Bonferroni inequality or Simes' procedure. As noted in chapters nine and eleven, all indications are that Simes' procedure is better. These procedures avoid the difficulties discovered by Agresti and Pendergast, and they control the experimentwise Type I error probability. Also recall from chapter nine that pairwise comparisons made contingent upon a significant F test, can be expected to lower the Type I error probability, and so if the Bonferroni inequality is used, perform the tests regardless of whether the F test is significant. Note that this approach differs from the Fisher-type procedure suggested by Conover.

For the problem at hand, to apply Simes' procedure, simply perform Iman's procedure to every pair of distributions and rank the significance levels. Next you examine the lowest significance level that was observed. The null hypothesis is rejected for the two groups having the lowest significance level if the significance level is less than α/C where $C=J(J-1)/2$ is the number of comparisons being performed and α is the desired experimentwise Type I error probability. For the two treatment groups having the second lowest significance level, you reject if the significance level is less than $2\alpha/C$. For the third lowest significance level you reject if the significance level is less than $3\alpha/C$, etc. Once you fail to reject, stop testing and fail to reject the remaining hypotheses.

For example, if you want to compare three treatment groups, C=3. Suppose you perform all pairwise comparisons using Imans procedure and find that for $H_0:F_1(x)=F_2(x)$, $H_0:F_1(x)=F_3(x)$, and $H_0:F_2(x)=F_3(x)$, the corresponding significance levels are .035, .01, and .06. Also suppose $\alpha=.05$. Because $.01<.05/3$, you reject $H_0:F_1(x)=F_3(x)$. But $.035>2(.05)/3$, so testing stops and you do not reject the other two hypotheses.

15.9 COMPARING MEDIANS

One of the more important procedures in this chapter deals with the problem of comparing the medians corresponding to two independent treatment groups. It is often argued that the median is a better measure of central location than the mean. The argument goes that if a distribution is symmetric, the mean and median are equal, but if a distribution is asymmetric, the median is closer to the center or "bulk" of the distribution in which case it is more "typical" of possible observed values. Another argument for comparing medians in addition or instead of the means is that the sample median is less sensitive to outliers (i.e., extreme values). It is known that "heavy-tailed" distributions are fairly common in practice. Relative to other distributions, outliers have a relatively high probability of occurring when a distribution is heavy-tailed. Outliers can also occur when errors are made when recording data. Also, for some distributions, such as the exponential distribution, the mean and median can be nearly one standard deviation apart, and so there may be practical situations where comparing medians will yield different conclusions than would be obtained when comparing means.

Although procedures have been devised for comparing medians, they are rarely used. One good reason for this is that the best known procedure (Mood, 1954) has several undesirable properties. For instance, it may not provide adequate control over the probability of a Type I error (Fligner & Rust, 1982). Fligner and Rust mention several other procedures for testing the hypothesis of equal medians, all of which are unsatisfactory.

Fligner and Rust (1982) proposed a method for comparing medians and their simulation results indicated that their procedure should work well when the distributions corresponding to the two treatment groups are symmetric. Their procedure appears to work well when the distributions are asymmetric provided the sample sizes are equal. However, for asymmetric distributions and unequal sample sizes, their procedure may not provide adequate control over the probability of a Type I error (Wilcox & Charlin, 1986). The procedure described here works about as well as the Fligner and Rust procedure when the distributions are symmetric, but it has the advantage of also working well in the asymmetric case. However, for equal sample sizes and at least 25 observations in each group, it appears that the Fligner-Rust procedure will not exceed the nominal α level in most practical situations, even for asymmetric distributions, provided both distributions are continuous. For discrete distributions the Fligner-Rust procedure can be highly unsatisfactory in situations like that described at the end of this section. For continuous distributions and equal sample sizes, the procedure described below can exceed the nominal α level. Moreover, the probability of a Type I error under the Fligner-Rust procedure is generally closer to the nominal level. The main point here is that for unequal sample sizes, the Fligner-Rust procedure can exceed the nominal α level by a substantial amount. For example, with sample sizes of 25 and 11, Wilcox and Charlin (1986) report α levels as high as .22 with a nominal α level of .05.

The procedure described below for comparing medians was suggested by Wilcox and Charlin (1986) and is based on results in Maritz and Jarrett (1978). Maritz and Jarrett provided a small sample estimate of the variance of the sample median. The approach here is to apply their estimate of the variance, assume this estimate is indeed equal to the actual variance, and apply the Z test. In addition to the results in Wilcox and Charlin (1986), results in McKean and Schrader (1984) support the use of this procedure as well.

The Incomplete Beta Function

Application of the procedure requires the evaluation of the incomplete beta function $I_p(a,b)$, where $0 \le p \le 1$, $a>0$, and $b>0$. Here attention can be restricted to $a=b=r$, say. If r is an odd integer,

$$I_p(r,r)=\Sigma_{j=r}^{n}\binom{n}{j}p^j(1-p)^{n-j}.$$

If r is an even integer, evaluating $I_p(r,r)$ is more complicated. In particular,

$$I_p(r,r)=Pr(Y \le p)$$

where Y is a beta random variable with probability density function

$$f(y)=\{\Gamma(a+b)/[\Gamma(a)\Gamma(b)]\}p^{a-1}(1-p)^{b-1}.$$

(The symbol Γ refers to the gamma function. When r is an integer, $\Gamma(r)=(r-1)!$ You won't need to evaluate the Γ function, so further details about Γ are omitted.)

One way to evaluate $I_p(r,r)$ is with the FORTRAN subroutine MDBETA available through IMSL (1975). If you are unable to write a FORTRAN program, you can approximate $I_p(a,b)$ fairly accurately by computing

$$m=a+b-1,$$

$$A=[b-1/2-m(1-p)],$$

$$B=2/[1+1/6m],$$

$$d=b-1/3-(m+1/3)(1-p),$$

$$D=(b-1/2)/[m(1-p)],$$

$$E=(a-1/2)/(mp),$$

$$z=(d/A)\{B[(b-1/2)\underline{ln}(D)+(a-1/2)\underline{ln}(E)]\},$$

where <u>ln</u> is the natural logarithm. Then $I_p(a,b) \doteq Pr(Z \le z)$ where Z is a standard normal random variable (Peizzer & Pratt, 1966). That is, you use Table A1 to evaluate I_p. An even more accurate approximation can be had by replacing d with

$$d'=d+(1/50)[(p/b)-(1-p)/a+(p-1/2)/(a+b)].$$

Estimating the Variance of the Sample Median

Consider a single treatment group having n observations, say $X_1, \ldots, X_n$. The next goal is to describe the Maritz-Jarrett estimate of the variance of M, the sample median.

Let

$$W_i(r,r)=I_{i/n}(r,r)-I_{(i-1)/n}(r,r),\ i=1,\ldots,n.$$

Also let $X_{(1)},\ldots,X_{(n)}$ be the X_i's written in ascending order.

That is, $X_{(1)}$ is the smallest of the X_i's, $X_{(2)}$ is the second

smallest, etc., and let

$$A_k=\Sigma_i X_{(i)}^k W_k(r,r),\ k=1,2,\ldots \tag{15.9.1}$$

If n is odd, set r=(n-1)/2+1 in (15.9.1) in which case the estimated variance of the sample median is

$$\hat{\sigma}^2=A_2-A_1^2.$$

For n even set m=n/2, and for notational convenience set

$$U_i=W_i(m,m),\ i=1,\ldots,n.$$

Next let

$$A_k=\Sigma X_{(i)}^k U_i$$

$$C_i=(i/n)^m,$$

$$D_i=[(n-i)/n]^m$$

$$E_i=[(i-1)/n)]^m$$

$$G_i=[(n+1-i)/n]^m$$

and compute

$$U_{ii}=U_i-(n!/(2(m!)^2)\{C_iD_i+E_iG_i-2E_iD_i\},\ \text{for } i=1,\ldots,n,$$

$$U_{ij}=(n!/(m!)^2)\{C_i-E_i\}\{G_j-D_j\},\ \text{for all } i\neq j,$$

and

$$H=\Sigma\Sigma U_{ij}X_{(i)}X_{(j)}.$$

The calculations are simplified by noting that $U_{ij}=U_{ji}$. The estimate of the variance of the sample median is

$$\hat{\sigma}^2=(1/2)(A_2+H)-A_1^2.$$

Testing Whether Two Medians Are Equal

Finally, let θ_1 and θ_2 be the population medians corresponding to two independent treatment groups. To test $H_0:\theta_1=\theta_2$, compute the sample medians corresponding to each group, say M_1 and M_2, estimate the variance of M_1 and M_2 with

$$\hat{\sigma}_1^2 \text{ and } \hat{\sigma}_2^2$$

using the method described above, and then compute

$$Z=(M_1-M_2)/(\hat{\sigma}_1^2+\hat{\sigma}_2^2)^{1/2}.$$

When H_0 is true, Z has, approximately, a standard normal distribution, and so you reject H_0 if

$$|Z|>z_{1-\alpha/2},$$

where $z_{1-\alpha/2}$ is read from Table A1.

The Case J>2

The procedure just described can be extended to the case J>2 using known results related to the chi-square distribution. (See, for example, Dijkstra and Werter, 1981.) Compute

$$\omega_j=1/\hat{\sigma}_j^2$$

where $\hat{\sigma}_j{}^2$ is the estimate of the variance of the j<u>th</u> sample median. Next compute

$$\omega=\Sigma\omega_j,$$

$$\bar{M}=\Sigma\omega_j M_j/\omega,$$

and

$$X^2=\Sigma\omega_j(M_j-\bar{M})^2,$$

where $\bar{M}$ is mean of the J sample medians.
When

$$H_0:\theta_1=\ldots=\theta_J$$

is true, X^2 has, approximately, a chi-square distribution with J-1 degrees of freedom. You reject H_0 if $X^2>c$ where c is the 1-α quantile of a chi-square distribution with J-1 degrees of freedom.

The Fligner and Rust Procedure

While the procedure described above generally works well when comparing medians, the Fligner and Rust procedure gives even better results when the sample sizes are equal and when there are at least 25 observations in each group. However, as already indicated, the Fligner and Rust procedure is not recommended when you have unequal sample sizes, and it can give unsatisfactory results when there are ties.

Let $X_1,\ldots,X_m$ and $Y_1,\ldots,Y_n$ be the observations in the two groups. As already noted, it is assumed that m=n. To apply the Fligner and Rust procedure, pool all m and n observations, as was done in the Mann-Whitney test, and compute the median, say M. For example, suppose the observations are

Group 1: 5 10 20

Group 2: 8 15 25.

The pooled observations, written in ascending order, are

5 8 10 15 20 and 25.

Thus, the median of the pooled observations is M=(10+15)/2=12.5. Next, for X_i, the ith observation in the first group, set $w_i=1$ if $X_i<M$, set $w_i=1/2$ if $X_i=M$, set $w_i=0$ if $X_i>M$, and compute

$$T=\Sigma w_i/n.$$

In the example, T=2/3.

Let N=n+m, and set

$$B=[.5(N+1) + \surd N]^\dagger$$

where $[.5(N+1) + \surd n]^\dagger$ is the greatest integer less than or equal to $.5(N+1)+\surd N$. In the example, N=6, and $B=[7/2 + \surd 6]^\dagger=5$. Let L be the (N-B)th largest value of the pooled observations. In the example, N-B=1, so L=5. Also let U be the Bth largest of the pooled observations which in the example is 20. Let F(x) be the proportion of observations in the first group that are less than or equal to x, and let G(x) be the corresponding proportion for the second group. Compute

$$R=[F(U)-F(L)]/[G(U)-G(L)].$$

In the example,

$$R=[1.0 - 1/3]/[2/3 - 0]=1.0$$

If G(U)-G(L)>0, set

$$\hat{\sigma}^2=.25(1+R^2)/(1+R)^2,$$

otherwise set

$$\hat{\sigma}^2=.25.$$

In the example, $\hat{\sigma}^2=.125$. Finally you compute

$$Q=(\sqrt{n})(T-.5)/\hat{\sigma}$$

which in the example is

$$(\sqrt{3})(2/3 - .5)/\sqrt{.125} = .82.$$

When H_0 is true, Q has, approximately, a standard normal distribution. Thus, the critical value is read from Table A1. In the illustration, with $\alpha=.05$, you do not reject. Fligner and Rust describe a slight generalization of this procedure for $m \neq n$, but because this procedure may not work well in practice, it is not described. For m and n large, the Fligner and Rust procedure may give satisfactory results when $m \neq n$, but it is not known just how large they must be for this to be the case. Also, if there is more than one X_i such that $X_i=M$, or more than one $Y_i=M$ -- a situation that might occur when comparing discrete distributions -- the Fligner-Rust procedure should not be used because in some cases it can give absurd results. For example, it is possible to have equal sample medians and yet reject H_0.

EXERCISES

15.1 You have the following data for two independent groups

Group 1: 34, 73, 27, 17

Group 2: 73, 62, 19, 36, 45

Perform a Mann-Whitney test with $\alpha=.05$.

15.2 Apply the Iman procedure to the data in problem 15.1.

15.3 In problem 15.1, let X be an observation from the first group, and let Y be an observation form the second. Estimate Pr(X<Y).

15.4 If you get a significant result with the Quade procedure, does this mean that the means corresponding to the treatments are not all equal?

15.5 Using the data in exercise 15.1, test the hypothesis of equal medians using the procedure on p. 340. Use α=.05.

References

Agresti, A. & Pendergast, J (1986) Comparing mean ranks for repeated measures data. Communications in Statistics--Theory and Methods, 15, 1417-1433.

Conover, W. J. (1980) Practical nonparametric statistics, New York: Wiley

Dijkstra, J. & Werter, P. (1981) Testing the equality of several means when the population variance are unequal. Communications in Statistics, B10, 557-569.

Fligner, M. A. & Rust S. W. (1982) A modification of Mood's median test for the generalized Behrens-Fisher problem. Biometrika, 69, 221-226.

Friedman, M. (1937) The use of ranks to avoid the assumption of normality implicit in the analysis of variance. Journal of the American Statistical Association, 32, 675-701.

Glasser, G. J. & Winter R. F. (1961) Critical values of rank correlation for testing the hypothesis of independence Biometrika, 48, 444-448.

Hays, W. L. (1981) Statistics New York: Holt, Rinehart and Winston.

Iman, R. L. (1974) A power study of a rank transform for the two-way classification model when interaction may be present. Canadian Journal of Statistics, 2, 227-239

Iman, R. L. & Davenport, J. M. (1980) Approximations of the critical region of the Friedman statistic. Communications in Statistics, A9, 571-595.

Iman, R. L., Hora, S. & Conover. W. J. (1984) Comparison of asymptotically distribution-free procedures for the analysis of complete blocks Journal of the American Statistical Association, 79, 674-685.

Iman, R. L., Quade, D. & Alexander. D. A. (1975) Exact probability levels for the Kruskal-Wallis test.

Selected tables in mathematical statistics, 3, 329-384.
IMSL (1975) Library 1, Vol. II Houston: International Mathematical and Statistical Libraries.
Kendall, M. G. (1970) Rank correlation methods New York: Hafner
Kendall, M. G. & Buckland, W. R. (1982) A dictionary of statistical terms. New York: Longman Group.
Kruskal, W. H. & Wallis, W. A. (1952) Use of ranks on one-criterion variance analysis. Journal of the American Statistical Associaiton, 47, 583-621 (With corrections Vol 48 pp. 907-911)
Maritz, J. S. & Jarrett, R. G. (1978) A note on estimating the variance of the sample median. Journal of the American Statistical Association, 73, 194-196.
McKean, J. W. & Schrader, R. M. (1984) A comparison of methods for studentizing the sample median. Communications in Statistics--Simulation and Computation, 13, 751-773.
Milton, R. C. (1964) An extended table of critical values for the Mann-Whitney (Wilcoxon) two-sample statistic. Journal of the American Statistical Association, 59, 925-934.
Mood, A. M. (1954) On the asymptotic efficiency of certain non-parametric two-sample tests. Annals of Mathematical Statistics, 25, 514-522.
Peizzer, D. B. & Pratt, J. W. (1966) Approximating the binomial, F and commonly used related distributions, I. Technical report No.12, Dept of Statistics, Harvard University.
Quade, D. (1979) Using weighted rankings in the analysis of complete blocks with additive block effects. Journal of the American Statistical Association, 74, 680-683.
Sandvik, L. & Olsson, B. (1982) A nearly distribution-free test for comparing dispersion in paired samples. Biometrika, 69, 484-485.
Verdooren, L. R. (1963) Extended tables of critical values for Wilcoxon's test statistic. Biometrika, 50, 177-186.
Wilcox, R. R. & Charlin, V. (1986) Comparing medians: A monte carlo study. Journal of Educational Statistics, 11, 263-274
Yu, M. C. & Dunn, O. J. (1982) Robust tests for the equality of two correlation coefficients: A monte carlo study. Educational and Psychological Measurement, 42, 987-1004.

APPENDIX A
LIST OF TABLES

Table A1
Standard Normal Distribution

z	Pr(Z≤z)	z	Pr(Z≤z)	z	Pr(Z≤z)
0.0	0.5000000	0.86	0.8051055	1.72	0.9572838
0.01	0.5039894	0.87	0.8078498	1.73	0.9581849
0.02	0.5079783	0.88	0.8105703	1.74	0.9590705
0.03	0.5119665	0.89	0.8132671	1.75	0.9599408
0.04	0.5159534	0.90	0.8159399	1.76	0.9607961
0.05	0.5199388	0.91	0.8185887	1.77	0.9616364
0.06	0.5239222	0.92	0.8212136	1.78	0.9624620
0.07	0.5279032	0.93	0.8238145	1.79	0.9632730
0.08	0.5318814	0.94	0.8263912	1.80	0.9640697
0.09	0.5358564	0.95	0.8289439	1.81	0.9648521
0.10	0.5398278	0.96	0.8314724	1.82	0.9656205
0.11	0.5437953	0.97	0.8339768	1.83	0.9663750
0.12	0.5477584	0.98	0.8364569	1.84	0.9671159
0.13	0.5517168	0.99	0.8389129	1.85	0.9678432
0.14	0.5556700	1.00	0.8413447	1.86	0.9685572
0.15	0.5596177	1.01	0.8437524	1.87	0.9692581
0.16	0.5635595	1.02	0.8461358	1.88	0.9699460
0.17	0.5674949	1.03	0.8484950	1.89	0.9706210
0.18	0.5714237	1.04	0.8508300	1.90	0.9712834
0.19	0.5753454	1.05	0.8531409	1.91	0.9719334
0.20	0.5792597	1.06	0.8554277	1.92	0.9725711
0.21	0.5831662	1.07	0.8576903	1.93	0.9731966
0.22	0.5870644	1.08	0.8599289	1.94	0.9738102
0.23	0.5909541	1.09	0.8621434	1.95	0.9744119
0.24	0.5948349	1.10	0.8643339	1.96	0.9750021
0.25	0.5987063	1.11	0.8665005	1.97	0.9755808
0.26	0.6025681	1.12	0.8686431	1.98	0.9761482
0.27	0.6064199	1.13	0.8707619	1.99	0.9767045
0.28	0.6102612	1.14	0.8728568	2.00	0.9772499
0.29	0.6140919	1.15	0.8749281	2.01	0.9777844
0.30	0.6179114	1.16	0.8769756	2.02	0.9783083
0.31	0.6217195	1.17	0.8789995	2.03	0.9788217
0.32	0.6255158	1.18	0.8809999	2.04	0.9793248
0.33	0.6293000	1.19	0.8829768	2.05	0.9798178
0.34	0.6330717	1.20	0.8849303	2.06	0.9803007
0.35	0.6368307	1.21	0.8868606	2.07	0.9807738
0.36	0.6405764	1.22	0.8887676	2.08	0.9812372
0.37	0.6443088	1.23	0.8906514	2.09	0.9816911
0.38	0.6480273	1.24	0.8925123	2.10	0.9821356
0.39	0.6517317	1.25	0.8943502	2.11	0.9825708
0.40	0.6554217	1.26	0.8961653	2.12	0.9829970

Table A1 (continued)

0.41	0.6590970	1.27	0.8979577	2.13	0.9834142
0.42	0.6627573	1.28	0.8997274	2.14	0.9838226
0.43	0.6664022	1.29	0.9014747	2.15	0.9842224
0.44	0.6700314	1.30	0.9031995	2.16	0.9846137
0.45	0.6736448	1.31	0.9049021	2.17	0.9849966
0.46	0.6772419	1.32	0.9065825	2.18	0.9853713
0.47	0.6808225	1.33	0.9082409	2.19	0.9857379
0.48	0.6843863	1.34	0.9098773	2.20	0.9860966
0.49	0.6879331	1.35	0.9114920	2.21	0.9864474
0.50	0.6914625	1.36	0.9130850	2.22	0.9867906
0.51	0.6949743	1.37	0.9146565	2.23	0.9871263
0.52	0.6984682	1.38	0.9162067	2.24	0.9874545
0.53	0.7019440	1.39	0.9177356	2.25	0.9877755
0.54	0.7054015	1.40	0.9192433	2.26	0.9880894
0.55	0.7088403	1.41	0.9207302	2.27	0.9883962
0.56	0.7122603	1.42	0.9221962	2.28	0.9886962
0.57	0.7156612	1.43	0.9236415	2.29	0.9889893
0.58	0.7190427	1.44	0.9250663	2.30	0.9892759
0.59	0.7224047	1.45	0.9264707	2.31	0.9895559
0.60	0.7257469	1.46	0.9278550	2.32	0.9898296
0.61	0.7290691	1.47	0.9292191	2.33	0.9900969
0.62	0.7323711	1.48	0.9305634	2.34	0.9903581
0.63	0.7356527	1.49	0.9318879	2.35	0.9906133
0.64	0.7389137	1.50	0.9331928	2.36	0.9908625
0.65	0.7421539	1.51	0.9344783	2.37	0.9911060
0.66	0.7453731	1.52	0.9357445	2.38	0.9913437
0.67	0.7485711	1.53	0.9369916	2.39	0.9915758
0.68	0.7517478	1.54	0.9382198	2.40	0.9918025
0.69	0.7549029	1.55	0.9394292	2.41	0.9920237
0.70	0.7580363	1.56	0.9406201	2.42	0.9922397
0.71	0.7611479	1.57	0.9417924	2.43	0.9924506
0.72	0.7642375	1.58	0.9429466	2.44	0.9926564
0.73	0.7673049	1.59	0.9440826	2.45	0.9928572
0.74	0.7703500	1.60	0.9452007	2.46	0.9930531
0.75	0.7733726	1.61	0.9463011	2.47	0.9932443
0.76	0.7763727	1.62	0.9473839	2.48	0.9934309
0.77	0.7793501	1.63	0.9484493	2.49	0.9936128
0.78	0.7823046	1.64	0.9494974	2.50	0.9937903
0.79	0.7852361	1.65	0.9505285	2.51	0.9939634
0.80	0.7881446	1.66	0.9515428	2.52	0.9941323
0.81	0.7910299	1.67	0.9525403	2.53	0.9942969
0.82	0.7938919	1.68	0.9535213	2.54	0.9944574
0.83	0.7967306	1.69	0.9544860	2.55	0.9946139
0.84	0.7995458	1.70	0.9554345	2.56	0.9947664
0.85	0.8023375	1.71	0.9563671	2.57	0.9949151

This table was computed with IMSL subroutine MDNOR

Table A2
Value of x such that $P=Pr(\chi_{\nu}^{2} \leq x)$

ν P:	.01	.025	.05	.10	.25	.50
2	0.0201	0.0507	0.1025	0.2107	0.5754	1.3861
3	0.1148	0.2158	0.3518	0.5843	1.2126	2.3663
4	0.2971	0.4839	0.7107	1.0636	1.9226	3.3570
5	0.5530	0.8310	1.1452	1.6101	2.6745	4.3518
6	0.8715	1.2364	1.6345	2.2036	3.4541	5.3485
7	1.2372	1.6876	2.1671	2.8330	4.2548	6.3462
8	1.6422	2.1789	2.7320	3.4893	5.0706	7.3445
9	2.0860	2.6987	3.3239	4.1677	5.8987	8.3431
10	2.5546	3.2439	3.9383	4.8643	6.7370	9.3421
11	3.0473	3.8145	4.5741	5.5764	7.5837	10.3412
12	3.5676	4.4018	5.2249	6.3035	8.4378	11.3405
13	4.1022	5.0056	5.8902	7.0410	9.2982	12.3399
14	4.6532	5.6241	6.5681	7.7888	10.1642	13.3393
15	5.2256	6.2601	7.2600	8.5457	11.0365	14.3389
16	5.8067	6.9047	7.9603	9.3108	11.9121	15.3385
17	6.4000	7.5600	8.6699	10.0833	12.7918	16.3385
18	7.0042	8.2251	9.3880	10.8644	13.6751	17.3366
19	7.6268	8.9038	10.1138	11.6502	14.5618	18.3377
20	8.2523	9.5871	10.8495	12.4417	15.4515	19.3375
21	8.8864	10.2781	11.5896	13.2384	16.3440	20.3373
22	9.5285	10.9761	12.3358	14.0400	17.2392	21.3371
23	10.1874	11.6854	13.0877	14.8462	18.1368	22.3370
24	10.8457	12.3971	13.8449	15.6565	19.0367	23.3368
25	11.5103	13.1146	14.6071	16.4708	19.9387	24.3367
26	12.1898	13.8375	15.3772	17.2910	20.8427	25.3366
27	12.8679	14.5654	16.1490	18.1129	21.7486	26.3365
28	13.5514	15.3036	16.9250	18.9380	22.6562	27.3364
29	14.2401	16.0418	17.7049	19.7663	23.5655	28.3363
30	14.9429	16.7843	18.4885	20.5975	24.4764	29.3362
40	22.1394	24.4229	26.5080	29.0555	33.6676	39.3370
50	29.6845	32.3485	34.7634	37.6933	42.9486	49.3363
60	37.4646	40.4739	43.1874	46.4633	52.2998	59.3358
70	45.4230	48.7504	51.7389	55.3331	61.7038	69.3354
80	53.5226	57.1466	60.3912	64.2818	71.1497	79.3352
90	61.7377	65.6405	69.1259	73.2949	80.6295	89.3350
100	70.0494	74.2162	77.9294	82.3618	90.1378	99.3348

Table A2 (continued)

ν P:	.75	.9	.95	.975	.99	.995
2	2.7723	4.6035	5.9948	7.3790	9.2205	10.5895
3	4.1085	6.2525	7.8167	9.3563	11.3247	12.8192
4	5.3856	7.7815	9.4917	11.1502	13.2797	14.8242
5	6.6262	9.2375	11.0733	12.8383	15.0876	16.7617
6	7.8416	10.6464	12.5961	14.4589	16.8104	18.5495
7	9.0382	12.0197	14.0702	16.0203	18.4705	20.2700
8	10.2202	13.3629	15.5117	17.5458	20.0820	21.9379
9	11.3891	14.6855	16.9252	19.0315	21.6542	23.5634
10	12.5493	15.9897	18.3112	20.4954	23.1940	25.1537
11	13.7012	17.2782	19.6806	21.9295	24.7545	26.7142
12	14.8460	18.5510	21.0297	23.3493	26.2460	28.2489
13	15.9846	19.8140	22.3668	24.7455	27.7167	29.8779
14	17.1178	21.0667	23.6908	26.1316	29.1692	31.3761
15	18.2460	22.3103	24.9997	27.4982	30.6054	32.8566
16	19.3699	23.5456	26.3011	28.8578	32.0269	34.3211
17	20.4899	24.7710	27.5932	30.2007	33.4352	35.7711
18	21.6062	25.9917	28.8767	31.5385	34.8314	37.2079
19	22.7192	27.2063	30.1484	32.8673	36.2165	38.6326
20	23.8293	28.4151	31.4163	34.1813	37.5914	40.0461
21	24.9365	29.6187	32.6776	35.4931	38.9570	41.4494
22	26.0411	30.8175	33.9327	36.7918	40.3138	42.8430
23	27.1432	32.0117	35.1780	38.0890	41.6625	44.2278
24	28.2432	33.1987	36.4215	39.3800	43.0036	45.6042
25	29.3410	34.3844	37.6600	40.6590	44.3375	46.9728
26	30.4368	35.5664	38.8938	41.9380	45.6648	48.3340
27	31.5308	36.7448	40.1191	43.2062	46.9857	49.6883
28	32.6230	37.9199	41.3439	44.4746	48.3007	51.0361
29	33.7136	39.0919	42.5647	45.7383	49.6101	52.3777
30	34.8004	40.2610	43.7817	46.9920	50.9141	53.7134
40	45.6097	51.7963	55.7534	59.3447	63.7104	66.8024
50	56.3279	63.1594	67.5006	71.4232	76.1719	79.5229
60	66.9762	74.3900	79.0783	83.3007	88.3961	91.9820
70	77.5717	85.5206	90.5279	95.0262	100.4408	104.2431
80	88.1256	96.5723	101.8765	106.6315	112.3435	116.3475
90	98.6455	107.5595	113.1425	118.1388	124.1303	128.3240
100	109.1370	118.4928	124.3396	129.5640	135.8201	140.1933

This table was computed with IMSL subroutine MDCHI

Table A3
Values of f such that Pr(F≤f)=.95 where F has an F distribution with ν_1 and ν_2 degrees of freedom

ν_2

ν_1	1	2	3	4	5	6	7	8	9	10
5	6.61	5.79	5.41	5.19	5.05	4.95	4.88	4.82	4.77	4.73
6	5.99	5.14	4.76	4.53	4.39	4.28	4.21	4.15	4.10	4.06
7	5.59	4.74	4.35	4.12	3.97	3.87	3.79	3.73	3.68	3.64
8	5.32	4.46	4.07	3.84	3.69	3.58	3.50	3.44	3.39	3.35
9	5.12	4.26	3.86	3.63	3.48	3.37	3.29	3.23	3.18	3.14
10	4.96	4.10	3.71	3.48	3.33	3.22	3.14	3.07	3.02	2.98
11	4.84	3.98	3.59	3.36	3.20	3.09	3.01	2.95	2.90	2.85
12	4.75	3.89	3.49	3.26	3.11	3.00	2.91	2.85	2.80	2.75
13	4.67	3.81	3.41	3.18	3.03	2.92	2.83	2.77	2.71	2.67
14	4.60	3.74	3.34	3.11	2.96	2.85	2.76	2.70	2.65	2.60
15	4.54	3.68	3.29	3.06	2.90	2.79	2.71	2.64	2.59	2.54
16	4.49	3.63	3.24	3.01	2.85	2.74	2.66	2.59	2.54	2.49
17	4.45	3.59	3.20	2.96	2.81	2.70	2.61	2.55	2.49	2.45
18	4.41	3.55	3.16	2.93	2.77	2.66	2.58	2.51	2.46	2.41
19	4.38	3.52	3.13	2.90	2.74	2.63	2.54	2.48	2.42	2.38
20	4.35	3.49	3.10	2.87	2.71	2.60	2.51	2.45	2.39	2.35
21	4.32	3.47	3.07	2.84	2.68	2.57	2.49	2.42	2.37	2.32
22	4.30	3.44	3.05	2.82	2.66	2.55	2.46	2.40	2.34	2.30
23	4.28	3.42	3.03	2.80	2.64	2.53	2.44	2.37	2.32	2.27
24	4.26	3.40	3.01	2.78	2.62	2.51	2.42	2.36	2.30	2.25
25	4.24	3.39	2.99	2.76	2.60	2.49	2.40	2.34	2.28	2.24
26	4.23	3.37	2.98	2.74	2.59	2.47	2.39	2.32	2.27	2.22
27	4.21	3.35	2.96	2.73	2.57	2.46	2.37	2.31	2.25	2.20
28	4.20	3.34	2.95	2.71	2.56	2.45	2.36	2.29	2.24	2.19
29	4.18	3.33	2.93	2.70	2.55	2.43	2.35	2.28	2.22	2.18
30	4.17	3.32	2.92	2.69	2.53	2.42	2.33	2.27	2.21	2.16
40	4.08	3.23	2.84	2.61	2.45	2.34	2.25	2.18	2.12	2.08
60	4.00	3.15	2.76	2.53	2.37	2.25	2.17	2.10	2.04	1.99
120	3.92	3.07	2.68	2.45	2.29	2.18	2.09	2.02	1.96	1.91
400	3.86	3.02	2.63	2.39	2.24	2.12	2.03	1.96	1.90	1.85
∞	3.84	3.00	2.60	2.37	2.21	2.10	2.01	1.94	1.88	1.83

Table A3 (continued)

ν_1 \ ν_2	11	12	15	20	24	30	40	60	120	400
5	4.70	4.68	4.62	4.56	4.53	4.50	4.46	4.43	4.40	4.38
6	4.03	4.00	3.94	3.87	3.84	3.81	3.77	3.74	3.70	3.68
7	3.60	3.57	3.51	3.44	3.41	3.38	3.34	3.31	3.27	3.24
8	3.31	3.28	3.22	3.15	3.12	3.08	3.04	3.00	2.97	2.94
9	3.10	3.07	3.01	2.94	2.90	2.86	2.83	2.79	2.75	2.72
10	2.94	2.91	2.85	2.77	2.74	2.70	2.66	2.62	2.58	2.55
11	2.82	2.79	2.72	2.65	2.61	2.57	2.53	2.49	2.45	2.42
12	2.72	2.69	2.62	2.54	2.51	2.47	2.43	2.38	2.34	2.31
13	2.63	2.60	2.53	2.46	2.42	2.38	2.34	2.30	2.25	2.22
14	2.57	2.53	2.46	2.39	2.35	2.31	2.27	2.22	2.18	2.15
15	2.51	2.48	2.40	2.33	2.29	2.25	2.20	2.16	2.11	2.08
16	2.46	2.42	2.35	2.28	2.24	2.19	2.15	2.11	2.06	2.02
17	2.41	2.38	2.31	2.23	2.19	2.15	2.10	2.06	2.01	1.98
18	2.37	2.34	2.27	2.19	2.15	2.11	2.06	2.02	1.97	1.93
19	2.34	2.31	2.23	2.16	2.11	2.07	2.03	1.98	1.93	1.89
20	2.31	2.28	2.20	2.12	2.08	2.04	1.99	1.95	1.90	1.86
21	2.28	2.25	2.18	2.10	2.05	2.01	1.96	1.92	1.87	1.83
22	2.26	2.23	2.15	2.07	2.03	1.98	1.94	1.89	1.84	1.80
23	2.24	2.20	2.13	2.05	2.00	1.96	1.91	1.86	1.81	1.77
24	2.22	2.18	2.11	2.03	1.98	1.94	1.89	1.84	1.79	1.75
25	2.20	2.16	2.09	2.01	1.96	1.92	1.87	1.82	1.77	1.73
26	2.18	2.15	2.07	1.99	1.95	1.90	1.85	1.80	1.75	1.71
27	2.17	2.13	2.06	1.97	1.93	1.88	1.84	1.79	1.73	1.69
28	2.15	2.12	2.04	1.96	1.91	1.87	1.82	1.77	1.71	1.67
29	2.14	2.10	2.03	1.94	1.90	1.85	1.81	1.75	1.70	1.66
30	2.13	2.09	2.01	1.93	1.89	1.84	1.79	1.74	1.68	1.64
40	2.04	2.00	1.92	1.84	1.79	1.74	1.69	1.64	1.58	1.53
60	1.95	1.92	1.84	1.75	1.70	1.65	1.59	1.53	1.47	1.41
120	1.87	1.83	1.75	1.66	1.61	1.55	1.50	1.43	1.35	1.29
400	1.81	1.78	1.69	1.60	1.54	1.49	1.42	1.35	1.26	1.18
∞	1.79	1.75	1.67	1.57	1.52	1.46	1.39	1.32	1.22	1.00

This Table was computed with IMSL subroutine MDFI

Table A3 (continued)

Values of f such that $Pr(F \le f) = .99$ where F has an F distribution with ν_1 and ν_2 degrees of freedom

ν_1	ν_2 = 1	2	3	4	5	6	7	8	9	10
5	16.26	13.27	12.06	11.39	10.97	10.67	10.46	10.29	10.16	10.05
6	13.75	10.92	9.78	9.15	8.75	8.47	8.26	8.10	7.98	7.87
7	12.25	9.55	8.45	7.85	7.46	7.19	6.99	6.84	6.72	6.62
8	11.26	8.65	7.59	7.01	6.63	6.37	6.18	6.03	5.91	5.81
9	10.56	8.02	6.99	6.42	6.06	5.80	5.61	5.47	5.35	5.26
10	10.04	7.56	6.55	5.99	5.64	5.39	5.20	5.06	4.94	4.85
11	9.65	7.21	6.22	5.67	5.32	5.07	4.89	4.74	4.63	4.54
12	9.33	6.93	5.95	5.41	5.06	4.82	4.64	4.50	4.39	4.30
13	9.07	6.70	5.74	5.21	4.86	4.62	4.44	4.30	4.19	4.10
14	8.86	6.51	5.56	5.04	4.69	4.46	4.28	4.14	4.03	3.94
15	8.68	6.36	5.42	4.89	4.56	4.32	4.14	4.00	3.89	3.80
16	8.53	6.23	5.29	4.77	4.44	4.20	4.03	3.89	3.78	3.69
17	8.40	6.11	5.18	4.67	4.34	4.10	3.93	3.79	3.68	3.59
18	8.29	6.01	5.09	4.58	4.25	4.01	3.84	3.71	3.60	3.51
19	8.18	5.93	5.01	4.50	4.17	3.94	3.77	3.63	3.52	3.43
20	8.10	5.85	4.94	4.43	4.10	3.87	3.70	3.56	3.46	3.37
21	8.02	5.78	4.87	4.37	4.04	3.81	3.64	3.51	3.40	3.31
22	7.95	5.72	4.82	4.31	3.99	3.76	3.59	3.45	3.35	3.26
23	7.88	5.66	4.76	4.26	3.94	3.71	3.54	3.41	3.30	3.21
24	7.82	5.61	4.72	4.22	3.90	3.67	3.50	3.36	3.26	3.17
25	7.77	5.57	4.68	4.18	3.85	3.63	3.46	3.32	3.22	3.13
26	7.72	5.53	4.64	4.14	3.82	3.59	3.42	3.29	3.18	3.09
27	7.68	5.49	4.60	4.11	3.78	3.56	3.39	3.26	3.15	3.06
28	7.64	5.45	4.57	4.07	3.75	3.53	3.36	3.23	3.12	3.03
29	7.60	5.42	4.54	4.04	3.73	3.50	3.33	3.20	3.09	3.00
30	7.56	5.39	4.51	4.02	3.70	3.47	3.30	3.17	3.07	2.98
40	7.31	5.18	4.31	3.83	3.51	3.29	3.12	2.99	2.89	2.80
60	7.08	4.98	4.13	3.65	3.34	3.12	2.95	2.82	2.72	2.63
120	6.85	4.79	3.95	3.48	3.17	2.96	2.79	2.66	2.56	2.47
400	6.70	4.66	3.83	3.37	3.06	2.85	2.68	2.56	2.45	2.37
∞	6.63	4.61	3.78	3.32	3.02	2.80	2.64	2.51	2.41	2.32

Table A3 (continued)

ν_1 \ ν_2	11	12	15	20	24	30	40	60	120	400
5	9.96	9.89	9.72	9.55	9.46	9.38	9.30	9.20	9.11	9.05
6	7.79	7.72	7.56	7.40	7.31	7.23	7.15	7.06	6.97	6.91
7	6.54	6.47	6.31	6.16	6.07	5.99	5.91	5.82	5.74	5.68
8	5.73	5.67	5.52	5.36	5.28	5.20	5.12	5.03	4.95	4.89
9	5.18	5.11	4.96	4.81	4.73	4.65	4.57	4.48	4.40	4.34
10	4.77	4.71	4.56	4.41	4.33	4.25	4.17	4.08	4.00	3.94
11	4.46	4.40	4.25	4.10	4.02	3.94	3.86	3.78	3.69	3.63
12	4.22	4.16	4.01	3.86	3.78	3.70	3.62	3.54	3.45	3.39
13	4.02	3.96	3.82	3.66	3.59	3.51	3.43	3.34	3.25	3.19
14	3.86	3.80	3.66	3.51	3.43	3.35	3.27	3.18	3.09	3.03
15	3.73	3.67	3.52	3.37	3.29	3.21	3.13	3.05	2.96	2.90
16	3.62	3.55	3.41	3.26	3.18	3.10	3.02	2.93	2.84	2.78
17	3.52	3.46	3.31	3.16	3.08	3.00	2.92	2.83	2.75	2.68
18	3.43	3.37	3.23	3.08	3.00	2.92	2.84	2.75	2.66	2.59
19	3.36	3.30	3.15	3.00	2.92	2.84	2.76	2.67	2.58	2.52
20	3.29	3.23	3.09	2.94	2.86	2.78	2.69	2.61	2.52	2.45
21	3.24	3.17	3.03	2.88	2.80	2.72	2.64	2.55	2.46	2.39
22	3.18	3.12	2.98	2.83	2.75	2.67	2.58	2.50	2.40	2.34
23	3.14	3.07	2.93	2.78	2.70	2.62	2.54	2.45	2.35	2.29
24	3.09	3.03	2.89	2.74	2.66	2.58	2.49	2.40	2.31	2.24
25	3.06	2.99	2.85	2.70	2.62	2.54	2.45	2.36	2.27	2.20
26	3.02	2.96	2.81	2.66	2.58	2.50	2.42	2.33	2.23	2.16
27	2.99	2.93	2.78	2.63	2.55	2.47	2.38	2.29	2.20	2.13
28	2.96	2.90	2.75	2.60	2.52	2.44	2.35	2.26	2.17	2.10
29	2.93	2.87	2.73	2.57	2.49	2.41	2.33	2.23	2.14	2.07
30	2.91	2.84	2.70	2.55	2.47	2.39	2.30	2.21	2.11	2.04
40	2.73	2.66	2.52	2.37	2.29	2.20	2.11	2.02	1.92	1.84
60	2.56	2.50	2.35	2.20	2.12	2.03	1.94	1.84	1.73	1.64
120	2.40	2.34	2.19	2.03	1.95	1.86	1.76	1.66	1.53	1.43
400	2.29	2.23	2.08	1.92	1.84	1.75	1.64	1.53	1.39	1.26
∞	2.24	2.18	2.04	1.88	1.79	1.70	1.59	1.47	1.32	1.00

Table A4
Binomial

x	p: .10	.15	.20	.25	.30	.35	.40	.45	.50
					n=2				
0	0.8100	0.7225	0.6400	0.5625	0.4900	0.4225	0.3600	0.3025	0.2500
1	0.1800	0.2550	0.3200	0.3750	0.4200	0.4550	0.4800	0.4950	0.5000
2	0.0100	0.0225	0.0400	0.0625	0.0900	0.1225	0.1600	0.2025	0.2500
					n=3				
0	0.7290	0.6141	0.5120	0.4219	0.3430	0.2746	0.2160	0.1664	0.1250
1	0.2430	0.3251	0.3840	0.4219	0.4410	0.4436	0.4320	0.4084	0.3750
2	0.0270	0.0574	0.0960	0.1406	0.1890	0.2389	0.2880	0.3341	0.3750
3	0.0010	0.0034	0.0080	0.0156	0.0270	0.0429	0.0640	0.0911	0.1250
					n=4				
0	0.6561	0.5220	0.4096	0.3164	0.2401	0.1785	0.1296	0.0915	0.0625
1	0.2916	0.3685	0.4096	0.4219	0.4116	0.3845	0.3456	0.2995	0.2500
2	0.0486	0.0975	0.1536	0.2109	0.2646	0.3105	0.3456	0.3675	0.3750
3	0.0036	0.0115	0.0256	0.0469	0.0756	0.1115	0.1536	0.2005	0.2500
4	0.0001	0.0005	0.0016	0.0039	0.0081	0.0150	0.0256	0.0410	0.0625
					n=5				
0	0.5905	0.4437	0.3277	0.2373	0.1681	0.1160	0.0778	0.0503	0.0312
1	0.3280	0.3915	0.4096	0.3955	0.3602	0.3124	0.2592	0.2059	0.1562
2	0.0729	0.1382	0.2048	0.2637	0.3087	0.3364	0.3456	0.3369	0.3125
3	0.0081	0.0244	0.0512	0.0879	0.1323	0.1811	0.2304	0.2757	0.3125
4	0.0005	0.0022	0.0064	0.0146	0.0284	0.0488	0.0768	0.1128	0.1562
5	0.0000	0.0001	0.0003	0.0010	0.0024	0.0053	0.0102	0.0185	0.0312
					n=6				
0	0.5314	0.3771	0.2621	0.1780	0.1176	0.0754	0.0467	0.0277	0.0156
1	0.3543	0.3993	0.3932	0.3560	0.3025	0.2437	0.1866	0.1359	0.0937
2	0.0984	0.1762	0.2458	0.2966	0.3241	0.3280	0.3110	0.2780	0.2344
3	0.0146	0.0415	0.0819	0.1318	0.1852	0.2355	0.2765	0.3032	0.3125
4	0.0012	0.0055	0.0154	0.0330	0.0595	0.0951	0.1382	0.1861	0.2344
5	0.0001	0.0004	0.0015	0.0044	0.0102	0.0205	0.0369	0.0609	0.0937
6	0.0000	0.0000	0.0001	0.0002	0.0007	0.0018	0.0041	0.0083	0.0156
					n=7				
0	0.4783	0.3206	0.2097	0.1335	0.0824	0.0490	0.0280	0.0152	0.0078
1	0.3720	0.3960	0.3670	0.3115	0.2471	0.1848	0.1306	0.0872	0.0547
2	0.1240	0.2097	0.2753	0.3115	0.3177	0.2985	0.2613	0.2140	0.1641
3	0.0230	0.0617	0.1147	0.1730	0.2269	0.2679	0.2903	0.2918	0.2734
4	0.0026	0.0109	0.0287	0.0577	0.0972	0.1442	0.1935	0.2388	0.2734
5	0.0002	0.0012	0.0043	0.0115	0.0250	0.0466	0.0774	0.1172	0.1641
6	0.0000	0.0001	0.0004	0.0013	0.0036	0.0084	0.0172	0.0320	0.0547
7	0.0000	0.0000	0.0000	0.0001	0.0002	0.0006	0.0016	0.0037	0.0078

x	p: .10	.15	.20	.25	.30	.35	.40	.45	.50
					n=8				
0	0.4305	0.2725	0.1678	0.1001	0.0576	0.0319	0.0168	0.0084	0.0039
1	0.3826	0.3847	0.3355	0.2670	0.1977	0.1373	0.0896	0.0548	0.0312
2	0.1488	0.2376	0.2936	0.3115	0.2965	0.2587	0.2090	0.1569	0.1094
3	0.0331	0.0839	0.1468	0.2076	0.2541	0.2786	0.2787	0.2568	0.2187
4	0.0046	0.0185	0.0459	0.0865	0.1361	0.1875	0.2322	0.2627	0.2734
5	0.0004	0.0026	0.0092	0.0231	0.0467	0.0808	0.1239	0.1719	0.2187
6	0.0000	0.0002	0.0011	0.0038	0.0100	0.0217	0.0413	0.0703	0.1094
7	0.0000	0.0000	0.0001	0.0004	0.0012	0.0033	0.0079	0.0164	0.0312
8	0.0000	0.0000	0.0000	0.0000	0.0001	0.0002	0.0007	0.0017	0.0039
					n=9				
0	0.3874	0.2316	0.1342	0.0751	0.0404	0.0207	0.0101	0.0046	0.0020
1	0.3874	0.3679	0.3020	0.2253	0.1556	0.1004	0.0605	0.0339	0.0176
2	0.1722	0.2597	0.3020	0.3003	0.2668	0.2162	0.1612	0.1110	0.0703
3	0.0446	0.1069	0.1762	0.2336	0.2668	0.2716	0.2508	0.2119	0.1641
4	0.0074	0.0283	0.0661	0.1168	0.1715	0.2194	0.2508	0.2600	0.2461
5	0.0008	0.0050	0.0165	0.0389	0.0735	0.1181	0.1672	0.2128	0.2461
6	0.0001	0.0006	0.0028	0.0087	0.0210	0.0424	0.0743	0.1160	0.1641
7	0.0000	0.0000	0.0003	0.0012	0.0039	0.0098	0.0212	0.0407	0.0703
8	0.0000	0.0000	0.0000	0.0001	0.0004	0.0013	0.0035	0.0083	0.0176
9	0.0000	0.0000	0.0000	0.0000	0.0000	0.0001	0.0003	0.0008	0.0020
					n=10				
0	0.3487	0.1969	0.1074	0.0563	0.0282	0.0135	0.0060	0.0025	0.0010
1	0.3874	0.3474	0.2684	0.1877	0.1211	0.0725	0.0403	0.0207	0.0098
2	0.1937	0.2759	0.3020	0.2816	0.2335	0.1757	0.1209	0.0763	0.0439
3	0.0574	0.1298	0.2013	0.2503	0.2668	0.2522	0.2150	0.1665	0.1172
4	0.0112	0.0401	0.0881	0.1460	0.2001	0.2377	0.2508	0.2384	0.2051
5	0.0015	0.0085	0.0264	0.0584	0.1029	0.1536	0.2007	0.2340	0.2461
6	0.0001	0.0012	0.0055	0.0162	0.0368	0.0689	0.1115	0.1596	0.2051
7	0.0000	0.0001	0.0008	0.0031	0.0090	0.0212	0.0425	0.0746	0.1172
8	0.0000	0.0000	0.0001	0.0004	0.0014	0.0043	0.0106	0.0229	0.0439
9	0.0000	0.0000	0.0000	0.0000	0.0001	0.0005	0.0016	0.0042	0.0098
10	0.0000	0.0000	0.0000	0.0000	0.0000	0.0000	0.0001	0.0003	0.0010
					n=11				
0	0.3138	0.1673	0.0859	0.0422	0.0198	0.0088	0.0036	0.0014	0.0005
1	0.3835	0.3248	0.2362	0.1549	0.0932	0.0518	0.0266	0.0125	0.0054
2	0.2131	0.2866	0.2953	0.2581	0.1998	0.1395	0.0887	0.0513	0.0269
3	0.0710	0.1517	0.2215	0.2581	0.2568	0.2254	0.1774	0.1259	0.0806
4	0.0158	0.0536	0.1107	0.1721	0.2201	0.2428	0.2365	0.2060	0.1611
5	0.0025	0.0132	0.0388	0.0803	0.1321	0.1830	0.2207	0.2360	0.2256
6	0.0003	0.0023	0.0097	0.0268	0.0566	0.0985	0.1471	0.1931	0.2256
7	0.0000	0.0003	0.0017	0.0064	0.0173	0.0379	0.0701	0.1128	0.1611
8	0.0000	0.0000	0.0002	0.0011	0.0037	0.0102	0.0234	0.0462	0.0806
9	0.0000	0.0000	0.0000	0.0001	0.0005	0.0018	0.0052	0.0126	0.0269
10	0.0000	0.0000	0.0000	0.0000	0.0000	0.0002	0.0007	0.0021	0.0054
11	0.0000	0.0000	0.0000	0.0000	0.0000	0.0000	0.0000	0.0002	0.0005

x	p: .10	.15	.20	.25	.30	.35	.40	.45	.50
					n=12				
0	0.2824	0.1422	0.0687	0.0317	0.0138	0.0057	0.0022	0.0008	0.0002
1	0.3766	0.3012	0.2062	0.1267	0.0712	0.0368	0.0174	0.0075	0.0029
2	0.2301	0.2924	0.2835	0.2323	0.1678	0.1088	0.0639	0.0339	0.0161
3	0.0852	0.1720	0.2362	0.2581	0.2397	0.1954	0.1419	0.0923	0.0537
4	0.0213	0.0683	0.1329	0.1936	0.2311	0.2367	0.2128	0.1700	0.1208
5	0.0038	0.0193	0.0532	0.1032	0.1585	0.2039	0.2270	0.2225	0.1934
6	0.0005	0.0040	0.0155	0.0401	0.0792	0.1281	0.1766	0.2124	0.2256
7	0.0000	0.0006	0.0033	0.0115	0.0291	0.0591	0.1009	0.1489	0.1934
8	0.0000	0.0001	0.0005	0.0024	0.0078	0.0199	0.0420	0.0762	0.1208
9	0.0000	0.0000	0.0001	0.0004	0.0015	0.0048	0.0125	0.0277	0.0537
10	0.0000	0.0000	0.0000	0.0000	0.0002	0.0008	0.0025	0.0068	0.0161
11	0.0000	0.0000	0.0000	0.0000	0.0000	0.0001	0.0003	0.0010	0.0029
12	0.0000	0.0000	0.0000	0.0000	0.0000	0.0000	0.0000	0.0001	0.0002
					n=13				
0	0.2542	0.1209	0.0550	0.0238	0.0097	0.0037	0.0013	0.0004	0.0001
1	0.3672	0.2774	0.1787	0.1029	0.0540	0.0259	0.0113	0.0045	0.0016
2	0.2448	0.2937	0.2680	0.2059	0.1388	0.0836	0.0453	0.0220	0.0095
3	0.0997	0.1900	0.2457	0.2517	0.2181	0.1651	0.1107	0.0660	0.0349
4	0.0277	0.0838	0.1535	0.2097	0.2337	0.2222	0.1845	0.1350	0.0873
5	0.0055	0.0266	0.0691	0.1258	0.1803	0.2154	0.2214	0.1989	0.1571
6	0.0008	0.0063	0.0230	0.0559	0.1030	0.1546	0.1968	0.2169	0.2095
7	0.0001	0.0011	0.0058	0.0186	0.0442	0.0833	0.1312	0.1775	0.2095
8	0.0000	0.0001	0.0011	0.0047	0.0142	0.0336	0.0656	0.1089	0.1571
9	0.0000	0.0000	0.0001	0.0009	0.0034	0.0101	0.0243	0.0495	0.0873
10	0.0000	0.0000	0.0000	0.0001	0.0006	0.0022	0.0065	0.0162	0.0349
11	0.0000	0.0000	0.0000	0.0000	0.0001	0.0003	0.0012	0.0036	0.0095
12	0.0000	0.0000	0.0000	0.0000	0.0000	0.0000	0.0001	0.0005	0.0016
13	0.0000	0.0000	0.0000	0.0000	0.0000	0.0000	0.0000	0.0000	0.0001
					n=14				
0	0.2288	0.1028	0.0440	0.0178	0.0068	0.0024	0.0008	0.0002	0.0001
1	0.3559	0.2539	0.1539	0.0832	0.0407	0.0181	0.0073	0.0027	0.0009
2	0.2570	0.2912	0.2501	0.1802	0.1134	0.0634	0.0317	0.0141	0.0056
3	0.1142	0.2056	0.2501	0.2402	0.1943	0.1366	0.0845	0.0462	0.0222
4	0.0349	0.0998	0.1720	0.2202	0.2290	0.2022	0.1549	0.1040	0.0611
5	0.0078	0.0352	0.0860	0.1468	0.1963	0.2178	0.2066	0.1701	0.1222
6	0.0013	0.0093	0.0322	0.0734	0.1262	0.1759	0.2066	0.2088	0.1833
7	0.0002	0.0019	0.0092	0.0280	0.0618	0.1082	0.1574	0.1952	0.2095
8	0.0000	0.0003	0.0020	0.0082	0.0232	0.0510	0.0918	0.1398	0.1833
9	0.0000	0.0000	0.0003	0.0018	0.0066	0.0183	0.0408	0.0762	0.1222
10	0.0000	0.0000	0.0000	0.0003	0.0014	0.0049	0.0136	0.0312	0.0611
11	0.0000	0.0000	0.0000	0.0000	0.0002	0.0010	0.0033	0.0093	0.0222
12	0.0000	0.0000	0.0000	0.0000	0.0000	0.0001	0.0005	0.0019	0.0056
13	0.0000	0.0000	0.0000	0.0000	0.0000	0.0000	0.0001	0.0002	0.0009
14	0.0000	0.0000	0.0000	0.0000	0.0000	0.0000	0.0000	0.0000	0.0001

x	p: .10	.15	.20	.25	.30	.35	.40	.45	.50
					n=15				
0	0.2059	0.0874	0.0352	0.0134	0.0047	0.0016	0.0005	0.0001	0.0000
1	0.3432	0.2312	0.1319	0.0668	0.0305	0.0126	0.0047	0.0016	0.0005
2	0.2669	0.2856	0.2309	0.1559	0.0916	0.0476	0.0219	0.0090	0.0032
3	0.1285	0.2184	0.2501	0.2252	0.1700	0.1110	0.0634	0.0318	0.0139
4	0.0428	0.1156	0.1876	0.2252	0.2186	0.1792	0.1268	0.0780	0.0417
5	0.0105	0.0449	0.1032	0.1651	0.2061	0.2123	0.1859	0.1404	0.0916
6	0.0019	0.0132	0.0430	0.0917	0.1472	0.1906	0.2066	0.1914	0.1527
7	0.0003	0.0030	0.0138	0.0393	0.0811	0.1319	0.1771	0.2013	0.1964
8	0.0000	0.0005	0.0035	0.0131	0.0348	0.0710	0.1181	0.1647	0.1964
9	0.0000	0.0001	0.0007	0.0034	0.0116	0.0298	0.0612	0.1048	0.1527
10	0.0000	0.0000	0.0001	0.0007	0.0030	0.0096	0.0245	0.0515	0.0916
11	0.0000	0.0000	0.0000	0.0001	0.0006	0.0024	0.0074	0.0191	0.0417
12	0.0000	0.0000	0.0000	0.0000	0.0001	0.0004	0.0016	0.0052	0.0139
13	0.0000	0.0000	0.0000	0.0000	0.0000	0.0001	0.0003	0.0010	0.0032
14	0.0000	0.0000	0.0000	0.0000	0.0000	0.0000	0.0000	0.0001	0.0005
15	0.0000	0.0000	0.0000	0.0000	0.0000	0.0000	0.0000	0.0000	0.0000
					n=16				
0	0.1853	0.0743	0.0281	0.0100	0.0033	0.0010	0.0003	0.0001	0.0000
1	0.3294	0.2097	0.1126	0.0535	0.0228	0.0087	0.0030	0.0009	0.0002
2	0.2745	0.2775	0.2111	0.1336	0.0732	0.0353	0.0150	0.0056	0.0018
3	0.1423	0.2285	0.2463	0.2079	0.1465	0.0888	0.0468	0.0215	0.0085
4	0.0514	0.1311	0.2001	0.2252	0.2040	0.1553	0.1014	0.0572	0.0278
5	0.0137	0.0555	0.1201	0.1802	0.2099	0.2008	0.1623	0.1123	0.0667
6	0.0028	0.0180	0.0550	0.1101	0.1649	0.1982	0.1983	0.1684	0.1222
7	0.0004	0.0045	0.0197	0.0524	0.1010	0.1524	0.1889	0.1969	0.1746
8	0.0001	0.0009	0.0055	0.0197	0.0487	0.0923	0.1417	0.1812	0.1964
9	0.0000	0.0001	0.0012	0.0058	0.0185	0.0442	0.0840	0.1318	0.1746
10	0.0000	0.0000	0.0002	0.0014	0.0056	0.0167	0.0392	0.0755	0.1222
11	0.0000	0.0000	0.0000	0.0002	0.0013	0.0049	0.0142	0.0337	0.0667
12	0.0000	0.0000	0.0000	0.0000	0.0002	0.0011	0.0040	0.0115	0.0278
13	0.0000	0.0000	0.0000	0.0000	0.0000	0.0002	0.0008	0.0029	0.0085
14	0.0000	0.0000	0.0000	0.0000	0.0000	0.0000	0.0001	0.0005	0.0018
15	0.0000	0.0000	0.0000	0.0000	0.0000	0.0000	0.0000	0.0001	0.0002
16	0.0000	0.0000	0.0000	0.0000	0.0000	0.0000	0.0000	0.0000	0.0000

x	p: .10	.15	.20	.25	.30	.35	.40	.45	.50
					n=17				
0	0.1668	0.0631	0.0225	0.0075	0.0023	0.0007	0.0002	0.0000	0.0000
1	0.3150	0.1893	0.0957	0.0426	0.0169	0.0060	0.0019	0.0005	0.0001
2	0.2800	0.2673	0.1914	0.1136	0.0581	0.0260	0.0102	0.0035	0.0010
3	0.1556	0.2359	0.2393	0.1893	0.1245	0.0701	0.0341	0.0144	0.0052
4	0.0605	0.1457	0.2093	0.2209	0.1868	0.1320	0.0796	0.0411	0.0182
5	0.0175	0.0668	0.1361	0.1914	0.2081	0.1849	0.1379	0.0875	0.0472
6	0.0039	0.0236	0.0680	0.1276	0.1784	0.1991	0.1839	0.1432	0.0944
7	0.0007	0.0065	0.0267	0.0668	0.1201	0.1685	0.1927	0.1841	0.1484
8	0.0001	0.0014	0.0084	0.0279	0.0644	0.1134	0.1606	0.1883	0.1855
9	0.0000	0.0003	0.0021	0.0093	0.0276	0.0611	0.1070	0.1540	0.1855
10	0.0000	0.0000	0.0004	0.0025	0.0095	0.0263	0.0571	0.1008	0.1484
11	0.0000	0.0000	0.0001	0.0005	0.0026	0.0090	0.0242	0.0525	0.0944
12	0.0000	0.0000	0.0000	0.0001	0.0006	0.0024	0.0081	0.0215	0.0472
13	0.0000	0.0000	0.0000	0.0000	0.0001	0.0005	0.0021	0.0068	0.0182
14	0.0000	0.0000	0.0000	0.0000	0.0000	0.0001	0.0004	0.0016	0.0052
15	0.0000	0.0000	0.0000	0.0000	0.0000	0.0000	0.0001	0.0003	0.0010
16	0.0000	0.0000	0.0000	0.0000	0.0000	0.0000	0.0000	0.0000	0.0001
17	0.0000	0.0000	0.0000	0.0000	0.0000	0.0000	0.0000	0.0000	0.0000
					n=18				
0	0.1501	0.0536	0.0180	0.0056	0.0016	0.0004	0.0001	0.0000	0.0000
1	0.3002	0.1704	0.0811	0.0338	0.0126	0.0042	0.0012	0.0003	0.0001
2	0.2835	0.2556	0.1723	0.0958	0.0458	0.0190	0.0069	0.0022	0.0006
3	0.1680	0.2406	0.2297	0.1704	0.1046	0.0547	0.0246	0.0095	0.0031
4	0.0700	0.1592	0.2153	0.2130	0.1681	0.1104	0.0614	0.0291	0.0117
5	0.0218	0.0787	0.1507	0.1988	0.2017	0.1664	0.1146	0.0666	0.0327
6	0.0052	0.0301	0.0816	0.1436	0.1873	0.1941	0.1655	0.1181	0.0708
7	0.0010	0.0091	0.0350	0.0820	0.1376	0.1792	0.1892	0.1657	0.1214
8	0.0002	0.0022	0.0120	0.0376	0.0811	0.1327	0.1734	0.1864	0.1669
9	0.0000	0.0004	0.0033	0.0139	0.0386	0.0794	0.1284	0.1694	0.1855
10	0.0000	0.0001	0.0008	0.0042	0.0149	0.0385	0.0771	0.1248	0.1669
11	0.0000	0.0000	0.0001	0.0010	0.0046	0.0151	0.0374	0.0742	0.1214
12	0.0000	0.0000	0.0000	0.0002	0.0012	0.0047	0.0145	0.0354	0.0708
13	0.0000	0.0000	0.0000	0.0000	0.0002	0.0012	0.0045	0.0134	0.0327
14	0.0000	0.0000	0.0000	0.0000	0.0000	0.0002	0.0011	0.0039	0.0117
15	0.0000	0.0000	0.0000	0.0000	0.0000	0.0000	0.0002	0.0009	0.0031
16	0.0000	0.0000	0.0000	0.0000	0.0000	0.0000	0.0000	0.0001	0.0006
17	0.0000	0.0000	0.0000	0.0000	0.0000	0.0000	0.0000	0.0000	0.0001
18	0.0000	0.0000	0.0000	0.0000	0.0000	0.0000	0.0000	0.0000	0.0000

x	p: .10	.15	.20	.25	.30	.35	.40	.45	.50
					n=19				
0	0.1351	0.0456	0.0144	0.0042	0.0011	0.0003	0.0001	0.0000	0.0000
1	0.2852	0.1529	0.0685	0.0268	0.0093	0.0029	0.0008	0.0002	0.0000
2	0.2852	0.2428	0.1540	0.0803	0.0358	0.0138	0.0046	0.0013	0.0003
3	0.1796	0.2428	0.2182	0.1517	0.0869	0.0422	0.0175	0.0062	0.0018
4	0.0798	0.1714	0.2182	0.2023	0.1491	0.0909	0.0467	0.0203	0.0074
5	0.0266	0.0907	0.1636	0.2023	0.1916	0.1468	0.0933	0.0497	0.0222
6	0.0069	0.0374	0.0955	0.1574	0.1916	0.1844	0.1451	0.0949	0.0518
7	0.0014	0.0122	0.0443	0.0974	0.1525	0.1844	0.1797	0.1443	0.0961
8	0.0002	0.0032	0.0166	0.0487	0.0981	0.1489	0.1797	0.1771	0.1442
9	0.0000	0.0007	0.0051	0.0198	0.0514	0.0980	0.1464	0.1771	0.1762
10	0.0000	0.0001	0.0013	0.0066	0.0220	0.0528	0.0976	0.1449	0.1762
11	0.0000	0.0000	0.0003	0.0018	0.0077	0.0233	0.0532	0.0970	0.1442
12	0.0000	0.0000	0.0000	0.0004	0.0022	0.0083	0.0237	0.0529	0.0961
13	0.0000	0.0000	0.0000	0.0001	0.0005	0.0024	0.0085	0.0233	0.0518
14	0.0000	0.0000	0.0000	0.0000	0.0001	0.0006	0.0024	0.0082	0.0222
15	0.0000	0.0000	0.0000	0.0000	0.0000	0.0001	0.0005	0.0022	0.0074
16	0.0000	0.0000	0.0000	0.0000	0.0000	0.0000	0.0001	0.0005	0.0018
17	0.0000	0.0000	0.0000	0.0000	0.0000	0.0000	0.0000	0.0001	0.0003
18	0.0000	0.0000	0.0000	0.0000	0.0000	0.0000	0.0000	0.0000	0.0000
19	0.0000	0.0000	0.0000	0.0000	0.0000	0.0000	0.0000	0.0000	0.0000

x	p: .10	.15	.20	.25	.30	.35	.40	.45	.50
					n=20				
0	0.1216	0.0388	0.0115	0.0032	0.0008	0.0002	0.0000	0.0000	0.0000
1	0.2702	0.1368	0.0576	0.0211	0.0068	0.0020	0.0005	0.0001	0.0000
2	0.2852	0.2293	0.1369	0.0669	0.0278	0.0100	0.0031	0.0008	0.0002
3	0.1901	0.2428	0.2054	0.1339	0.0716	0.0323	0.0123	0.0040	0.0011
4	0.0898	0.1821	0.2182	0.1897	0.1304	0.0738	0.0350	0.0139	0.0046
5	0.0319	0.1028	0.1746	0.2023	0.1789	0.1272	0.0746	0.0365	0.0148
6	0.0089	0.0454	0.1091	0.1686	0.1916	0.1712	0.1244	0.0746	0.0370
7	0.0020	0.0160	0.0545	0.1124	0.1643	0.1844	0.1659	0.1221	0.0739
8	0.0004	0.0046	0.0222	0.0609	0.1144	0.1614	0.1797	0.1623	0.1201
9	0.0001	0.0011	0.0074	0.0271	0.0654	0.1158	0.1597	0.1771	0.1602
10	0.0000	0.0002	0.0020	0.0099	0.0308	0.0686	0.1171	0.1593	0.1762
11	0.0000	0.0000	0.0005	0.0030	0.0120	0.0336	0.0710	0.1185	0.1602
12	0.0000	0.0000	0.0001	0.0008	0.0039	0.0136	0.0355	0.0727	0.1201
13	0.0000	0.0000	0.0000	0.0002	0.0010	0.0045	0.0146	0.0366	0.0739
14	0.0000	0.0000	0.0000	0.0000	0.0002	0.0012	0.0049	0.0150	0.0370
15	0.0000	0.0000	0.0000	0.0000	0.0000	0.0003	0.0013	0.0049	0.0148
16	0.0000	0.0000	0.0000	0.0000	0.0000	0.0000	0.0003	0.0013	0.0046
17	0.0000	0.0000	0.0000	0.0000	0.0000	0.0000	0.0000	0.0002	0.0011
18	0.0000	0.0000	0.0000	0.0000	0.0000	0.0000	0.0000	0.0000	0.0002
19	0.0000	0.0000	0.0000	0.0000	0.0000	0.0000	0.0000	0.0000	0.0000
20	0.0000	0.0000	0.0000	0.0000	0.0000	0.0000	0.0000	0.0000	0.0000

Table A5

Values of $\delta/\surd d$ for Controlling power in Chapman's Procedure

ν_1	ν_2	$1-\beta$:	$\alpha=.05$		$\alpha=.01$	
			.8	.9	.8	.9
5	5		5.06	5.77	6.74	7.67
6	5		4.94	5.68	6.59	7.45
6	6		4.82	5.59	6.32	7.07
7	5		4.88	5.59	6.45	7.25
7	6		4.77	5.50	6.20	6.90
7	7		4.66	5.42	6.09	6.90
8	5		4.82	5.59	6.32	7.07
8	6		4.71	5.42	6.09	6.90
8	7		4.61	5.35	5.98	6.74
8	8		4.56	5.27	5.87	6.59
9	5		4.77	5.50	6.32	7.07
9	6		4.66	5.42	6.09	6.74
9	7		4.56	5.27	5.87	6.59
9	8		4.52	5.27	5.77	6.59
9	9		4.52	5.20	5.77	6.45
10	5		4.71	5.50	6.20	7.07
10	6		4.61	5.35	5.98	6.74
10	7		4.56	5.27	5.87	6.59
10	8		4.52	5.20	5.77	6.45
10	9		4.52	5.20	5.68	6.45
10	10		4.52	5.13	5.68	6.32
12	5		4.71	5.42	6.20	6.90
12	6		4.56	5.27	5.98	6.74
12	7		4.52	5.20	5.77	6.45
12	8		4.52	5.20	5.68	6.45
12	9		4.52	5.13	4.30	6.32
12	10		4.52	5.06	5.59	6.32
12	12		4.52	5.06	5.50	6.20
15	5		4.66	5.35	6.09	6.90
15	6		4.56	5.27	5.87	6.59
15	7		4.52	5.20	5.77	6.45
15	8		4.52	5.13	5.59	6.32
15	9		4.52	5.06	5.59	6.20
15	10		4.52	5.06	5.50	6.20
15	12		4.52	5.00	5.42	6.09
15	15		4.52	4.94	5.35	5.98
20	5		4.61	5.35	6.09	6.74
20	6		4.52	5.20	5.87	6.59

Table A5 (continued)

20	7	4.52	5.13	5.68	6.32
20	8	4.52	5.06	5.59	6.32
20	9	4.52	5.00	5.50	6.20
20	10	4.52	5.00	5.42	6.09
20	12	4.52	4.94	5.35	6.09
20	15	4.52	4.88	5.27	5.98
20	20	4.52	4.88	5.20	5.87
30	5	4.56	5.27	5.98	6.74
30	6	4.52	5.20	5.77	6.45
30	7	4.52	5.06	5.59	6.32
30	8	4.52	5.00	5.50	6.20
30	9	4.52	5.00	5.42	6.09
30	10	4.52	4.94	5.35	6.09
30	12	4.52	4.88	5.27	5.98
30	15	4.52	4.88	5.20	5.87
30	20	4.52	4.82	5.13	5.77
30	30	4.52	4.77	5.06	5.77
40	5	4.56	5.27	5.98	6.74
40	6	4.52	5.13	5.77	6.45
40	7	4.52	5.06	5.59	6.32
40	8	4.52	5.00	5.50	6.20
40	9	4.52	4.94	5.42	6.09
40	10	4.52	4.94	5.35	5.98
40	12	4.52	4.88	5.27	5.98
40	15	4.52	4.82	5.20	5.87
40	20	4.52	4.77	5.13	5.77
40	30	4.52	4.77	5.06	5.68
40	40	4.52	4.71	5.00	5.68
60	5	4.56	5.27	5.98	6.74
60	6	4.52	5.13	5.68	6.45
60	7	4.52	5.06	5.59	6.20
60	8	4.52	5.00	5.42	6.20
60	9	4.52	4.94	5.35	6.09
60	10	4.52	4.94	5.35	5.98
60	12	4.52	4.88	5.27	5.87
60	15	4.52	4.82	5.13	5.87
60	20	4.52	4.77	5.06	5.77
60	30	4.52	4.71	5.00	5.68
60	40	4.52	4.71	5.00	5.68
60	60	4.52	4.66	5.00	5.59

Table A5 (continued)

120	5	4.52	5.20	5.98	6.74
120	6	4.52	5.13	5.68	6.45
120	7	4.52	5.00	5.50	6.20
120	8	4.52	5.00	5.42	6.09
120	10	4.52	4.88	5.27	5.98
120	12	4.52	4.82	5.20	5.87
120	15	4.52	4.82	5.13	5.77
120	20	4.52	4.77	5.06	5.68
120	30	4.52	4.71	5.00	5.68
120	40	4.52	4.66	5.00	5.59
120	60	4.52	4.66	4.94	5.59
120	120	4.52	4.66	4.94	5.59

Table A6
Critical Values for $\tilde{F}$

	J=3		J=4		J=5		J=6	
n α:	.05	.01	.05	.01	.05	.01	.05	.01
11	7.78	13.37	10.29	16.81	12.59	19.86	14.76	22.66
13	7.46	12.55	9.85	15.71	12.04	18.50	14.10	21.08
15	7.23	11.97	9.53	14.94	11.63	17.57	13.62	20.00
17	7.06	11.56	9.29	14.39	11.34	16.91	13.26	19.23
19	6.93	11.25	9.11	13.98	11.11	16.42	12.99	18.67
21	6.83	11.01	8.97	13.67	10.93	16.04	12.78	18.24
26	6.65	10.60	8.72	13.14	10.62	15.41	12.41	17.51
31	6.53	10.34	8.56	12.80	10.41	15.01	12.16	17.05
41	6.39	10.04	8.36	12.41	10.17	14.53	11.87	16.51
61	6.25	9.75	8.17	12.03	9.93	14.09	11.60	16.01
81	6.18	9.61	8.08	11.85	9.82	13.88	11.46	15.77
101	6.14	9.52	8.03	11.75	9.75	13.75	11.38	15.63
∞	5.99	9.21	7.82	11.35	9.49	13.28	11.07	15.09

Reprinted, with permission, from "Percentage points of a quadratic form in Student t variates" by T. Bishop, E. Dudewicz, J. Juritz & M Stevens, Biometrika, 1978, 65, 435-439.

Table A7
Dunn's Procedure (The Bonferroni t-test)
For C Comparisons and an Experimentwise Type I Error=α

α=.05

Degrees of Freedom ν

C \	6	8	10	12	15	20	24	30	40	60	120	∞
2	2.97	2.75	2.63	2.56	2.49	2.42	2.39	2.36	2.33	2.30	2.27	2.24
3	3.29	3.02	2.87	2.78	2.69	2.61	2.57	2.54	2.50	2.46	2.43	2.39
4	3.52	3.21	3.04	2.93	2.84	2.74	2.70	2.66	2.62	2.58	2.54	2.50
5	3.71	3.36	3.17	3.05	2.95	2.85	2.80	2.75	2.70	2.66	2.62	2.58
6	3.86	3.48	3.28	3.15	3.04	2.93	2.88	2.82	2.78	2.73	2.68	2.64
7	4.00	3.58	3.37	3.24	3.11	3.00	2.94	2.89	2.84	2.79	2.74	2.69
8	4.12	3.68	3.45	3.31	3.18	3.06	3.00	2.94	2.89	2.83	2.78	2.74
9	4.22	3.76	3.52	3.37	3.23	3.11	3.05	2.99	2.93	2.88	2.82	2.77
10	4.32	3.83	3.58	3.43	3.29	3.15	3.09	3.03	2.97	2.91	2.86	2.81
15	4.70	4.12	3.83	3.65	3.48	3.33	3.26	3.19	3.12	3.06	3.00	2.94
20	4.98	4.33	4.00	3.81	3.62	3.46	3.38	3.30	3.23	3.16	3.09	3.02
25	5.21	4.50	4.14	3.93	3.73	3.55	3.47	3.39	3.31	3.23	3.16	3.09
30	5.40	4.64	4.26	4.03	3.82	3.63	3.54	3.45	3.37	3.29	3.22	3.15
35	5.56	4.76	4.36	4.12	3.90	3.70	3.60	3.51	3.43	3.34	3.26	3.19
40	5.71	4.86	4.44	4.19	3.96	3.75	3.66	3.56	3.47	3.39	3.31	3.23
45	5.84	4.96	4.52	4.26	4.02	3.80	3.70	3.61	3.51	3.43	3.34	3.26
50	5.96	5.04	4.59	4.32	4.07	3.85	3.75	3.65	3.55	3.46	3.37	3.29
100	6.79	5.62	5.05	4.72	4.42	4.15	4.02	3.90	3.79	3.68	3.58	3.48
250	8.02	6.44	5.69	5.26	4.88	4.54	4.38	4.23	4.09	3.96	3.84	3.72

α=.01

C \	6	8	10	12	15	20	24	30	40	60	120	∞
2	4.32	3.83	3.58	3.43	3.29	3.15	3.09	3.03	2.97	2.91	2.86	2.81
3	4.70	4.12	3.83	3.65	3.48	3.33	3.26	3.19	3.12	3.06	3.00	2.94
4	4.98	4.33	4.00	3.81	3.62	3.46	3.38	3.30	3.23	3.16	3.09	3.02
5	5.21	4.50	4.14	3.93	3.73	3.55	3.47	3.39	3.31	3.23	3.16	3.09
6	5.40	4.64	4.26	4.03	3.82	3.63	3.54	3.45	3.37	3.29	3.22	3.15
7	5.56	4.76	4.36	4.12	3.90	3.70	3.60	3.51	3.43	3.34	3.26	3.19
8	5.71	4.86	4.44	4.19	3.96	3.75	3.66	3.56	3.47	3.39	3.31	3.23
9	5.84	4.96	4.52	4.26	4.02	3.80	3.70	3.61	3.51	3.43	3.34	3.26
10	5.96	5.04	4.59	4.32	4.07	3.85	3.75	3.65	3.55	3.46	3.37	3.29
15	6.43	5.37	4.85	4.55	4.27	4.02	3.91	3.80	3.69	3.59	3.49	3.40
20	6.79	5.62	5.05	4.72	4.42	4.15	4.02	3.90	3.79	3.68	3.58	3.48
25	7.07	5.81	5.20	4.85	4.53	4.24	4.11	3.98	3.86	3.75	3.64	3.54
30	7.31	5.97	5.33	4.96	4.62	4.32	4.18	4.05	3.92	3.81	3.69	3.59
35	7.52	6.11	5.44	5.05	4.70	4.39	4.24	4.11	3.98	3.85	3.74	3.63

40	7.71	6.23	5.53	5.13	4.77	4.44	4.29	4.15	4.02	3.89	3.78	3.66
45	7.87	6.34	5.62	5.20	4.83	4.49	4.34	4.20	4.06	3.93	3.81	3.69
50	8.02	6.44	5.69	5.26	4.88	4.54	4.38	4.23	4.09	3.96	3.84	3.72
100	9.08	7.12	6.21	5.69	5.24	4.84	4.65	4.48	4.32	4.17	4.03	3.89
250	10.67	8.10	6.94	6.29	5.73	5.24	5.02	4.81	4.62	4.43	4.27	4.11

These critical values were obtained with IMSL subroutine MDSTI which has a reported accuracy of five decimal places.

Table A8
Orthogonal Contrasts

J=3

Degree of
Polynomial

| 1 | -1 | 0 | 1 |
| 2 | 1 | -2 | 1 |

J=4

1	-3	-1	1	3
2	1	-1	-1	1
3	-1	3	-3	1

J=5

1	-2	-1	0	1	2
2	2	-1	-2	-1	2
3	-1	2	0	-2	1
4	1	-4	6	-4	1

J=6

1	-5	-3	-1	1	3	5
2	5	-1	-4	-4	-1	5
3	-5	7	4	-4	-7	5
4	1	-3	2	2	-3	1
5	-1	5	-10	10	-5	1

J=7

1	-3	-2	-1	0	1	2	3
2	5	0	-3	-4	-3	0	5
3	-1	1	1	0	-1	-1	1
4	3	-7	1	6	1	-7	3
5	-1	4	-5	0	5	-4	1
6	1	-6	15	-20	15	-6	1

J=8

1	-7	-5	-3	-1	1	3	5	7
2	7	1	-3	-5	-5	-3	1	7
3	-7	5	7	3	-3	-7	-5	7
4	7	-13	-3	9	9	-3	-13	7
5	-7	23	-17	-15	15	17	-23	7
6	1	-5	9	-5	-5	9	-5	1

Table A9
Studentized Range Statistic, q, for α=.05

ν	J: 2	3	4	5	6	7	8	9	10	11
3	4.50	5.91	6.82	7.50	8.04	8.48	8.85	9.18	9.46	9.72
4	3.93	5.04	5.76	6.29	6.71	7.05	7.35	7.60	7.83	8.03
5	3.64	4.60	5.22	5.68	6.04	6.33	6.59	6.81	6.99	7.17
6	3.47	4.34	4.89	5.31	5.63	5.89	6.13	6.32	6.49	6.65
7	3.35	4.17	4.69	5.07	5.36	5.61	5.82	5.99	6.16	6.30
8	3.27	4.05	4.53	4.89	5.17	5.39	5.59	5.77	5.92	6.06
9	3.19	3.95	4.42	4.76	5.03	5.25	5.44	5.59	5.74	5.87
10	3.16	3.88	4.33	4.66	4.92	5.13	5.31	5.47	5.59	5.73
11	3.12	3.82	4.26	4.58	4.83	5.03	5.21	5.36	5.49	5.61
12	3.09	3.78	4.19	4.51	4.76	4.95	5.12	5.27	5.39	5.52
13	3.06	3.73	4.15	4.45	4.69	4.88	5.05	5.19	5.32	5.43
14	3.03	3.70	4.11	4.41	4.64	4.83	4.99	5.13	5.25	5.36
15	3.01	3.67	4.08	4.37	4.59	4.78	4.94	5.08	5.20	5.31
16	3.00	3.65	4.05	4.33	4.56	4.74	4.90	5.03	5.15	5.26
17	2.98	3.63	4.02	4.30	4.52	4.70	4.86	4.99	5.11	5.21
18	2.97	3.61	4.00	4.28	4.49	4.67	4.83	4.96	5.07	5.17
19	2.96	3.59	3.98	4.25	4.47	4.65	4.79	4.93	5.04	5.14
20	2.95	3.58	3.96	4.23	4.45	4.62	4.77	4.90	5.01	5.11
24	2.92	3.53	3.90	4.17	4.37	4.54	4.68	4.81	4.92	5.01
30	2.89	3.49	3.85	4.10	4.30	4.46	4.60	4.72	4.82	4.92
40	2.86	3.44	3.79	4.04	4.23	4.39	4.52	4.63	4.73	4.82
60	2.83	3.40	3.74	3.98	4.16	4.31	4.44	4.55	4.65	4.73
120	2.80	3.36	3.68	3.92	4.10	4.24	4.36	4.47	4.56	4.64
∞	2.77	3.31	3.63	3.86	4.03	4.17	4.29	4.39	4.47	4.55

Table A9 (continued)

					α=.01					
2	14.0	19.0	22.3	24.7	26.6	28.2	29.5	30.7	31.7	32.6
3	8.26	10.6	12.2	13.3	14.2	15.0	15.6	16.2	16.7	17.8
4	6.51	8.12	9.17	9.96	10.6	11.1	11.5	11.9	12.3	12.6
5	5.71	6.98	7.81	8.43	8.92	9.33	9.67	9.98	10.24	10.48
6	5.25	6.34	7.04	7.56	7.98	8.32	8.62	8.87	9.09	9.30
7	4.95	5.92	6.55	7.01	7.38	7.68	7.94	8.17	8.37	8.55
8	4.75	5.64	6.21	6.63	6.96	7.24	7.48	7.69	7.87	8.03
9	4.59	5.43	5.96	6.35	6.66	6.92	7.14	7.33	7.49	7.65
10	4.49	5.28	5.77	6.14	6.43	6.67	6.88	7.06	7.22	7.36
11	4.39	5.15	5.63	5.98	6.25	6.48	6.68	6.85	6.99	7.13
12	4.32	5.05	5.51	5.84	6.11	6.33	6.51	6.67	6.82	6.94
13	4.26	4.97	5.41	5.73	5.99	6.19	6.38	6.53	6.67	6.79
14	4.21	4.89	5.32	5.63	5.88	6.08	6.26	6.41	6.54	6.66
15	4.17	4.84	5.25	5.56	5.80	5.99	6.16	6.31	6.44	6.55
16	4.13	4.79	5.19	5.49	5.72	5.92	6.08	6.22	6.35	6.46
17	4.10	4.74	5.14	5.43	5.66	5.85	6.01	6.15	6.27	6.38
18	4.07	4.70	5.09	5.38	5.60	5.79	5.94	6.08	6.20	6.31
19	4.05	4.67	5.05	5.33	5.55	5.73	5.89	6.02	6.14	6.25
20	4.02	4.64	5.02	5.29	5.51	5.69	5.84	5.97	6.09	6.19
24	3.96	4.55	4.91	5.17	5.37	5.54	5.69	5.81	5.92	6.02
30	3.89	4.45	4.80	5.05	5.24	5.40	5.54	5.65	5.76	5.85
40	3.82	4.37	4.69	4.93	5.10	5.26	5.39	5.49	5.60	5.69
60	3.76	4.28	4.59	4.82	4.99	5.13	5.25	5.36	5.45	5.53
120	3.70	4.20	4.50	4.71	4.87	5.01	5.12	5.21	5.30	5.37
∞	3.64	4.12	4.40	4.60	4.76	4.88	4.99	5.08	5.16	5.23

The values in this table were computed with the IBM SSP subroutines DQH32, which performs 32-point Gauss-Hermite numerical quadrature, and DQG32, which performs 32-point Gaussian quadrature.

Table A10

Studentized Maximum Modulus Distribution

(C is the number of comparisons being performed.)

ν	α	C: 2	3	4	5	6	7	8	9	10
2	.05	5.57	6.34	6.89	7.31	7.65	7.93	8.17	8.83	8.57
	.01	12.73	14.44	15.65	16.59	17.35	17.99	18.53	19.01	19.43
3	.05	3.96	4.43	4.76	5.02	5.23	5.41	5.56	5.69	5.81
	.01	7.13	7.91	8.48	8.92	9.28	9.58	9.84	10.06	10.27
4	.05	3.38	3.74	4.01	4.20	4.37	4.50	4.62	4.72	4.82
	.01	5.46	5.99	6.36	6.66	6.89	7.09	7.27	7.43	7.57
5	.05	3.09	3.39	3.62	3.79	3.93	4.04	4.14	4.23	4.31
	.01	4.70	5.11	5.39	5.63	5.81	5.97	6.11	6.23	6.33
6	.05	2.92	3.19	3.39	3.54	3.66	3.77	3.86	3.94	4.01
	.01	4.27	4.61	4.85	5.05	5.20	5.33	5.45	5.55	5.64
7	.05	2.80	3.06	3.24	3.38	3.49	3.59	3.67	3.74	3.80
	.01	3.99	4.29	4.51	4.68	4.81	4.93	5.03	5.12	5.19
8	.05	2.72	2.96	3.13	3.26	3.36	3.45	3.53	3.60	3.66
	.01	3.81	4.08	4.27	4.42	4.55	4.65	4.74	4.82	4.89
9	.05	2.66	2.89	3.05	3.17	3.27	3.36	3.43	3.49	3.55
	.01	3.67	3.92	4.10	4.24	4.35	4.45	4.53	4.61	4.67
10	.05	2.61	2.83	2.98	3.10	3.19	3.28	3.35	3.41	3.47
	.01	3.57	3.80	3.97	4.09	4.20	4.29	4.37	4.44	4.50
11	.05	2.57	2.78	2.93	3.05	3.14	3.22	3.29	3.35	3.40
	.01	3.48	3.71	3.87	3.99	4.09	4.17	4.25	4.31	4.37
12	.05	2.54	2.75	2.89	3.01	3.09	3.17	3.24	3.29	3.35
	.01	3.42	3.63	3.78	3.89	3.99	4.08	4.15	4.21	4.26
14	.05	2.49	2.69	2.83	2.94	3.02	3.09	3.16	3.21	3.26
	.01	3.32	3.52	3.66	3.77	3.85	3.93	3.99	4.05	4.10
16	.05	2.46	2.65	2.78	2.89	2.97	3.04	3.09	3.15	3.19
	.01	3.25	3.43	3.57	3.67	3.75	3.82	3.88	3.94	3.99
18	.05	2.43	2.62	2.75	2.85	2.93	2.99	3.05	3.11	3.15
	.01	3.19	3.37	3.49	3.59	3.68	3.74	3.80	3.85	3.89
20	.05	2.41	2.59	2.72	2.82	2.89	2.96	3.02	3.07	3.11
	.01	3.15	3.32	3.45	3.54	3.62	3.68	3.74	3.79	3.83
24	.05	2.38	2.56	2.68	2.77	2.85	2.91	2.97	3.02	3.06
	.01	3.09	3.25	3.37	3.46	3.53	3.59	3.64	3.69	3.73
30	.05	2.35	2.52	2.64	2.73	2.80	2.87	2.92	2.96	3.01
	.01	3.03	3.18	3.29	3.38	3.45	3.50	3.55	3.59	3.64
40	.05	2.32	2.49	2.60	2.69	2.76	2.82	2.87	2.91	2.95
	.01	2.97	3.12	3.22	3.30	3.37	3.42	3.47	3.51	3.55
60	.05	2.29	2.45	2.56	2.65	2.72	2.77	2.82	2.86	2.90
	.01	2.91	3.06	3.15	3.23	3.29	3.34	3.38	3.42	3.46
∞	.05	2.24	2.39	2.49	2.57	2.63	2.68	2.73	2.77	2.79
	.01	2.81	2.93	3.02	3.09	3.14	3.19	3.23	3.26	3.29

Table A10 (continued)

ν	α	C: 11	12	13	14	15	16	17	18	19
2	.05	8.74	8.89	9.03	9.16	9.28	9.39	9.49	9.59	9.68
	.01	19.81	20.15	20.46	20.75	20.99	20.99	20.99	20.99	20.99
3	.05	5.92	6.01	6.10	6.18	6.26	6.33	6.39	6.45	6.51
	.01	10.45	10.61	10.76	10.90	11.03	11.15	11.26	11.37	11.47
4	.05	4.89	4.97	5.04	5.11	5.17	5.22	5.27	5.32	5.37
	.01	7.69	7.80	7.91	8.01	8.09	8.17	8.25	8.32	8.39
5	.05	4.38	4.45	4.51	4.56	4.61	4.66	4.70	4.74	4.78
	.01	6.43	6.52	6.59	6.67	6.74	6.81	6.87	6.93	6.98
6	.05	4.07	4.13	4.18	4.23	4.28	4.32	4.36	4.39	4.43
	.01	5.72	5.79	5.86	5.93	5.99	6.04	6.09	6.14	6.18
7	.05	3.86	3.92	3.96	4.01	4.05	4.09	4.13	4.16	4.19
	.01	5.27	5.33	5.39	5.45	5.50	5.55	5.59	5.64	5.68
8	.05	3.71	3.76	3.81	3.85	3.89	3.93	3.96	3.99	4.02
	.01	4.96	5.02	5.07	5.12	5.17	5.21	5.25	5.29	5.33
9	.05	3.60	3.65	3.69	3.73	3.77	3.80	3.84	3.87	3.89
	.01	4.73	4.79	4.84	4.88	4.92	4.96	5.01	5.04	5.07
10	.05	3.52	3.56	3.60	3.64	3.68	3.71	3.74	3.77	3.79
	.01	4.56	4.61	4.66	4.69	4.74	4.78	4.81	4.84	4.88
11	.05	3.45	3.49	3.53	3.57	3.60	3.63	3.66	3.69	3.72
	.01	4.42	4.47	4.51	4.55	4.59	4.63	4.66	4.69	4.72
12	.05	3.39	3.43	3.47	3.51	3.54	3.57	3.60	3.63	3.65
	.01	4.31	4.36	4.40	4.44	4.48	4.51	4.54	4.57	4.59
14	.05	3.30	3.34	3.38	3.41	3.45	3.48	3.50	3.53	3.55
	.01	4.15	4.19	4.23	4.26	4.29	4.33	4.36	4.39	4.41
16	.05	3.24	3.28	3.31	3.35	3.38	3.40	3.43	3.46	3.48
	.01	4.03	4.07	4.11	4.14	4.17	4.19	4.23	4.25	4.28
18	.05	3.19	3.23	3.26	3.29	3.32	3.35	3.38	3.40	3.42
	.01	3.94	3.98	4.01	4.04	4.07	4.10	4.13	4.15	4.18
20	.05	3.15	3.19	3.22	3.25	3.28	3.31	3.33	3.36	3.38
	.01	3.87	3.91	3.94	3.97	3.99	4.03	4.05	4.07	4.09
24	.05	3.09	3.13	3.16	3.19	3.22	3.25	3.27	3.29	3.31
	.01	3.77	3.80	3.83	3.86	3.89	3.91	3.94	3.96	3.98
30	.05	3.04	3.07	3.11	3.13	3.16	3.18	3.21	3.23	3.25
	.01	3.67	3.70	3.73	3.76	3.78	3.81	3.83	3.85	3.87
40	.05	2.99	3.02	3.05	3.08	3.09	3.12	3.14	3.17	3.18
	.01	3.58	3.61	3.64	3.66	3.68	3.71	3.73	3.75	3.76
60	.05	2.93	2.96	2.99	3.02	3.04	3.06	3.08	3.10	3.12
	.01	3.49	3.51	3.54	3.56	3.59	3.61	3.63	3.64	3.66
∞	.05	2.83	2.86	2.88	2.91	2.93	2.95	2.97	2.98	3.01
	.01	3.32	3.34	3.36	3.38	3.40	3.42	3.44	3.45	3.47

Table A10 (continued)

ν	α	C: 20	21	22	23	24	25	26	27	28
2	.05	9.77	9.85	9.92	10.00	10.07	10.13	10.20	10.26	10.32
	.01	22.11	22.29	22.46	22.63	22.78	22.93	23.08	23.21	23.35
3	.05	6.57	6.62	6.67	6.71	6.76	6.80	6.84	6.88	6.92
	.01	11.56	11.65	11.74	11.82	11.89	11.97	12.07	12.11	12.17
4	.05	5.41	5.45	5.49	5.52	5.56	5.59	5.63	5.66	5.69
	.01	8.45	8.51	8.57	8.63	8.68	8.73	8.78	8.83	8.87
5	.05	4.82	4.85	4.89	4.92	4.95	4.98	5.00	5.03	5.06
	.01	7.03	7.08	7.13	7.17	7.21	7.25	7.29	7.33	7.36
6	.05	4.46	4.49	4.52	4.55	4.58	4.60	4.63	4.65	4.68
	.01	6.23	6.27	6.31	6.34	6.38	6.41	6.45	6.48	6.51
7	.05	4.22	4.25	4.28	4.31	4.33	4.35	4.38	4.39	4.42
	.01	5.72	5.75	5.79	5.82	5.85	5.88	5.91	5.94	5.96
8	.05	4.05	4.08	4.10	4.13	4.15	4.18	4.19	4.22	4.24
	.01	5.36	5.39	5.43	5.45	5.48	5.51	5.54	5.56	5.59
9	.05	3.92	3.95	3.97	3.99	4.02	4.04	4.06	4.08	4.09
	.01	5.10	5.13	5.16	5.19	5.21	5.24	5.26	5.29	5.31
10	.05	3.82	3.85	3.87	3.89	3.91	3.94	3.95	3.97	3.99
	.01	4.91	4.93	4.96	4.99	5.01	5.03	5.06	5.08	5.09
11	.05	3.74	3.77	3.79	3.81	3.83	3.85	3.87	3.89	3.91
	.01	4.75	4.78	4.80	4.83	4.85	4.87	4.89	4.91	4.93
12	.05	3.68	3.70	3.72	3.74	3.76	3.78	3.80	3.82	3.83
	.01	4.62	4.65	4.67	4.69	4.72	4.74	4.76	4.78	4.79
14	.05	3.58	3.59	3.62	3.64	3.66	3.68	3.69	3.71	3.73
	.01	4.44	4.46	4.48	4.50	4.52	4.54	4.56	4.58	4.59
16	.05	3.50	3.52	3.54	3.56	3.58	3.59	3.61	3.63	3.64
	.01	4.29	4.32	4.34	4.36	4.38	4.39	4.42	4.43	4.45
18	.05	3.44	3.46	3.48	3.50	3.52	3.54	3.55	3.57	3.58
	.01	4.19	4.22	4.24	4.26	4.28	4.29	4.31	4.33	4.34
20	.05	3.39	3.42	3.44	3.46	3.47	3.49	3.50	3.52	3.53
	.01	4.12	4.14	4.16	4.17	4.19	4.21	4.22	4.24	4.25
24	.05	3.33	3.35	3.37	3.39	3.40	3.42	3.43	3.45	3.46
	.01	4.00	4.02	4.04	4.05	4.07	4.09	4.10	4.12	4.13
30	.05	3.27	3.29	3.30	3.32	3.33	3.35	3.36	3.38	3.39
	.01	3.89	3.91	3.92	3.94	3.95	3.97	3.98	4.00	4.01
40	.05	3.20	3.22	3.24	3.25	3.27	3.28	3.29	3.31	3.32
	.01	3.78	3.80	3.81	3.83	3.84	3.85	3.87	3.88	3.89
60	.05	3.14	3.16	3.17	3.19	3.20	3.21	3.23	3.24	3.25
	.01	3.68	3.69	3.71	3.72	3.73	3.75	3.76	3.77	3.78
∞	.05	3.02	3.03	3.04	3.06	3.07	3.08	3.09	3.11	3.12
	.01	3.48	3.49	3.50	3.52	3.53	3.54	3.55	3.56	3.57

This table was computed using the FORTRAN program described in R. Wilcox, "Improved simultaneous confidence intervals for linear contrasts and regression parameters", Communications in Statistics -- Simulation and Computation, 1986, 15, 917-932.

Table A11
Critical values for Tamhane's Procedure
(Percentage points of the range of
J independent Student's t variates)

α	ν: 5	6	7	8	9	14	19	24	29	39	59
					J=2						
.05	3.63	3.45	3.33	3.24	3.18	3.01	2.94	2.91	2.89	2.85	2.82
.01	5.37	4.96	4.73	4.51	4.38	4.11	3.98	3.86	3.83	3.78	3.73
					J=3						
.05	4.49	4.23	4.07	3.95	3.87	3.65	3.55	3.50	3.46	3.42	3.39
.01	6.32	5.84	5.48	5.23	5.07	4.69	5.54	4.43	4.36	4.29	4.23
					J=4						
.05	5.05	4.74	4.54	4.40	4.30	4.03	3.92	3.85	3.81	3.76	3.72
.01	7.06	6.40	6.01	5.73	5.56	5.05	4.89	4.74	4.71	4.61	4.54
					J=5						
.05	5.47	5.12	4.89	4.73	4.61	4.31	4.18	4.11	4.06	4.01	3.95
.01	7.58	6.76	6.35	6.05	5.87	5.33	5.12	5.01	4.93	4.82	4.74
					J=6						
.05	5.82	5.42	5.17	4.99	4.86	4.52	4.38	4.30	4.25	4.19	4.14
.01	8.00	7.14	6.70	6.39	6.09	5.53	5.32	5.20	5.12	4.99	4.91
					J=7						
.05	6.12	5.68	5.40	5.21	5.07	4.70	4.55	4.46	4.41	4.34	4.28
.01	8.27	7.50	6.92	6.60	6.30	5.72	5.46	5.33	5.25	5.16	5.05
					J=8						
.05	6.37	5.90	5.60	5.40	5.25	4.86	4.69	4.60	4.54	4.47	4.41
.01	8.52	7.73	7.14	6.81	6.49	5.89	5.62	5.45	5.36	5.28	5.16
					J=9						
.05	6.60	6.09	5.78	5.56	5.40	4.99	4.81	4.72	4.66	4.58	4.51
.01	8.92	7.96	7.35	6.95	6.68	6.01	5.74	5.56	5.47	5.37	5.28
					J=10						
.05	6.81	6.28	5.94	5.71	5.54	5.10	4.92	4.82	4.76	4.68	4.61
.01	9.13	8.14	7.51	7.11	6.83	6.10	5.82	5.68	5.59	5.46	5.37

Reprinted, with permission, from R. Wilcox, "A table of percentage points of the range of independent t variables", Technometrics, 25, 201-204.

Table A12
Percentage points of $T=T_1+T_2$ where T_1 and T_2 are independent t random variables having ν_1 and ν_2 degrees of freedom
(For $\nu_1=\nu_2=1$, see the end of this table.)

ν_1	α	ν_2: 2	3	4	5	6	7	8	9	10
2										
	.05	4.565								
	.025	6.539								
	.01	10.276								
	.005	14.417								
3										
	.05		3.495							
	.025		4.588							
	.01		6.307							
	.005		7.917							
4										
	.05			3.107						
	.025			3.941						
	.01			5.135						
	.005			6.152						
5										
	.05	3.667	3.193	3.007	2.909	2.850	2.810	2.781	2.760	2.743
	.025	4.998	4.097	3.783	3.627	3.536	3.476	3.434	3.403	3.379
	.01	7.477	5.460	4.869	4.602	4.453	4.360	4.296	4.251	4.217
	.005	10.441	6.702	5.775	5.386	5.180	5.056	4.974	4.917	4.875
6										
	.05	3.599	3.129	2.946	2.850	2.791	2.751	2.723	2.702	2.685
	.025	4.905	4.002	3.690	3.536	3.444	3.385	3.343	3.312	3.288
	.01	7.373	5.234	4.723	4.453	4.303	4.208	4.144	4.097	4.063
	.005	10.329	6.529	5.578	5.180	4.968	4.841	4.756	4.696	4.651
7										
	.05	3.554	3.087	2.905	2.810	2.751	2.712	2.684	2.663	2.646
	.025	4.846	3.942	3.630	3.476	3.385	3.325	3.283	3.252	3.229
	.01	7.317	5.234	4.631	4.360	4.208	4.113	4.048	4.001	3.965
	.005	10.278	6.431	5.461	5.056	4.841	4.710	4.623	4.561	4.515
8										
	.05	3.523	3.057	2.876	2.781	2.723	2.684	2.656	2.635	2.618
	.025	4.804	3.899	3.588	3.434	3.343	3.283	3.241	3.210	3.187
	.01	7.285	5.178	4.570	4.296	4.144	4.048	3.982	3.935	3.899
	.005	10.251	6.372	5.386	4.974	4.756	4.623	4.534	4.471	4.424

Table A12 (continued)

ν_1	α	ν_2: 2	3	4	5	6	7	8	9	10
9										
	.05	3.499	3.035	2.854	2.760	2.702	2.663	2.635	2.614	2.597
	.025	4.780	3.868	3.557	3.403	3.312	3.252	3.210	3.179	3.156
	.01	7.264	5.139	4.526	4.251	4.097	4.001	3.935	3.878	3.851
	.005	10.234	6.332	5.333	4.917	4.696	4.561	4.471	4.407	4.360
10										
	.05	3.482	3.018	2.838	2.743	2.685	2.646	2.618	2.597	2.581
	.025	4.759	3.845	3.533	3.379	3.288	3.229	3.187	3.156	3.132
	.01	7.249	5.110	4.493	4.217	4.063	3.965	3.899	3.851	3.814
	.005	10.222	6.305	5.296	4.875	4.651	4.515	4.424	4.360	4.312
11										
	.05	3.467	3.004	2.824	2.730	2.672	2.633	2.605	2.584	2.568
	.025	4.744	3.826	3.514	3.360	3.269	3.210	3.168	3.137	3.113
	.01	7.239	5.089	4.468	4.190	4.035	3.938	3.871	3.823	3.786
	.005	10.213	6.285	5.267	4.842	4.617	4.480	4.388	4.323	4.275
12										
	.05	3.456	2.993	2.813	2.719	2.661	2.622	2.595	2.574	2.557
	.025	4.731	3.812	3.499	3.345	3.254	3.195	3.153	3.122	3.098
	.01	7.231	5.072	4.448	4.169	4.014	3.916	3.849	3.800	3.763
	.001	10.207	6.270	5.245	4.817	4.590	4.452	4.360	4.294	4.245
13										
	.05	3.447	2.983	2.804	2.710	2.652	2.613	2.586	2.565	2.549
	.025	4.721	3.800	3.487	3.332	3.242	3.182	3.140	3.109	3.085
	.01	7.225	5.058	4.432	4.152	3.996	3.898	3.830	3.782	3.745
	.005	10.201	6.258	5.227	4.797	4.569	4.430	4.337	4.271	4.221
14										
	.05	3.439	2.976	2.796	2.702	2.645	2.606	2.578	2.557	2.541
	.025	4.713	3.789	3.476	3.322	3.231	3.171	3.129	3.098	3.075
	.01	7.221	5.047	4.419	4.137	3.981	3.882	3.815	3.766	3.729
	.005	10.197	6.248	5.213	4.780	4.551	4.411	4.318	4.251	4.202
15										
	.05	3.432	2.969	2.790	2.696	2.638	2.599	2.572	2.551	2.535
	.025	4.706	3.781	3.467	3.313	3.222	3.162	3.120	3.089	3.065
	.01	7.217	5.038	4.407	4.125	3.969	3.870	3.802	3.753	3.716
	.005	10.193	6.241	5.201	4.767	4.536	4.396	4.302	4.235	4.185
20										
	.05	3.409	2.946	2.767	2.674	2.616	2.578	2.550	2.529	2.513
	.025	4.684	3.752	3.438	3.283	3.192	3.132	3.090	3.059	3.035
	.01	7.204	5.009	4.371	4.086	3.928	3.828	3.759	3.710	3.673
	.005	10.181	6.217	5.164	4.722	4.488	4.345	4.249	4.181	4.131

Table A12 (continued)

ν_1	α	ν_2: 2	3	4	5	6	7	8	9	10
30										
	.05	3.388	2.925	2.746	2.652	2.595	2.557	2.529	2.508	2.492
	.025	4.665	3.726	3.410	3.255	3.163	3.104	3.061	3.030	3.006
	.01	7.194	4.983	4.338	4.050	3.890	3.789	3.720	3.670	3.632
	.005	10.170	6.197	5.131	4.683	4.445	4.300	4.203	4.133	4.082
40										
	.05	3.379	2.915	2.736	2.642	2.585	2.547	2.519	2.498	2.482
	.025	4.656	3.714	3.397	3.241	3.150	3.090	3.048	3.016	2.992
	.01	7.189	4.972	4.323	4.033	3.873	3.771	3.702	3.652	3.614
	.005	10.165	6.189	5.117	4.665	4.425	4.279	4.181	4.111	4.059
60										
	.05	3.369	2.904	2.726	2.632	2.575	2.537	2.509	2.488	2.472
	.025	4.648	3.702	3.384	3.228	3.137	3.077	3.034	3.003	2.979
	.01	7.184	4.961	4.309	4.018	3.856	3.754	3.684	3.634	3.596
	.005	10.160	6.181	5.104	4.649	4.407	4.259	4.161	4.090	4.038
120										
	.05	3.360	2.895	2.716	2.623	2.565	2.527	2.499	2.479	2.463
	.025	4.640	3.691	3.372	3.216	3.124	3.064	3.022	2.990	2.966
	.01	7.180	4.951	4.296	4.003	3.840	3.738	3.668	3.617	3.578
	.005	10.155	6.173	5.091	4.633	4.390	4.241	4.141	4.070	4.018
240										
	.05	3.355	2.890	2.711	2.618	2.561	2.522	2.495	2.474	2.458
	.025	4.636	3.685	3.366	3.210	3.118	3.058	3.015	2.984	2.960
	.01	7.178	4.947	4.289	3.995	3.832	3.730	3.659	3.609	3.750
	.005	10.153	6.170	5.085	4.626	4.381	4.232	4.132	4.061	4.008

For $\nu_1=\nu_2=1$ the 1-α percentage points for α=.05, .025, .01 and .005 are 12.628, 25.412, 63.641. 127.313 (Ghosh, 1975, *Journal of the American Statisical Association*, 70, 463-467).

Table A13
The Multivariate Studentized Range Distribution

$J=2,\ \alpha=.05$

ν	K: 2	3	4	5	6	7	8	9	10
5	4.38	5.38	6.01	6.47	6.83	7.12	7.37	7.59	7.78
6	4.13	5.03	5.59	6.01	6.34	6.59	6.83	7.02	7.19
7	3.97	4.79	5.33	5.71	6.01	6.25	6.46	6.64	6.79
8	3.85	4.64	5.13	5.49	5.77	5.99	6.19	6.37	6.52
9	3.76	4.52	4.99	5.33	5.59	5.82	5.99	6.16	6.31
10	3.69	4.42	4.88	5.19	5.46	5.67	5.85	5.99	6.14
11	3.64	4.35	4.79	5.09	5.35	5.55	5.73	5.88	6.01
12	3.59	4.29	4.71	5.02	5.26	5.46	5.63	5.77	5.89
13	3.56	4.24	4.65	4.95	5.19	5.38	5.54	5.68	5.81
14	3.53	4.19	4.59	4.89	5.12	5.31	5.47	5.61	5.73
15	3.49	4.16	4.55	4.84	5.07	5.25	5.41	5.54	5.66
16	3.48	4.12	4.52	4.79	5.02	5.19	5.36	5.49	5.61
17	3.46	4.09	4.48	4.76	4.98	5.16	5.31	5.44	5.56
18	3.44	4.07	4.45	4.73	4.94	5.12	5.27	5.39	5.51
19	3.43	4.05	4.43	4.69	4.91	5.08	5.23	5.36	5.47
20	3.41	4.03	4.39	4.67	4.88	5.05	5.19	5.32	5.44
24	3.37	3.97	4.33	4.59	4.79	4.96	5.09	5.22	5.32
30	3.33	3.91	4.26	4.51	4.69	4.86	4.99	5.11	5.21
40	3.28	3.85	4.18	4.42	4.61	4.76	4.89	4.99	5.09
60	3.23	3.78	4.09	4.33	4.51	4.66	4.78	4.89	4.98
120	3.21	3.74	4.05	4.27	4.44	4.58	4.69	4.79	4.89
240	3.19	3.71	4.01	4.23	4.39	4.54	4.65	4.75	4.83

$J=2,\ \alpha=.01$

ν	K: 2	3	4	5	6	7	8	9	10
5	6.65	7.99	8.86	9.49	9.99	10.39	10.75	11.05	11.32
6	6.05	7.19	7.91	8.45	8.87	9.22	9.52	9.77	9.99
7	5.66	6.67	7.31	7.79	8.16	8.47	8.73	8.96	9.16
8	5.39	6.31	6.89	7.33	7.67	7.95	8.19	8.39	8.58
9	5.19	6.05	6.59	6.99	7.31	7.57	7.79	7.98	8.15
10	5.05	5.86	6.37	6.74	7.03	7.28	7.49	7.67	7.83
11	4.93	5.69	6.18	6.54	6.82	7.05	7.25	7.42	7.57
12	4.84	5.58	6.04	6.38	6.64	6.87	7.05	7.22	7.36
13	4.76	5.47	5.92	6.24	6.49	6.71	6.89	7.05	7.19
14	4.69	5.39	5.82	6.13	6.38	6.59	6.76	6.91	7.05
15	4.64	5.31	5.73	6.04	6.28	6.48	6.65	6.79	6.92

Table A13 (continued)

ν	K: 2	3	4	5	6	7	8	9	10
16	4.59	5.25	5.66	5.96	6.19	6.39	6.55	6.69	6.82
17	4.55	5.19	5.59	5.89	6.12	6.29	6.47	6.59	6.73
18	4.52	5.15	5.54	5.82	6.05	6.23	6.39	6.53	6.65
19	4.49	5.11	5.49	5.77	5.99	6.17	6.32	6.46	6.58
20	4.46	5.07	5.45	5.72	5.94	6.11	6.27	6.39	6.51
24	4.37	4.95	5.31	5.57	5.77	5.94	6.08	6.21	6.32
30	4.28	4.84	5.18	5.42	5.62	5.77	5.91	6.02	6.12
40	4.19	4.72	5.04	5.27	5.45	5.59	5.72	5.83	5.93
60	4.07	4.57	4.88	5.09	5.27	5.39	5.52	5.62	5.71
120	4.05	4.53	4.81	5.02	5.17	5.29	5.41	5.51	5.59
240	3.99	4.47	4.75	4.94	5.09	5.22	5.33	5.42	5.49

$J=3$, $\alpha=.05$

5	4.81	5.83	6.46	6.92	7.27	7.56	7.81	8.02	8.21
6	4.52	5.43	5.99	6.41	6.73	6.99	7.22	7.41	7.58
7	4.33	5.17	5.69	6.08	6.37	6.62	6.82	6.99	7.16
8	4.19	4.98	5.48	5.83	6.11	6.34	6.54	6.71	6.85
9	4.09	4.84	5.31	5.65	5.92	6.14	6.32	6.48	6.62
10	4.01	4.74	5.19	5.51	5.77	5.98	6.16	6.31	6.44
11	3.94	4.65	5.08	5.39	5.65	5.85	6.02	6.17	6.29
12	3.89	4.58	4.99	5.31	5.55	5.74	5.91	6.05	6.18
13	3.85	4.52	4.93	5.23	5.46	5.66	5.82	5.96	6.08
14	3.81	4.47	4.87	5.17	5.39	5.58	5.74	5.88	5.99
15	3.78	4.43	4.82	5.11	5.33	5.52	5.67	5.81	5.92
16	3.75	4.39	4.78	5.06	5.28	5.46	5.61	5.75	5.86
17	3.73	4.36	4.74	5.02	5.23	5.41	5.56	5.69	5.81
18	3.71	4.33	4.71	4.98	5.19	5.37	5.52	5.64	5.76
19	3.69	4.29	4.68	4.95	5.16	5.33	5.48	5.59	5.71
20	3.67	4.28	4.65	4.92	5.13	5.29	5.44	5.56	5.67
24	3.62	4.21	4.57	4.82	5.02	5.19	5.33	5.45	5.55
30	3.57	4.14	4.49	4.73	4.92	5.08	5.21	5.33	5.43
40	3.52	4.07	4.39	4.64	4.82	4.97	5.09	5.21	5.31
60	3.46	3.99	4.31	4.54	4.72	4.86	4.98	5.08	5.18
120	3.43	3.94	4.25	4.47	4.63	4.77	4.88	4.98	5.07
240	3.39	3.91	4.21	4.42	4.58	4.72	4.83	4.92	5.01

Table A13 (continued)

ν	K: 2	3	4	5	6	7	8	9	10
				J=3, α=.01					
5	7.23	8.59	9.47	10.09	10.59	11.01	11.36	11.66	11.92
6	6.53	7.69	8.43	8.96	9.39	9.73	10.03	10.28	10.51
7	6.08	7.11	7.76	8.24	8.61	8.92	9.18	9.41	9.61
8	5.77	6.71	7.29	7.73	8.08	8.36	8.59	8.79	8.98
9	5.55	6.42	6.97	7.37	7.68	7.94	8.16	8.36	8.52
10	5.38	6.19	6.71	7.09	7.38	7.63	7.83	8.01	8.17
11	5.25	6.02	6.51	6.87	7.15	7.38	7.58	7.75	7.89
12	5.14	5.88	6.35	6.69	6.96	7.18	7.37	7.53	7.67
13	5.05	5.77	6.21	6.54	6.79	7.01	7.19	7.35	7.49
14	4.98	5.67	6.09	6.42	6.67	6.87	7.05	7.19	7.33
15	4.91	5.59	6.01	6.31	6.56	6.76	6.92	7.07	7.19
16	4.86	5.52	5.93	6.23	6.46	6.65	6.82	6.96	7.09
17	4.81	5.46	5.86	6.15	6.38	6.57	6.73	6.86	6.99
18	4.77	5.39	5.79	6.08	6.29	6.49	6.64	6.78	6.89
19	4.74	5.36	5.74	6.02	6.24	6.42	6.57	6.71	6.82
20	4.69	5.31	5.69	5.96	6.18	6.36	6.51	6.64	6.76
24	4.59	5.18	5.54	5.79	5.99	6.17	6.31	6.43	6.54
30	4.51	5.06	5.39	5.64	5.83	5.98	6.12	6.23	6.33
40	4.39	4.92	5.24	5.47	5.65	5.79	5.92	6.03	6.12
60	4.27	4.76	5.06	5.28	5.45	5.59	5.69	5.79	5.89
120	4.24	4.71	4.99	5.19	5.34	5.47	5.58	5.67	5.75
240	4.19	4.64	4.92	5.11	5.26	5.38	5.48	5.57	5.65
				J=4, α=.05					
5	5.12	6.14	6.77	7.23	7.58	7.87	8.11	8.32	8.51
6	4.79	5.71	6.28	6.69	7.01	7.27	7.49	7.68	7.85
7	4.58	5.43	5.95	6.33	6.63	6.87	7.07	7.25	7.39
8	4.43	5.23	5.72	6.07	6.35	6.58	6.77	6.94	7.08
9	4.31	5.07	5.54	5.88	6.14	6.36	6.54	6.69	6.84
10	4.22	4.95	5.39	5.73	5.98	6.19	6.37	6.52	6.65
11	4.15	4.86	5.29	5.61	5.85	6.05	6.22	6.37	6.49
12	4.09	4.78	5.19	5.51	5.75	5.94	6.11	6.25	6.38
13	4.05	4.72	5.13	5.43	5.66	5.85	6.01	6.15	6.27
14	4.01	4.66	5.06	5.36	5.58	5.77	5.93	6.06	6.18
15	3.97	4.62	5.01	5.29	5.52	5.69	5.85	5.99	6.09

Table A13 (continued)

ν	K: 2	3	4	5	6	7	8	9	10
16	3.94	4.58	4.96	5.24	5.46	5.64	5.79	5.92	6.04
17	3.92	4.54	4.92	5.19	5.41	5.59	5.74	5.87	5.98
18	3.89	4.51	4.89	5.16	5.37	5.54	5.69	5.82	5.93
19	3.87	4.48	4.85	5.12	5.33	5.49	5.65	5.77	5.88
20	3.85	4.46	4.82	5.09	5.29	5.46	5.61	5.73	5.84
24	3.79	4.38	4.73	4.99	5.19	5.35	5.49	5.59	5.71
30	3.74	4.29	4.64	4.89	5.08	5.23	5.37	5.48	5.58
40	3.68	4.23	4.55	4.79	4.97	5.12	5.24	5.35	5.45
60	3.62	4.14	4.46	4.68	4.85	4.99	5.12	5.22	5.31
120	3.58	4.08	4.38	4.59	4.76	4.89	5.01	5.11	5.19
240	3.55	4.05	4.34	4.55	4.71	4.84	4.95	5.05	5.13

$J=4,\ \alpha=.01$

ν	K: 2	3	4	5	6	7	8	9	10
5	7.64	9.03	9.89	10.53	11.03	11.44	11.78	12.08	12.34
6	6.87	8.05	8.79	9.32	9.75	10.09	10.38	10.63	10.85
7	6.38	7.42	8.08	8.55	8.93	9.23	9.49	9.72	9.92
8	6.05	6.99	7.59	8.02	8.36	8.64	8.88	9.08	9.27
9	5.79	6.68	7.23	7.63	7.94	8.19	8.42	8.62	8.78
10	5.62	6.44	6.95	7.33	7.63	7.87	8.08	8.26	8.42
11	5.47	6.25	6.74	7.09	7.38	7.61	7.81	7.98	8.13
12	5.35	6.09	6.57	6.91	7.18	7.39	7.58	7.75	7.89
13	5.26	5.97	6.42	6.75	7.01	7.22	7.39	7.56	7.69
14	5.18	5.87	6.29	6.62	6.87	7.07	7.25	7.39	7.53
15	5.11	5.78	6.19	6.51	6.75	6.95	7.12	7.27	7.39
16	5.05	5.71	6.12	6.41	6.65	6.84	7.01	7.15	7.27
17	4.99	5.64	6.04	6.33	6.56	6.75	6.91	7.05	7.17
18	4.95	5.58	5.97	6.26	6.48	6.67	6.82	6.96	7.08
19	4.91	5.53	5.91	6.19	6.41	6.59	6.75	6.88	6.99
20	4.88	5.49	5.86	6.14	6.35	6.53	6.68	6.81	6.92
24	4.77	5.35	5.69	5.96	6.16	6.33	6.47	6.59	6.69
30	4.66	5.21	5.54	5.79	5.98	6.13	6.26	6.38	6.48
40	4.55	5.06	5.38	5.61	5.78	5.93	6.05	6.16	6.26
60	4.41	4.89	5.19	5.41	5.58	5.71	5.83	5.93	6.01
120	4.37	4.83	5.11	5.29	5.46	5.58	5.69	5.78	5.86
240	4.32	4.76	5.03	5.22	5.37	5.49	5.59	5.68	5.76

Table A13 (continued)

J=5, α=.05

ν	K: 2	3	4	5	6	7	8	9	10
5	5.36	6.38	7.01	7.46	7.81	8.09	8.34	8.54	8.72
6	5.01	5.93	6.49	6.89	7.22	7.48	7.69	7.88	8.05
7	4.78	5.63	6.15	6.53	6.82	7.06	7.26	7.44	7.59
8	4.61	5.41	5.89	6.26	6.53	6.76	6.95	7.11	7.26
9	4.49	5.25	5.71	6.05	6.32	6.53	6.71	6.87	7.01
10	4.39	5.12	5.57	5.89	6.15	6.35	6.53	6.68	6.81
11	4.32	5.02	5.45	5.77	6.01	6.21	6.38	6.52	6.65
12	4.25	4.94	5.36	5.66	5.89	6.09	6.26	6.39	6.52
13	4.19	4.87	5.28	5.57	5.81	5.99	6.16	6.29	6.42
14	4.16	4.81	5.21	5.49	5.73	5.91	6.07	6.19	6.32
15	4.12	4.76	5.15	5.44	5.66	5.84	5.99	6.13	6.24
16	4.09	4.72	5.09	5.38	5.59	5.78	5.93	6.06	6.17
17	4.06	4.68	5.06	5.33	5.55	5.72	5.87	5.99	6.11
18	4.03	4.65	5.02	5.29	5.49	5.67	5.82	5.95	6.06
19	4.01	4.62	4.99	5.25	5.46	5.63	5.77	5.89	6.01
20	3.99	4.59	4.96	5.22	5.42	5.59	5.73	5.86	5.96
24	3.93	4.51	4.86	5.11	5.31	5.47	5.61	5.72	5.83
30	3.87	4.43	4.76	5.01	5.19	5.35	5.48	5.59	5.69
40	3.79	4.33	4.66	4.89	5.08	5.22	5.35	5.46	5.55
60	3.74	4.25	4.57	4.79	4.96	5.09	5.22	5.32	5.41
120	3.69	4.19	4.49	4.69	4.86	4.99	5.11	5.19	5.29
240	3.66	4.15	4.44	4.65	4.81	4.93	5.04	5.14	5.22

J=5, α=.01

ν	K: 2	3	4	5	6	7	8	9	10
5	7.96	9.36	10.23	10.86	11.35	11.76	12.09	12.39	12.66
6	7.14	8.32	9.06	9.59	10.02	10.36	10.65	10.89	11.12
7	6.62	7.67	8.32	8.79	9.17	9.47	9.73	9.96	10.16
8	6.26	7.21	7.81	8.24	8.58	8.86	9.09	9.29	9.48
9	5.99	6.88	7.43	7.83	8.15	8.39	8.62	8.81	8.98
10	5.79	6.63	7.14	7.52	7.82	8.06	8.26	8.44	8.59
11	5.64	6.43	6.92	7.27	7.55	7.79	7.98	8.15	8.29
12	5.52	6.27	6.73	7.08	7.34	7.57	7.75	7.92	8.06
13	5.42	6.14	6.58	6.91	7.17	7.38	7.56	7.72	7.86
15	5.26	5.93	6.35	6.66	6.89	7.09	7.27	7.41	7.54

Table A13 (continued)

ν	K: 2	3	4	5	6	7	8	9	10
16	5.19	5.85	6.26	6.56	6.79	6.99	7.15	7.29	7.42
17	5.14	5.78	6.18	6.47	6.69	6.89	7.05	7.19	7.31
18	5.09	5.72	6.11	6.39	6.62	6.79	6.96	7.09	7.21
19	5.05	5.67	6.05	6.33	6.55	6.73	6.88	7.01	7.13
20	5.01	5.62	5.99	6.27	6.48	6.66	6.81	6.94	7.06
24	4.89	5.47	5.82	6.08	6.28	6.45	6.59	6.71	6.82
30	4.78	5.33	5.66	5.89	6.09	6.24	6.38	6.49	6.59
40	4.66	5.17	5.49	5.71	5.89	6.04	6.16	6.26	6.36
60	4.52	4.99	5.29	5.51	5.67	5.81	5.92	6.02	6.11
120	4.47	4.93	5.19	5.39	5.55	5.67	5.78	5.87	5.95
240	4.41	4.86	5.12	5.31	5.46	5.57	5.68	5.76	5.84

J=6, α=.05

ν	K: 2	3	4	5	6	7	8	9	10
5	5.56	6.58	7.19	7.65	7.99	8.28	8.52	8.73	8.91
6	5.19	6.09	6.67	7.07	7.39	7.64	7.86	8.04	8.21
7	4.94	5.79	6.31	6.68	6.97	7.21	7.41	7.59	7.74
8	4.76	5.56	6.05	6.39	6.68	6.89	7.09	7.26	7.39
9	4.63	5.39	5.86	6.19	6.45	6.67	6.85	6.99	7.14
10	4.53	5.26	5.69	6.03	6.28	6.48	6.66	6.81	6.94
11	4.45	5.15	5.58	5.89	6.14	6.34	6.49	6.65	6.78
12	4.38	5.06	5.48	5.79	6.02	6.21	6.38	6.52	6.64
13	4.33	4.99	5.39	5.69	5.92	6.11	6.27	6.41	6.53
14	4.28	4.93	5.33	5.62	5.84	6.03	6.18	6.32	6.43
15	4.24	4.88	5.27	5.55	5.77	5.95	6.11	6.24	6.35
16	4.19	4.83	5.22	5.49	5.71	5.89	6.04	6.17	6.28
17	4.17	4.79	5.17	5.44	5.66	5.83	5.98	6.11	6.22
18	4.15	4.76	5.13	5.39	5.61	5.78	5.93	6.05	6.16
19	4.12	4.73	5.09	5.36	5.57	5.74	5.88	5.99	6.11
20	4.09	4.69	5.06	5.32	5.53	5.69	5.84	5.96	6.07
24	4.04	4.61	4.96	5.21	5.41	5.57	5.69	5.82	5.92
30	3.97	4.53	4.86	5.09	5.29	5.44	5.57	5.69	5.78
40	3.89	4.44	4.76	4.99	5.17	5.32	5.44	5.55	5.64
60	3.85	4.36	4.67	4.89	5.06	5.19	5.31	5.41	5.49
120	3.79	4.28	4.57	4.78	4.94	5.07	5.18	5.41	5.49
240	3.75	4.24	4.52	4.73	4.88	5.01	5.12	5.21	5.29

Table A13 (continued)

J=6, α=.01

ν	K: 2	3	4	5	6	7	8	9	10
5	8.22	9.63	10.49	11.12	11.62	12.02	12.36	12.66	12.92
6	7.36	8.55	9.29	9.82	10.24	10.58	10.86	11.11	11.33
7	6.81	7.86	8.52	8.99	9.36	9.67	9.93	10.15	10.35
8	6.44	7.39	7.98	8.42	8.76	9.03	9.27	9.48	9.66
9	6.16	7.04	7.59	7.99	8.31	8.57	8.79	8.97	9.14
10	5.95	6.78	7.29	7.67	7.97	8.21	8.41	8.59	8.75
11	5.79	6.57	7.06	7.42	7.69	7.93	8.12	8.29	8.44
12	5.65	6.39	6.87	7.21	7.48	7.69	7.89	8.05	8.19
13	5.55	6.27	6.72	7.04	7.29	7.51	7.69	7.85	7.99
14	5.46	6.15	6.59	6.89	7.15	7.36	7.53	7.68	7.81
15	5.38	6.05	6.47	6.78	7.02	7.22	7.39	7.53	7.66
16	5.31	5.97	6.38	6.68	6.91	7.09	7.27	7.41	7.53
17	5.25	5.89	6.29	6.59	6.82	6.99	7.16	7.29	7.42
18	5.19	5.83	6.22	6.51	6.73	6.91	7.07	7.21	7.32
19	5.16	5.78	6.16	6.44	6.66	6.84	6.99	7.12	7.24
20	5.12	5.73	6.09	6.38	6.59	6.77	6.92	7.05	7.16
24	4.99	5.57	5.92	6.18	6.38	6.55	6.69	6.81	6.92
30	4.88	5.42	5.75	5.99	6.18	6.34	6.47	6.58	6.68
40	4.75	5.26	5.57	5.79	5.98	6.12	6.24	6.35	6.44
60	4.59	5.08	5.38	5.59	5.75	5.89	5.99	6.09	6.19
120	4.55	4.99	5.27	5.47	5.62	5.74	5.85	5.94	6.02
240	4.49	4.93	5.19	5.38	5.52	5.64	5.74	5.83	5.89

J=7, α=.05

ν	K: 2	3	4	5	6	7	8	9	10
5	5.72	6.74	7.36	7.81	8.16	8.44	8.68	8.88	9.06
6	5.33	6.25	6.81	7.21	7.52	7.78	7.99	8.18	8.34
7	5.07	5.92	6.44	6.81	7.09	7.34	7.54	7.71	7.86
8	4.89	5.69	6.17	6.52	6.79	7.02	7.21	7.37	7.52
9	4.75	5.51	5.97	6.31	6.57	6.78	6.96	7.12	7.25
10	4.64	5.37	5.82	6.14	6.39	6.59	6.77	6.91	7.05
11	4.56	5.26	5.69	5.99	6.24	6.44	6.61	6.75	6.88
12	4.49	5.17	5.59	5.89	6.12	6.32	6.48	6.62	6.74
13	4.43	5.09	5.49	5.79	6.02	6.21	6.37	6.51	6.63
14	4.38	5.03	5.43	5.72	5.94	6.12	6.28	6.41	6.53
15	4.34	4.98	5.37	5.65	5.87	6.05	6.19	6.33	6.45

Table A13 (continued)

ν	K: 2	3	4	5	6	7	8	9	10
16	4.29	4.93	5.31	5.59	5.79	5.98	6.13	6.26	6.37
17	4.27	4.89	5.26	5.54	5.75	5.92	6.07	6.19	6.31
18	4.24	4.85	5.22	5.49	5.69	5.87	6.01	6.14	6.25
19	4.22	4.82	5.19	5.45	5.66	5.82	5.97	6.09	6.19
20	4.19	4.79	5.15	5.41	5.62	5.78	5.92	6.04	6.15
24	4.13	4.69	5.05	5.29	5.49	5.65	5.79	5.89	6.01
30	4.06	4.61	4.94	5.18	5.37	5.52	5.65	5.76	5.86
40	3.99	4.52	4.84	5.07	5.25	5.39	5.52	5.62	5.72
60	3.91	4.42	4.73	4.95	5.12	5.25	5.37	5.47	5.56
120	3.86	4.35	4.64	4.85	5.01	5.14	5.25	5.34	5.43
240	3.83	4.31	4.59	4.79	4.95	5.07	5.18	5.27	5.35
				J=7, α=.01					
5	8.45	9.85	10.72	11.34	11.84	12.24	12.58	12.88	13.14
6	7.55	8.74	9.47	10.01	10.42	10.76	11.04	11.29	11.49
7	6.98	8.03	8.68	9.16	9.53	9.83	10.09	10.31	10.51
8	6.58	7.54	8.13	8.57	8.89	9.18	9.42	9.62	9.79
9	6.29	7.18	7.73	8.13	8.44	8.69	8.92	9.11	9.27
10	6.08	6.91	7.42	7.79	8.09	8.34	8.54	8.72	8.87
11	5.91	6.69	7.18	7.54	7.82	8.05	8.24	8.41	8.56
12	5.77	6.52	6.99	7.33	7.59	7.82	7.99	8.16	8.31
13	5.66	6.38	6.83	7.15	7.41	7.62	7.79	7.96	8.09
14	5.56	6.26	6.69	7.01	7.26	7.46	7.63	7.78	7.92
15	5.48	6.16	6.58	6.88	7.12	7.32	7.49	7.64	7.76
16	5.41	6.07	6.48	6.78	7.01	7.19	7.37	7.51	7.63
17	5.35	5.99	6.39	6.68	6.91	7.09	7.26	7.39	7.52
18	5.29	5.93	6.32	6.59	6.82	7.01	7.16	7.29	7.42
19	5.25	5.87	6.25	6.53	6.75	6.93	7.08	7.21	7.33
20	5.21	5.82	6.19	6.47	6.68	6.86	7.01	7.13	7.25
24	5.08	5.66	6.01	6.27	6.47	6.63	6.77	6.89	6.99
30	4.96	5.49	5.83	6.07	6.26	6.41	6.54	6.66	6.76
40	4.83	5.34	5.65	5.87	6.05	6.19	6.31	6.42	6.51
60	4.67	5.15	5.45	5.66	5.82	5.95	6.07	6.16	6.25
120	4.62	5.07	5.34	5.53	5.68	5.79	5.89	5.99	6.07
240	4.56	4.99	5.25	5.44	5.58	5.69	5.79	5.88	5.96

Table A13 (continued)

J=8, α=.05

ν	K: 2	3	4	5	6	7	8	9	10
5	5.87	6.88	7.49	7.94	8.29	8.57	8.81	9.01	9.19
6	5.46	6.38	6.93	7.33	7.64	7.89	8.11	8.29	8.45
7	5.19	6.04	6.55	6.92	7.21	7.45	7.65	7.82	7.97
8	4.99	5.79	6.28	6.63	6.89	7.12	7.31	7.47	7.62
9	4.86	5.61	6.07	6.41	6.67	6.88	7.06	7.21	7.35
10	4.74	5.47	5.91	6.23	6.48	6.69	6.86	7.01	7.14
11	4.65	5.36	5.78	6.09	6.33	6.53	6.69	6.84	6.97
12	4.58	5.26	5.68	5.98	6.21	6.39	6.56	6.69	6.83
13	4.52	5.18	5.59	5.88	6.11	6.29	6.45	6.59	6.71
14	4.47	5.12	5.51	5.79	6.02	6.21	6.36	6.49	6.61
15	4.43	5.06	5.45	5.73	5.95	6.13	6.28	6.41	6.52
16	4.39	5.01	5.39	5.67	5.88	6.06	6.21	6.34	6.45
17	4.35	4.97	5.35	5.62	5.83	5.99	6.15	6.27	6.38
18	4.33	4.93	5.29	5.57	5.78	5.95	6.09	6.22	6.32
19	4.29	4.89	5.26	5.53	5.73	5.89	6.04	6.16	6.27
20	4.28	4.87	5.23	5.49	5.69	5.86	5.99	6.12	6.22
24	4.19	4.77	5.12	5.37	5.56	5.72	5.86	5.97	6.08
30	4.13	4.68	5.01	5.25	5.44	5.59	5.72	5.83	5.93
40	4.06	4.59	4.89	5.13	5.31	5.46	5.58	5.68	5.78
60	3.98	4.49	4.79	5.01	5.18	5.32	5.43	5.53	5.62
120	3.93	4.41	4.69	4.91	5.06	5.19	5.29	5.39	5.48
240	3.89	4.37	4.65	4.85	4.99	5.13	5.23	5.32	5.39

J=8, α=.01

5	8.64	10.04	10.91	11.53	12.03	12.43	12.77	13.07	13.33
6	7.71	8.89	9.63	10.16	10.58	10.91	11.19	11.43	11.65
7	7.12	8.17	8.82	9.29	9.67	9.97	10.22	10.45	10.64
8	6.71	7.67	8.26	8.69	9.03	9.31	9.54	9.75	9.93
9	6.41	7.29	7.85	8.25	8.56	8.82	9.04	9.22	9.39
10	6.19	7.02	7.53	7.91	8.19	8.44	8.65	8.82	8.98
11	6.01	6.79	7.29	7.64	7.92	8.15	8.35	8.51	8.66
12	5.87	6.62	7.09	7.43	7.69	7.91	8.09	8.26	8.39
13	5.75	6.47	6.92	7.25	7.51	7.72	7.89	8.05	8.19
14	5.65	6.35	6.78	7.09	7.35	7.55	7.72	7.87	8.01
15	5.57	6.25	6.67	6.97	7.21	7.41	7.58	7.72	7.85

Table A13 (continued)

ν	K: 2	3	4	5	6	7	8	9	10
16	5.49	6.16	6.56	6.86	7.09	7.29	7.45	7.59	7.72
17	5.44	6.08	6.48	6.77	6.99	7.18	7.34	7.48	7.59
18	5.38	6.01	6.39	6.68	6.91	7.09	7.24	7.38	7.49
19	5.33	5.95	6.33	6.61	6.83	7.01	7.16	7.29	7.41
20	5.29	5.89	6.27	6.54	6.76	6.93	7.08	7.21	7.33
24	5.16	5.73	6.08	6.34	6.54	6.69	6.84	6.97	7.07
30	5.03	5.57	5.89	6.14	6.33	6.48	6.61	6.72	6.82
40	4.89	5.39	5.71	5.93	6.11	6.25	6.37	6.48	6.57
60	4.74	5.21	5.49	5.71	5.88	6.01	6.12	6.22	6.31
120	4.68	5.12	5.39	5.58	5.73	5.85	5.96	6.04	6.12
240	4.61	5.04	5.29	5.49	5.63	5.75	5.85	5.93	6.01

Let Z_{jk} ($j=1,\ldots,J$; $k=1,\ldots,K$) be JK independent normal random variables with means μ and variances σ^2, let $R_j = \max_k Z_{jk} - \min_k Z_{jk}$, and let S^2 be the usual mean square within groups. The values in this table, say c, satisfy $\Pr\{R_1/S \le c, \ldots, R_J/S \le c\} = 1-\alpha$.

Table A14
Student's t distribution

$P=Pr(T_\nu \le t)$ where T_ν is a Student's t random variable with ν degrees of freedom

ν	P=.6	P=.75	P=.9	P=.95	P=.975	P=.99	P=.995	P=.999
1	0.325	1.000	3.078	6.314	12.706	31.821	63.657	318.313
2	0.289	0.816	1.886	2.920	4.303	6.965	9.925	22.327
3	0.277	0.765	1.638	2.353	3.182	4.541	5.841	10.215
4	0.271	0.741	1.533	2.132	2.776	3.747	4.604	7.173
5	0.267	0.727	1.476	2.015	2.571	3.365	4.032	5.893
6	0.265	0.718	1.440	1.943	2.447	3.143	3.707	5.208
8	0.262	0.706	1.397	1.860	2.306	2.896	3.355	4.501
10	0.260	0.700	1.372	1.812	2.228	2.764	3.169	4.144
12	0.259	0.695	1.356	1.782	2.179	2.681	3.055	3.930
15	0.258	0.691	1.341	1.753	2.131	2.602	2.947	3.733
20	0.257	0.687	1.325	1.725	2.086	2.528	2.845	3.552
24	0.256	0.685	1.318	1.711	2.064	2.492	2.797	3.467
30	0.256	0.683	1.310	1.697	2.042	2.457	2.750	3.385
40	0.255	0.681	1.303	1.684	2.021	2.423	2.704	3.307
60	0.254	0.679	1.296	1.671	2.000	2.390	2.660	3.232
120	0.254	0.677	1.289	1.658	1.980	2.358	2.617	3.160
∞	0.253	0.674	1.282	1.645	1.960	2.326	2.576	3.090

This table was computed with IMSL subroutine MDSTI

Table A15

Two-tailed Comparisons with a Control

		Number of Treatment Means, Including the Control							
ν	α	2	3	4	5	6	7	8	9
5	.05	2.57	3.03	3.29	3.48	3.62	3.73	3.82	3.90
	.01	4.03	4.63	4.98	5.22	5.41	5.56	5.69	5.80
6	.05	2.45	2.86	3.10	3.26	3.39	3.49	3.57	3.64
	.01	3.71	4.21	4.51	4.71	4.87	5.00	5.10	5.20
7	.05	2.36	2.75	2.97	3.12	3.24	3.33	3.41	3.47
	.01	3.50	3.95	4.21	4.39	4.53	4.64	4.74	4.82
8	.05	2.31	2.67	2.88	3.02	3.13	3.22	3.29	3.35
	.01	3.36	3.77	4.00	4.17	4.29	4.40	4.48	4.56
9	.05	2.26	2.61	2.81	2.95	3.05	3.14	3.20	3.26
	.01	3.25	3.63	3.85	4.01	4.12	4.22	4.30	4.37
10	.05	2.23	2.57	2.76	2.89	2.99	3.07	3.14	3.19
	.01	3.17	3.53	3.74	3.88	3.99	4.08	4.16	4.22
11	.05	2.20	2.53	2.72	2.84	2.94	3.02	3.08	3.14
	.01	3.11	3.45	3.65	3.79	3.89	3.98	4.05	4.11
12	.05	2.18	2.50	2.68	2.81	2.90	2.98	3.04	3.09
	.01	3.05	3.39	3.58	3.71	3.81	3.89	3.96	4.02
13	.05	2.16	2.48	2.65	2.78	2.87	2.94	3.00	3.06
	.01	3.01	3.33	3.52	3.65	3.74	3.82	3.89	3.94
14	.05	2.14	2.46	2.63	2.75	2.84	2.91	2.97	3.02
	.01	2.98	3.29	3.47	3.59	3.69	3.76	3.83	3.88
15	.05	2.13	2.44	2.61	2.73	2.82	2.89	2.95	3.00
	.01	2.95	3.25	3.43	3.55	3.64	3.71	3.78	3.83
16	.05	2.12	2.42	2.59	2.71	2.80	2.87	2.92	2.97
	.01	2.92	3.22	3.39	3.51	3.60	3.67	3.73	3.78
17	.05	2.11	2.41	2.58	2.69	2.78	2.85	2.90	2.95
	.01	2.90	3.19	3.36	3.47	3.56	3.63	3.69	3.74
18	.05	2.10	2.40	2.56	2.68	2.76	2.83	2.89	2.94
	.01	2.88	3.17	3.33	3.44	3.53	3.60	3.66	3.71
19	.05	2.09	2.39	2.55	2.66	2.75	2.81	2.87	2.92
	.01	2.86	3.15	3.31	3.42	3.50	3.57	3.63	3.68
20	.05	2.09	2.38	2.54	2.65	2.73	2.80	2.86	2.90
	.01	2.85	3.13	3.29	3.40	3.48	3.55	3.60	3.65

Table A15 (continued)

ν	α	2	3	4	5	6	7	8	9
24	.05	2.06	2.35	2.51	2.61	2.70	2.76	2.81	2.86
	.01	2.80	3.07	3.22	3.32	3.40	3.47	3.52	3.57
30	.05	2.04	2.32	2.47	2.58	2.66	2.72	2.77	2.82
	.01	2.75	3.01	3.15	3.25	3.33	3.39	3.44	3.49
40	.05	2.02	2.29	2.44	2.54	2.62	2.68	2.73	2.77
	.01	2.70	2.95	3.09	3.19	3.26	3.32	3.37	3.41
60	.05	2.00	2.27	2.41	2.51	2.58	2.64	2.69	2.73
	.01	2.66	2.90	3.03	3.12	3.19	3.25	3.29	3.33
120	.05	1.98	2.24	2.38	2.47	2.55	2.60	2.65	2.69
	.01	2.62	2.85	2.97	3.06	3.12	3.18	3.22	3.26
∞	.05	1.96	2.21	2.35	2.44	2.51	2.57	2.61	2.65
	.01	2.58	2.79	2.92	3.00	3.06	3.11	3.15	3.19

The values in this table were computed using a slight modification of the computer program used to generate Table A21

Table A16

Values of h for Rinott's Selection Procedure

$P^{*}=.95$

n_0	J: 2	3	4	5	6	7	8
3	4.565	6.136	7.304	8.205	8.928	9.525	10.033
4	3.497	4.530	5.190	5.685	6.091	6.434	6.732
5	3.107	3.908	4.390	4.746	5.025	5.260	5.463
6	2.910	3.603	4.021	4.305	4.533	4.721	4.885
7	2.792	3.426	3.792	4.053	4.252	4.419	4.560
8	2.713	3.309	3.648	3.889	4.073	4.226	4.352
9	2.657	3.227	3.549	3.774	3.950	4.091	4.211
10	2.615	3.165	3.476	3.692	3.859	3.994	4.106
11	2.583	3.118	3.420	3.628	3.789	3.918	4.026
12	2.555	3.083	3.376	3.578	3.733	3.859	3.965
13	2.534	3.051	3.341	3.539	3.690	3.813	3.915
14	2.518	3.027	3.310	3.505	3.654	3.774	3.874
15	2.502	3.007	3.285	3.477	3.622	3.741	3.839
16	2.490	2.989	3.265	3.452	3.597	3.713	3.810
17	2.478	2.972	3.244	3.432	3.575	3.690	3.785
18	2.469	2.960	3.230	3.414	3.555	3.669	3.763
19	2.460	2.948	3.215	3.399	3.540	3.651	3.745
20	2.453	2.937	3.203	3.385	3.523	3.634	3.728
30	2.406	2.875	3.130	3.303	3.435	3.539	3.625
40	2.387	2.846	3.095	3.265	3.392	3.495	3.580
50	2.373	2.828	3.074	3.241	3.367	3.468	3.552

Table A16 (continued)

$P^*=.99$

n_0	J: 2	3	4	5	6	7	8
3	10.276	11.570	12.922	13.812	14.320	14.711	14.984
4	6.307	7.918	8.969	9.828	10.609	11.234	11.859
5	5.135	6.133	6.742	7.211	7.602	7.914	8.188
6	4.602	5.359	5.852	6.180	6.461	6.695	6.883
7	4.294	4.961	5.359	5.641	5.863	6.039	6.203
8	4.106	4.703	5.055	5.301	5.500	5.664	5.805
9	3.986	4.527	4.844	5.078	5.254	5.406	5.523
10	3.884	4.398	4.708	4.914	5.078	5.219	5.324
11	3.815	4.305	4.586	4.797	4.949	5.078	5.184
12	3.764	4.234	4.504	4.703	4.844	4.973	5.066
13	3.713	4.176	4.445	4.621	4.773	4.879	4.984
14	3.679	4.129	4.387	4.563	4.703	4.820	4.914
15	3.645	4.082	4.340	4.516	4.645	4.762	4.844
16	3.160	4.047	4.293	4.469	4.598	4.715	4.797
17	3.593	4.023	4.270	4.434	4.563	4.668	4.750
18	3.576	4.000	4.234	4.398	4.527	4.633	4.715
19	3.560	3.977	4.211	4.375	4.504	4.598	4.691
20	3.542	3.953	4.188	4.352	4.469	4.574	4.656
30	3.442	3.836	4.045	4.203	4.320	4.414	4.492
40	3.409	3.781	4.000	4.140	4.250	4.344	4.414
50	3.375	3.750	3.961	4.102	4.211	4.297	4.375

This table is reprinted, with permission, from R. Wilcox, "A table for Rinott's selection procedure", Journal of Quality Technology, 16, 97-100.

Table A17
Critical Values for the Wilcoxon Signed Ranks Test

n α:	.005	.01	.025	.05
4	0	0	0	0
5	0	0	0	1
6	0	0	1	3
7	0	1	3	4
8	1	2	4	6
9	2	4	6	9
10	4	6	9	11
11	6	8	11	14
12	8	10	14	18
13	10	13	18	22
14	13	16	22	26
15	16	20	26	31
16	20	24	30	36
17	24	28	35	42
18	28	33	41	48
19	33	38	47	54
20	38	44	53	61
21	44	50	59	68
22	49	56	67	76
23	55	63	74	84
24	62	70	82	92
25	69	77	90	101
26	76	85	111	125
27	84	94	108	120
28	92	102	117	131
29	101	111	127	141
30	110	121	138	152
31	119	131	148	164
32	129	141	160	176
33	139	152	171	188
34	149	163	183	201
35	160	175	196	214
36	172	187	209	228
37	184	199	222	242
38	196	212	236	257
39	208	225	250	272
40	221	239	265	287

This table was computed by noting that the distribution of the Wilcoxon signed ranks statistic is the same as the distribution of $V=\Sigma V_i$ where the V_i's are independent and $Pr(V_i=i)=Pr(V_i=-i)=1/2$ (R. Hogg, and A. Craig, Introduction to Mathematical Statistics, New York: Macmillan, 1970, p. 361). A FORTRAN program was written to generate all possible values of V and the corresponding probabilities. The calculations were checked against Table A13 in W. Conover, Practical Nonparametric Statistics, Wiley, 1980.

Table A18
Selecting the Best Treatment (known variances)

J	P_0: .75	.90	.95	.99
2	.9539	1.8124	2.3262	3.2900
3	1.4338	2.2302	2.7101	3.6173
4	1.6822	2.4516	2.9162	3.7970
5	1.8463	2.5997	3.0552	3.9196
6	1.9674	2.7100	3.1591	4.0121
7	2.0626	2.7972	3.2417	4.0860
8	2.1407	2.8691	3.3099	4.1475
9	2.2067	2.9301	3.3679	4.1999
10	2.2637	2.9829	3.4182	4.2456

This table was computed by evaluating equation equation (19) in R. Bechhofer, "A single-sample multiple decision procedure for ranking means of normal populations with known variances", Annals of Statistics, 1954, 25, 16-39. This was done with IMSL subroutine MDNORD and IBM subroutine DQH32.

Table A19
Selecting the Best Treatment (Equal but Unknown Variances)

$P_0 = .95$

ν	J: 2	3	4	5	6	7	8	9	10
5	2.01	2.44	2.68	2.85	2.98	3.08	3.16	3.24	3.30
6	1.94	2.34	2.56	2.71	2.83	2.92	3.00	3.06	3.12
7	1.89	2.27	2.48	2.62	2.73	2.81	2.89	2.95	3.00
8	1.86	2.22	2.42	2.55	2.66	2.74	2.81	2.87	2.92
9	1.83	2.18	2.37	2.50	2.60	2.68	2.75	2.81	2.86
10	1.81	2.15	2.34	2.47	2.56	2.64	2.70	2.76	2.81
12	1.78	2.11	2.29	2.41	2.50	2.58	2.64	2.69	2.73
14	1.76	2.08	2.25	2.37	2.46	2.53	2.59	2.64	2.69
16	1.75	2.06	2.23	2.34	2.43	2.50	2.56	2.61	2.65
18	1.73	2.04	2.21	2.32	2.41	2.48	2.53	2.58	2.62
20	1.72	2.03	2.19	2.30	2.39	2.46	2.51	2.56	2.60
25	1.71	2.00	2.16	2.27	2.36	2.42	2.48	2.52	2.56
30	1.70	1.99	2.15	2.25	2.33	2.40	2.45	2.50	2.54
60	1.67	1.95	2.10	2.21	2.28	2.35	2.39	2.44	2.48
120	1.66	1.93	2.08	2.18	2.26	2.32	2.37	2.41	2.45
∞	1.64	1.92	2.06	2.16	2.23	2.29	2.34	2.38	2.42

Table A19 (continued)

$P_0 = .99$

ν	J: 2	3	4	5	6	7	8	9	10
5	3.36	3.90	4.21	4.43	4.60	4.73	4.85	4.94	5.03
6	3.14	3.61	3.88	4.06	4.21	4.32	4.42	4.51	4.58
7	3.00	3.42	3.66	3.83	3.96	4.06	4.15	4.22	4.29
8	2.90	3.29	3.51	3.66	3.78	3.88	3.96	4.03	4.09
9	2.82	3.19	3.40	3.54	3.66	3.75	3.82	3.89	3.94
10	2.76	3.11	3.31	3.45	3.56	3.64	3.72	3.78	3.83
12	2.68	3.01	3.19	3.32	3.42	3.50	3.56	3.62	3.67
14	2.62	2.93	3.11	3.23	3.32	3.40	3.46	3.51	3.56
16	2.58	2.88	3.05	3.17	3.26	3.33	3.39	3.44	3.48
18	2.55	2.84	3.01	3.12	3.20	3.27	3.33	3.38	3.42
20	2.53	2.81	2.97	3.08	3.16	3.23	3.29	3.34	3.38
25	2.48	2.76	2.91	3.01	3.10	3.16	3.21	3.26	3.30
30	2.46	2.72	2.87	2.97	3.05	3.11	3.16	3.20	3.24
60	2.39	2.64	2.78	2.87	2.94	3.00	3.04	3.08	3.12
120	2.36	2.60	2.73	2.82	2.89	2.94	2.99	3.03	3.06
∞	2.33	2.56	2.68	2.77	2.84	2.89	2.93	2.97	3.00

This table was computed using a slight modification of the FORTRAN program used to generate Table A21.

Table A20
Comparisons with a Control when the Variances are Unequal

α=.05

n′	J: 2	3	4	5	6	7	8	9	10
4	3.50	4.29	4.80	5.20	5.53	5.81	6.06	6.29	6.50
5	3.11	3.75	4.14	4.42	4.66	4.85	5.03	5.18	5.32
6	2.91	3.48	3.81	4.05	4.25	4.41	4.54	4.66	4.77
7	2.79	3.32	3.62	3.84	4.01	4.15	4.27	4.37	4.47
8	2.71	3.21	3.50	3.70	3.86	3.98	4.09	4.19	4.27
9	2.66	3.14	3.41	3.60	3.75	3.87	3.97	4.06	4.14
10	2.61	3.08	3.34	3.53	3.67	3.79	3.88	3.96	4.04
15	2.50	2.94	3.17	3.34	3.40	3.57	3.65	3.72	3.79
20	2.45	2.87	3.10	3.26	3.38	3.47	3.55	3.62	3.68
25	2.42	2.84	3.06	3.21	3.33	3.42	3.50	3.56	3.62
30	2.41	2.81	3.03	3.18	3.30	3.39	3.46	3.53	3.18

α=.01

n′	J: 2	3	4	5	6	7	8	9	10
4	6.31	7.44	8.21	8.82	9.34	9.79	10.20	10.58	10.92
5	5.14	5.91	6.40	6.78	7.09	7.35	7.58	7.79	7.98
6	4.60	5.23	5.62	5.90	6.13	6.32	6.49	6.64	6.77
7	4.30	4.86	5.19	5.43	5.62	5.78	5.91	6.03	6.14
8	4.11	4.62	4.92	5.13	5.30	5.44	5.56	5.66	5.75
9	3.98	4.46	4.74	4.93	5.09	5.21	5.32	5.41	5.49
10	3.89	4.34	4.60	4.79	4.93	5.05	5.15	5.23	5.31
15	3.64	4.04	4.27	4.43	4.55	4.64	4.73	4.80	4.86
20	3.54	3.92	4.13	4.28	4.39	4.48	4.55	4.62	4.68
25	3.48	3.85	4.05	4.20	4.30	4.39	4.46	4.53	4.58
30	3.45	3.81	4.01	4.14	4.25	4.33	4.40	4.46	4.51

Table A21

Percentage Points of a k-variate Student's t Distribution with correlations $\rho_{12}=\rho$ and $\rho_{jm}=0$ otherwise, $j\neq m$

k=2

ν	α	ρ: .1	.3	.5	.7	.9	.95
2	.10	3.83	3.79	3.72	3.59	3.34	3.23
	.05	5.57	5.52	5.42	5.24	4.89	4.73
	.01	12.73	12.61	12.39	11.99	11.23	10.88
3	.10	2.99	2.96	2.91	2.82	2.65	2.57
	.05	3.96	3.93	3.87	3.76	3.55	3.45
	.01	7.12	7.07	6.97	6.79	6.45	6.28
4	.10	2.66	2.64	2.59	2.52	2.38	2.31
	.05	3.38	3.36	3.31	3.23	3.06	2.99
	.01	5.46	5.43	5.36	5.25	5.02	4.91
5	.10	2.49	2.47	2.43	2.37	2.24	2.18
	.05	3.09	3.07	3.03	2.96	2.82	2.76
	.01	4.69	4.68	4.63	4.54	4.36	4.28
6	.10	2.38	2.37	2.33	2.27	2.15	2.09
	.05	2.91	2.89	2.86	2.79	2.68	2.62
	.01	4.27	4.25	4.21	4.14	3.99	3.92
7	.10	2.31	2.29	2.26	2.21	2.09	2.04
	.05	2.79	2.78	2.75	2.69	2.58	2.52
	.01	3.99	3.98	3.95	3.89	3.76	3.69
8	.10	2.26	2.25	2.22	2.16	2.05	2.00
	.05	2.72	2.71	2.67	2.62	2.51	2.46
	.01	3.81	3.79	3.77	3.71	3.59	3.53
9	.10	2.22	2.21	2.18	2.12	2.02	1.97
	.05	2.66	2.64	2.61	2.56	2.46	2.41
	.01	3.67	3.66	3.63	3.58	3.47	3.42

Table A21 (continued)

ν	α	ρ: .1	.3	.5	.7	.9	.95
10	.10	2.19	2.18	2.15	2.09	1.99	1.95
	.05	2.61	2.59	2.57	2.52	2.42	2.37
	.01	3.57	3.56	3.53	3.48	3.38	3.33
11	.10	2.17	2.15	2.13	2.08	1.98	1.93
	.05	2.57	2.56	2.53	2.48	2.39	2.34
	.01	3.48	3.47	3.45	3.41	3.31	3.26
12	.10	2.15	2.13	2.11	2.06	1.96	1.91
	.05	2.54	2.53	2.51	2.46	2.36	2.31
	.01	3.42	3.41	3.39	3.35	3.25	3.21
14	.10	2.12	2.10	2.08	2.03	1.94	1.89
	.05	2.49	2.48	2.46	2.41	2.32	2.28
	.01	3.32	3.31	3.29	3.25	3.17	3.12
16	.10	2.09	2.08	2.06	2.01	1.92	1.87
	.05	2.46	2.45	2.42	2.38	2.29	2.25
	.01	3.24	3.24	3.22	3.19	3.11	3.06
18	.10	2.08	2.07	2.04	1.99	1.90	1.86
	.05	2.43	2.42	2.39	2.36	2.27	2.23
	.01	3.19	3.18	3.17	3.13	3.05	3.01
20	.10	2.06	2.05	2.03	1.98	1.89	1.85
	.05	2.41	2.41	2.38	2.34	2.25	2.21
	.01	3.15	3.14	3.13	3.09	3.02	2.98
24	.10	2.04	2.03	2.01	1.96	1.88	1.83
	.05	2.38	2.37	2.35	2.31	2.23	2.19
	.01	3.09	3.08	3.07	3.04	2.96	2.92
30	.10	2.02	2.01	1.99	1.95	1.86	1.82
	.05	2.35	2.34	2.32	2.28	2.21	2.16
	.01	3.03	3.02	3.01	2.98	2.91	2.87
40	.10	2.01	1.99	1.97	1.93	1.84	1.80
	.05	2.32	2.31	2.29	2.26	2.18	2.14
	.01	2.97	2.96	2.95	2.93	2.86	2.82
60	.10	1.99	1.97	1.95	1.91	1.83	1.79
	.05	2.29	2.28	2.27	2.23	2.15	2.12
	.01	2.91	2.90	2.89	2.87	2.81	2.77
∞	.10	1.95	1.94	1.92	1.88	1.79	1.76
	.05	2.24	2.23	2.21	2.18	2.11	2.07
	.05	2.80	2.80	2.79	2.77	2.72	2.68

Table A21 (continued)

k=3

ν	α	ρ: .1	.3	.5	.7	.9	.95
2	.10	4.38	4.35	4.31	4.22	4.07	4.01
	.05	6.34	6.31	6.24	6.12	5.91	5.82
	.01	14.43	14.36	14.21	13.95	13.48	13.27
3	.10	3.37	3.35	3.32	3.26	3.16	3.11
	.05	4.43	4.41	4.37	4.29	4.17	4.11
	.01	7.91	7.88	7.81	7.69	7.48	4.38
4	.10	2.97	2.96	2.93	2.89	2.81	2.76
	.05	3.74	3.73	3.69	3.65	3.55	3.51
	.01	5.98	5.96	5.92	5.85	5.71	5.64
5	.10	2.77	2.76	2.73	2.69	2.62	2.58
	.05	3.40	3.39	3.36	3.32	3.23	3.19
	.01	5.11	5.09	5.06	5.01	4.89	4.84
6	.10	2.64	2.63	2.61	2.57	2.51	2.47
	.05	3.19	3.18	3.16	3.12	3.04	3.01
	.01	4.61	4.59	4.57	4.53	4.44	4.39
7	.10	2.55	2.54	2.52	2.49	2.42	2.39
	.05	3.05	3.05	3.03	2.99	2.92	2.89
	.01	4.29	4.29	4.26	4.23	4.14	4.11
8	.10	2.49	2.48	2.46	2.43	2.37	2.34
	.05	2.96	2.95	2.93	2.89	2.83	2.81
	.01	4.08	4.07	4.05	4.02	3.94	3.91
9	.10	2.45	2.44	2.42	2.39	2.33	2.29
	.05	2.88	2.88	2.86	2.83	2.77	2.74
	.01	3.92	3.91	3.89	3.87	3.79	3.76
10	.10	2.41	2.41	2.38	2.35	2.29	2.27
	.05	2.83	2.82	2.81	2.77	2.71	2.69
	.01	3.81	3.79	3.78	3.75	3.69	3.66
11	.10	2.38	2.37	2.35	2.32	2.27	2.24
	.05	2.78	2.78	2.76	2.73	2.67	2.65
	.01	3.71	3.71	3.69	3.66	3.59	3.57
12	.10	2.36	2.35	2.33	2.31	2.25	2.22
	.05	2.75	2.74	2.72	2.69	2.64	2.62
	.01	3.63	3.62	3.61	3.59	3.53	3.49
14	.10	2.32	2.31	2.29	2.27	2.21	2.19
	.05	2.69	2.68	2.67	2.64	2.59	2.56
	.01	3.52	3.51	3.49	3.48	3.42	3.39

Table A21 (continued)

ν	α	ρ: .1	.3	.5	.7	.9	.95
16	.10	2.29	2.28	2.27	2.24	2.19	2.16
	.05	2.65	2.64	2.63	2.61	2.55	2.53
	.01	3.43	3.43	3.42	3.39	3.35	3.32
18	.10	2.27	2.26	2.25	2.22	2.17	2.15
	.05	2.62	2.61	2.59	2.57	2.52	2.51
	.01	3.37	3.37	3.36	3.34	3.29	3.26
20	.10	2.25	2.25	2.23	2.21	2.16	2.13
	.05	2.59	2.59	2.58	2.55	2.51	2.48
	.01	3.32	3.32	3.31	3.29	3.24	3.22
24	.10	2.23	2.22	2.21	2.18	2.13	2.11
	.05	2.56	2.55	2.54	2.52	2.47	2.45
	.01	3.25	3.25	3.24	3.22	3.18	3.15
30	.10	2.21	2.19	2.19	2.16	2.11	2.09
	.05	2.52	2.52	2.51	2.48	2.44	2.41
	.01	3.18	3.18	3.17	3.16	3.12	3.09
40	.10	2.18	2.18	2.16	2.14	2.09	2.07
	.05	2.49	2.48	2.47	2.45	2.41	2.38
	.01	3.12	3.12	3.11	3.09	3.05	3.03
60	.10	2.16	2.15	2.14	2.12	2.07	2.05
	.05	2.45	2.45	2.44	2.42	2.37	2.35
	.01	3.05	3.05	3.05	3.03	2.99	2.97
∞	.10	2.11	2.11	2.09	2.07	2.03	2.01
	.05	2.39	2.38	2.37	2.36	2.32	2.29
	.01	2.93	2.93	2.93	2.92	2.88	2.86

k=4

ν	α	ρ: .1	.3	.5	.7	.9	.95
2	.10	4.76	4.75	4.71	4.65	4.54	4.49
	.05	6.88	6.86	6.81	6.73	6.58	6.51
	.01	15.65	15.59	15.49	15.29	14.96	14.81
3	.10	3.64	3.62	3.60	3.56	3.49	3.45
	.05	4.76	4.75	4.72	4.67	4.58	5.54
	.01	8.48	8.45	8.41	8.32	8.16	8.09
4	.10	3.19	3.19	3.17	3.13	3.07	3.05
	.05	4.01	3.99	3.97	3.93	3.86	3.83
	.01	6.36	6.35	6.31	6.26	6.16	6.11
5	.10	2.96	2.96	2.94	2.91	2.86	2.83
	.05	3.62	3.61	3.59	3.56	3.49	3.47
	.01	5.39	5.39	5.36	5.32	5.24	5.21

Table A21 (continued)

ν	α	ρ: .1	.3	.5	.7	.9	.95
6	.10	2.82	2.81	2.79	2.77	2.72	2.69
	.05	3.39	3.38	3.36	3.34	3.28	3.26
	.01	4.85	4.85	4.83	4.79	4.73	4.69
7	.10	2.72	2.72	2.70	2.68	2.63	2.61
	.05	3.24	3.23	3.21	3.19	3.14	3.12
	.01	4.51	4.51	4.49	4.46	4.41	4.37
8	.10	2.65	2.65	2.63	2.61	2.57	2.55
	.05	3.13	3.12	3.11	3.08	3.04	3.02
	.01	4.27	4.27	4.25	4.23	4.18	4.15
9	.10	2.60	2.59	2.58	2.56	2.52	2.49
	.05	3.05	3.04	3.03	3.01	2.96	2.94
	.01	4.09	4.09	4.08	4.06	4.01	3.99
10	.10	2.56	2.56	2.54	2.52	2.48	2.46
	.05	2.98	2.98	2.97	2.94	2.90	2.88
	.01	3.97	3.96	3.95	3.93	3.89	3.86
11	.10	2.53	2.52	2.51	2.49	2.45	2.43
	.05	2.93	2.93	2.92	2.89	2.86	2.84
	.01	3.86	3.86	3.85	3.83	3.79	3.77
12	.10	2.50	2.49	2.48	2.46	2.42	2.41
	.05	2.89	2.89	2.88	2.86	2.82	2.79
	.01	3.78	3.78	3.77	3.75	3.71	3.69
14	.10	2.46	2.45	2.44	2.42	2.38	2.37
	.05	2.83	2.82	2.81	2.79	2.76	2.74
	.01	3.66	3.65	3.64	3.63	3.59	3.57
16	.10	2.43	2.42	2.41	2.39	2.36	2.34
	.05	2.78	2.78	2.77	2.75	2.72	2.69
	.01	3.57	3.56	3.56	3.54	3.51	3.49
18	.10	2.40	2.39	2.39	2.37	2.33	2.32
	.05	2.75	2.74	2.74	2.72	2.68	2.67
	.01	3.49	3.49	3.49	3.47	3.44	3.42
20	.10	2.39	2.38	2.37	2.35	2.32	2.30
	.05	2.72	2.72	2.71	2.69	2.66	2.64
	.01	3.45	3.44	3.44	3.42	3.39	3.37
24	.10	2.36	2.35	2.34	2.33	2.29	2.27
	.05	2.68	2.68	2.67	2.65	2.62	2.61
	.01	3.37	3.37	3.36	3.35	3.32	3.29

Table A21 (continued)

ν	α	ρ: .1	.3	.5	.7	.9	.95
30	.10	2.33	2.33	2.32	2.29	2.27	2.25
	.05	2.64	2.64	2.63	2.61	2.58	2.57
	.01	3.29	3.29	3.29	3.28	3.25	3.23
40	.10	2.30	2.29	2.29	2.27	2.24	2.23
	.05	2.61	2.59	2.59	2.58	2.55	2.53
	.01	3.22	3.22	3.22	3.21	3.18	3.16
60	.10	2.28	2.27	2.26	2.25	2.22	2.20
	.05	2.56	2.56	2.55	2.54	2.51	2.49
	.01	3.15	3.15	3.15	3.14	3.11	3.09
∞	.10	2.23	2.22	2.21	2.19	2.17	2.15
	.05	2.49	2.49	2.48	2.47	2.44	2.43
	.01	3.02	3.02	3.02	3.01	2.99	2.97
				k=5			
2	.10	5.06		5.02		4.89	
	.05	7.31		7.25		7.07	
	.01	16.59		16.46		16.06	
3	.10	3.84		3.82		3.73	
	.05	5.02		4.99		4.88	
	.01	8.92		8.86		8.67	
4	.10	3.37		3.34		3.27	
	.05	4.21		4.18		4.09	
	.01	6.65		6.62		6.49	
5	.10	3.12		3.09		3.03	
	.05	3.79		3.77		3.69	
	.01	5.62		5.59		5.51	
6	.10	2.96		2.94		2.88	
	.05	3.54		3.52		3.46	
	.01	5.04		5.02		4.95	
7	.10	2.86		2.84		2.78	
	.05	3.38		3.36		3.31	
	.01	4.68		4.66		4.59	
8	.10	2.78		2.76		2.71	
	.05	3.26		3.24		3.19	
	.01	4.42		4.41		4.35	
9	.10	2.72		2.71		2.66	
	.05	3.17		3.16		3.11	
	.01	4.24		4.23		4.17	

Table A21 (continued)

ν	α	ρ: .1	.3	.5	.7	.9	.95
10	.10	2.68		2.66		2.61	
	.05	3.11		3.09		3.04	
	.01	4.09		4.09		4.03	
11	.10	2.64		2.63		2.58	
	.05	3.05		3.04		2.99	
	.01	3.99		3.98		3.93	
12	.10	2.61		2.59		2.55	
	.05	3.01		2.99		2.95	
	.01	3.89		3.89		3.84	
14	.10	2.57		2.55		2.51	
	.05	2.94		2.92		2.88	
	.01	3.77		3.76		3.71	
16	.10	2.53		2.52		2.48	
	.05	2.89		2.88		2.83	
	.01	3.67		3.66		3.62	
18	.10	2.51		2.49		2.45	
	.05	2.85		2.84		2.79	
	.01	3.59		3.59		3.55	
20	.10	2.49		2.47		2.43	
	.05	2.82		2.81		2.77	
	.01	3.54		3.53		3.49	
24	.10	2.46		2.44		2.40	
	.05	2.77		2.77		2.73	
	.01	3.46		3.45		3.42	
30	.10	2.43		2.42		2.38	
	.05	2.73		2.72		2.69	
	.01	3.38		3.37		3.34	
40	.10	2.39		2.39		2.35	
	.05	2.69		2.68		2.65	
	.01	3.31		3.29		3.27	
60	.10	2.37		2.36		2.32	
	.05	2.65		2.64		2.61	
	.01	3.23		3.22		3.19	
∞	.10	2.31		2.31		2.29	
	.05	2.57		2.56		2.53	
	.01	3.09		3.09		3.06	

Table A21 (continued)

ν	α	ρ: .1	.3	.5	.7	.9	.95
				k=6			
2	.10	5.30		5.27		5.17	
	.05	7.64		7.59		7.45	
	.01	17.35		17.24		16.92	
3	.10	4.01		3.99		3.92	
	.05	5.23		5.21		5.12	
	.01	9.27		9.23		9.08	
4	.10	3.51		3.49		3.43	
	.05	4.37		4.34		4.28	
	.01	6.89		6.87		6.77	
5	.10	3.24		3.22		3.17	
	.05	3.93		3.91		3.85	
	.01	5.81		5.79		5.71	
6	.10	3.07		3.06		3.01	
	.05	3.66		3.65		3.59	
	.01	5.21		5.18		5.12	
7	.10	2.96		2.95		2.90	
	.05	3.49		3.48		3.43	
	.01	4.81		4.79		4.74	
8	.10	2.88		2.87		2.83	
	.05	3.36		3.35		3.31	
	.01	4.55		4.53		4.48	
9	.10	2.82		2.81		2.77	
	.05	3.27		3.26		3.22	
	.01	4.35		4.34		4.29	
10	.10	2.77		2.76		2.72	
	.05	3.19		3.19		3.15	
	.01	4.21		4.19		4.15	
11	.10	2.73		2.72		2.68	
	.05	3.14		3.13		3.09	
	.01	4.09		4.08		4.04	
12	.10	2.70		2.69		2.65	
	.05	3.09		3.08		3.05	
	.01	3.99		3.99		3.95	
14	.10	2.65		2.64		2.61	
	.05	3.02		3.01		2.98	
	.01	3.85		3.85		3.81	

Table A21 (continued)

ν	α	ρ: .1	.3	.5	.7	.9	.95
16	.10	2.62		2.61		2.57	
	.05	2.97		2.96		2.93	
	.01	3.75		3.75		3.71	
18	.10	2.59		2.58		2.55	
	.05	2.93		2.92		2.89	
	.01	3.68		3.67		3.64	
20	.10	2.57		2.56		2.52	
	.05	2.89		2.89		2.86	
	.01	3.62		3.61		3.58	
24	.10	2.53		2.53		2.49	
	.05	2.85		2.84		2.81	
	.01	3.53		3.53		3.49	
30	.10	2.50		2.49		2.46	
	.05	2.81		2.79		2.77	
	.01	3.45		3.44		3.42	
40	.10	2.47		2.46		2.43	
	.05	2.76		2.75		2.73	
	.01	3.37		3.36		3.34	
60	.10	2.44		2.43		2.40	
	.05	2.72		2.71		2.68	
	.01	3.29		3.29		3.26	
∞	.10	2.38		2.37		2.34	
	.05	2.63		2.63		2.60	
	.01	3.14		3.14		3.12	
				k=8			
2	.10	5.67		5.65		5.58	
	.05	8.17		8.14		8.03	
	.01	18.53		18.46		18.22	
3	.10	4.27		4.26		4.20	
	.05	5.56		5.54		5.48	
	.01	9.84		9.81		9.69	
4	.10	3.72		3.71		3.67	
	.05	4.62		4.61		4.56	
	.01	7.27		7.25		7.18	
5	.10	3.43		3.42		3.38	
	.05	4.14		4.13		4.09	
	.01	6.11		6.09		6.03	

Table A21 (continued)

ν	α	ρ: .1	.3	.5	.7	.9
6	.10	3.25		3.24		3.20
	.05	3.86		3.85		3.81
	.01	5.45		5.44		5.39
7	.10	3.13		3.12		3.09
	.05	3.67		3.66		3.62
	.01	5.03		5.02		4.98
8	.10	3.04		3.03		2.99
	.05	3.53		3.52		3.49
	.01	4.74		4.73		4.69
9	.10	2.97		2.96		2.93
	.05	3.43		3.42		3.39
	.01	4.53		4.52		4.49
10	.10	2.92		2.91		2.88
	.05	3.35		3.34		3.31
	.01	4.37		4.37		4.33
11	.10	2.87		2.87		2.84
	.05	3.29		3.28		3.25
	.01	4.25		4.24		4.21
12	.10	2.84		2.83		2.81
	.05	3.24		3.23		3.21
	.01	4.15		4.14		4.11
14	.10	2.79		2.78		2.75
	.05	3.16		3.15		3.13
	.01	3.99		3.99		3.96
16	.10	2.75		2.74		2.71
	.05	3.09		3.09		3.07
	.01	3.88		3.88		3.86
18	.10	2.72		2.71		2.68
	.05	3.05		3.05		3.03
	.01	3.81		3.79		3.78
20	.10	2.69		2.68		2.66
	.05	3.02		3.01		2.99
	.01	3.74		3.73		3.71
24	.10	2.65		2.65		2.63
	.05	2.97		2.96		2.94
	.01	3.64		3.64		3.62

Table A21 (continued)

ν	α	ρ: .1	.3	.5	.7	.9	.95
30	.10	2.62		2.61		2.59	
	.05	2.92		2.91		2.89	
	.01	3.55		3.55		3.53	
40	.10	2.58		2.58		2.56	
	.05	2.87		2.86		2.84	
	.01	3.47		3.47		3.45	
60	.10	2.55		2.54		2.52	
	.05	2.82		2.82		2.79	
	.01	3.38		3.38		3.37	
∞	.10	2.48		2.48		2.46	
	.05	2.73		2.72		2.71	
	.01	3.23		3.22		3.21	

The percentage points, h, in this table satisfy

$$\int I(sh)g(s;\nu)\,ds=1-\alpha$$

where $g(s;\nu)$ is the density of the standard deviation, s, with ν degrees of freedom, $I(sh)=Pr(|Z_1|\le sh,\ldots|Z_k|\le sh)$, and the Z_i's are standard normal random variables with correlations $\rho_{12}=\rho$ and $\rho_{ij}=0$ otherwise for $i\ne j$. Details of the calculations are described in "Improved simultaneous confidence intervals for linear constrasts and regression parameters" by R. Wilcox, Communications in Statistics -- Simulation and Computation, 1986, 15, 917-932.

APPENDIX B

MATRIX ALGEBRA

The purpose of this appendix is to summarize the basic rules of matrix algebra. The important point about matrices is that they greatly simplify the mathematics and description of various statistical problems. There were a few instances in this book where this was the case, and so this appendix was added to help readers apply these procedures.

A matrix is just a two dimensional array of numbers or variables having r rows and c columns. For example,

$$\begin{bmatrix} 2 & 4 & 7 \\ 3 & 2 & -6 \end{bmatrix} \qquad (B.1)$$

is a matrix having r=2 rows and c=3 columns. More briefly, a matrix having r rows and c columns is called an r x c matrix. The matrix is said to be square if r=c. A matrix with r=1 (c=1) is called a row (column) vector.

Let A be an r x c matrix. The value in the ith row and the jth column is denoted by a_{ij}. The quantity a_{ij} is called the (i,j)th element of the matrix A. For the matrix in equation (B.1), $a_{11}=2$, $a_{23}=-6$, etc. Some books write $\{a_{ij}\}$ indicating that you are working with a matrix where a_{ij} is the (i,j)th element.

The transpose of the r x c matrix A, written A', is just a c x r matrix where the ith row of A' is the ith column of A, and the jth column of A' is the jth row of A. For example, the transpose of the matrix in equation (B.1) is

$$\begin{bmatrix} 2 & 3 \\ 4 & 2 \\ 7 & -6 \end{bmatrix} \qquad (B.2)$$

Another way of describing the transpose of matrix $A=\{a_{ij}\}$ is that $A'=\{a_{ji}\}$.

Two r x c matrices, say A and B, are equal if $a_{ij}=b_{ij}$ for all i and j. The sum of A and B is the matrix C where

$$c_{ij}=a_{ij}+b_{ij}.$$

For example,

$$\begin{bmatrix} 1 & 3 \\ 4 & -1 \\ 9 & 2 \end{bmatrix} + \begin{bmatrix} 8 & 2 \\ 4 & 9 \\ 1 & 6 \end{bmatrix} = \begin{bmatrix} 9 & 5 \\ 8 & 8 \\ 10 & 8 \end{bmatrix}$$

Multiplication of a matrix, A, by a scalar, say w, results in the matrix $wA=\{wa_{ij}\}$. For example,

$$2\begin{bmatrix} 2 & 3 \\ 4 & 5 \end{bmatrix} = \begin{bmatrix} 4 & 6 \\ 8 & 10 \end{bmatrix}$$

Let A be an r by d matrix, and let B be a d x c matrix. That is, A has d columns while B has d rows. The product of A and B is defined to be the r x c matrix C=AB where

$$c_{ij}=\Sigma_k a_{ik}b_{kj}.$$

For example,

$$[2 \quad 4] \begin{bmatrix} 3 & 1 \\ 5 & 3 \end{bmatrix} = [26 \quad 14]$$

As another example, one that is more relevant to this book, suppose you randomly sample n=3 subjects and observe (X_i, Y_i) for the ith subject. The linear regression model is that $Y_i=\beta_1 X_i+\beta_0$. To write this model in matrix notation, let

$$X = \begin{bmatrix} 1 & X_1 \\ 1 & X_2 \\ 1 & X_3 \end{bmatrix}, \quad \beta = \begin{bmatrix} \beta_0 \\ \beta_1 \end{bmatrix} \quad \text{and} \quad Y=\begin{bmatrix} Y_1 \\ Y_2 \\ Y_3 \end{bmatrix}$$

The linear regression model is

$$Y=X\beta.$$

The sum of squares is easily represented in matrix notation. Let the matrix

$$Y'=[Y_1, \ldots, Y_n] \qquad \text{(B.3)}$$

be the observations corresponding to n randomly sampled subjects. The product of the two matrices Y′ and Y is

$$Y'Y = Y_1^2 + Y_2^2 + \ldots + Y_n^2 = \Sigma Y_i^2.$$

Let the matrix X be defined by

$$X' = \begin{bmatrix} 1 & 1 & \ldots & 1 \\ X_1 & X_2 & \ldots & X_n \end{bmatrix} \qquad (B.4)$$

The product X'X is important in regression, and it is equal to

$$\begin{bmatrix} n & \Sigma X_i \\ \Sigma X_i & \Sigma X_i^2 \end{bmatrix}$$

Another important product in regression is

$$X'Y = \begin{bmatrix} \Sigma Y_i \\ \Sigma X_i Y_i \end{bmatrix}$$

By definition, a matrix A is said to be symmetric if A'=A. A diagonal matrix is an r x r matrix A where $a_{ij}=0$ for all $i \neq j$. The diagonal matrix where $a_{ii}=1$ for $i=1,\ldots,r$ is called the identity matrix, and it is usually written as I. The indentity matrix has the property that for any r x r matrix A, IA=AI=A. Verification of this statement is left as an exercise.

The matrix A^{-1} is called the inverse of the matrix A if $AA^{-1}=I$. Numerical methods are available for finding the inverse of a matrix, but they are not described here. A description of the method can be found in most books on multivariate statistics, and widely available computer programs can be used to carry out the necesary computations. Here it is merely noted that if the matrix X is defined as above, the inverse of the matrix X'X is the 2 by 2 matrix given by

$$(X'X)^{-1} = \begin{bmatrix} \Sigma X_i^2/[n\Sigma(X_i-\bar{X})^2] & -\bar{X}/\Sigma(X_i-\bar{X})^2 \\ -\bar{X}/\Sigma(X_i-\bar{X})^2 & 1/\Sigma(X_i-\bar{X})^2 \end{bmatrix}$$

This matrix plays an important role in regression.

ANSWERS

1.1 a) 1, b) 0, c) 15, d) 1, e) -14, f) 1/4, g) 14.75, h) 12, i) 9
1.2 a) 160, b) 10, c) 20, d) 18, e) 8
1.3 a) 1, b) 2.1, c) 4.7, d) 3, e) .29
1.4 a)1, b) .2, c) .3, d) 1.6, e) .85, f) 2.9
1.5 $\Sigma(X_i-\bar{X})^2=\Sigma(X_i{}^2-2X_i\bar{X}+\bar{X}^2)$
$=\Sigma X_i{}^2-2\bar{X}\Sigma X_i+\Sigma\bar{X}^2=\Sigma X_i{}^2-2\bar{X}(n\bar{X})+n\bar{X}^2$
$=\Sigma X_i{}^2-n\bar{X}^2$

2.1 All real numbers greater than or equal to 6.
2.2 b) {8,10}, c) {3,5}, d) 0, e) 0, g) {0,1,7,9,11,12}
2.5 $C=\bar{A}\cap B$
2.6 $Pr(B)=Pr[A+(\bar{A}\cap B)]=Pr(A)+Pr(\bar{A}\cap B)\geq Pr(A)$ since $Pr(\bar{A}\cap B)\geq 0$
2.8 a) .1/.6, b) (.1+.2)/.6=1/2
2.10 Let A=red marble on first draw, B=blue marble on first draw, and C=blue marble on second draw. Pr(A)=30/100, Pr(B)=20/100, Pr(C |A)=20/99, Pr(C|B)=19/99,
Pr(C)=(80/100)(20/99)+(20/100)(19/99)=.2,
so $Pr(A+C)=Pr(A)+Pr(C)-Pr(A\cap C)=.3+.2-.0606=.4394$
2.11 b) 2(.3)(.5)=.3, c)3(.3)(.3)(.5)=.135
2.12 a) Pr(Red, Green)≥1-.7-.5=-.2, so the Bonferroni inequality gives no useful information in this case.
b)1-.2-.2=.6

3.1 a) .5, b) .3, c), .5, d)1.0, 3) .2
3.2 a) .15, b) .48, c) .5, d) .13
3.3 No. They measure different things, and so their probability functions are likely to be different, and X and Y are probably dependent measures.
3.4 In contrast to exercise 3.3, the issue is whether the ten pairs of values $(X_1,Y_1),\ldots,(X_n,Y_n)$ are independent and have the same joint distribution.
The answer is yes, and the pairs of values are a random sample of size 10. That is, you have a random sample of 10 pairs.
3.5 a) .02, b) .29, c) .29, d) .68, e) .65, f) .32, g) .08/.5, h) 0
3.6 a) .125, b) .125, c) .25, d) .96
3.7 $\mu=.2$, $\sigma^2=.76$
3.8 $\sigma^2=(1/3)-(1/2)^2=1/12$. a) 11/2, b) 3
3.9 a)2.0, b) .2 c) 8
3.10 a)16, b) 1.6, c) 30 $1/\mu=.625$ E(1/X)=.733
3.11 c)50, d) 10
3.12 $100-9^2=19$
3.15 $\bar{X}=8$, $s^2=5$. Unbiased estimate of σ is 2.376

4.1 26!/22!
4.2 $(26)^4$
4.3 a) 12!/[3!9!], b) $(12)^3$, c) 12
4.4 10!/7!
4.5 Sample space contains $(365)^5$ points. Number of ways you can have all five birthdays different is 365(364)(363)(362)(361)= 365!/360! So the answer is $1-(365!/360!)(1/365)^5$.
4.6 With p=.7,
$Pr(X\geq5)=Pr(X=5)+Pr(X=6)+...+Pr(X=10)$
$=.1029+...+.0282 = .9526$.
4.7 Want $Pr(X\geq.5n)=Pr(X/n\geq.5)=.99$ when p=.55.
Want $Pr\{Z\geq(.5-.55)/\surd[.55(.45)/n]\}=.99$.
$Pr(Z\geq-2.33)=.99$ so choose n such that
$(.5-.55)/\surd[.55(.45)/n]=-2.33$. n=537.
4.8 1-.069=.931
4.9 a) 12/20, b) .25
4.10 F(z)=.4 is not in Table A1 so use F(z)=1-F(-z)=.4. So F(-z)=.6, -z=.25, z=-.25.
4.11 $Pr(Z\leq1.11)=.87$
4.12 a) .953, b) .797-.203=.594, c) $80\pm1.96(6)/\surd25$
4.14 From theorem 4.5.2, $X=X_1+2X_2-3X_3$ is normally distributed with mean $\mu=\mu_1+2\mu_2-3\mu_3$ and variance $1^2(4)+2^2(9)+3^2(16)=184$.
The observed value of X is 200+2(240)-3(300)=-220.
A .95 confidence interval is $-220\pm1.96\surd184$.

5.1 C={7,8,9}
5.2 The significance level is .0703+.0176+.002=.0899.
Power=.2668+.1556+.0404=.4628
5.3 C={0,1,8,9}
5.4 yes
5.5 $\alpha=.0132$ and $1-\beta=.0404$
5.6 Increase n.
5.7 $H_0:\mu\geq18$, $\alpha=.05$, so c=-1.645, $(\surd n)(\bar{X}-\mu_0)/\sigma=(\surd5)(9.8-18)/5.8$
=-3.16, reject H_0.
5.9 $Power=Pr(Z\leq-1.645 - (\surd5)(16-18)/5.8)=.19$
5.10 c=2.576 Fail to reject.
5.11 .28
5.12 $[(-1.645-1.28)(5.8)/(-2)]^2=72$
5.13 52
5.14 Choose n such that $\{.2(\surd n)/\surd.25\} - 1.645\surd[.3(.7)/.25]=.84$.
Solving for n gives n=34.4
5.15 100
5.16 36.45
5.17 From Table A4, 1-.5987=.4013.

6.1 .75
6.2 $Pr\{4s_1{}^2+9s_2{}^2\leq221.52\} = Pr\{(4s_1{}^2/8)+(9s_2{}^2/8\leq27.69\} =$

$\Pr\{\chi_4{}^2+\chi_9{}^2\leq 27.69\}=\Pr\{\chi_{13}{}^2\leq 27.69\}=.99$

6.3 $\Pr\{s_1{}^2\leq y\}=\Pr\{4s_1{}^2/8\leq 4y/8\}=\Pr\{\chi_4{}^2\leq 4y/8\}=.9$, so $4y/8=7.78$, $y=15.56$.

6.5 $\nu=13$, $y''=29.82$, $y'=3.565$, $[(n-1)s^2/y'', (n-1)s^2/y'] = (4.36,36.47)$

6.6 The 95% confidence interval is (5.26, 25.955) which contains the value 12. Do not reject.

6.7 With $\nu=14$, critical value is $c=29.17$, $14s^2/12=35$, reject.

6.8 F distribution with 1 and ν degrees of freedom.

6.9 $|T|=|(\surd 25)(30-34)/2|=|-10|>2.797$.

6.10 $T=(\surd 24)(42-36)/3=9.798>2.79$, reject.

6.11 $\Pr\{T_{23}\leq 1.714\}=.95$. A 90% confidence interval is $42\pm 1.714(\surd 9)/(\surd 24)=(40.95,43.05)$

6.12 $A=2/2=1$, $t=2.069$, $d=(A/t)^2=.23$, $n=\max\{24,40\}=40$. Need 40-24 additional observations.

6.13 $t=2.069$. From equation (6.3.11), choose d so that $2.069-2/(\surd d)=-1.319$, $d=.3486$ and $n=26$.

6.15 $F=1.8/2.3=.783$, $f_{.975}=3.85$, $f_{.025}=1/4.3=.232$,

$.232<.783<3.85$, fail to reject

7.1 $T=(\surd 5)(580-560)/\{[9(100)+9(121)]/18\}^{1/2}=4.254$, $\nu=18$, $t=2.101$ reject H_0

7.2 $T=(\surd 8)(5-8)/\{[15(3)+15(4.5)]/30\}^{1/2}=-4.83$, $\nu=30$, $t=-2.457$, reject.

7.3 $A=\max\{(7/9)^{1/2}(2.262), (7/9)^{1/2}2.262\}=1.995$, $B=5.33$. The 95% confidence interval is 20 ± 10.6

7.4 From Table A14, $\Pr(T_9>-1.383)=.9$, so consider $a=-1.383$. Since $\alpha=.05$, the critical value is $t=2.262$, and since $\delta_0=40$, $d=120$, and $n=\max\{10, [200/120]^{\dagger}+1\}=10$. No additional observations are required.

7.6 $\nu=28$, $t=2.048$, $\delta=1.5/(2/15)^{1/2}=4.108$. From (7.3.6), $\Pr(T_\nu(\delta)\geq 2.048)\doteq\Pr(Z\geq -1.98)=.976$. $\Pr(T_\nu(\delta)<-2.048)=0$, so power = .976.

7.7 It's impossible to determine the sample size prior to collecting your data when the power requirement is specified in terms of $\mu_1-\mu_2$ and σ is unknown.

7.8 $\bar{D}=.83$, $s_d{}^2=3.37$, $\nu=5$, $t=4.032$ and $T=1.11$ Fail to reject

7.9 Critical value is $t=1.96(\surd 2)[1+(.2+.2)(1.96^2+5)/16]=3.38$

7.10 $t=1.96(\surd 2)[1+(.2+.5)(1.96^2+5)/16]=3.84$.

7.11 $w_1=10-(\surd 2/\surd 3)(10)=1.835$, $w_2=14-(\surd 2/\surd 3)(12)=4.2$, $\bar{w}=3.018$ $n_1=2$, $s_2{}^2=2.79$, $T=.97$ The approximate critical value is $1.96(\surd 2)[1+(.25+1)(1.96^2+5)/16]=4.68$

7.13 From the Lin-Stiver procedure $\bar{Y}_1=10.25$, $\bar{Y}_2=10.43$, so an unbiased estimate of δ is $10.25-10.43=-.18$.

7.14 If $\delta=\delta_0$, $Y_i=X_{i1}-X_{i2}-\delta_0$ is normally distributed with mean zero. Apply Stein's procedure to the Y_i's.

8.1	DF	SS	MS	F
BETWEEN	2	233.6	116.8	6.08
WITHIN	6	115.3	19.2	
TOTAL	8	348.9		

Critical value is 5.14, reject. The estimate of σ^2 is 19.2

8.2 $M_1=28$, $M_2=34$, $M_3=24$,
$Z_{11}=0$, $Z_{21}=10$, $Z_{31}=2$, $Z_{12}=0$, $Z_{13}=4$,
$Z_{22}=1$, $Z_{23}=0$, $Z_{32}=4$ and $Z_{33}=2$.
W=4.778/12.111=.395, do not reject.

8.3 $\bar{X}_{.1}=25.33$, $\bar{X}_{.2}=35$, $\bar{X}_{.3}=23.33$, N=9, $\bar{X}_{..}=27.89$, $w_1=.073$,

$w_2=.429$, $w_3=.322$, u=.824, $\tilde{X}=29.58$.
W=11.2, $\nu_2=3.7$, the critical value is 6.94, reject.

For F^*, $c_1=.716$, $c_2=.122$, $c_3=.162$, $\nu_2=3.78$, $F^*=6.08$, critical value is 6.94, do not reject.

H=21.04 and the critical value is 5.995. Reject.

Using James' second order method, Q=26.44 and the critical value is $c_a=15.305$. Reject.

8.4 .530

8.5 $\hat{\sigma}^2_A=(116.8-19.2)/3=32.53$,
$\rho_I=32.53/(32.53+19.2) = .629$,
A=-.054, B=80.778, confidence interval is (-.057, .988).

8.6 c=11.98

8.7a z=-1.04, c=14.94 (using Table A6), so b=12.806,

$A=[1.04(2^{1/2}) + \{2(-1.04)^2+4(25.6-4+2\}^{1/2}]/2=5.649$,
$B=(5.649)^2-12.806=19.102$, d=.0449.

8.7b $n_1=31$, $n_2=103$, $n_3=308$ and $n_4=718$.

8.9 ν is approximately equal to 20. Using chi-square, c=15.61 while for the Hochberg approximation, c=16.29. d=.0428.

9.1 a) For $H_0:\mu_1=\mu_3$ and equal sample sizes, MSWG=(8+10+6)/3=8,

$$|T|=(13-20)/[8(1/10 + 1/10)]^{1/2}=5.53.$$

There are C=2 comparisons, $\nu=27$, so the critical value is approximately 2.38. Reject.
b) From Table A9, with J=3, $q \doteq 3.51$, so $T=3.51(8/10)^{1/2}=3.14$.
Confidence interval for $\mu_1-\mu_2$ is $-3\pm3.14=(-6.14, .14)$ do not reject
c) From Table A10, with C=2, the critical value is

approximately 2.365. Reject $H_0:\mu_1=\mu_2$
d) From Table A9, q=3.95. For Dunnett's C,

$$Q=[(3.95)(8)/10 + 3.95(10)/10]/[.8+1.0]^{1/2}$$
$$=7.11/1.342=5.299.$$

The confidence interval for $\mu_1-\mu_2$ is $-3\pm5.299/\surd2=-3\pm3.747$. Do not reject.
e) For Scheffe's procedure, from Table A3, f=3.35, S=3.274. For $\mu_1-\mu_2$ the confidence interval is -3 ± 3.274. Don't reject. For Kaiser-Bowden and $H_0:\mu_1=\mu_2$,

$$\nu_2'=17.78.$$

The critical value is f=3.55, A=7.499. Confidence interval is -3 ± 3.674. Do not reject.

9.2 a) If the tests were independent, the probability that both would yield a Type I error would be $(.05)^2$. But they are not independent because each t-test has MSWG in its denominator.
b) Use Dunn-Sidak
c) $\nu=76$, With $\alpha=.05$, J=4, critical value is q=3.73. For $H_0:\mu_1=\mu_2$,

$$T=3.73[8(1/15 + 1/20)/2]^{1/2}=2.55$$

$(26-32)\pm2.55=-4\pm2.55$. Reject
d) For Dunnett's T3 and $H_0:\mu_1=\mu_2$

$$\nu_{12}=[8/15 +20/20]^2/\{8^2/[15^2(15-1)] + 20^2/[20^2(20-1]\}$$
$$=32.21$$

If all pairwise comparisons are made, C=J(J-1)/2=6, so V=2.80 Confidence interval for $\mu_1-\mu_2$ is $-6\pm2.80\surd(8/15 +20/20)= -6\pm3.47$.

9.6 a) Dunn-Sidak

9.7 a) $\nu=15-1=14$. From Table A11, h=3.65, m=1.5, so $d=(1.5/3.65)^2 =.169$. $n_1=\max\{16, (5/.169)^\dagger+1\}=30$. Need 30-15 more observations from first group. $n_2=36$
b) $b_1=.0373$, $\tilde{X}_1=.44$
c) $\bar{X}_1=(T_1+U_1)/n_1=.467$, $\bar{X}_2=.5$ For J=3, h=3.65, confidence interval for $\mu_1-\mu_2$ is $(.467-.5)\pm3.65\max\{.41,.41\}=.033\pm1.46$

9.8 m=20/2=10, q=4.7, d=4.527, $n=\max\{10, 8/4.527)^\dagger+1\}=10$
$(10-14)\pm10=(-14, 6)$ don't reject.

10.1

Source	DF	SS	MS	F
A	1	92.0	92.0	3.85
B	2	81.1	40.5	1.695
INTER	2	106.2	53.0	2.22
WITHIN	18	430.7	23.9	

TOTAL	23	710.0

Critical value for factor A is 4.41. Do not reject. Similarly, factor B and interaction are not significant. The unbiased estimate of σ^2 is 23.9.

b) $\bar{Y}_1=\bar{X}_{11}+\bar{X}_{21}=18.75$, $\bar{Y}_2=14.5$, $\bar{Y}_3=23.5$, $q=4.70$ (with $\alpha=.01$ and $\nu=18$), so
$T=4.70[2(23.9)/4]^{1/2}=16.25$.
For $\mu_{.1}$ and $\mu_{.2}$ the confidence interval is 4.25 ± 16.25. Do not reject.
For $\bar{\mu}_{.1}=\bar{\mu}_{.2}$, $T=8.12$ and the confidence interval is 2.125 ± 8.12. Do not reject. The test of $H_0:\mu_{.1}=\mu_{.2}$ will always be consistent with the test of $H_0:\bar{\mu}_{.1}=\bar{\mu}_{.2}$.

c) There are $C=2$ comparisons with $\nu=18$. From Table A10 the critical value is 2.43. $T=-1.81$. Do not reject.

d) To test $H_0:\mu_{11}=\mu_{13}$ with the Welch-Bonferroni or the Welch-Dunn-Sidak procedure, $\nu=34.88$ and $T=-1.78$.

e) For the first hypothesis $T=-1.99$.

f) The unbiased estimate of $\Sigma\alpha_j{}^2$ is $(92-23.9)/12=5.675$.

g) yes

10.2 For factor A, $F=92/53=1.736$. Do not reject.

b) $(92-53)/12=3.25$

10.3 Because power is to be controlled in terms of $\Sigma\beta_k{}^2$, a two-stage procedure must be used. From Table A2, $\Pr\{\chi_2^2\le5.99\}=.95$, so $c=3(5.99)/1=17.97$.

b) $z=-1.28$, $\eta=K-1=2$, $b=5.99$,
$A=(.5)\{1.28(\surd2)+[2(1.28^2+4(2(5.99)-2+1)]^{1/2}\}=4.34$,
$\delta=10$, $d=.26$, $n_{11}=\max\{5, (8.33/.26)^{\dagger}+1\}=33$
You need 33-4=29 more observations from the first group.

c) For the first group $n_{11}=5$, $b=.98$, $a=.005$,
$\tilde{X}_{11}=.005(18)+.98(10)=9.89$, $\tilde{X}_{12}=.09(29)+.64(4)=5.17$.

d) $\tilde{F}=2.0$. Do not reject.

e) $\tilde{F}=4$. The critical value is approximately 28. Do not reject.

11.1 $\hat{\epsilon}=.83$
11.2 F=53.5833/6.6071=8.1

13.1 a) $Y'=.33+.155X$, b) $.155\pm.015$
c) Use equations (13.2.10c) and (13.2.10b), but read t from Table A10

e) $T=.98(13-2)^{1/2}/(1-.98^2)^{1/2}=16.3$, $\nu=n-2=11$, t=2.201, reject

13.2 $Y'=-12.1+0.265X$
13.3 With J=5 groups, the test for linear trends is based on $\Psi=-2\mu_1-\mu_2+\mu_4+2\mu_5$.
Because equal variances are assumed, the critical value is read from Table A10. With $\nu=75$ and C=2 contrasts being tested, $t\doteq2.27$
13.4. Only if the power of Tan's procedure is reasonably high.
13.6 $\nu=(20-2)+(20-2)=36$. You are performing C=2 tests, one for $H_0:\tau_{112}=0$ and one for $H_0:\tau_{212}=0$.
From Table A10 the critical value is approximately 2.33.
For $H_0:\tau_{112}=0$, $D_{112}\pm2.33(2)\surd(.03)=(3.2,4.8)$, so reject.
For $H_0:\tau_{212}=0$ $D_{212}\pm2.33(2)\surd(.06)=(-7.1,-4.85)$, reject.
Because the D's have opposite signs, i.e., one is positive and the other is negative, and because both hypotheses were rejected, conclude that the regression lines cross.

14.1 $X^2=13$
14.2 Using (14.1.3), $X^2=5.2$. Using (14.1.4), $X^2=5.0$.
You can expect the chi-square approximation to be accurate since $n/k\geq.25$, $k\geq3$, $n\geq10$ and $n^2/k\geq10$.
14.3 $X^2=26.67$
14.4 $X^2=5.074$
14.5 Z=.0333/.12213=.273

15.1 Note that there are ties, G=1, S=28.5, U=13.5, $\sigma_u{}^2=13.19$, Z=.96, fail to reject.
15.3 .675

15.5 $\hat{\sigma}_1{}^2=429.88$, $\hat{\sigma}_2{}^2=175.78$, Z=-.589, do not reject.

AUTHOR INDEX

SUBJECT INDEX